The Organization and Administration of Physical Education

The Organization and Administration of Physical Education

Fifth Edition

Edward F. Voltmer

Arthur A. Esslinger

Betty Foster McCue
University of Oregon

Kenneth G. Tillman
Trenton State College

PRENTICE-HALL, INC., Englewood Cliffs, New Jersey 07632

Library of Congress Cataloging in Publication Data
Main entry under title:

The Organization and administration of physical education

    First-4th ed., by E. F. Voltmer and A. A. Esslinger,
published under title: The organization and administration
of physical education.
    Includes bibliographies and index.
    1. Physical education and training—Administration.
I. Voltmer, Edward Frank. The organization and
administration of physical education.
GV343.O73 1978   375′.6′37   78-18724
ISBN 0-13-641100-2

© 1979 by Prentice-Hall, Inc., Englewood Cliffs, N.J. 07632

Printed in the United States of America

10 9 8 7 6 5 4

PRENTICE-HALL INTERNATIONAL, INC., *London*
PRENTICE-HALL OF AUSTRALIA PTY. LIMITED, *Sydney*
PRENTICE-HALL OF CANADA, LTD., *Toronto*
PRENTICE-HALL OF INDIA PRIVATE LIMITED, *New Delhi*
PRENTICE-HALL OF JAPAN, INC., *Tokyo*
PRENTICE-HALL OF SOUTHEAST ASIA PTE. LTD., *Singapore*
WHITEHALL BOOKS LIMITED, *Wellington, New Zealand*

Contents

The social and emotional development objective.
Physical education an integral part of education.

Preface

The study of administration of physical education and related fields is of value not only to those who become administrators; every teacher must know how to work within the framework of an organization under the guidance of an administrator. The teacher's success and advancement is dependent not only upon good teaching but also upon cooperative effort in working within the organization. In addition, almost every teacher must carry out certain administrative responsibilities in connection with teaching assignments.

Every effort has been made to make this textbook inclusive and practical. The basic problems of organization and administration were ascertained by job analyses. Surveys of the duties of physical education administrators in public schools, colleges, and universities have provided the basis for the administrative assignments treated. This approach has resulted, we hope, in a balanced text including all important phases of organization and administration.

This fifth edition of the Voltmer and Esslinger book is updated, revised and includes a new chapter on managing of personnel and one on related programs which are becoming ever more common in the broadening and strengthening of physical education.

In this edition the authors wish to recognize those who generously contributed their time and expertise: colleagues at the University of

Oregon—Corlee Munson, Richard J. Smith and Louis Osternig who rewrote parts of chapter 8, Richard G. Schlaadt who gave valuable suggestions on school health education, Becky Sisley who wrote the section on women's intercollegiate athletics, Wilfred Ewens who assisted with the rewriting of chapter 2, Boyd Baker, University of Arizona, who rewrote the chapter on legal liability and Patricia S. Butcher of the Trenton State College, Roscoe L. West Library who provided resource material for several chapters. Our thanks to Jean Shepherd for proof reading some of the copy, and the authors are most grateful to Marge Rice and Dee Tillman for the typing of many chapters.

B. F. M.
K. G. T.

one

Administrative Theory and Management

1

The Nature and Importance of Administration

One of the characteristics of our modern way of life is the great prevalence of organizations. Although organizations have existed for thousands of years, only in recent decades have they multiplied with such spectacular speed. We have only to contrast the living conditions of today with those of a century ago to appreciate how much more our lives are influenced by organizations. Wherever one turns there are organizations of varying sizes and purposes.

Organizations are created when a group of people come together to accomplish certain objectives that as individuals they could not do for themselves or could not do as well. It is immediately apparent that such organizations as schools, hospitals, factories, banks, churches, department stores, and governmental departments can render a quality of service that could never be offered by individuals working independently.

Organizations do not automatically function smoothly and efficiently. Their success depends largely upon a specialized type of leadership which is known as administration. In common usage the term "administration" is synonymous with "management." Drucker[1] states that there are specific skills which are essential in the leadership of an organization. These managerial skills include the ability to communicate within the organization, to make decisions under conditions of uncertainty, and to plan strategically and effectively in order to do the right things.

Drucker says that the manager or administrator "has to create tomorrow." Thus, administration is largely concerned with guiding human behavior toward some goal. Whatever the nature of the organization it is through human behavior that necessary tasks are accomplished.

In physical education, the administrator is expected to accomplish the purposes of the organization with the human and material resources available. Whether one is the chairperson of a high school department or a director of a college department, or college of physical education, one's responsibility is to lead, guide, direct, and control those individuals who are members of the unit to achieve the objectives for which the organization was created.

DEVELOPMENT OF ADMINISTRATIVE THOUGHT

Administration is an ancient human activity. It probably had its origin when two primitive men learned while trying to lift a heavy log that it was better for one to give a signal so they could lift simultaneously. The need for an administrator became apparent when primitive man started to congregate into groups and to engage in projects too large for one person to accomplish. Building and operating the world's earliest armies, churches, governments, empires and other complex enterprises required organizations and their administrators. The Bible comments briefly upon the administrative problems of Moses as the leader of the Children of Israel. The pyramids have revealed the administrative as well as the engineering skills of the ancient Egyptians.

Over these many centuries a great deal of thought has been given to organizations and their management. However, it is only in the present century that administration has emerged as a field of study, research, and abstract theory. An increasing volume of written materials and many concepts, generalizations, and methods have been developed and studied in the last two decades.

IMPORTANCE OF ADMINISTRATION

The importance of administration in general is well expressed by a simple statement by Massie and Douglas[2] who say: "Managers are people who are primarily responsible for seeing to it that work gets done in an organization." Tead[3] further elaborates this point:

Indeed, so pervasive in influence, so valuable, so adroitly constituted is this skill that it (administration) deserves to be recognized as a fine art. If work with paints or clay, with combinations of sounds in music, with combinations of words and ideas in literature—if these are fine arts, we are certainly entitled to call that labor also a fine art which would bring closer together in purpose the organized relationships of individuals and groups to each other. It is indeed, an art of the highest order to be able to bring about the most fruitful collaboration in a world where associated effort is the typical expression of individuals who seek to be productively alive. And this art becomes in all good sense a social undertaking of fundamental public importance.

The quality of the physical education program in an institution depends more upon the administration than any other factor. It is true that what can be accomplished is dependent on the facilities, equipment, personnel, and time allotment available; but in any given situation, a good administrator produces a substantially better program than a poor one. Likewise, over a period of time an excellent administrator is much more successful in bringing about improvements in facilities, equipment, time allotment, and personnel than a poor or mediocre one. Despite excellent resources many physical education departments are considered weak because of poor administration. Likewise, many departments that have inadequate facilities, equipment, and manpower do surprisingly well because of the ability of their administrators. It has been demonstrated repeatedly that it is the administrator who makes the difference between a successful and unsuccessful program.

The administrator achieves the goal of a department to the extent that he or she is familiar with the recommended standards and practices in all aspects of the program and can obtain optimal performance from all of the personnel. Two variables are involved here. First, the administrator must have a target at which to shoot. In other words, he or she must be familiar with the best practices in the various aspects of the program, and must have in view the standards which the department is to try to achieve. In addition, the administrator has the responsibility of achieving results with associates. This role becomes more difficult as the size of the organization increases. Problems are frequently encountered because individuals do not always work together harmoniously. In fact, jealousies, frictions, and antagonisms frequently prevail. The administrator must direct, guide, coordinate, and control these variable factors and be able to relate to staff in such a way as to elicit the best efforts of every member. Morale and teamwork are essential if the objectives of the department are to be realized.

JUSTIFICATION FOR STUDY OF ADMINISTRATION

In virtually all programs of professional preparation in physical education one or more courses in administration are required. These courses have come to be regarded as essential in the preparation of physical educators for several reasons. In the first place, all physical educators find themselves working in an organization under the direction of an administrator. In the elementary and small secondary schools their immediate superior is likely to be the principal. In larger secondary schools, colleges, and universities a departmental organization exists in which the departmental chairperson or director is the administrator. In either case, physical educators must know how to operate within an organization and under the direction of an administrator. It is important for them to understand how organizations operate in order that they may function more effectively. They are expected to fit into the organization and to conform to the administrative pattern that exists. The administrator assigns the staff members' duties, works out schedules, supervises performance, provides the necessary supplies and equipment, enforces existing policies, evaluates work, determines whether salary increases and tenure are to be recommended, and the like. This relationship of the administrator and teacher bears heavily upon the success and satisfaction that the teacher experiences. Consequently, it is incumbent upon the teacher to understand the nature of administration and his or her role in relation to it.

In the second place, many physical educators eventually become administrators themselves. This assignment cannot be undertaken and discharged successfully unless the individual has had considerable professional preparation for it. It is possible for an individual to be a very successful teacher and coach and yet be quite unprepared to become an administrator. Administration is a large, involved field of specialization with its own philosophy, principles, and techniques; these must be acquired before one can become a skilled administrator. The rapid development of special courses in executive development and management indicate the growth and importance of this field of study.

ORGANIZATIONAL PURPOSES

Gross[4] has developed a category of purposes which are typical of all organizations. He states:

Organizations aim at (1) satisfying human interests, of both members and non-members; by (2) producing services or goods with (3) an efficient use of scarce inputs; by (4) investing in their own viability; (5) mobilizing the resources needed as inputs, and doing all these things (6) in conformance with certain codes of behavior; and (7) in a rational manner.

1. Satisfaction of Interests

Organizations exist for the purpose of satisfying human interests. If the members of a physical education department find it impossible to obtain satisfaction of their interests in the organization, they will either seek another position or try to bring about changes which will enable them to obtain satisfaction. The interest of students who are involved in the program must be satisfied or they will either agitate against it or try to get out of it. The interests of their parents and the general public must be served or opposition to the program will be created. The interests of school administrators and the governing board must be satisfied or their support of the program may be reduced or withdrawn.

2. Output of Services

The output of physical education organizations consists almost entirely of services. Output is why the organization exists. The services are teaching or coaching. In the case of intramural athletics the output is leadership in the conduct of the program. In other words, the quality and quantity of the services of all departmental personnel represents the output of the department. From this output comes the achievement of the objectives of the physical education program.

3. Efficiency

The input of an organization really refers to the cost of the program. The input of a physical education program consists chiefly of the costs of personnel, equipment, supplies, facilities, maintenance, and repairs. It is apparent that the input must be used efficiently. The physical education administrator must get maximum output from the resources available. Physical education organizations both at the secondary school and higher education levels rarely have sufficient budgets, personnel, and equipment. They must get maximum mileage out of what they have.

4. Investment in Organizational Viability

If all the inputs are devoted solely to the production of output, the vigor, strength and vitality of the organization will suffer. If the organization is to live and grow, some of the inputs must be diverted from the production of output and used to maintain the facilities and equipment and revitalize and strengthen the people in the organization. If all the resources are expended on production and nothing on maintaining the strength, vigor and vitality of the organization, it will eventually deteriorate.

5. Mobilization of Resources

It is apparent that the administrator must mobilize all available resources in order to produce the expected outputs and to maintain the organization's viability. Resources are invariably inadequate and much of the organization's success depends upon the administrator's ability to mobilize what is needed at the right time and right place.

6. Observance of Codes

The organizations of which physical education departments are a part always have various regulations and policies that must be observed. The administrator has no alternative but to conform to these regulations which are established by higher authority. In addition, there are professional ethics and standards established by educational and physical education professional organizations that govern the behavior of the administrator. These codes recommend certain behavior and prohibit other activities.

7. Rationality

Gross[5] treats rationality from the standpoint of its technical and administrative aspects. "Technical rationality involves use of the best methods developed by science and technology. Administrative rationality involves the use of the best methods of governing organizations."

The above list of organizational purposes should not be confused with the objectives of the basic instruction, or the undergraduate and graduate professional programs in physical education in colleges and universities. The purposes described by Gross are, in reality, universal purposes characteristic of all organizations whether business, industrial, military, governmental, or educational in nature. The specific objectives of a physical education program at any school level are the anticipated outcomes of the second of Gross' purposes, namely, the output of services.

THE TASK OF ADMINISTRATION

As the leader of an organization it is obvious the administrator should accomplish the goals for which the organization was created and for which it exists. For the chairperson of a physical education department this involves achieving the objectives of the service, intramural and inter-school athletic programs. For the administrator at the college or university level it may also include the objectives of the program of professional preparation in physical education. However, the accomplishment of the purposes of the various programs really represents only part of the administrator's task. There is also responsibility for the individuals who are associated with the administrator in the organization. Their commitment and effort in behalf of the organization's objectives must be secured.

Many administrations have erroneously believed that if their staff members had high morale and satisfaction with their jobs that production would take care of itself. As Likert[6] put it:

It is not sufficient merely to measure morale and the attitudes of employees toward the organization, their supervision, and their work. Favorable attitudes and excellent morale do not necessarily assure high motivation, high performance, and an effective human organization. A good deal of research indicates that this relationship is much too simple.

Likert and his associates have found organizations with all the logical possibilities—high morale with low productivity, low productivity with low morale, etc.

It is easy to conceive of an organization in which the friendliness, favorable attitudes and sociability of all members is so high that the purposes of the organization are neglected. High morale is a desirable state of affairs in an organization but it must be accompanied by a commitment on the part of all staff members to the organization's objectives.

It is also possible for the administrator to put a great deal of pressure on subordinates to increase their output and to ignore the human relations among subordinates. Research studies have shown that technically competent, job-centered, insensitive, and tough administrators may achieve impressive production records for a period of a year or two. However, the results of this approach are invariably lowered morale, dissension, lack of motivation and a high rate of turnover of personnel.

It is because of this seemingly incompatible task of the administrator that Bennis[7] observes:

9

It is my contention that effective leadership depends primarily on mediating between the individual and the organization in such a way that both can obtain maximum satisfaction.

This is the task of the administrator.

Essential Skills of Administration

Katz[8] has indicated that the skills of effective administrators are: (1) technical skill, (2) human skill, and (3) conceptual skill.

Technical Skill. Katz[9] defines technical skill as ". . . an understanding of, and proficiency in, a specific kind of activity, particularly one involving methods, processes, procedures, or techniques. Technical skill involves specialized knowledge, analytical ability within that specialty, and facility in the use of the tools and techniques of the specific discipline."

The technical skills of a physical education administrator include a wide variety of items such as budget making, equipment purchase and care, planning and maintenance of facilities, scheduling athletic contests, drawing up and running of tournaments, certifying the eligibility of athletes, establishing policies, curriculum planning, supervision of instruction, office management, public relations and evaluation.

Human Skill. Katz[10] defines human skill as: "The executive's ability to work effectively as a group member and to build co-operative effort within the team he leads." This involves understanding other people and being able to work effectively with them. As the term implies, it signifies skill in human relations. Implicit in this skill is a realistic understanding of self.

Conceptual Skill. This is defined by Katz[11] as: "The ability to see the enterprise as a whole; it includes recognizing how the various functions of the organization depend on one another, and how changes in any one part affect all the others."

Conceptual skill increases in importance with the size of the staff and the scope of the operation. For the physical education administrator of a very large secondary school, of a city-wide program, or of a department or school in a large college or university, conceptual skill is essential. Little conceptual skill is required in a small school in which the physical education department includes only three or four individuals.

Griffiths[12] refers to a study of the differences between successful and unsuccessful school administrators. It was discovered that there were very few differences between the two groups in their technical skills. The difference between the successful and unsuccessful administrators in their human skills was very great. The difference between the two groups in those practices called conceptual was even greater. He concludes that "it is evident that success in administration is related to the degree of human and conceptual skill the individual brings to the job."

TEACHING VERSUS ADMINISTRATION

Ordinarily newly graduated staff members devote their efforts largely to teaching. After they have had some years of teaching experience many will have an opportunity to assume some administrative responsibilities. They will be confronted eventually with the decision of whether or not to enter administration, to which they would devote increasing amounts of time and energy. They will need to evaluate all aspects of this type of service because administration has its disadvantages as well as its advantages.

In a position in which at least half of the responsibilities are administrative in nature the individual should understand the following limitations.

1. Administration is more time-consuming than teaching. The task of the administrator is never finished because the responsibilities are so numerous that it is a rare occasion when there is nothing more to be done. The administrator is concerned with every aspect of the department's operation and is obligated to see that everything functions smoothly.

2. Administration is involved with countless details. The individual who abhors details should not consider being an administrator. In a large organization the administrator may be able to delegate details to some other staff member but this is not ordinarily possible in the great majority of school situations.

3. Because of the heavy demands upon the administrator's time, there are few opportunities for stimulating exchanges with students. For many individuals such relationships represent one of the most rewarding aspects of teaching.

4. The responsibilities of the administrator are great. This person is responsible for the achievements and failures of the department. In addition, the problems that staff members are unable to handle finally come to the administrator for solution. In large organizations there is frequently much tension and pressure on the administrator.

5. If an individual enjoys teaching, research, or writing, it must be recognized that administrative responsibilities will probably make it

necessary to curtail these activities. The extent to which this is necessary depends upon the percentage of total workload devoted to administration.

6. At times the administrator must make decisions that affect others adversely. Inevitably, promotions, merit salary increases and tenure will have to be denied to some staff members who, in the administrator's opinion, do not deserve them. These actions usually result in disappointment, criticism, and at times embitterment on the part of those concerned. At times staff members must be disciplined, a usually unpleasant experience. There is no way to avoid such problems.

7. The administrator must relate to all staff members in such a way that each serves with maximum effectiveness. This requires much tact and diplomacy. Adjustment to the peculiarities and idiosyncrasies of associates must be made. Some excellent teachers may be unreasonable and demanding. Tolerance and patience are usually necessary to handle such individuals.

8. Administration is frequently a lonely assignment. Because of relationship to staff members, the administrator cannot be partial to any one of them. If a preference is shown for some staff members, socially as well as professionally, others will feel discriminated against.

9. Conflict is an inevitable part of administration. Some inexperienced administrators labor under the delusion that the frictions and disturbances which occur are due to faulty administration. However, conflict is inextricably wound up in the life of any organization. The administrator must face it and resolve it to allow the work of the organization to proceed.

These points represent an imposing list of administrative responsibilities. What then are other aspects of the administrator's assignment, aspects which may seem like more rewarding factors? They can be enumerated as follows:

1. Ordinarily, the administrator receives an excellent salary, usually higher than that of any member of the teaching staff, in recognition of the importance of the leadership role.

2. The administrator has greater security than that of any staff members and is less likely to be released or transferred. For some individuals, this is an important consideration.

3. One of the greatest satisfactions of the administrator is the opportunity to help young staff members grow and develop into professional leaders. Through guidance, direction, and supervision the administrator can play an important role in their future success. The administrator must

provide the climate in which staff members advance, otherwise, the organization will not succeed.

4. The satisfaction of achieving the purposes of the organization is a very rewarding feature of the administrator's work. The administrator is able to make a larger contribution to these purposes than any other staff member for the power and authority to influence is far greater than that of any one teacher.

ADMINISTRATIVE LEADERSHIP

Years ago much research was conducted to identify the universal characteristics of successful leaders. If such characteristics could be determined the identification of potential leaders would be greatly simplified. Many outstanding leaders were analyzed to determine the qualities instrumental to their success. As a consequence of these studies an extensive list of desirable attributes of personality and character was compiled. In fact, the number of such qualities is almost endless. It is possible to conclude that virtually all positive, wholesome, commendable human qualities are assets to prospective administrators.

More recent research however, has exploded the idea of the existence of universal leadership traits. The data do not substantiate a single basic pattern of character and personality traits characteristic of all leaders. McGregor[13] points out:

> There are at least four major variables now known to be involved in leadership: (1) the characteristics of the leader; (2) the attitudes, needs, and other personal characteristics of the followers; (3) characteristics of the organization, such as its purpose, its structure, and the nature of the tasks to be performed; and (4) the social, economic, and political mileau. The personal characteristics required for effective performance as a leader vary, depending on the other factors.

This is an important research finding. *It means that leadership is not a property of the individual, but a complex relationship among these variables.*

The implication of these studies for physical education is that the personal characteristics that enabled an administrator to be a success in one situation may not necessarily ensure success in another. Different styles of leadership are called for to meet the different situations which prevail in organizations.

This does not imply that the personality and character qualities of the administrator are unimportant. Qualities such as sincerity, integrity, unselfishness, sympathy, patience, and kindliness cannot help but be assets to the physical education administrator.

WHAT ADMINISTRATORS SHOULD LEARN

This vitally important topic is effectively covered by Gross.[14] An outline of his ideas follow:

I. Knowledge
 A. *General Background.* The importance of a strong general education background as part of the professional preparation of all physical educators has been stressed by professional physical education leaders. It is even more important to those who become involved in administration, the larger the administrative responsibility, the more essential it becomes.

 Particularly, physical educators have been deficient in the fields of psychology, sociology, and social psychology. These behavioral sciences provide the best preparation for the most important of the administrator's responsibilities, namely, the human aspects of administration.

 B. *Technical Knowledge.* This aspect of the preparation of the administrator is intimately involved with the duties that they are called upon to perform. Analyses have been made of the various things which physical education administrators at the secondary school and college and university levels do. Such duties are listed under essential skills earlier in this chapter.

 C. *Jobs and Organization.* In addition to the technical knowledge the physical education administrator must understand the job and its relationships within the institution and the wider educational programs in the community and state. The administrator needs to be aware of how the departmental role fits into the aim and purposes of education in the educational system of which it is a part and must relate to the efforts of the state, regional and national physical education professional organizations.

 D. *Administrative Concepts and Theories.* "It is particularly important that administrators acquire something more than tacit knowledge concerning organizations and their management. They should become familiar with the growing set of explicit concepts in the language of modern administrative thought, with the diverse and rapidly expanding body of currently useful generalizations and with the major values that govern administrative behavior."[15]

 E. *Self-Knowledge.* A good understanding of one's self is a valuable asset to any administrator. It helps one to understand how he or she affects associates. Furthermore, the knowledge of one's strengths and limitations enables the administrator to be more realistic of what one can and cannot do. In many instances the revelation of one's limitations provides the incentive to eliminate them. The essence of Greek wisdom was "Know Thyself." This is certainly applicable to administrators.

II. Abilities
 A. *Working With Others.* It is evident that the administrator must have the ability to work with others. One probably would not last long as an

administrator if unable to get along with staff members. The ability to get along with superiors is also a necessity. Likewise, good relations with colleagues in other departments and with clients (students and parents) is most important.

How does one develop the ability to work successfully with others? Gross[16] suggests that "Wisdom in this area can probably be achieved only by genuine understanding of others and interest in them."

B. *Handling Conflict.* Every administrator must face the inevitability of conflict. Ability to cope with it provides a measure of one's managerial skill. Some manage to avoid conflict although this approach might not be the best solution in the long run. Compromise is often used to settle a conflict; however, integration is the best way to resolve a conflict even though it is frequently difficult to accomplish. Integration is achieved by finding a solution which is acceptable to both sides involved in the conflict with neither side losing anything.

C. *Intuitive Thought.* Intuition is the immediate apprehension of truth or reality. It involves the act of grasping the meaning, significance, or structure of a problem or situation without reasoning or inferring. Quick and ready insight or "hunch" also are used to explain intuitive thought.

The importance of intuitive thought is emphasized by Gross.[17] "This objective of promoting intuitive thinking is increasingly recognized in the teaching of mathematics and physics. In administration, where greater uncertainties must be dealt with and the tools of analysis are weaker, this objective is still more important. Without intuitive thinking administrative decision-making can never get beyond mere skill and reach the heights of art, judgment and wisdom."

D. *Communication.* Communication is an indispensable ability of the administrator. By means of written and verbal expression the administrator activates and motivates associates. (See also Chapter 3 on communication.)

E. *Learning.* The administrator need not stop learning after formal education is completed. Experience is a great teacher and much can be learned from it as well as from the experience of others.

III. Interests

A. *Action-Orientation.* The life of an administrator is an extremely busy one. There are so many decisions to make, people to see, correspondence to answer, conferences and meetings to participate in that it is extremely difficult to get everything done in a normal working day. This is hardly the kind of position for the person who is not action-oriented. The life of the administrator is so filled that it is difficult to find time for serious reflection and contemplation.

B. *Self-Confidence.* The importance of self-confidence for the administrator is immediately apparent. It would be difficult to think of a leader without it. As Gross[18] states: "The overwhelming importance of self-confidence is that without it an administrator cannot stand up to the rigors of decision-making in the face of change and opposition. Without it, one cannot have sufficient confidence in others to encourage the

self-development of subordinates, stand up to superiors, and cooperate with colleages."
C. *Responsibility.* By the very nature of the job the administrator accepts
responsibility for the performance of the organization. No one should
accept an administrative position unless willing to assume the responsibility for its functions. Whenever the organization fails to meet satisfactory standards of performance, when mistakes are made, the
administrator is accountable to his superior.

KEY ADMINISTRATIVE CONCEPTS

It is not possible to understand administration unless one knows the
meaning of authority, power, and responsibility. These concepts are not
only significant for administrators but for their staff members as well.

Authority. Webster defines authority as "legal or rightful power; a
right to command or to act; power exercised by a person by virtue of office
or trust." According to Simon[19] "authority is the power to make decisions
which guide the actions of others."

For public education and for public institutions of higher education
the source of authority is the state. For the public schools the local board
of education is the agent of the state. The board of education grants
authority to the superintendent who in turn delegates the necessary
authority to the principal of a school. From the principal comes the
authority to departmental chairpersons. For private institutions of higher
education the state grants them authority via a charter. From then on the
line of authority goes from the board of trustees to the president, the dean
and then to departmental chairpersons.

The nature of authority in organizations has been spelled out by
Gross:[20]

> The authority of administrators consists of the rights to engage in certain
> actions needed for the guidance of organizations or units thereof. These
> rights may be subdivided in various ways—such as rights to (a) receive,
> request, and transmit certain kinds of information, (b) make certain kinds of
> decisions, (c) initiate action through commands and other forms of activa-
> tion, and (d) allot certain types of rewards and punishments.

When an individual accepts a position as chairperson or director of
a department or division of physical education, the authority which is
attached to that position falls to the individual. In this position one has
clearly defined powers and responsibilities; authority may be supple-
mented if the individual has charisma. Consequently, it is extremely
important that when administrators are selected, that in addition to their

professional qualifications, they also possess exceptional qualities of leadership and personality.

Power. Power exerts influences. It is the ability to employ force or to produce action, make decisions and initiate action with the expectation that staff members will comply. If they are disposed not to comply they know that the administrator has the power to do something about it such as to take punitive action. Thus, power is a latent force which sustains and supports the authority of the administrator.

Some administrators have great power and others little or virtually none. Great power is usually associated with long tenure, prestige and admiration both within and without the school system, success in professional endeavors, confidence and support from superiors and proven leadership. When these factors do not apply the administrator obviously has a minimum of power. Some administrators are "administrators in name only." This is because they have little power to support their authority. They have failed to realize that power must be achieved by their own efforts.

Responsibility. Gross[21] defines responsibility as "the obligation to act in a certain way." He points out that there are two dimensions to responsibility, namely, responsibility *for* and responsibility *to*. Responsibility *for* is the obligation of the administrator to provide the services and leadership which will accomplish the goals of the organization. This means responsibility not only for all personal actions but also what all subordinates do. Responsibility *to* usually involves satisfying the expectations of one's superiors but it also includes the obligation to one's own staff members.

An administrator may delegate authority to one or more colleagues for a specific assignment. However, it should be understood that the administrator is still held responsible by superiors for all of the activities of the department. The administrator cannot evade responsibility if a staff member bungles the assignment.

An important consideration in regard to responsibility is that authority and power should be commensurate to it. The responsibility for running an intramural track meet does not require nearly the authority —and power—that the administration of the state interscholastic track and field meet does. A formula for failure would be a position with much responsibility but with little authority and power.

DUTIES OF PHYSICAL EDUCATION ADMINISTRATORS

Over the period of the past 20 years extensive job analyses of the duties of physical education administrators have been made by Humphrey,[22] Mackey,[23] Kelliher,[24] Bridgeman,[25] and Hansan.[26] By the processes of reviewing the literature on administration of physical education and holding interviews with physical education administrators, Hansan developed a list of 119 duties of physical education administrators. These are indicated in the Appendix C.

The various job analyses indicated above reveal a striking similarity of the duties of physical education administrators in secondary schools and colleges and universities. One factor, however, causes a variation in these duties. This factor is the size of the department they administer. In the smaller secondary schools and institutions of higher education the physical education administrator spends most of his or her time teaching or coaching or both. In such instances the administrative aspects of the position are not as varied and time-consuming as they would be in a larger institution.

The administrative duties of physical education are encompassed in the following categories:

1. Personnel administration.
2. Physical education objectives.
3. Program administration.
   (a) The school physical education program.
   (b) Health educational program.
   (c) Intramural athletic program.
   (d) Interschool athletic program.
4. Facilities.
5. Purchase and care of equipment.
6. Budget and finance.
7. Public relations.
8. Office management.
9. Evaluation.
10. Legal liability.

Each of the above duties will be considered in detail in subsequent chapters.

SELECTED REFERENCE

STEPHEN J. KNEZEVICH, *Administration of Public Education* (New York: Harper & Row, Publishers, 1975), Ch. 1.

1. Peter F. Drucker, *Management* (New York: Harper and Row Publishers Inc., 1974), pp. 17 and 45.

2. Joseph L. Massie and John Douglas, *Managing, a Contemporary Introduction,* 2nd ed. (Englewood Cliffs, N.J.: Prentice-Hall, Inc., 1977), p. 9.

3. Ordway Tead, *The Art of Administration* (New York: McGraw-Hill Book Company, Inc., 1951), p. 4.

4. Bertram M. Gross, *Organizations and Their Managing* (New York: The Free Press, 1964), p. 276.

5. Gross, *Organizations,* p. 274.

6. Rensis Likert, "Measuring Organizational Performance," *Harvard Business Review,* Vol. 36, (March–April, 1958), pp. 41–50.

7. Warren Bennis, *Changing Organizations* (New York: McGraw-Hill Book Company, Inc.), 1966, p. 66.

8. Robert Katz, "Skills of an Effective Administrator," *Harvard Business Review,* Vol. 33, No. 1 (January–February, 1955), pp. 33–42.

9. Katz, "Skills of an Effective Administrator," p. 34.

10. Katz, "Skills" p. 34.

11. Katz, "Skills" p. 35.

12. Daniel Griffiths, *Human Relations in School Administration* (New York: Appleton-Century-Crofts, 1956), p. 12.

13. Douglas McGregor, *The Human Side of Enterprise* (New York: McGraw-Hill Book Company, Inc., 1960), p. 182.

14. Gross, *Organizations,* pp. 616–620.

15. Gross, *Organizations,* p. 617.

16. Gross, *Organizations,* p. 618.

17. Gross, *Organizations,* p. 619.

18. Gross, *Organizations,* p. 620.

19. Herbert Simon, *Administrative Behavior* (New York: The Macmillan Book Company, 1950), p. 125.

20. Gross, *Organizations,* p. 88.

21. Gross, *Organizations,* p. 94.

22. James Humphrey, "A Job Analysis of Selected Public School Physical Education Directors" (unpublished Doctoral dissertation, Boston University, 1958).

23. Helen T. Mackey, "Job Analysis of Women Supervisors of Physical Education in the United States Public Schools," *Research Quarterly* of the American Association for Health, Physical Education and Recreation, XVI (March, 1956) 32.40.

24. Mayville Kelliher, "A Job Analysis of the Duties of Selected Athletic Directors in Colleges and Universities," (unpublished Doctoral dissertation, University of Oregon, 1956).

25. Donald Bridgeman, "A Study of the Job Competencies Utilized by Directors of Health, Physical Education and Recreation," (unpublished Doctoral dissertation, Springfield College, 1959).

26. John Hansan, "A Job Analysis of Secondary School Men Physical Education Administrators," (unpublished Doctoral dissertation, University of Oregon, 1969).

2

Basic Considerations
for Administration

It is essential that administration be seen as a process and not an end in itself. Administration is the process by which an organization attempts to achieve its goals. The more efficient the administrative process the more likely it is that the goals will be achieved.

Two different concepts can be used to describe the processes of administration. One way is to consider the tasks which confront the leader. The following questions can then form the basis on which to work:

1. What is the purpose of the group? (the objectives)

2. How will the purpose be achieved? (policies, rules and procedures to be used)

3. What resources will be necessary to undertake the operation? (personnel, facilities, equipment)

4. How will members be organized? (allocation of people to jobs)

5. What time lines will guide progress?

6. How and when will evaluation of progress take place?

A second and perhaps more common way to study theory of administration is to identify the processes by using descriptive terminology. While there are variations in the terms used by the different writers, similarities in the patterns are obvious. A classification developed by Gulick and Urwick[1] in 1937 still provides a meaningful pattern for the administration of physical education. The processes listed by Gulick and Urwick are: planning, organizing, staffing, directing, coordinating, reporting and budgeting.

Planning

Planning is deciding in advance what is to be done. It is a method or technique of looking ahead to devise a basis for a course of future action. It is an intellectual activity involving facts, ideas, and objectives. Knowledge, logical thinking and good judgment are, or should be, involved in planning if it is to be effective.

Organizing

Bartky[2] defines organizing as "the process or state of being in which two or more people coordinate their efforts and pool their resources to achieve given purposes." Newman[3] provides further understanding of the nature of organizing by his statement: "The administrative process of organizing an enterprise or any of its parts consists of (1) dividing and grouping the work that should be done (including administration) into individual jobs, and (2) defining the established relationships between individuals filling these jobs."

Organizing involves consideration of such subjects as grouping of activities, departmentalization, delegation of work, and use of committees and administrative staff.

Staffing

Staffing is employing appropriate personnel to accomplish the various tasks which have been identified as necessary for the success of the organization. Consideration must be given to items such as the number of staff required, the particular talents needed, and the manner in which the members of the staff will interact with each other. The operational efficiency of a physical education department will, to a large measure, depend upon how well members of the staff work together.

Directing

Direction initiates action. It occurs when the executive "gives the signals to act, orders or empowers others to act, indicates what the action is to be and when it is to start and stop. In its essence, direction is authority on the move, guided and controlled by the will of the officer."[4] It occurs after the preparation stage, which involves planning, organizing, and assembling personnel and other resources.

Direction is important because when it is done effectively it enhances the chances of a successful operation. When it is done poorly it threatens the progress and success of the enterprise. The manner in which direction is conducted has a marked effect upon the behavior of those being directed. Both the quantity and quality of their performance depends upon their reaction to the directions they receive.

Coordinating

The problems of coordination multiply as the size and complexity of the organization increases. The close and constant contact of individuals in a small department simplifies the organizational setup, promotes communication among staff members, and facilitates supervision and control. While all of these factors make coordination easier it would be incorrect to assume that the physical education administrator of a small high school or college department need not be concerned with coordination. It has been pointed out that even two individuals who are lifting a heavy log need to coordinate their efforts.

Reporting

Administrators in physical education are middle management leaders. They are not only responsible for the operation of the department and the welfare of the teachers and students in the program, but they must also answer to presidents, principals and/or school boards who have responsibilities for the broader institutional function. The administrator therefore must report in two directions: downwards and upwards. An ability to give a clear, concise and accurate report of the status of the department or particular aspects of it, is an important factor of effective administration.

Budgeting

The budgeting process includes planning a budget to meet program requirements, updating and maintaining budget records, and monitoring the accounting system. Budget plans for expenditures must of course be reconciled with available resources. As competition for the available funds increases, skill in budgetary matters will assume ever more importance for the administrator.

Whatever method a chairperson adopts in establishing budgetary processes,[5] he or she must clearly define the way in which the department will operate. The decisions made will affect all of the program and operations within the department.

FUNCTIONAL ADMINISTRATION

Historically administrative theory has developed from a position which stressed the importance of particular traits a successful leader should possess to the current functional approach. This latter approach emphasizes that administration is primarily concerned with interpersonal relationships that develop the most effective use of the human and material resources of the organization. Everyday experiences show that effective administration is not the result of a unique solution of a problem but the result of a relationship between the elements involved. These elements of the organization are: the external environment (the school and the society), the structure (the form of the department), the work force (the faculty), and the leader or administrator (departmental chairperson).

Functional administration is consistent with the concept that administration is a dynamic process and as such it should be recognized that no one particular type of individual has the unique ability to succeed in a given circumstance. Leaders may use different techniques yet be equally successful in similar situations. Effective leadership occurs when the elements work in harmony to maximize achievement and staff self-satisfaction. To attain the ultimate goal of the organization requires the sequential completion of a number of subgoals. It is essential that the administrator recognize that effectiveness is not only concerned with the completion of particular short-term tasks but is also concerned with the continued well-being of all the people in the department.

The External Environment

The external environment is made up of all the factors that fall outside the boundaries of the organization under consideration. Massie and Douglas[6] state that the external environment "contains all those forces, factors and information in the world that interact with the manager's organization."

A department of physical education within a school has its external environment divided into two parts: one part is closely related to the department, and one is more distant. The immediate environment, external to the department, is the school, the district administration, the school board, the parents and citizens of the district. The more distant or general external environment consists of the entire society or culture in which the department and school operate as well as that society's values, mores, laws, politics and economy. The immediate environment, in many ways, acts as a partial screen against the broader external influences. As an outcome of pressures exerted by laws, economic constraints and other social changes, the school board, the superintendent and the principal establish policies. It is within the framework of these policies that the chairperson is obliged to operate.

The significance of the external environment is that its many components often have conflicting objectives. The principal requires the physical education program to be an integrated segment of the total school curriculum, the school board is concerned with limited budget and may fail to provide adequate facilities, and the parents may demand a winning athletic program. As no organization operates within a vacuum the external environment is an important consideration for any administrator. For an organization to be effective it must be able to exist harmoniously within the wider sphere of general society.

The departmental chairperson is often required to make decisions which affect all or most of the external elements. It is not an easy task and the more sensitive he or she is to the various pressures and their influence upon the achievement of the departmental objectives, the better the position to make a reasoned decision. This relationship does not preclude opportunities for a physical education chairperson and faculty to initiate change within the school, or indeed society at large. However, the astute administrator must be ever conscious of the changing attitudes and values of the external environment.

The Structure

Organizations have a particular form depending upon how authority and responsibility are assigned and the way in which lines of communication are established. An organization has two types of structure, the formal structure and the informal structure.

Formal structure refers to the formal roles that members occupy; it establishes the authority of one role over another. This structure is relatively constant even when the personnel changes. Massie and Douglas[7] suggest that the formal structure has the following purposes:

1. To establish efficient and logical patterns of interrelationships among members of the group.

2. To secure advantages of specialization or division of labor whereby the optimum utilization of talents can be realized.
3. To coordinate activities of the component parts in order to facilitate the realization of the goals of the organization.

The larger and more complex the organization the more need there is for formal structure. Small departments generally operate on a simple structure and informal relationships.

The informal structure develops from the human relationships and communication networks that evolve naturally and spontaneously as a result of the members being brought together under the formal framework. While the formal organization can design the roles of a chairperson or a teacher, it must be remembered that these roles are filled by individuals who have abilities, personalities, interests, and goals of their own. Therefore friendships are formed and lines of informal communication and rapport are established within the formal structure. The relevance of the informal structure is explained by Owens[8] in this way:

> In the final analysis, in order to get the organization's work done the people in the various roles . . . must meet face-to-face and interact: they must communicate, make decisions, plan, and so forth. This requires interaction between *people*, not just interaction between *roles*.

Ideally the formal and informal structures would be synonymous, but rarely are the two systems perfectly matched. The administrator must be aware of the presence and importance of the informal organization, he or she must be alert to the positive contribution it can make and at the same time guard against the formation of unhealthy cliques and subgroups.

One might ask if it is wise for a leader to become closely associated with the informal organization. The degree to which the administrator socializes with members of the faculty while off the job will require careful deliberation in terms of the relationships both real and perceived. Real or imagined favoritism must not be perceived by the faculty. Therefore must the leader or administrator be aware of, but detatched from, the informal structure? If the leader becomes too involved with parts of the informal organization do other members feel reluctant to discuss matters openly? If this was the case the administrator could lose an important avenue of feedback and/or positive contributions from staff members. Thus the administrator must determine how involved he or she can become in the informal structure since this can affect organizational achievement.

Both the formal and the informal structures are important and must be understood by the administrator. The effectiveness of a physical education department will in large measure depend upon the appropriateness of the formal structure and the compatibility of the informal organization.

The Work Force

In a physical education department the work force is made up of the departmental faculty members. While it may be important for members of the faculty to get along together, to enjoy working with one another, this is not the real reason for their participation in the organization. The criterion is, hopefully, their ability to provide professional competencies in teaching consistent with the purposes of the organization.

Administrators should attempt to develop esprit de corps among the staff, but high morale may not necessarily lead to high productivity. High morale may be related to social groupings which have little to do with the departmental goals. Such a basis for group cohesiveness could be the result of reaction against the way a leader perceives administrative procedures. This negative reaction is usually to the detriment of the organization.

Morale which is most effective is that which is related to the achievement of the organization's goal (task oriented). If this is the case it means that the organization's goals and the personal goals of organization members will be closely interrelated. Good leadership will create a climate which allows members to fulfill their own ambitions and at the same time work for departmental goals.

The Administrator

Of all the elements of an organization, the administrator is the most influential. The administrator bears the responsibility for all departmental operations. The leader's effectiveness is based on the premise that two dimensions of leader behavior are significant in administration: task oriented behavior and people oriented behavior. Halpin[9] defines these dimensions as follows:

> "Initiating Structure" refers to the leader's behavior in delineating the relationship between himself and members of the work group, and in endeavoring to establish well-defined patterns of organization, channels of communication, and methods of procedure . . . "Consideration" refers to behavior indicative of friendship, mutual trust, respect and warmth in relationships between the leader and members of his staff.

Support for this concept is widespread. Ratsay, Holdaway and Miklos[10] cite 18 studies which support the task orientation/person orientation nature of administration.

The manner in which a leader perceives his or her role is based on personal philosophy. The word "philosophy" has been defined in many ways. Its simplest definition is "the pursuit of wisdom," or "the eternal search for truth." A fuller definition is "the love of wisdom; a science which investigates the facts, principles and problems of reality in an attempt to describe, analyze and evaluate them."

Importance of a Philosophy. The philosophy of the administrator is of crucial importance. It is significantly related to the kind of administrator one is. It serves as a directional post to guide the administrator's steps. All administrators become involved in philosophical problems. They can never become successful unless they can formulate a valid philosophical foundation for their actions.

Every administrator has a philosophy whether or not he or she realizes it and decisions are based upon the beliefs and values that constitute this philosophy. One's philosophy is the result of all past experiences. It may be mature or immature, consistent or inconsistent, logical or illogical, rational or irrational.

Sources of Philosophy. The philosophy of the physical education administrator grows out of at least three factors, namely, (1) a philosophy of life, (2) a philosophy of education, and (3) a philosophy of physical education. Perhaps other considerations are also involved but the administrative philosophy of the executive in physical education will be strongly affected by each of these aspects.

Philosophy of Life. It would be impossible to have a philosophy of administration entirely disassociated from one's philosophy of life. The life purposes, the ideals, the values an individual holds, reactions to people and their response are all part of one's personal philosophy, which inevitably exerts a powerful influence upon philosophy of administration.

A philosophy of life relates significantly to the manner in which an individual works with subordinates. Administrators have power. It comes from two sources, namely, that which is ascribed to the office and that which is achieved by the manner in which he or she relates to staff members. Formal power or authority is delegated and vested in the office regardless of the person who happens to fill it. Informal power or influence is earned or achieved irrespective of the office held. It depends upon the personality and character of the administrator and the manner in which the individual works with staff members.

It is apparent that the administrator who supplements the formal authority of position with the informal power or influence that was earned by personal leadership is the better executive. Experience has demonstrated that the administrator must earn the respect and cooperation of subordinates. To rely solely upon the authority that is vested in the office is to court certain failure.

The administrator's relationship to students is also governed largely by a philosophy of life. Associations with superiors, with other faculty members and with department staff members, and responsibilities for budget, equipment, facilities, office management, and the like may be regarded as far more important than relationships with students. As a consequence, the administrator becomes virtually inaccessible to them. If on the other hand, the students are regarded as having a high priority, this point of view is well expressed by the following statements:

1. A student is the most important person in our business.

2. A student is not dependent upon us—we are dependent upon the student.

3. A student is not an interruption of our business—a student is the purpose of it.

4. A student does us a favor when he or she calls—we are not doing a favor by serving the student.

5. A student is part of our business, not an outsider.

6. A student is deserving of the most courteous and attentive treatment we can give.

7. A student is one who brings us wants—it is our job to fill them.

8. A student is the lifeblood of any school.

Philosophy of Education. A philosophy of education is of crucial importance to the individual who serves as an educational administrator. The beliefs entertained concerning the aims, objectives, and principles of education will govern attitudes and decisions regarding school matters. Every educational executive's thinking and action receive their purpose and direction from a philosophy of education.

Philosophy of Physical Education. A philosophy of physical education grows out of one's philosophy of education. While the ultimate aim is the same, the approach and the program of physical education are different. The administrator's philosophy of physical education undergirds thoughts and actions concerning such matters as outcomes, standards, methods, curriculum, evaluation, and the like. A philosophy enables the administrator to evaluate accomplishments as opposed to what is supposed to be done. It gives direction to actions and keeps one on the track.

TYPES OF ADMINISTRATION

Early studies of administration developed categories for administrative styles. The categories were based on the leader's conception of the power and authority they possess and how they will employ it. Griffiths[11] classified administrators into four types: the laissez-faire administrator, the autocrat, the benevolent dictator, and the democratic administrator. Each of these types represents a different philosophy of administration.

1. The Laissez-faire Administrator. This type of person is really not an executive at all, making little use of the formal power of the position and no effort to obtain informal power. This type never exerts any leadership—never takes a stand. Faculty members do what they want. Complete abdication of authority and direction by the administrator is characteristic of this type of executive. The consequence of this type of leadership is an attitude of hopelessness and very low morale on the part of the individual staff members.

2. The Autocrat. This type of administrator relies solely upon the formal power of the position, is arbitrary, inconsiderate, and coercive. He or she employs close and continuous supervision and tight and inflexible controls over individual and group behavior. This person acts upon the concept that inasmuch as the teacher is being paid, the teacher should do everything he or she is told to do and do it unquestioningly. The administrator is not interested in the opinions of subordinates and never solicits their suggestions. Someone had said: "Administrators hold power, and where humans hold power, there is temptation to tyranny; and where there is temptation there is yielding." The autocratic administrator is one who has yielded to the temptation.

Such administrators are rarely successful in a democratic society. Staff members have a smoldering resentment, lack of morale, and loss of initiative and enthusiasm. Staff turnover is high. The abuse of power which characterizes such an administrator is the cause of more administrative failures than any other single factor.

3. The Benevolent Dictator. This type of administrator is friendly, approachable, and understanding, looks after the needs of staff members and wants to know their problems. Interest is manifested in each individual and excellent work is praised by this type of administrator. Morale and productivity under such an administrator are excellent.

The negative aspect of such executive leadership is the loss of initiative and creativity on the part of staff members. So much reliance is placed upon the administrator's judgment and wisdom that faculty members lose their independence. Also, because such an administrator assumes possession of more wisdom and more experience than the members of the staff, the important decisions and policies are made solely by the administrator without taking advantage of staff experience and insight.

4. The Democratic Administrator. This type of administrator makes the fullest possible use of the formal power of the position and the informal power of personal leadership. The democratic administrator respects the personalities of subordinates and relates to each staff member to obtain maximum contribution to the objectives of the organization. This type of administrator solicits the opinions of staff members and involves them in decision making on certain issues. Group participation is encouraged. Freedom of action prevails. Regular staff meetings are scheduled. Periodic evaluation of programs and progress toward goals is made. Effective communication is provided. Good human relations are stressed.

It would seem logical to expect that the democratic administration would be the most appropriate administrative style for all activity within an organization. However, experience in the administrative world does not always support this notion. It is possible for a leader to use one type of administration more than another, but it is wise to remember that leaders generally will, at one time or another, use most, if not all, of these approaches in reaching decisions about the organizational operations. It is therefore more appropriate to consider Griffith's classification as one relating to the decision-making process rather than to specifically typing administrators.

In all situations it should be the administrator's objective to obtain the fullest use of each individual's best talents on behalf of the organization. This is a difficult and challenging task which will require the administrator to take action at times without conferring with members of the faculty. Nevertheless the principles of democratic administration provide greater opportunities for those who make up the organization to contribute more fully in the decision making and the implementation of the decision and therefore gives them greater commitment to the organization and its objectives.

MISCONCEPTIONS OF DEMOCRATIC ADMINISTRATION

A great deal of misunderstanding exists about what democratic administration actually is. Many individuals believe that it means that staff members vote on all issues that arise. Some believe that the administrator acts autocratically in making any decision alone. These are erroneous concepts of the nature of democratic administration.

The administrator has the prerogative of deciding to what extent staff members are involved in decision making and is entitled to administer in the way he or she believes will produce the best results. The responsibility for the success of the organization rests with the administrator; superiors hold him or her accountable for results. The administrator has the authority to make decisions or to delegate this authority to staff members. It should be understood that the use of the democratic method does not relieve the administrator of responsibility. If the decision should have a disastrous result, the administrator cannot escape responsibility by claiming that "it was a group decision." Responsibility must be centered upon one individual and not an entire group.

The following six statements by Griffith[12] will aid in clarifying the concept of democratic administration:

Six Mistaken Meanings of Democratic Administration

"Democracy is the most misunderstood term in educational administration. Many schoolmen do not grasp its limitations. In the name of democracy, as they misunderstand it, they justify their blundering, indecisiveness, and buck-passing.

Six mistaken meanings of educational democracy need to be swept away so that the true meaning of democratic administration can be perceived.

Error 1: Democratic administration is a laissez-faire procedure. Democracy in school management does not mean autonomy for the classroom teacher or school principal. It does not mean that a teacher can do as he pleases in his classroom so long as instruction goes forward. It does not mean that a principal can follow whatever practices he chooses so long as his school operates smoothly.

A measure of freedom is desirable in teaching and administration but it must be exercised in a framework of established policy, and all school activities must be subject to inspection and evaluation. The administrator who allows his teachers to do as they please on the ground that he is being democratic is shirking his legal responsibility.

A good school does not run by itself. Confusion is not an ingredient of freedom. Leadership and authority are essential.

Teachers respect a principal who makes and announces clean-cut decisions even when they disagree with them. They like the security of definiteness, as long as they have a chance to be heard before policies are promulgated and the right to advocate modification or discontinuance after new policies have been put into effect.

Error 2: Democratic administration means guiding persons to accept an administrator's viewpoint. Democratic administration is not an exercise in human engineering. It does not mean influencing subordinates to adopt a policy reached in advance of consultation. It does not mean adroitly manipulating persons to think and act as an administrator wants them to.

The gentle guidance of others into acceptance of a predetermined course of action is a perversion of democracy. Democratic group discussion is a procedure for hammering out truth, for testing the merit of proposals by submitting them to critical analysis, and for creative thinking.

Error 3: Democratic administration avoids the firm exercise of authority and insistence on obedience. Some administrators confuse firmness with authoritarianism. The reasoned and reasonable use of power is a far cry from authoritarianism. Authority is legitimately used when it takes into account the rights of those whom it affects and when it employs means appropriate to, and commensurate with, the ends it seeks to attain.

No organization can be effective without direction from above and compliance from below. A successful administrator must be firm. He cannot discharge the duties of his office unless he coordinates and directs the activities of his subordinates. The higher his position, the fewer orders he has to issue, for a suggestion often has the force of an order; but whether he is at the top of an echelon or in one of its lower ranks he must exercise control, with due regard for each individual, if he is to run his school smoothly.

He should expect his subordinates to comply promptly and completely, if not willingly. While his orders are being complied with, he should permit the expression of dissent and never interpret opposition to a policy as disrespect or a personal affront. He must be careful not to stifle independent thinking, look on individuals as cogs in a machine, or make a virtue of blind acceptance.

Error 4: Democratic administration means majority rule. Voting, which is an essential part of political democracy, is not an essential part of educational democracy. Educational problems cannot be solved by majority rule. An administrator proposed solution may be sound even though his faculty considers it fallacious and unworkable. A majority's opposition may be based on ignorance, fear of change, or an incomplete knowledge of the elements in a situation.

A skillful administrator should always be receptive to advice and suggestion from every source, but he is under no obligation to follow it if it is at odds with his own best thinking. He must consider the general good rather than individual preferences.

He may, if he wishes, call for a show of hands at a faculty conference or committee meeting to guide him in his decision-making, but he should make it clear beforehand that the poll is only advisory and that the final decision will be his alone. If he is wise, he will only rarely call on his faculty to vote.

Few educational matters are so urgent that they require immediate attention. For reasons of expediency, an administrator may defer action when a poll shows widespread opposition to a proposal he favors. He may continue to try to convince his teachers and supervisors of the wisdom of a proposal, realizing that it will fail unless his subordinates are convinced of its validity.

An administrator who determines his actions by the votes of his faculty substitutes their judgment for his own. He abdicates his responsibility by following rather than leading.

Error 5: Democratic administration is a means of avoiding unpleasant decisions. Every administrator faces at least one problem which requires an unpopular solution. A mature administrator will reflect on it thoroughly, discuss it with his associates and those affected, and after due consideration announce his ruling accompanied by a statement of his reasons therefor. He should not be concerned with the effect on his popularity; he should enter some field other than school administration.

How does an insecure administrator act when faced with a problem which has only disagreeable solutions? He usually turns it over to a committee, ostensibly for study and recommendation, but actually to get himself off a hook. Sometimes he rigs the committee's membership so that its recommendations are a foregone conclusion. When the committee submits its report, he accepts it and thereafter rejects complaints on the grounds that he has followed a democratic procedure and that the decision was not of his making.

When problems are important and complex, committees are indispensable instruments in school administration. But when committees are used to evade responsibility, they negate rather than promote democratic administration.

Error 6: Democratic administration means the absence of formality. A school in which every staff member is on a first-name basis with his fellow teachers and superiors is not necessarily democratic. A school in which the principal addresses everyone as "Mr.," "Mrs.," or "Miss" may be more truly democratic than one in which the principal backslaps his teachers, calls them by their first names, and discusses their personal affairs with them.

Democratic administration is not a matter of externals. It is characterized by a professional attitude, a spirit of mutual concern and helpfulness, and a willingness to work together toward clearly perceived and valued goals. Glad-handing, boisterous camaraderie, and other informalities sometimes hide a benevolent despot.

Every administrator needs to be aware of these six pitfalls. Democracy is a term which has been bandied about so much that it is assuming strange connotations. The beginning administrator, particularly, should distinguish between democracy's trappings and democracy's essence—a respect for every individual."

SUMMARY

The effective administration of a department of physical education within a school or college is a complex phenomena. It does not evolve as a result of a "cook book" type formula which can account for all propositions, but as a result of the relationships between the environment, the organizational structure, the group members and the leader.

To establish and continue to maintain a productive organization the leader must not only be concerned with short-range task achievement but he or she must develop an atmosphere that gives staff members personal satisfaction and the incentive to continue to work towards the ultimate organizational goals.

An administrative style which provides opportunities for staff members to participate in decision making is conducive to efficient management. Nevertheless, the administrator must accept the responsibility and vested authority to guide the operations of the enterprise. To fail to provide positive leadership will have negative consequences.

SELECTED REFERENCES

ALBANESE, ROBERT, *Management: Toward Accountability for Performance.* Homewood, Illinois: Richard D. Irwin, Inc., 1975.

HAIMANN, THEO and WILLIAM G. SCOTT, *Management in the Modern Organization.* (2nd ed.), Boston: Houghton Mifflin Company, 1974.

OWENS, ROBERT, *Organizational Behavior in the Schools.* Englewood Cliffs, N.J.: Prentice-Hall, Inc., 1970, Ch. 10.

NOTES

1. Luther Gulick, and Lyndall Urwick, eds., *Papers on the Science of Administration* (New York: Institute of Public Administration, 1937).

2. John Bartky, *Administration as Educational Leadership* (Stanford, Calif.: Stanford University Press, 1956).

3. William H. Newman, *Administrative Action: the Techniques of Organization and Management,* 2nd ed. (Englewood Cliffs, N.J.: Prentice-Hall, 1963), p. 143.

4. Jesse B. Sears, *The Nature of the Administrative Process* (New York: McGraw-Hill Book Company, 1950), p. 127.

5. James M. Lipham and James A. Hoeh, Jr., *The Principalship: Foundations and Functions* (New York: Harper & Row, Publ., 1974), pp. 297–319 on financial-physical resources.

6. Joseph L. Massie & John Douglas, *Managing, a Contemporary Introduction,* 2nd ed. (Englewood Cliffs, N.J.: Prentice-Hall, Inc., 1977), p. 12.

7. Massie and Douglas, *Managing,* p. 131.

8. Robert G. Owens, *Organizational Behavior in Schools* (Englewood Cliffs, N.J., Prentice-Hall, Inc., 1970), p. 50.

9. Andrew W. Halpin, *Theory and Research in Administration* (New York: The Macmillan Book Company, 1966), p. 86.

10. E. Ratsay, E. Holdaway and E. Milkos, Editors, *Leader Behavior in Educational Organizations* (Edmonton, Canada: University of Alberta, 1974), p. 65.

11. Daniel Griffiths, *Human Relations in School Administration* (New York: Appleton-Century-Crofts, 1956), pp. 148–154

12. Francis Griffith, "Six Mistaken Meanings of Democratic Administration," *Phi Delta Kappan* (October, 1966), pp. 59–61. Reproduced with permission of the editor and author.

3

Management of Personnel

MANAGEMENT OF PEOPLE IS THE HEART OF THE ADMINISTRATIVE PROCESS

Administration involves two major aspects: namely, the human and the technical. The human dimension of administration is concerned with the managing of all the people in the organization. The technical aspects involve such considerations as budget-making, purchase and care of equipment, construction and maintenance of facilities, office management, curriculum construction, and other responsibilities which require technical knowledge and skill.

Of these two phases of administration it is generally considered that the administration of the human component in an organization is the most important and difficult. As Likert[1] has expressed it:

Of all the tasks of management, managing the human component is the central and most important task, because all else depends upon how well it is done.

Basically, the manager's job consists of getting jobs done for, with, and through people. The most important skill to learn is the management of people rather than the administration of things. The administrator must relate to staff members in such a way that 100 percent effort is obtained from 100 percent of the people 100 percent of the time. This is a challenging prospect for a period of several months, but it is the administrator's obligation to achieve this goal not only for the entire school year, but for all the succeeding years during which he or she has the administrative responsibility.

That this goal is not often achieved is well expressed by Marrow:[2]

Management has come increasingly to recognize that the daily waste of men's capacity to produce on the job, and of their capacity to feel satisfied with their work, is the failure to apply the knowledge which psychology, among the behavioral sciences, could make available. The valuable chemicals that spew from chimneys of refineries, the fertile elements in garbage dumped into the waterways of a great city, the rejects that are carried from factory floor to the scrap heap—these are needless drains at a huge price to our economy. But the human capacity to do useful things that go up in smoke every day and everywhere is a far greater waste.

THE NECESSITY OF UNDERSTANDING HUMAN BEHAVIOR

Since the behavior of people is at the very heart of the administrative process, it follows that the administrator must understand human beings. People are very complex and a genuine understanding of them is invaluable in getting them to work together to accomplish the organization's purposes. Some administrators develop an excellent insight into human nature by broad and varied experience with people, but even this is not a substitute for an academic preparation in the behavioral sciences. For the physical education administrator, a strong background in psychology and sociology is as important as an adequate preparation in human anatomy and physiology. The study of administration depends upon nothing less than the study of man.

In the last half of the twentieth century an explosion of knowledge and technology occurred in the behavioral sciences. A vast amount of research that has profound implications for physical education administrators has become available. Any administrator who does not become familiar with this literature will be seriously handicapped.

McGregor[3] provides an excellent example of the unfortunate consequences when the administrator lacks an understanding of subordinates. He describes two types of administrators who operate upon different assumptions or hypotheses about human behavior. The Theory X administrator is the traditional type whose assumptions about human nature are not in accord with the facts of modern psychology. The Theory Y administrator manages personnel in a manner consistent with more recent psychological interpretations of human behavior.

The Theory X Administrator

The Theory X administrator assumes that the average person has an inherent dislike for work and will avoid it if possible; must be coerced, controlled, directed, and threatened with punishment to get the work done; prefers to be directed, wishes to avoid responsibility, has relatively little ambition, and wants security above all.

As a consequence, the Theory X administrator operates on the assumption that organizational requirements take precedence over the needs of individual members. Coercive, autocratic and arbitrary, this administrator uses authority to obtain the commitment of staff members to the organization's objectives, orders staff members on what to do, evaluates their performance and rewards or punishes them on the basis of how well they perform their assignments. Economic rewards are perceived as the major motivator of human behavior. The primary means of control is the reliance upon authority. The effectiveness of authority depends largely upon the administrator's ability to enforce it through the use of punishment.

The Theory Y Administrator

The Theory Y administrator operates upon an entirely different set of assumptions about human behavior than the Theory X administrator does. According to McGregor,[4] these are:

1. The expenditure of physical and mental effort in work is as natural as play or rest.
2. External control and the threat of punishment are not the only means for bringing about effort toward organizational objectives. Man will exercise self-direction and self-control in the service of objectives to which he is committed.
3. Commitment to objectives is a function of the rewards associated with their achievement.
4. The average human being learns, under proper conditions, not only to accept but to seek responsibility.
5. The capacity to exercise a relatively high degree of imagination, ingenuity, and creativity in the solutions of organizational problems is widely, not narrowly, distributed in the population.
6. Under the conditions of modern industrial life, the intellectual potentialities of the average human being are only partially utilized.

Upon the basis of the above assumptions McGregor[5] postulates that people will exercise self-control and self-direction in the achievement of organizational objectives to the extent that they are committed to these objectives.

"The central principle which derives from Theory Y is that of integration: the creation of conditions such that the members of the organization can achieve their own goals *best* by directing their efforts toward the success of the enterprise."

Consequently, the Theory Y administrator strives to create an environment which will encourage commitment to organizational objectives and which will provide opportunities for the maximum exercise of initiative, ingenuity, and self-direction in achieving them. This type of administrator has a genuine concern for the welfare of subordinates on the one hand and productivity on the other.

M For Management

Allen,[6] in a 1973 article, restudied McGregor's X and Y types of behavior and suggested that most managers avoid extremes in their beliefs about people. Allen developed what he called Theory M (for management) and stated that "people are motivated to work by highly complex factors that may be biological, psychological, social, or economic, to name only a few possibilities. Such factors vary in relative importance according to conditions at the time." He further stated: "Some people dislike responsibility and prefer to be led; others are ambitious and want to be leaders; the majority fall somewhere in between." These ideas would suggest two points in relation to administration: (1) X and Y type administrators represent only the extremes and the majority of administrators are somewhere between the extremes, and (2) the successful administrator recognizes that no two persons nor problems are identical; thus different types of behavior are needed at different times in order to best help the work group to accomplish team goals.

MOTIVATION

One of the physical education administrator's most important responsibilities is to motivate all staff members to their best efforts in behalf of the organization's objectives. Whenever an individual gives less than his or her best effort to the organization, it weakens the organization. It has been repeatedly demonstrated in athletic competition that a team of players, each of whom gives maximum effort, frequently defeats an opposing team which is superior but not highly motivated. By the same token, a physical education organization is weaker and less successful in its operations when every member fails to give less than optimal performance.

Similarly, the physical education administrator is often held responsible when a high level of motivation does not exist among the staff members. At times, the factors affecting motivation adversely may be beyond the power of the administrator to remedy. Inadequate facilities and equipment, an insufficient number of staff members, low salaries, few promotions, and a second-class citizen status within the institution are considerations which may diminish motivation. These are factors which the administrator is frequently unable to correct. However, there is no doubt that it is the administrator who is the leading factor affecting the motivation of staff members.

To accomplish a highly motivated, cooperative attitude toward the organization and its objectives on the part of the staff, the administrator must harness effectively all the major motivational forces which are available. Some of these major motivational forces are the basic needs or interests which are universally characteristic of people. Maslow[7] developed a hierarchy of human needs which he listed from low to high level needs: physiological needs (food, shelter, clothing), safety needs, then social (belonginess), esteem (self-respect), and finally self-actualization (self-fulfillment).

A number of behavioral scientists have supported the thesis that human needs or interests are organized in a hierarchy, with the physiological needs for survival at the base. At progressively higher levels are the needs for belonginess, esteem, and self-actualization. However, Albanese[8] cautions: "there is some evidence to support the model's predictions that satisfaction of lower level needs *causes* the strengths of those needs to decrease . . . the model has to be further tested before managers can utilize the concept of human behavior being motivated by a step-by-step satisfaction of five levels of needs."

The mistake which countless administrators have made is to assume that their staff members are solely interested in the economic motives. There should be no question that money is a powerful motivator of human beings. It is a prerequisite for meeting the survival needs. It contributes to the satisfaction of the higher level needs. However, it is not the only motivator. The administrator can achieve maximum motivation only by tapping all the motives which yield favorable and cooperative attitudes. The superior who relies primarily on the economic motives of buying an individual's time and then telling the person precisely what to do, how to do it, and at what level to produce is disregarding what behavioral science has learned about human behavior.

Other Variables Related to Motivation

In addition to employing the right motives to affect human behavior there are other factors involved in motivation. The manner in which organizational decision making is done is significantly related to motivation. The effectiveness of communication within the organization is another important consideration. The leadership processes employed by the administrator have a strong influence upon motivation. Motivation is also affected by the control processes employed.

Various behavioral scientists have emphasized the importance of the way in which the superior supervises subordinates. Productivity and job satisfaction, and thus motivation, can be increased. A summary is presented from Likert's[9] studies of organizational performance:

   a. Personnel are favorably disposed toward their superiors who try to get their ideas and do something about them.
   b. Administrators who are highly rated by their superiors hold more group meetings than those who hold few meetings.
   c. In organizations where group meetings are held, the personnel perform as usual when the supervisor is absent.
   d. A supportive attitude on the part of the supervisor, as well as the constructive use of group meetings, leads to group pride and loyalty.
   e. Higher production goals and more actual production with less sense of strain or pressure occur when group meetings are held.
   f. Supervisors who employ group meetings have higher peer group loyalty among their staff members. In turn, high peer group loyalty results in a feeling of less tension at work; a more favorable attitude toward their superior; better interpersonal relationships; a lower absence rate and a sense of group responsibility for getting the work done.

The Organizational Climate

In the last two decades the concept of organizational climate has assumed a position of increasing importance among organizational theorists. The climate of the relationships between the superior and subordinates has significant implications for the motivation of the people in an organization. For this reason it is an extremely important responsibility of an administrator to create the proper climate of the superior-subordinate relationship.

LEADERSHIP PROCESSES

The administrator, more than anyone else, affects the human relations in a physical education organization. He or she is so intimately involved with motivation, communication, personnel, daily operations, and the decision-making process, that this is the key position to affect the human resources in an organization. This is not to say that there are not other factors which may enter the picture. Unfortunately, there are, at times, other elements over which the chairperson has no control, that may affect staff members adversely.

Some administrators are "job-centered"; others are "employee-centered." Administrators who are "job-centered" are only interested in the productivity of their subordinates. Those who are "employee-centered" are interested both in their subordinates and their productivity. They identify with them and trust their colleagues who reciprocate by having confidence and trust in their superior.

Mutual trust and confidence are indispensable ingredients in the relationship between the administrator and staff members. For the subordinate to feel that the superior does not have a genuine concern for the worker's welfare and is not likely to give all a fair break is extremely damaging to morale.

Subordinates also doubt that they will get a fair break from a superior who has little upward influence. Research studies have shown the importance of the administrator having substantial influence with his or her own superior. Staff members look to their chairperson to obtain salary increases, promotions, improved facilities, adequate equipment and supplies, and better working conditions for them. When their administrator cannot deliver the needed resources, subordinates lose confidence. This is particularly true when other departmental chairpersons and directors are having more success than their own.

Staff members will not expect to get a fair break when their chairperson is incompetent. This is particularly true when the chairperson is not conversant with the technical aspects of the work. No one expects the administrator to be expert with every detail of every job but staff members expect their leader to be technically competent. If this is not the case, they lose confidence in their leader.

Neither will staff members hope to get a fair break from their superior when they have reason to doubt his or her integrity. If the administrator is devious, insincere, selfish, vain, arrogant, unscrupulous and disloyal, colleagues will soon find out. No matter how technically competent or whatever assets the administrator might have, if staff members cannot trust their administrator, the climate in the organization will not be healthy.

COMMUNICATION

Communication is an essential process of administration. An organization could not function without it. An administrator's decisions are meaningless unless they can be communicated to others. As a matter of fact, most administrative decisions depend upon data transmitted by others in the organization to the superior. The breakdown in communications has caused serious problems in countless organizations.

Likert[10] points out that:

> Communication is a complex process involving many dimensions. One is the transmission of material from the sender to the target audience. Another is its reception and comprehension. A third is its acceptance or rejection . . . Another complicating factor in the process of communication is the diverse nature of the material to be transmitted. There is:
> Cognitive material, such as:
> > information or facts as to the current situation, problems, progress toward goals, etc.
> > ideas, suggestions, experiences
> > knowledge with regard to objectives, policies, actions; and
>
> Motivational and emotional material, such as:
> > emotional climate or atmosphere
> > attitudes and reactions
> > loyalties and hostilities
> > feelings of support, appreciation, or rejection
> > goals and objectives.

Channels of Communication

A variety of channels of communication are available. The most direct is face-to-face communication. In small departments this type predominates. It has the advantage of providing an exchange between the sender and receiver which could be enlightening to both. When people do not meet face-to-face indirect communication may be provided by intermediaries or by written messages. The latter are extensively used in the larger organizations. The telephone and the loudspeaker system are indirect channels which enable the parties to discuss the message.

Blockages

Blockages in communications occur at a number of points in the system. The administrator frequently causes the problem when he or she forgets to communicate or sends incomplete, inaccurate or contradictory messages. Some are unwilling to share information with their colleagues. In this latter case staff members become bitter and frustrated when they are denied information to which they are entitled and which staff members in other departments receive.

Receivers themselves may cause a blockage of communication. They may ignore or carelessly receive messages. In these instances face-to-face communication is needed.

Flow of Information

The flow of information may be downward, upward, and sideward. Traditionally, communication was only thought of as orders or instructions initiated by the administrator for the subordinates. The sideward and upward flow of information was virtually ignored. Research investigations, however, have revealed the importance of sideward communication to the other teachers and upward communication to the administrator. Data shows that the lack of upward communication is more serious than the deficiencies in downward communication.

Upward communication is facilitated when the climate of the organization encourages it. All staff members should feel a responsibility for initiating upward—or sideward—communication that is pertinent and accurate. The administrator needs such information, particularly in larger organizations, to know what is going on in all aspects of the operation. The administrator may be unaware that some facilities are in need of repair or that certain items of equipment are defective or inadequate. Such problems should be reported immediately so that corrective action may be taken. As decisions of the superior are being implemented, he or she needs to know how they are working out. Some actions may be creating unnecessary difficulties for staff members or they may be unreasonable or unfair. Upward communication provides the best way for such matters to be brought to the attention of the administrator. Unless these problems are resolved, the consequences might prove detrimental to the organization. Not only is inefficiency encouraged but faculty morale is undermined.

DECISION MAKING

Decision making is another administrative process which has important implications for the human relations in an organization. Many authorities regard it as the most important administrative activity because it is involved in all of the other processes of administration such as planning, organizing, controlling, directing, coordinating and evaluating. Every administrator wants to have sound decisions and effective implementation of those decisions. In fact, this is what administration is all about. It is understandable why decision making is becoming generally recognized as the heart of organization and the process of administration.

A multitude of decisions are made in physical education organizations. These decisions may be categorized as personal and organizational. Personal decisions are those which every staff member makes in discharging duties. They relate to such matters as to what will be taught, how taught, what teaching aids to employ, evaluation of pupil progress, discipline and the like. Organizational decisions, on the other hand, relate to the operations of the entire organization and generally are of concern to all members of the department.

The Decision-Making Process

Griffiths[11] believes that the decision-making process involves the following steps:

1. Recognize, define and limit the problem.
2. Analyze and evaluate the problem.
3. Establish criteria or standards by which the solution will be evaluated or judged as acceptable and adequate to the need.
4. Collect data.
5. Formulate and select the preferred solution or solutions. Test them in advance.
6. Put into effect the preferred solution.
   a. Program the solution.
   b. Control the activities in the program.
   c. Evaluate the results and the process.

Faculty Participation in Departmental Decision Making

In educational circles the principle that all who might be affected by a decision should share in making it has wide currency. No aspect of the decision-making process is more widely misunderstood and improperly implemented. One interpretation is that all concerned faculty members should participate fully in the discussion and then finally make the decision on the issue by a formal vote. Another view is that after full discussion of the matter by the concerned faculty members, the administrator would then make the final decision. A third point of view holds that all faculty members should discuss the problem and then be delegated by the administrator to make some of the decisions with the administrator reserving the right to make the remainder of the decisions. Finally, there is the procedure whereby the administrator makes the decision without referring the matter to staff members.

The principle that all personnel who might be affected by a decision should share in making it is subject to a variety of interpretations. The term "share" causes the confusion. It is the consensus that all affected by a decision should participate in discussing it. Two advantages accrue from such a procedure. The first is that such discussion provides maximum input in regard to the decision. Staff members provide a larger number of ways of looking at a problem, a larger number of suggestions for a solution, and a larger number of criticisms of each proposed plan. The administrator would be remiss in not making full use of the talents of the members of his staff. Vital information or the best idea for solving the problem could come from some unexpected source.

The second advantage of involving those affected by a decision in a discussion of it is that staff members will implement the decision better when they have had such an opportunity. In connection with this point, Likert[12] says:

> Without question, wise decisions are important and necessary to the success of an enterprise, but it is equally true that no decision is any better than the motivation used in carrying it out. An excellent decision poorly executed because of hostile or apathetic motivation is no better in its consequences for the organization than a poor decision. It is well to keep in mind the formula:
> Results achieved = quality of the decision $\times$ motivation to implement the decision.
> If either term in the right half of the equation is low, the action performed will be unsatisfactory.

To give the concerned staff members an opportunity to discuss the issue and to express their convictions and concerns is definitely "sharing" in the decision-making process. However, to some the term "share" goes beyond this point. They believe that the decisions should be made by a vote of those concerned. They conceive this as "democratic administration."

The authority for making organizational decisions belongs to the organizational administrator. It has been delegated by a superior. If the administrator wants to delegate the authority to make decisions to the faculty, he or she may do so. However, this act does not remove the responsibility for the results of the decision from the administrator. Decisions which might well be made by faculty members, since they are directly involved with implementation, include such matters as curriculum, purchase and use of audio-visual and other instructional aids, teaching methods, classroom discipline and evaluation of student performance.

In the last decade the students are a segment of the school population who have become increasingly involved in the decision-making process. As consumers in the educational scene, this seems a right and natural function for students. Not only do they have more options in determining their own course work, but students have also shown interest in serving on policy-making committees with faculty members. Thus many students have been conscientious and concerned and have contributed fresh and worthwhile ideas to the educational scene.

SELECTED REFERENCES

FRENCH, WENDELL L., and DON HELLRIEGEL, *Personnel Management and Organization: Fields in Transition.* Boston: Houghton Mifflin Company, 1971.

MASSIE, JOSEPH L. and JOHN DOUGLAS, *Managing a Contemporary Introduction,* 2nd ed. Englewood Cliffs, N.J.: Prentice-Hall, Inc., 1977.

MINER, MARY GREEN and JOHN B. MINER, *A Guide to Personnel Management.* Washington, D.C.: The Bureau of National Affairs, Inc., 1973.

OWENS, ROBERT G., *Organizational Behavior in Schools.* Englewood Cliffs, N.J.: Prentice-Hall, Inc., 1970, Ch. 4 and 6.

NOTES

1. Rensis Likert, *The Human Organization* (New York: McGraw-Hill Book Company, Inc., 1961), p. 1.

2. Alfred Marrow, *Making Management Human* (New York: McGraw-Hill Book Company, Inc., 1957), p. 1.

3. Douglas McGregor, *The Human Side of Enterprise* (New York: McGraw-Hill Book Company, Inc., 1960), pp. 33–34.

4. McGregor, *The Human Side,* p. 47.

5. McGregor, *The Human Side,* p. 49

6. Louis A. Allen, "M for Management: Theory Y Updated," *Personnel Journal,* December 1973, pp. 1061–1067.

7. Abraham H. Maslow, "A Theory of Human Motivation" *Psychological Review* 50 (1943): pp. 370–396.

8. Robert Albanese, *Management Toward Accountability for Performance* (Homewood, Illinois: Richard D. Irwin, Inc., 1975), p. 425.

9. Rensis Likert, *New Patterns of Management* (New York: McGraw-Hill Book Company, Inc., 1967), pp. 26–43.

10. Likert, *New Patterns,* p. 44.

11. Daniel Griffiths, *Administrative Theory* (New York: Appleton-Century-Crofts, Inc., 1959), p. 94.

12. Likert, *New Patterns,* p. 212.

4

The Physical Education Staff

SIGNIFICANCE OF STAFF

James A. Garfield, former President of the United States, said, "Give me a log hut, with only a simple bench, Mark Hopkins on one end and I on the other and you may have all the buildings, apparatus, and libraries without him." Possibly this quotation comes closer to overemphasizing the importance of the faculty in the total school setup than it does to presenting all the factors in correct proportion. However, it points to a significant truth that has at times been overlooked: no school can be greater than its staff, nor can a program advance beyond the vision of those who administer it. The program must rely upon the staff to put it into efficient operation. Any philosophy that dictates the selection of staff members on the basis of friendship or politics rather than upon adequate qualifications can only fulfill its program in a mediocre way.

Before 1925 well-trained people in the field of physical education were comparatively scarce. Except for a brief decline during the depression years, the supply of men graduating from college with majors in the field rose gradually from 1925 to 1941, then dwindled to just a few during the war years. From 1946 to 1952 the number increased rapidly, after which there was a noticeable decline followed by a slight rise in 1956. Calls from the armed forces during the Korean and Vietnamese conflicts temporarily removed from teaching some of the graduates during the late 1950s and the 60s. However, the supply of men with bachelor's degrees adequately met the demand during these years. Declining student enrollments during the 1970s resulted in an oversupply of male physical educators in most areas. The situation concerning women with bachelor's degrees in physical education has had a different history. For many years there was a shortage of women physical educators. Not until the pupil decline starting in the mid 1970s were there sufficient women teachers to meet the demand and eventually create a surplus. Although there is a decreased demand for physical educators, it should be pointed out that many school districts would be understaffed if they had optimal physical education programs. All physical educators need to work diligently for daily physical education for grades K–12 in our schools, comprehensive programs for the exceptional students, and programs for the out of school population. When these goals are met, a dramatic increase in job opportunities will result.

The supply of women and men with graduate preparation was inadequate in the late 1940s. The steady growth of graduate education has resulted in an impressive number of physical education teachers who now have at least a master's degree. By 1976 there was already an oversupply of men with doctor's degrees. As a result of Title IX of the Education Amendments of 1972 and the implementation of affirmative action plans in the early and mid 70s, many education positions that had been closed to women and other minority groups were opened. This resulted in a significant increase in the number of women and other minorities receiving equal opportunity to pursue master's and doctor's degrees and thereby educationally qualify for administrative and higher education positions in physical education.

Since requirements for physical education majors vary widely from state to state and from school to school, it does not follow that all those who receive degrees are equally prepared. Semester hours required for a major in physical education vary from less than 20 to more than 60, and the type and quality of instruction differs considerably from school to school. Out of this varied training come graduates with varying qualifications. However, the administrator who really desires a well-prepared physical education faculty can have such a staff. It costs little more to secure good instructors than to secure poor ones. It is a matter of knowing adequate qualifications and being able to determine which of the candidates have these qualifications.

QUALIFICATIONS

There are many important characteristics that an administrator must consider when selecting a physical education instructor. Obviously, the job description will determine the type of technical skills that will be desired. If gymnastics is part of the teaching load, then competency in this area will be required. If administrative or coaching responsibilities are a part of the position, administrative or coaching skills of the applicant must be carefully evaluated. There are many other qualities, frequently more difficult to measure, that must also be considered. Of key importance is the ability of the person to relate positively to the students. Does the candidate enjoy teaching and working with students? Will the candidate continue to grow as a physical educator and strive to overcome weaknesses that might be present? Answers to this type of question must be carefully sought in order to obtain high quality staff members.

Several specific characteristics must be considered:

Personality. This is a complex area in that each person has a unique personality and different aspects of one's personality are typically exhibited in different situations. In nontechnical terms, personality can be viewed as an individual's way of behaving, experiencing, and thinking. These characteristics are of prime importance in determining whether or not a person should be selected for a physical education position. The close relationship which develops between the student and physical education teacher and the coach makes it critical for the physical education teacher and coach to have exemplary personality characteristics. For example, if a coach verbally expresses to the team members the value of following rules and then circumvents rules in the course of a season, the principle that the coach has been teaching will be discredited.

The importance of personality and character in the teacher is nowhere better expressed than by Pullias et al:[1]

> All of this is to say that the most fundamental principle of all we have considered about excellence in teaching is that if the teacher would effectively fulfill his role as a teacher, he must constantly grow in greatness as a person. In deepest essence, a teacher can be no greater as a teacher than he is as a person. The aphorism 'What you are speaks so loud I cannot hear what you say' is not more applicable anywhere in life than in teaching.

Emotional stability is an important personality attribute for the physical education teacher-coach. The pressures involved and the impact that this person has on students demands that a proper personal perspective be maintained. Self-control, acceptance of disappointments and criticisms, adaptation to changing situations, patience, an even temperament, and ability not to worry about trivial things are examples of qualities that physical educators need to possess.

Flexibility and Warmth. Heitzman and Starpoli reviewed research that investigated the characteristics of successful teachers.[2] They found flexibility and warmth to be key ingredients. Acceptance of student differences and varying moods requires physical educators to be flexible. Capitalizing on learning situations which develop suddenly or change from year to year places a premium on teacher flexibility. The spark of interest which surfaces when a student is motivated by something he or she has read, seen on television, or perhaps been shown by an older sister or brother, provides an optimum learning opportunity that will be utilized by the flexible teacher. The teacher's approach to each student must vary according to the personality of each student as well as with changes in the learning environment.

Warmth encompasses many things. It means accepting each student as a person and having a sincere interest in each student. Warmth permits the teacher to nurture even the student with strange and impulsive actions. It tells the student that someone cares. This is critical for student growth.

Health and physical fitness. This is a particularly important attribute for physical educators. The physical demands placed on a person teaching physical education are great and increase when after-school inter-scholastic and intramural responsibilities are included. Maintaining enthusiasm and handling the pressures associated with teaching physical education requires a satisfactory level of mental and physical health and physical fitness. The stamina to demonstrate, spot effectively, and teach physical skills requires a high level of health and physical fitness if the students are to learn in a safe climate.

One of the objectives of physical education programs is to develop physical fitness. The example set by the physical education teacher is an important influence on the students. This is another reason why physical fitness and health are important qualifications.

Intellectual ability. A teacher must have better than average intelligence. This is important for physical educators if they are going to grow as teachers and apply the principles of learning to their discipline. Mastery of teaching techniques and methodology changes based on research findings and implementing new approaches to the teaching process requires above average intellectual ability.

Communication skills. A physical educator must be able to communicate effectively, both orally and in writing. This is important for teachers of all disciplines. However, in physical education, communication skills are even more important. Physical educators frequently need to communicate with parents and other members of the community. This occurs when carrying out coaching and intramural responsibilities, presenting a sports night program, or being involved in some other school program that is promoting physical education.

Creativity. To make a physical education program come alive, creativity is needed. Meeting individual needs requires a creative person. Many physical educators find themselves teaching with insufficient equipment and inadequate facilities. The creative person will be able to overcome these disadvantages to the extent that a viable program can still be presented. This quality is also evident in successful athletic programs that are usually characterized by innovations and creative ideas in organizational pattern, practice procedures, and skill development.

Other Personal Characteristics

There are many other personal qualities that could be listed. Leadership ability, personal appearance, professional involvement, integrity, and resourcefulness are examples of characteristics that are desired.

Experience. Appropriate experience is important in the development and growth of a physical education teacher. Supervision is important during the formative years in order for the teacher or prospective teacher to profit from mistakes and failures. Experience can be counterproductive when the same errors are repeated. What one does about failure is the important factor. The true value of experience from the viewpoint of improving teachers is that it leads to better performances.

Experiences should be varied. The multifaceted nature of the physical education profession puts a premium on diversified skills and abilities. The student preparing to teach should strive to gain as many experiences as possible. Personal participation in sports, teaching skills to varied age groups, and working as camp counselors are examples of ways that experience can be obtained. The full-time teacher will continue to grow by participating in different aspects of the physical education field. In terms of experience, repetition of the same thing soon yields a rapidly diminishing return.

Experience serves as a testing device for those who select teachers. Analogously, by applying pressure from various directions, strong boxes can be selected out of a group of boxes varying in strength. The pressure does not make the strong boxes strong; rather, it provides a method of determining which ones are strong. Experience does the same thing and more for teachers. It furnishes a practical means of selecting the good ones, while giving all a chance to improve to a limited extent. Many good teachers have the essentials at the start, as do the strong boxes, and experience helps develop and classify them.

Preparation. From the standpoint of success as a teacher of physical education, an adequate professional preparation is of prime importance.

Granted equivalent personality qualifications, the teacher with a thorough preparation is worth much more than the one with poor professional preparation. Experience is a valuable asset, but it is doubtful that it can compensate for a weak professional preparation.

The basic and minimum requirements to be certified to teach physical education in public schools differ appreciably from state to state.[3] Less than 20 hours are required in some states, and other states require 30 or more hours. Assuming equivalence in such factors as the quality of teaching, equipment, facilities, and library in teacher education institutions, it is apparent that some states require a much higher standard of professional preparation than others.

What Constitutes a Strong Undergraduate Professional Preparation?

The American Association for Health, Physical Education and Recreation sponsored Professional Preparation Conferences in 1962 and again in 1973 to consider this question.[4,5] The 1962 Conference designated specific areas that were *strongly recommended* to develop the competencies needed by the beginning teacher. These areas are still pertinent, although changes in our field have resulted in the need for additions and a restructuring of the activities to comply with Title IX of the Education Amendments of 1972. The curricular areas that were recommended follow.

General Education:
1. English composition.
2. Physical science.
   a.   General chemistry
   b.   General physics.
3. Biological sciences.
   a.   General biology.
   b.   Human anatomy.
   c.   Human physiology.
4. Social science.
   a.   History.
   b.   General psychology.
   c.   General sociology.
5. Humanities.
   a.   Literature (English, American, or foreign).
   b.   Philosophy.
   c.   The arts (art, music, theater arts).

At the 1962 Professional Preparation Conference it was recommended that 50 percent of the undergraduate program be devoted to general education courses.

General professional education:

1. Social and philosophical foundations of education.
2. Educational psychology (growth and development).
3. Educational curriculum and instruction.
4. Directed teaching.

The number of credit hours to be devoted to course work in general professional education is from 15 to 17 percent of the total required for graduation.

Specialized professional preparation:

1. Introduction and orientation to physical education.
2. Administration and supervision of physical education.
3. Curriculum and instruction in physical education.
4. History, philosophy, and principles of physical education.
5. Measurement and evaluation in physical education.
6. Kinesiology.
7. Physiology of activity.
8. Adapted physical education.
9. Health education and safety education.
10. Recreation.
11. Physical activities.
    a. Fundamental skills and exercise:
       (1) Conditioning exercises.
       (2) Fundamental movements.
       (3) Exercise with apparatus.
       (4) Marching tactics.
       (5) Posture and body mechanics.
       (6) Weight training.
       (7) Individual self-testing events.
       (8) Stunts and tumbling.
    b. Sports and games:
       (1) Aquatics, including life saving and water safety.
       (2) Combatives—wrestling.
       (3) Team sports.
       (4) Individual and dual sports.
       (5) Mass or group games.

(6) Individual and group contests.

(7) Relays.

c.   Rhythms and dance activities.

No specific recommendations were made in regard to the amount of time and credit that should be allocated for the various courses recommended. However, the total hours for the specialized professional preparation area should represent about one third of the total. Thus, if 120 semester hours were required for graduation, 40 should be devoted to this area.

The academic courses listed under *Specialized professional preparation* are nearly always included among the requirements for major students in those institutions that are recognized for their strong programs in physical education. In regard to the area of physical activities, a conference of representatives of the institutions in the Northwest District, AAHPER,[6] recommended that 16 semester hours or 24 quarter hours be required of physical education majors.

Courses in motor learning, physical education and the law, human movement, aesthetics, and research foundations are examples of additional specialized courses that are in many professional preparation programs. A block of courses leading to nonteaching careers are also becoming prevalent. Specialized preparation for careers in athletic training, coaching, therapeutics, athletic administration, and various aspects of the sport communication field are prime examples.

The 1973 Professional Preparation Conference did not recommend specific courses. Instead members of the conference task force presented concepts that serve as goals for professional preparation programs. Behavioral competencies needed for student mastery of the concepts were presented to provide guidelines for college and university preparation programs. The emphasis was placed on student performance objectives.

The 1973 conference presented concepts and competencies which were consistent with the course recommendations of the 1962 conference. Competencies in general education, general professional education, and specialized professional preparation were included. The 1973 conference emphasized qualitative factors rather than the quantitative factors of the 1962 conference.

Some physical education departments have established areas of emphasis in their programs which permit students to specialize in one aspect of physical education. A student's program can place an emphasis on adaptive physical education, elementary physical education, gymnastics, team sports, motor learning, or some other similar area where a core of courses are offered. The advantage to this approach is that the student can become highly skilled in the area of specialization. The disadvantage is that most physical education positions in the elementary and secondary level require ability in a range of activities. There is also concern that some students do not obtain a solid, broad foundation which is needed for future specialization and growth as a physical educator.

With the abundance of physical education teachers, there is no justification for school districts to employ physical educators who have only a minor in physical education. Some school districts require a master's degree or at least a specified number of graduate hours for employment or tenure. To upgrade the quality of instruction, some states require graduate study in order to receive permanent certification. At the higher education level, the doctorate is generally required, either for employment or prior to attaining tenure.

The caliber of the physical education graduate is influenced significantly by the excellence of the preparation program. The quality of the program is determined by a number of factors. Of major importance are the standards for admission and retention of the physical education professional student. Screening of applicants on motor ability, intellectual competence, and activity background in high school should be a minimal standard for admittance to a professional preparation program. Satisfactory scholarship and performance standards should be required for retention in a program.

The quality of the teaching staff is another vitally important consideration. In certain institutions highly trained specialists are available to teach each professional course. There is a great difference between what students get out of courses taught by well-prepared teachers as compared with the same courses taught by instructors who have only a superficial background in the area. It is an unfortunate fact that in many institutions the professional courses are taught by staff members who lack the background and mastery of the subject matter. This applies equally to the activities and the classroom courses.

Another critical item is the pride that the department takes in the quality of its products. It is important for physical education departments to be proud of the reputation gained by graduating superior professional students. All the faculty members must be dedicated to producing quality products and making every effort to accomplish this objective.

The final consideration is the matter of sufficient resources for a superior operation. Such factors as the adequacy of the equipment, facilities, library, and number of faculty are all related to quality programs. The number of available faculty members is an important consideration. If the number is inadequate, staff members are either overloaded or their classes are overly large.

Selection of Staff

The administrator who is evaluating an applicant's qualifications must consider the type of behavior that would be consistent with school and departmental philosophy and would contribute positively to staff relationships. This does not mean that staff members should be from the same "mold." Divergence of opinion and different types of personalities add strength to a physical education staff and are critical factors in establishing relationships with the typical heterogeneous school population.

A carefully written job description should precede the search for a new staff member. The exact nature of the position, with a clear explanation of competencies needed, must be listed. The school district's affirmative action guidelines must also be followed to provide an equal employment opportunity for all qualified applicants.

It is preferable to involve staff members in the selection process. In a small department all members might be involved, whereas a larger department would select a committee to screen and interview applicants. As many members of a staff as possible should meet candidates to provide varying viewpoints and to minimize the possibility of hiring someone who would cause a major conflict in the department. Institutional policy will determine the role that is assumed by administrators in the selection process.

As many sources of information as possible should be used to evaluate applicants for a position. Initial screening should include an evaluation of the candidate's written application and pertinent records to determine whether the candidate has the performance competencies required for the position. A more rigorous evaluation should be used once the initial screening is completed. The following criteria and sources of information are commonly used:

College transcripts. Most employing officers are interested in examining transcripts of candidates. They provide certain insights that may prove helpful. Indications of strengths and weaknesses may be revealed. The academic ability of the candidates does have significance.

In this connection it should be pointed out that the institution attended by the candidate is an important consideration. Some colleges and universities are quality institutions and their physical education graduates are superbly prepared. Physical education departments in such institutions make every effort to eliminate weak candidates. While professional preparation is only one of the criteria to be assessed in employing new staff members its quality can be readily evaluated by determining the institution where the preparation was obtained.

Other college records. The extent of participation in various activities provides valuable information. Leadership responsibilities are listed and it is possible to get an indication of the candidate's interests.

Record of participation in sports. This is a particularly important consideration where coaching is involved.

Statement of philosophy of physical education. The philosophy of candidates is invariably requested. Ordinarily it is determined in the personal interview. At times a written statement is requested.

Professional activities. Information about professional activities is very important. Active membership in professional organizations and regular attendance at conventions and conferences indicates interest in the profession and personal growth.

Civic activities. Involvement in civic activities adds strength to a person's application.

Reference letters. Reference letters are usually involved in the selection of new teachers. They may be assets or liabilities. When they accurately portray the weaknesses as well as strengths of the candidates, they are invaluable. When weaknesses and undesirable characteristics are not mentioned where they exist, a letter of recommendation has little validity. It has happened occasionally that some administrators, in order to get rid of a weak or undesirable staff member, have not represented the person in a true light in a letter of recommendation.

In this situation the reputation of the writer is of major importance. The integrity of many individuals is so well-established that complete reliance may be placed on their recommendations. The same confidence cannot be felt in a recommendation if the writer's integrity is unknown. In this latter case one's confidence in a written recommendation is improved when the author holds a responsible position in an institution that has a professional program of recognized standing.

The Family Educational Rights and Privacy Act of 1974 provides that students over the age of 18 may not be denied the opportunity to review and inspect their education records. This has made it even more important to know the person who has written the recommendation. Follow-up telephone calls or personal discussions are highly recommended.

The crucial importance of the character of candidates has been pointed out. The best way to assess this quality is from information supplied by individuals who have been closely acquainted with the candidate. This information can be obtained via a letter of recommendation or a discussion either personally or by telephone. Of all the qualifications that must be evaluated fully and accurately none compares to character.

Written examinations. Some school systems use the results of the National Teacher Examinations to evaluate the candidate's general professional background and competence in the field of physical education. These are standard examinations available at various centers.

Performance of physical education skills. A few school systems require candidates to demonstrate their activity skills. This has proved a valuable procedure for many years. It is not extensively used because of various problems in administering the tests.

The personal interview. The personal interview is undoubtedly the most important of all procedures employed to select new staff members. It is exceptional when candidates are selected without being interviewed. If the expense of bringing the candidate to the community is prohibitive, an interview may be arranged at a convention or in the applicant's own community by a designated staff member who is traveling in the vicinity.

The interview should be carefully planned. It is designed to evaluate such factors as manner and appearance, poise, personality, verbal expression, personal philosophy of physical education, recreational interests, professional attitudes, and aspirations. The candidate should be encouraged to ask questions about any matters of concern. In addition to the formal interview, impressions may be obtained at luncheon and dinner meetings or during participation in a recreational activity.

Observation in a teaching situation. This is a very desirable procedure, but it is not extensively employed because of the problems of implementing it. It is so advantageous, however, to see candidates in action that the efforts to arrange for them to teach one or two classes are justified. Some administrators who are employing first-year teachers will make arrangements to visit classes during the applicant's student-teaching experience. If this is not possible, administrators will weigh heavily the recommendation of the public school teacher who has been observing the candidate's student-teaching performance.

Teaching Load

Sound administration requires thorough consideration of the amount of work assigned to each staff member, just as it does careful staff selection.

Teaching loads in secondary schools are reasonably well standarized. Five periods per day plus a study hall or preparation period will approximate the teaching load in most secondary schools. In small schools in rural areas the teaching load will generally be greater. Departmental chairpersons are usually relieved of part of the regular teaching load. A similar arrangement is made for athletic directors who are part of the physical education department. In many school systems the chairperson and athletic director also receive extra compensation for their administrative duties.

It should be recognized that teaching load involves more than the number of classes taught per day. Conferences with students, grading papers, and various clerical duties such as recording physical fitness test scores and preparation are all involved. All these factors are related to the total number of students handled by the teacher. It is possible for a teacher to have a heavier teaching load than a colleague even though the latter may teach one less class per day. This is due to differences in class size. For this reason another standard is frequently employed, namely, one teacher for every 190 pupils.

In most school districts the teacher's contract will specify the permitted teacher load. The administrator must abide by the contract when assigning classes and other duties.

On the higher education level 12 hours per week of undergraduate academic teaching is a widely prevalent standard. Eighteen hours of physical activity classes represents teaching loads in many colleges and universities. In small institutions the academic and activity teaching loads are appreciably larger.

No standard work load exists for administrators in institutions of higher education. In addition to their administrative assignment most will teach and a few will coach. They must spend whatever time it takes on administrative duties to make the department run efficiently. They must do that whether it requires 10 or 60 hours a week.

Proper class size depends on such factors as space and equipment available, type of activity, degree of classification of pupils for activity, and grade level. Even though there are many modifying factors, certain general conclusions regarding class size may prove valuable. Generally a class of 25 to 30 is not too large to provide an excellent teaching situation. When teaching activities requiring high levels of skill, smaller classes might be indicated. If a differentiated staffing plan is utilized, larger classes are feasible. The use of teacher-interns, paraprofessionals, and aides will permit classes of 50 to 60 if ample facilities are available. Differentiated staffing also makes it possible to utilize different teacher skills and to vary large and small group instruction according to the activity and the specific skills that are being taught. Incorporation of clerical and equipment personnel into the differentiated staffing plan provides more time for the teachers to spend on actual teaching responsibilities.

EVALUATION OF STAFF

Physical education administrators are obligated to assess the teaching effectiveness of their staff members. Their supervisory responsibilities require that they know the strengths and weaknesses of every one of their teachers. Such knowledge is needed in order to schedule their personnel most advantageously and to give them help and guidance where necessary. In addition, such data are needed for decisions on tenure, promotions, and salary increases.

The evaluation of teaching effectiveness has been a problem for years and the solution is nowhere in sight. A great deal of research in regard to teaching effectiveness has been done, but the results are inconclusive. Much effort has gone into the determination of qualities, traits, or behavioral characteristics which differentiate the effective from the ineffective teacher. These many investigations have failed to come up with any criterion or constellation of criteria which can be used to evaluate all teachers objectively. Despite the problems involved, the administrator has the responsibility to determine teacher effectiveness.

The best way to evaluate staff effectiveness is to determine the extent to which the departmental objectives are being achieved. If evidence is available that student performance on standard tests for the various physical education objectives has attained a satisfactory level, the administrator is justified in believing that the staff as a whole has met the most important criterion. This is not to say, however, that perfection has been attained. It is quite likely that an even better performance of students might be obtained. Likewise, some staff members are probably more effective in accomplishing the objectives than others. Consequently, the administrator must constantly evaluate the performance of every staff member.

Criteria of an Effective Staff

Some of the criteria of an effective staff are:

1. An adequate number of staff members are available to cover all assignments without being overloaded or without classes being too large.

2. Staff members meet the recognized standards of professional preparation.

3. Specialists are available for all positions requiring specialized preparation.

4. Each staff member has a mastery of the subject matter for which she or he is responsible.

5. Each staff member satisfactorily meets the needs of students through physical education.

6. Staff morale is high. Staff members are all loyal to each other and the department.

7. The staff is enthusiastic, neat, punctual, and dedicated to the welfare of students.

8. The staff members are respected by other faculty members; they command admiration and respect in the community.

9. The staff members are progressive; they keep abreast of the literature and research; they belong to the appropriate professional organizations and they regularly attend professional meetings.

10. Each staff member is conversant with the various methods of presenting the subject to students and is consistently successful in the methods employed.

11. Staff members use appropriate evaluative procedures.

12. Student interest and participation is enthusiastic. Absences, excuses, and disciplinary problems are at a minimum.

Appraising Staff Members

The increased emphasis on accountability has made it even more important for the administrator to assess accurately the performance of staff members. Performance criteria must be clearly designated to permit the administrator to precisely evaluate staff members on the basis of their ability as teachers. Competency-based criteria should form the basis for staff evaluation. The criteria should be established for each school so that staff members are aware of the performance standards that will be used to evaluate their teaching ability. Most states, many institutions of higher education, and numerous teacher education organizations are in the process of establishing performance criteria which can serve as a basis for a physical education department's competency requirements.

The best procedure for an administrator to use when evaluating staff members is to actually observe them in action. Several classes should be viewed to get a true picture. Videotape can also be an effective technique. It has the added advantage of allowing the administrator and the teacher who taught the class to view the session jointly. This procedure tends to contribute more to teacher growth and improvement and is not as likely to cause teacher resentment.

The administrator receives information about staff members from a variety of other sources. From parents, students, other faculty members, and citizens in the community will come unsolicited reports that may reflect favorably or unfavorably upon the performance of the teacher.

Students will spread information about their instructors; not infrequently, some of this comes back to the administrator. Legitimate student feedback is valuable. Student evaluations, anonymously submitted on a regular basis, for all faculty, are helpful to the administrator and can assist the teacher in pinpointing weaknesses.

In normal associations in and about the department, the administrator will gain many impressions of colleagues. Such factors as personal appearance, punctuality, thoroughness, attention to detail, cooperativeness, and professional attitude will be revealed to the observer.

It is important that the staff member receive a copy of the evaluation, whether it is an informal unstructured report of a class visit or a more extensive evaluation. Staff appraisal should be keyed to staff improvement.

Self-evaluation is too frequently overlooked as an evaluation technique in physical education. It is highly cherished by coaches who view films of their teams' performances over and over in order to gain insight for future improvement. Self-evaluation of teaching performance in the physical education class setting will also lead to improvement. The teacher having responsibility for carrying out a specific assignment must be significantly involved in the evaluation process if improved performance is to be achieved.

SELECTED REFERENCES

DAVIS, HOWARD, *State Requirements in Physical Education for Teachers and Students.* Washington, D.C.: AAHPER, 1973.

LOHSE, LOLA L., "What Makes a Good Teacher," *The Physical Educator,* (October 1974), p. 156.

PEASE, DEAN A., "Competency Based Teacher Education," *Journal of Physical Education and Recreation,* (May 1975), pp. 20–22.

Professional Preparation in Dance, Physical Education, Recreation Education, Safety Education and School Health Education. Washington, D.C.: AAHPER, 1974.

Professional Preparation in Health, Physical Education and Recreation. Washington, D.C.: AAHPER, 1962.

Title IX of the Education Amendments of 1972. Washington, D.C.: U.S. Department of Health, Education and Welfare.

NOTES

1. Earl Pullias et al., *Toward Excellence in College Teaching* (Dubuque, Iowa: William C. Brown Company, 1963), p. 44.

2. Ray Heitzman and Charles Starpoli, "Teacher Characteristics and Successful Teaching," *Education,* 95 (Spring 1975), pp. 298–299.

3. Howard Davis, *State Requirements in Physical Education for Teachers and Students* (Washington, D.C.: AAHPER, 1973).

4. *Professional Preparation in Health, Physical Education and Recreation* (Washington, D.C.: AAHPER, 1962), pp. 65–70.

5. *Professional Preparation in Dance, Physical Education, Recreation Education, Safety Education and School Health Education* (Washington, D.C.: AAHPER, 1974), pp. 23–51.

6. Northwest District, American Alliance for Health, Physical Education and Recreation and the Athletic Institute, *Proceedings of the Menucha Conference (1964),* p. 88.

5

Student Leaders
in Physical Education

Ours is a society in which everyone is granted the right to be a leader in any line of endeavor for which he or she can adequately prepare. We do not select certain classes as the ruling or leading groups and arbitrarily relegate others to the less desirable positions. We believe in giving and taking, in following in some aspects of life while leading in others.

Modern educational philosophy accepts and sponsors the proposition that we learn to do by doing; that is, by actually practicing or living out an experience we acquire more knowledge of it than by just hearing or reading about it. If the schools are to prepare students to live enriched lives during both school life and adult life, many opportunities must be provided for practice of the elements of successful living. One of these elements, certainly, is leadership, around which can be developed cooperation, loyalty, sociability, and many other desirable social qualities. Few, if any, other school subjects provide the number of leadership opportunities that are to be found in physical education. The instructor who does not take advantage of the outstanding opportunities offered is failing to make use of the possibilities which are available and is not putting to good use the talents that have been entrusted to the school by the community. The use of student leaders does not provide an opportunity for the teacher to rest while the students do the work; instead, it provides a more complete means of educating through physical education, since it permits the students to share in various aspects of leadership which the instructor directs.

EDUCATIONAL VALUES

In addition to providing invaluable opportunities to develop leadership, a student-leader program can also contribute to the improvement of the physical education program. The help the student leaders can give to the instructor is appreciable. They can assist with countless details, thus enabling the teacher to devote more time to important functions. Most important of all, student progress is facilitated. More individual attention is available and the level of accomplishment of the entire class is raised.

Physical education teachers carry a very heavy load. Almost invariably they have more students than they can handle adequately. Their responsibilities involve a multitude of details. To accomplish their objectives they urgently need more help; yet additional faculty personnel are difficult to obtain. The solution to the dilemma is to use student leaders. They can be an invaluable asset if utilized properly. The astonishing fact is that so many secondary schools fail to capitalize on this resource. What makes this all the more surprising is that countless schools have had great success with student-leader programs. Likewise, YMCAs and recreational agencies have had similar successful results. Out of all this experience has emerged the fact that student leader programs are indispensable.

Another advantage of a student-leader program is that it encourages some of the participants to consider physical education as a career. The experience provides a realistic introduction to physical education, and many physical educators entered this field because of an interest engendered while they participated as student leaders.

Ordinarily student leaders are highly motivated to improve their own performance in the activities included in the program. The last thing they want is to appear incompetent before their classmates. This extends also to their physical fitness and personal appearance. In every way they want to excel, and they are willing to pay the price of extra practice.

The best way to develop potential leadership ability is to have the opportunity of experiencing leadership. This opportunity enables students to develop poise and self-assurance. They can acquire a sense of responsibility and initiative. The ability to take charge of a group of peers and to accomplish the purposes of the program is a valuable educational experience. Tact, social sensitivity to the interests and needs of others, and thoughtfulness may be gained.

Student Leaders in Class Work

Since practically all students in the school are members of physical education classes for at least a part of their school career, the regular class work offers an opportunity to provide some type of leadership training for a large percentage of the students. The principles and procedures are essentially the same in middle or junior high school, senior high school, and college. They can be applied below these grade levels, but this involves more difficulties. Some minor modifications will need to be made at the various age levels and for different types of activity.

Presenting the plan. This should be done at the first meeting of the class. Some time might well be spent in pointing out the values and opportunities this type of procedure has for the class members. The general setup and procedure of the plan should be explained, and in this connection the authority and responsibility of a leader should be clearly designated. As a means of overcoming the possible objection that one student should not have the right to tell another what to do, it should be explained that there can be no leaders unless there are followers; and that, in order to have followers when one's turn comes to lead, it is only fair to serve as a follower for the other person's leadership.

Opportunities to lead. There are enough different leadership opportunities in a class of this type that each student should be able to find something in which he or she can lead reasonably well. Some of those opportunities are listed and discussed in brief:

1. Leader of squad or class group. There can be, quite conveniently, four or five such leaders in a class. This is one of the better leadership possibilities, for students in this position take charge of their group, under the instructor's direction, for many of the activities.

2. Activity leader. Student leaders can be of invaluable assistance to the instructor by demonstrating activities in which they are competent and by helping students to master skills which have been presented.

3. Individual assistant to slow-learning and physically weak students. A one-to-one basis is needed for such students to achieve satisfactory progress.

4. Leader of warming-up exercises. This should be passed around so that several class members have the chance to lead the group. These leaders must display enthusiasm and assurance tempered with friendliness.

5. Spotters. Spotters are necessary in gymnastics. Students selected for this purpose should be among the most highly skilled in the group.

6. Officials. A class should provide its own officials for the games that are to be played. Some of the better students can act as chief officials and those less experienced as assistants. These boys and girls should be granted the customary authority due officials of the game concerned.

7. Member of equipment and grounds committee. The activity area should be in condition to use, but it should be checked by someone to be sure that it is. Courts and fields need to be prepared for class use. In softball the bases may need to be placed and taken up later; in volleyball the nets may need to be put up, and in practically every sport the equipment needs to be brought out before class and returned after class.

8. Leader for games of lower organization. Every student in the class should have a turn at presenting a game of this type and directing the remainder of the class in it.

9. Assistant in the production of special programs such as demonstrations, exhibitions, and clinics.

10. Participant in a variety of ways in the testing program. Students can time and measure performance and check and record test results.

11. Assistant in maintaining the bulletin board.

12. Assistant in the supervision of the locker and shower rooms.

13. Assistant in administering the noon-hour recreation program.

14. Assistant to the instructor in planning the physical education program. Input from the students is valuable.

Methods of selecting leaders. In most cases the advantages of participation will be distributed more evenly, and the whole plan will work out more smoothly if the instructor appoints leaders and thus apportions opportunities. This is particularly true concerning officials, committee members, leaders for warming-up exercises and for games of lower organization.

The matter of selecting group leaders presents a somewhat different problem, for these students must conduct and manage their groups during a large portion of the class time. They must be the type that others will follow readily or the system will not function properly. For the first semester there will be but one-third to two-fifths of a normal class which can serve creditably as group leaders, and those are the students who should act in that capacity. Later, many more can learn the essential techniques. At the first meeting of the class the instructor should appoint leaders to serve for about three weeks until the class members have an opportunity to know one another. It should be announced that these leaders are to serve three weeks. If the instructor knows few or none of the students, he or she should still appoint the first group of leaders at about the end of the first meeting. This can be done on the basis of size, general appearance, apparent confidence, extrovertive tendencies shown by speaking up when the opportunity is offered, and on the basis of hunches. On these bases some few will be appointed who do not possess adequate qualifications, but the same would be true if the appointments were made a few meetings later. There is no value in hesitating, for all are new, and a weak leader will probably get along better at first while all are learning the routine than later when the routine is established. When the three weeks are up, the class members should elect their leaders for the next division of time—probably five or six weeks. All class members except the first group leaders are eligible. Each member should vote for as many fellow students as there are to be leaders. The old leaders should count the votes in the presence of the instructor and announce only the highest candidates. If five leaders are to be elected, the five highest become group leaders for the next period. At the end of their service period others are elected as above, with only those who have not served as group leaders eligible for election. The class members can be trusted to elect only those whom they consider leaders since the weight of group opinion will overbalance a few votes for personal friends. Those selected by the class are those whom the class will follow.

Methods of guiding leaders. This can be done in part by means of general instructions to all concerning the responsibilities and techniques of leadership, but it is done chiefly through leaders' conferences with the instructor. These may be group or individual conferences. For new leaders there should be group conferences at which the specific duties to be performed are discussed, additional suggestions are made, and questions are answered. As the leaders gain experience, the conferences should become less frequent and more individual in nature. A definite effort must be made to help the leader who needs help, but those who are having no difficulties need not be included in the later conferences.

Method of selecting group. Each leader should have the opportunity to choose his or her group. This should not be done in the presence of the rest of the class members, except for the first time, when the members do not know each other's abilities. Since the purpose here is to develop leadership instead of inferiority complexes, the poorer performers must be spared the depressing effect of being chosen from among the last. They need to have their confidence built up, not destroyed by being made to feel that they are the least desirable candidates. Except as stated above, the following method of selection is recommended. All class members' names except those choosing are written on the board. The right to choose first, second, third, and fourth (assuming four leaders) is determined by lot. On the second round the order is reversed, and the leader who chose fourth gets the chance to choose fifth; the person who chose third chooses sixth; the one who chose second chooses seventh; and the one who chose first chooses eighth and ninth. This method is followed in order to provide for more equal competition. The choices granted each leader are given in Table 5-1. As a student is chosen, that name is marked off the board and placed on the list of the leader who chose that individual. The teams should be posted on the bulletin board with the names arranged in alphabetical order; then none will be shown to have been chosen last or next to last.

Each new group of leaders will choose their squads from the class roll. This will tend to place the students each leader wants on his or her squad and give each class member a chance to become better acquainted with a larger percentage of the class.

TABLE 5-1.

First	1	8	9	16	17	24	25	32	33	40	41	
Second	2	7	10	15	18	23	26	31	34	39	42	
Third	3	6	11	14	19	22	27	30	35	38	43	
Fourth	4	5	12	13	20	21	28	29	36	37	44	45

Class control under leaders. Class control will not ordinarily present a problem because of the presence of the teacher. If a problem arises for a student leader, the instructor should if possible permit the leader to handle the situation. Only in extreme cases should the instructor step in and take charge of a group for control purposes; for when the teacher does, the confidence of the leader and the respect of the group for their leader is diminished. The instructor should provide control assistance, but it should be indirect.

Control problems usually involve failure to comply with the group leader's requests, objecting to officials' decisions, not following prescribed procedures, speaking out of turn in rules meeting, and any other acts that provide evidence of not being willing to accept the requests of those in charge. Individual conferences with the chronic offender and with the leader who has control difficulties are often helpful in improving control. Simply talking it over with the unadjusted student in private conference may clear up the matter. In the case of the leader, helpful suggestions and the building up of confidence are important. In some cases the plan of making anyone who objects to an official's decision the new official helps to maintain high standards of officiating.

Student Leaders in Intramural Activities

Historically, intramural activities furnished the outstanding opportunity for students to lead in physical education in the schools of this country. This still remains a particularly favorable area of operation for student leaders, under faculty guidance.

Student Leaders in Varsity Athletics

Interscholastic and intercollegiate athletics provide two distinct types of student leadership opportunities: those delegated to the students selected to direct their respective teams in action and those provided for managers and assistants. Captains of the various teams and other specific team leaders, such as the quarterback in football, the catcher in baseball, and the coxswain in crew, are the leaders of the first type. The captains may be elected by the letter winners of the previous year or appointed by the coach for a season or for a single contest. Many coaches prefer to have the captain serve for a season, especially if there is one student who is an outstanding leader, for this practice gives more stability to the team organization. If there is no student who really stands out as a leader, the team may function as well or better with a different captain for each contest. If the practice of having a different captain for each contest prevails, the coach almost always appoints the captain. Specific team leaders, other than captains, are appointed by the coach to fit the particular requirements of the position.

These positions of leadership in varsity athletics are some of the most desired and most valuable in the entire school. Consequently, it is not sound practice to permit one student to serve as captain in two or three sports or for two years in one sport, since others should also have an opportunity to receive the benefits of this experience. It should also be remembered that student leaders should be under the direction of the coach. If there is any value in training and experience, the coach certainly is better qualified to direct than students are. If the coach cannot be trusted with matters of supervising leadership, the remedy does not lie in turning the responsibility over to students but rather in dismissing that coach and securing one who can take care of normal responsibilities.

Opportunities for managers in varsity athletics (see Chapter 11 on interschool athletics).

Leaders Corps

Some schools have well-established leaders corps. They are somewhat differently organized and conducted than the student leader organization previously described. They represent an elite group in the school and membership is highly prized—in fact it may be considered one of the highest honors in the school.

Standards for membership are very high. Such criteria as the following are commonly established: (1) excellence in physical education activities, (2) a level of physical fitness which is appreciably above the average, (3) at least average academic achievement, (4) leadership ability, (5) good citizenship, and (6) interest and enthusiasm in physical education.

In a senior high school a common practice is to select only seniors for the leaders corps. They have the advantage of greater maturity and experience in this program. Ordinarily the selection is made in the spring of the year while the students are still juniors. All staff members should participate in the selection of the student leaders.

Members of the leaders corps usually wear a distinctive uniform and have a whistle. Often they wear a jacket or insignia in their academic classes which identifies them as members of the leaders corps. Unless financially unable to do so, the students ordinarily purchase their own clothing.

The duty of the members of the leaders corps is to assist the teacher in physical education classes. To render more valuable assistance they usually go through several sessions per week with the instructor. These extra meetings are held at times when students have free periods such as during activity periods. The purpose of such sessions is to provide the student leaders with a thorough understanding of the next lesson and the manner in which they will perform their role. In addition, they will have the opportunity to perfect their own skills.

The most successful leaders corps or clubs are formally organized with officers and a constitution and bylaws. Regular meetings are held and a carefully prepared agenda is followed. The induction of new members is formally executed with a dignified ceremony in the presence of all club members. High standards of performance must be maintained for continued membership in the organization. The aims and objectives of the program are carefully explained to inductees. The contributions of the members are publicized in appropriate ways.

Many physical education teachers select skilled performers in their classes to assist in demonstrations, spotting, and providing individualized help to students needing special attention. Likewise, the practice of using students to take attendance; assist in testing; securing the necessary equipment; and preparing the teaching stations, officiating, and the like are employed.

It should be pointed out, however, that the members of the leaders corps are equipped to provide a quality of service which is decidedly superior to that described above. Their increased maturity, careful selection, previous experience, and specialized preparation enable them to make an invaluable contribution to the teaching program.

6

Office Management

Every physical education administrator needs to understand the essentials of efficient office management. This need is obvious in large departments where secretaries, clerks, telephone operators, and receptionists are available to provide a variety of services for the public and department personnel. However, the same functions must be carried on in a one-person department, where no secretary or office equipment is available. Regardless of the size of the department, correspondence must be carried on, reports rendered, materials duplicated, equipment ordered, materials filed, and records maintained. Whether the department is large or small, the internal requirements are the same. The only difference is that in the small department the administrator must do more things, and in the large department the various duties are delegated to others to perform.

An effective office operation is important to the success of the department. The work of the administrator and the staff members is assisted materially by office personnel. Faculty members are relieved of a variety of duties that can be better performed by office employees. Services to students and the general public are improved. Communications are enhanced. As a consequence, better public relations are engendered.

There are proper and improper ways of performing all the office details in a physical education office. To do them correctly saves both time and money. The efficient operation of a department requires sound office procedures. Such procedures have been tested and proved in business and industry and may be readily adapted to school situations. No administrator can afford to fail to use them.

Office Unit Orientation

The administrative offices should be centrally located so as to be accessible to all who have business with the director or any of the staff members. Almost invariably the office is located near the entrance of the gymnasium or the physical education building. Staff offices should be located adjacent to the central office and close to the classrooms.

Office Facilities

The office facilities needed depend upon the size of the organization and the functions it serves. Although needs vary, a desirable physical education office arrangement should include the following facilities:

1. A waiting and reception room for visitors. Such a facility should be available for visitors, students, and other persons who have personal or business matters to discuss with the administrator. It should be large enough to accommodate the largest number of callers who are likely to occupy it at any one time. This space should be separated in some manner from the other office facilities.

2. A service area where students and the general public may be accommodated. This could be located at one side of the main office. With the availability of a window and counter space this area could serve as an information center and a place where students can make adjustments concerning their registration in physical education classes. Ordinarily, such matters can be handled by a member of the office staff.

3. A main office area. This is the space in which members of the clerical staff perform their services. This is where the desks, typewriters, filing cabinets, tables, and other office equipment are ordinarily located. Frequently faculty mail boxes are situated here. This area also serves as a repository for department records.

An important function of the office staff is to duplicate materials. This can be done in the central office, but it is advantageous to have a smaller separate area for this purpose as well as for storage space of office supplies.

The administrator should strive to obtain optimum working conditions in the office. It is impossible for the personnel to achieve maximum output in an environment where considerable noise, confusion, and distraction prevail. Unnecessary traffic and distraction must be eliminated.

4. A private office for the administrator. It is advantageous for the administrator to have an office in which he/she can hold private conferences and concentrate and develop the thinking vital to the organization. Another advantage of the private office is that visitors who talk loudly do not distract office workers.

5. A conference room adjacent to the main office is a desirable facility. It is needed for staff and committee meetings and as a place for the entertainment of guests.

Office Functions and Practices

The size of the physical education office usually varies with the size of the institution and the extensiveness of the program. In some very small secondary schools the physical education administrator is fortunate to have an office. In many other small schools the office is often shared with several other staff members. Office personnel, if any is available, usually consists of a part-time secretary or volunteer student secretary or clerk. At the other extreme are the physical education administrators in large colleges and universities who have several secretaries, a telephone operator, and perhaps even a receptionist—all housed in commodious offices with the latest equipment.

Regardless of the size of the office staff and facilities, there are many functions common to practically all offices. These are: (1) answering and placing telephone calls, (2) receiving visitors, (3) answering correspondence, (4) filing, (5) duplicating materials, (6) keeping appointments and meeting obligations, and (7) providing services to staff members. Each of these functions will be discussed briefly.

Answering and placing telephone calls. In larger offices telephone calls will be placed and answered by the secretary or telephone operator. The administrator without office assistance must perform this function. In either case standard telephone technique and courtesy should be observed. Favorable or unfavorable impressions of the department are readily created by the manner in which telephone calls are received. The proper procedures do not accidentally occur—they must be taught and insisted upon by the administrator.

The individual answering the telephone must be as friendly and as cordial as if the caller were a visitor in the office. Good public relations are created by courtesy and helpfulness. Sincerity of purpose and desire to be of service to people is the key to good telephone relationships. Since emotions are readily reflected in one's voice, care must be exercised not to show anger. When it is necessary to give a negative answer, the caller must have the feeling that he has been courteously treated.

The telephone should be answered promptly. The department should be identified immediately. The name of the person receiving the call is frequently given, for example, "Department of Physical Education, Mr. Smith speaking." Such terms as "Hello" and "Yes" are not used in answering telephone calls in a business office.

A pencil and telephone pad should be available to take messages or telephone numbers that are to be called. If the administrator is not available, the secretary may be able to provide the desired information. If the administrator is occupied, the secretary should have an understanding regarding interruptions. When the administrator leaves the office, the secretary should know where he or she can be located and when he or she expects to return. When the administrator is out of the office, a form similar to the one given in Figure 6-1 should be used to indicate that a call

Date_____19_____ Name_____

While you were out, there was a personal telephone call today.

Time_____ o'clock

From _____

Of_____

Who said_____

Telephone number is:_____

Signed_____

Figure 6-1. Form for Recording Phone Calls

has been received. If the person called is not in, the secretary should always offer to take a message. It is helpful to get the name of the caller. If the caller's name has not been given, such questions as "May I have him call you?" or "————is not in. Is there a message?" are in order.

The office telephone is made available for business purposes. There is no objection when personnel use it for local personal calls, but this privilege should not be abused. Lengthy personal calls should not be permitted. Business calls always should have priority over personal calls.

Receiving visitors. Every member of the clerical staff should be well versed in the common courtesies of greeting visitors as they call at the office. Needless to say, all visitors should be made welcome. They should be greeted cordially, and every effort should be made to meet their needs. In the event the caller has no appointment, the purpose of the visit should be determined. In some instances the office staff member may be able to supply the desired information. If it is necessary to wait to see the administrator, the caller should be comfortably seated and offered something to read. If the administrator is not available, either an appointment should be arranged or an effort made to have someone else provide the assistance the visitor desires. Visitors with appointments or important visitors should be announced immediately. A courteous procedure should be worked out whereby the secretary interrupts an unnecessarily long interview with a visitor, especially when other visitors are waiting. When there are no callers, an effective procedure for the administrator is to summarize what has been discussed and to inquire if there are other matters to be considered.

Answering correspondence. One of the quickest ways for an administrator to gain a poor reputation is to be negligent or careless about answering correspondence. Some administrators have a policy of answering every letter within twenty-four hours after it has been received. Although this may not be possible in all cases, it is a sound practice to answer correspondence promptly. Not only should the answer be prompt, but it should be complete as well. All questions and letters should be answered carefully and in good English.

Many letters the administrator receives can be answered better by some other member of the department. A form is usually employed, requesting the appropriate action by the staff member. Many letters of a routine nature can be answered directly by the secretary. This will save the valuable time of the administrator. In larger institutions letters of the same type are commonly received. These may be answered by a standard form reply.

It is standard procedure to proofread all outgoing letters to detect mistakes. The address should be checked for accuracy. Carbon copies are necessary, and they should be filed with the related correspondence.

In many small schools the administrator will have no secretarial help whatsoever and must handle his or her own correspondence. If the administrator is unable to type, the only recourse is to write out letters longhand. The opposite extreme is the availability of a full-time or part-time secretary to take shorthand. Between these extremes are the schools in which dictating machines are available. These machines have several advantages. They can be taken home and letters dictated at night or over the weekend. Administrators who have part-time secretaries can dictate at any time and have the completed tapes available for the time the secretary has available for this work. If the administrator is constantly interrupted during dictation or has difficulty composing a letter, much secretarial time can be saved by using a dictating machine.

Filing. An effective filing system is essential in any office. All correspondence, records, budgets, and reports must be filed in such a way that they can be located quickly. It is not difficult to locate recently filed material, but on occasions several years may elapse before it is needed. Reference to filed material is constantly necessary, and when it cannot be located, delay, inefficiency and, at times, embarrassment result. Filing is more accurately done when only one person does it.

A variety of filing systems are known, but in schools the alphabetical system is used almost invariably. The material to be filed is classified according to name, subject, or a combination of name and subject. Large physical education offices will probably use both a name and a subject file, but the majority will use the combination system.

The name file refers to names of people or organizations with whom correspondence or business is carried on. In this system a folder is made for each name or correspondent if there is sufficient material to justify starting a folder. From three to ten papers justify starting a folder. A lesser amount is filed in a miscellaneous folder. A miscellaneous folder is made for each letter of the alphabet and is located behind the last name folder under each alphabetical letter.

Subject filing refers to filing the material according to the subject matter with which it deals. The subject headings must be specific, significant, and technically correct. Nouns are generally used to refer to the subject. Subheadings are used in subject filing. A miscellaneous folder is also used in subject filing. The papers within each subject folder are arranged by date, with the latest date on top.

A subject file is necessary in any physical education office because of the nature of its operation. Items such as budgets, schedules, contracts, equipment orders, records, and reports must be filed according to subject. Since there are many more items that would be filed under subjects than under names, most physical education offices should file by subject into which names are incorporated.

In setting up a filing system for a medium-size school, the first step should be to segregate the total program into specific subjects, such as (1) physical education, (2) intramural sports, (3) health education, and (4) interscholastic sports. Each drawer of a four-drawer filing cabinet would refer to a specific area with the subareas listed in alphabetical order.

The physical education drawer could be subdivided into the following areas:

1. Annual reports. A folder for each annual report should be included.

2. Budget. A folder for each annual budget for each of the past five years should be maintained.

3. Committees. A folder for each committee should be filed.

4. Correspondence. Folders should be arranged alphabetically under this heading. All carbons and original copies of communications should be filed in the appropriate folder.

5. Departmental policies. The departmental policy file should be included in a folder. If desirable, a number of folders might be used with each including the policies in different areas.

6. Equipment. A folder should be included listing the equipment, excepting that included in the interscholastic athletic inventory. The new equipment on order should also be noted.

7. Financial matters. Duplicate copies of all requisitions and duplicate vouchers submitted for payment can be filed under this heading.

8. Personnel records. A folder for each student should be available. This should include medical examination records, correspondence with family physician, parents, and others. Excuses and the anecdotal record of student achievement and conduct can also be filed in this folder. Personnel records might be filed in a separate drawer. Content and availability to the student must conform to school policy.

9. Service program. A folder for each activity taught should be available. This might include lesson plans, rules, syllabus, examinations, and teaching aids, such as clippings from newspapers and magazines. In addition, a folder for the program and schedule for each year for the past three years should be included.

10. Student help. Records for all part-time and student help should be kept in this folder.

11. Test data. Complete data on physical fitness and other tests should be filed in folders according to the school year in which they apply.

The intramural sports drawer could be subdivided as follows:

1. Eligibility rules. The eligibility rules for participating in the different activities should be included.

2. Intramural activities. A folder for each sport included in the program should be available. These folders should include rules governing that activity. In addition, they might include past records and schedules.

3. Officials. A folder with the names, addresses, telephone numbers, and qualifications of all officials used in the program should be available.

4. Participation records. A complete record of the results of all competition should be maintained.

5. Programs. A folder should be available which would contain the details of each year's program for a period of five years. The details should cover such items as the participants and teams in each sport and the results of all the competition.

6. Publicity. A folder should be retained which has all the posters, announcements, news stories, and other publicity materials.

7. Schedules. This folder should contain schedules for all intramural activities for the current year.

The health education drawer might be arranged as follows:

1. Administrative policies. A folder under this heading should be included for each of the following areas: communicable disease control, emergency care and injuries, excuses, health of school personnel, and scheduling.

2. Health services. A folder under this subject heading should be included for each of the following areas: health examinations and followup, screening, counseling, communicable disease control, and sanitation of the school plant.

3. Health instruction. A separate folder under this subject heading should be available for each of the following areas: personal health, weight control, vision and hearing, dental health, communicable and non-communicable disease, first aid and safety, family life education, nutrition, exercise, rest and recreation, health services and products, community health, narcotics and alcohol education, mental health and personal adjustment, and smoking.

4. Healthful school living. A separate folder under this subject heading should be included for each of the following areas: school lunch, seating, heating, lighting, ventilation, swimming pool sanitation, and locker and shower room sanitation.

The interscholastic sports drawer might be subdivided as follows:

1. Budget. A folder should be filed for the interscholastic athletic budget for each year for the past five years.

2. Contracts. A folder is desirable for each sport that involves contracts.

3. Eligibility lists. For each sport, a folder should be available in which there is an eligibility list.

4. Equipment lists. A folder for each sport should be available in which data concerning equipment is filed. These data should include an equipment inventory plus a listing of new equipment that has been ordered.

5. Game reports. A folder for each sport should be included which would contain game reports for home games. The game reports should include such data as attendance, weather, gate receipts, opponent, and score.

6. Officials. All data relating to officials should be filed under this heading in folders arranged according to sports.

7. Schedules. Schedules for all sports in the current year should be included in a folder. Folders for previous years should also be maintained. In some schools a folder for future schedules is needed.

8. Sports. A folder for each interscholastic sport should be maintained. Included in such a folder will be squad personnel, current records, lesson plans, scouting reports, coaching aids, and the like.

9. Transportation. A folder should be developed for each sport. Every folder should contain all arrangements for travel by the respective team.

Duplicating materials. A constant need exists in a physical education office to have materials duplicated. In addition to the requirements in instructional classes for objective examinations, reading lists, syllabi, instructional materials, and outlines, coaches may wish to have plays duplicated for their players, and the intramural director will require numerous copies of rules and schedules. The administrator will also need to have various materials duplicated, such as departmental regulations, announcements, minutes of committee meetings, and instructions to staff members and students.

In most high schools and colleges the materials are mimeographed, dittoed, or copied by machine in a central office. However, when the volume justifies it, the physical education department has found it advantageous to possess its own duplicating equipment. Dittoing equipment is relatively inexpensive to purchase and to operate. Although the ditto and mimeographing machines are simple to operate, it is advisable to restrict their use to authorized individuals only. On staffs where little if any office personnel is available, staff members can learn how to operate the duplicating machine. They can then reproduce their own materials.

Keeping appointments and meeting obligations. On many occasions physical education administrators must make appointments to speak to people or to perform some task by a certain stipulated time. To meet these obligations the administrator must have some infallible reminder system. The administrator simply cannot afford to miss or to be late for an appointment nor forget details.

The administrator needs a pocket appointment book. This should include all the notations that are on the desk calendar. The administrator will make appointments when away from the office and will also need to know of office appointments when elsewhere.

A secretary, when available, should also maintain a desk calendar and see that the calendar and those of the administrator are accurate, identical, and up to date. To remind one's employer of a task to be done, the secretary should place the file on the administrator's desk. If it is obvious that the administrator has overlooked a call or appointment, the secretary should remind him or her of it. It is a sound practice to spend the first few minutes each morning with the secretary, discussing the daily schedule. Some secretaries place a typed schedule of the administrator's appointments on the desk every morning. When leaving the office at the end of the day, the administrator should check the calendar to see whether there are any early appointments for the following day.

The establishment of regular office hours facilitates the making and keeping of appointments. When staff members, students, tradespeople, and others know what the regular office hours are, they can usually arrange to see the administrator at a mutually convenient time. The administrator must keep the secretary informed concerning any changes in office hours, especially when he or she will be absent or late.

Faculty members should also have regular office hours when they would be available for conferences, meetings with students, colleagues, and anyone else who wishes to see them. These office hours should be posted and adhered to. The office personnel should be aware of these office hours in order to be helpful to those who wish to contact staff members.

When the necessity of performing a task occurs, many administrators endeavor to take care of it immediately. If the administrator is free for an immediate appointment, or can make a telephone call, write a letter or prepare a report at once, rather than defer it, there is no possibility of forgetting it. If the matter cannot be immediately disposed of, a notation should be made concerning it. Calendars are essential in any office to assure that appointments are kept and obligations met. The administrator needs a desk calendar with fifteen or thirty minute time designations. All appointments and obligations should be noted on the calendar.

It is a mistake for the administrator to rely upon memory for the conduct of daily affairs. It has been said that "the shortest pencil is better than the longest memory." Everything that cannot be taken care of immediately should be written down in such a way that it will not be forgotten.

A very helpful office device that may be combined with a desk calendar is known as the office tickler. The tickler carries reminders for certain routine activities. There are in every department many duties that recur each year. These can be indicated on the office tickler in advance. The tickler file usually consists of a box built to hold three by five inch memorandum cards. A tabbed guide for each month and thirty-one tabbed guides for each day of each month are needed. Each activity that is to be performed at a future date is noted on the appropriate card. The cards are filed according to dates. The tickler file should be checked every morning. Certain items that occur frequently throughout the year can be handled by a single card. Thus, if the payroll must be completed on the last day of each month, the same card may be used each month, rather than making twelve separate entries.

In larger offices secretaries make the necessary arrangements for committee meetings. To work out a convenient time and place for a number of people to meet is frequently a time-consuming process.

Providing services to staff members. A major function of the physical education office is to provide various services to staff members. The most important of these is to type examinations, reading lists, course outlines, reports, speeches, and letters. In many secondary schools such assistance is not available and the staff member either must do the typing or get along without it. Neither alternative is desirable. The time of staff members is too important to be spent laboriously typing essential materials. On the other hand, if typed materials are not available, the performance of the staff member may be diminished.

The secretarial personnel may also assist staff members by arranging appointments, gathering travel information, maintaining student personnel records, recording test data, contacting students, and the like. The more staff members can be relieved of these essential details, the more time will be available for them to perform their teaching, supervisory, and advisory functions.

Office Management in a Small High School

The heavy load of the administrator in a small school makes good organization and efficient methods of office management particularly necessary. He or she should have one period set aside every day for the conduct of departmental affairs. If such time is not provided, the administrator will need to use the free period or time before or after school.

Whatever assistance the administrator has may have to come from students. Fortunately, in most high schools it is possible to obtain senior students interested in office work who will volunteer their services to gain experience. It is not difficult to find students who can type; some are capable of taking shorthand as well. The administrator will probably have to use several students to accomplish all the necessary duties. In this way the duties that require special skill can be reserved for the period when the student with that skill is available.

It is relatively easy to teach the student clerks how to use the telephone, to receive visitors, to file materials, to use the mimeograph or ditto machines, or maintain records, and to perform the essential housekeeping duties of the office. They can render invaluable service if they are used wisely. They must be given recognition for their services, and care must be exercised not to exploit them.

In the small high school office equipment is usually limited. The minimum items in any office should consist of:

1. One desk for each teacher.
2. Desk tools (paper cutter, scissors, ruler, paste, blotter, pens, pencils, paper, stapler, and clips).
3. Calendar and memorandum pads.
4. A large work table for student assistants.
5. Extra chairs for guests.
6. A four or five drawer filing cabinet with lock.
7. Several card files of different sizes.
8. Bookshelves.
9. Magazine stand.
10. Ditto and/or mimeograph machine.

A typewriter and a typewriter table are very important items that are often unavailable in small high schools. If this equipment is not available, access to some other typewriter within the school should be obtained. If a telephone cannot be procured, the main office telephone may be used.

Office Management in a Medium-Size High School

In a medium-size high school the physical education administrator has the same duties as the administrator in the small school. However, he or she is much more likely to be allocated time for administrative duties.

The administrator may be relieved of one or two teaching periods per day for this purpose. More office equipment probably will be available. He or she will undoubtedly have more people to whom to delegate various duties. It might be possible to use the principal's clerical staff for dictation, typing, and mimeographing. Student assistants will continue to be needed. For part-time and student secretarial help, a specific job description will be helpful. If they can have recourse to written instructions and policies concerning their responsibilities, they will avoid many mistakes. A typewriter, typewriter table, telephone, and an alphabetical index to common telephone numbers should be available in the administrator's office.

Office Management in a Large Institution

In a large school where one or more clerical personnel are available the role of the administrator is that of office manager. All the activities carried on in the office are his or her responsibility. The duties of the different individuals are assigned and supervised by the administrator.

A standard procedure in large offices is to develop a job description for each member of the clerical staff. This lets the employee know specifically what is expected and that he or she is held responsible for demonstrating competence as it applies to these responsibilities. This does not mean that each employee is restricted from assuming other duties in the office as circumstances require.

In a large office a definite organizational structure might be necessary for the office personnel. Responsibility must be vested in some individual—usually the most experienced, the most mature, and the highest-ranking member. The administrator will not have the time to be concerned with the details of managing the office. The assignment of duties, distribution of work, and supervision of the work of all office personnel should be delegated to this head person.

The administrator is responsible for the development and maintenance of high morale and esprit de corps among the office personnel. This is accomplished by creating pleasant working conditions, by establishing reasonable standards of accomplishment, by providing suitable working tools, and by friendly, helpful supervision.

In large schools the matter of communication within the office and among the staff is a problem. The accepted practice is to use written interstaff memoranda. Special forms are available for this purpose. These memoranda are time saving and have the advantage of fixing responsibility. In addition, they reduce the risk of misunderstanding and error.

Figure 6-2 is an example of a form which facilitates communication within a larger organization. It also saves the time of the administrator.

```
                    Division of Health and Physical Education
    FROM:     Jane Abbott, Chairperson          DATE: _____

    TO: ____  Brown              For your files____
        ____  Flemming           For your information ____
        ____  Ford               Please see me ____
        ____  Jones              Please call me ____
        ____  Henry              Please handle____
        ____  Morgan             Please draft reply for:
        ____  Pastor                 My signature ____
        ____  Rogers                 Your signature____
        ____  Smith
        ____  White
        ____  Wilson
```

Figure 6-2. Form for Inter-Office Communication.

The major items of office equipment for a large organization include:

1. Calculator.
2. Ditto, mimeograph machine, and copying machines.
3. Typewriters.
4. Filing cabinets.
5. Staplers (including electrical stapler).
6. Paper cutter.
7. Collator.
8. Dictation machine and transcriber.
9. Three hole punch.

Centralization of stenographic services

Many organizations centralize their stenographic services. This is frequently called a stenographic pool. The services provided include typing, transcribing, duplicating, and filing. Leffingwell and Robinson[1] list the advantages of such centralization:

Economy: fewer employees needed, therefore less equipment and space.

Improved quality of work: better and closer supervision and control; easier to train employees and set standards.

Increased individual efficiency of employees: resulting from specialization and concentration.

Relief of department heads from supervisory responsibility: gives them more time for technical activities.

A stenographic pool may not be feasible or practical for a small high school but it is extensively used in larger organizations.

The Secretary[2]

An important asset that many administrators overlook in planning their work is a capable secretary. By working with an intelligent secretary and learning to delegate all the responsibility that the secretary is capable of assuming and by leaving many time-consuming routine matters in the secretary's hands, the administrator will find there is much more time for creative work. The wise administrator, then, should know what a good secretary is and how to make the best use of the secretary's abilities. Intelligence, personality, and character are the three general personal qualifications of a good secretary.

Intelligence should be practical and analytical, not merely abstract. The secretary should be able to comprehend the factors in any situation and make some reasonable decision about it, using sound logic to back up judgment. Intelligence must include a capacity for detail and an ability to deal with the almost endless routine matters that arise in any administrator's office. If this intelligence is to function to the best advantage for the secretary and the administrator, behind it must be a genuine interest and pride in the activities, welfare, and progress of the department. If the secretary is desultory and detached regarding the duties and performs them mechanically, he or she will be of no particular asset. When an administrator has a secretary who is dedicated to the position and takes a deep personal interest in the success of the department, the administrator is indeed fortunate.

The personality of the secretary is of critical importance. This person constantly encounters students, staff members, other faculty, and visitors, and it is vital that a favorable impression be created. Since the administrator will spend from one-third to three-fourths of his or her working hours in the company of the secretary, it is axiomatic that their personalities be compatible. The pleasant, cheerful, and sensible secretary is not only easier to work with than the temperamental one but will usually accomplish much more in the same amount of time.

The caller's first impression of the administrator comes from the front office, where he or she is received by the secretary. The secretary must display graciousness, cordiality, interest, and tact. By manner and appearance, the secretary should convey the impression of the well-run office where all demands are given courteous attention. Needing patience, good humor, and diplomacy in dealing with those who come to the office, the secretary must also exercise discrimination in determining which of them have legitimate business with the employer and which do not.

Telephone voice and manner should be as pleasant as office personality. The secretary should be able to convey to the person who calls that he or she is talking to a capable and willing person who, in most cases, can supply the information needed without troubling the administrator about it. To assume the somewhat belligerent "who wants to talk to him?" attitude is as rude as it is inexcusable.

The secretary who really becomes a part of the organization must be extremely adaptable and ready and willing to do whatever must be done, no matter how far it may seem to fall out of the sphere of activity. The position exists as a service to the administrator, and is never limited to the mere mechanics of letter writing.

To be worthy of the name, the secretary must be absolutely reliable in all situations so that the employer may trust this person as completely as the employer does himself or herself. The secretary's loyalty must be absolutely unquestionable. In the course of a day's work a secretary learns many things that are not for publication but must never gossip under any circumstances about office information, however trivial. The necessity for personal integrity is obvious.

The training of the good secretary should be more than a matter of shorthand, typing, filing, and office practice, although these, of course, are essential. Most important is the correct use of the English language, both written and spoken. Since the secretary composes numerous letters that go out over the signature of the employer, the secretary should know style and form in composition in order to make letters convincing. The secretary should know the essentials of order and have a systematic way of getting work done in the quickest, best possible way. The person in this job should sense task priorities.

It is desirable but not essential that the secretary have some training in the field in which the employer is interested. If this is not possible, the secretary should acquire at an early date a very real interest in that field and keep reasonably well informed about it. This will not only add to enjoyment of the work but will increase the secretary's value to the employer.

Having hired a secretary, many an administrator seems to feel that his or her responsibility is ended, and from then on it is up to the secretary. If the administrator takes that attitude, he or she will soon have not a capable secretary, but just another person working in the office. It is important that as soon as the secretary begins working, the administrator should see to it that all possible information concerning the work to be done is available for the secretary. In any organization there is almost endless red tape with which the secretary becomes entangled in the course of a day's activity; the workings of much of this will eventually be learned by trial and error. However, a knowledge of the regulations will save endless time and trouble. Do not expect the new secretary to immediately assume charge of all the routine matters that will arise, but gradually delegate all the responsibility the secretary is able to handle. This is the point at which most administrators fail. They cannot bear to see authority to act on matters, however trivial, placed in hands other than their own. Remember that this person is an intelligent adult; and having been given responsibility, this person can be trusted with it. The secretary's judgment soon may be almost as good as your own in those situations covered by departmental policies.

Much has been written of loyalty of the secretary to the employer, but much more might be written about the loyalty of the employer to the secretary. This person is, presumably, intelligent and capable of handling the job, and should be backed up by the employer in any reasonable situation—not made the scapegoat for all the mistakes that occur in the office. To humiliate the secretary in order to inflate one's ego before important callers is, of course, an inexcusable but not uncommon practice. A feeling of mutual loyalty and respect helps to create an office morale that makes the secretary feel an integral part of the organization;—he or she is working not *for* but *with* a wise and understanding person; not for a salary but for the good of the profession. It is this feeling that makes the person a real asset to the employer.

NOTES

1. William H. Leffingwell and Edwin M. Robinson. *Textbook of Office Management* (New York, McGraw-Hill Book Company, 1950), p. 36.

2. The authors are indebted to Miss Eleanor Metheny, Emeritus Professor, University of Southern California, for material in this section.

two

Organization
of the Program

7

The Objectives
of Physical Education

In order to proceed efficiently and with dispatch toward any goal it is essential that the goal be known. Nothing is more important for the physical education administrator to know than the objectives he or she is expected to achieve. Certain human and material resources have been provided with which the administrator is expected to accomplish various purposes. These purposes—or objectives—should dictate everything to be done. They give direction to the efforts of the administrator and staff and they provide the basis for evaluating the success of the department.

PHYSICAL EDUCATION DEFINED

Physical education is the process by which changes in the individual are brought about through movement experiences. Physical education aims not only at physical development but is concerned with the education of the whole person *through* physical activity. It would be erroneous to believe that only physical responses are involved in physical education activities. The whole organism interacts in any experience and this involves mental, emotional, and social, as well as physical reactions. Such behavior provides the physical educator with an exceptional opportunity to guide the responses of students so that valuable mental, emotional, social, and physical learnings accrue.

Spranger emphasizes the broader aspects of physical education in these words:[1]

> And we shall not be satisfied with a teacher of physical education who doesn't know anything but how to teach physical activities or, even worse, can only perform them. Teachers of physical education as we see them, must be part of the spirit and meaning of the cultural tasks with which they are confronted.

Whether or not all of the potentialities are realized depends upon the leadership. Unfortunately, some physical educators concern themselves only with the physical outcomes and ignore these other valuable aspects of development. All of the results are important and should be constantly sought. If physical education is to make its maximum contribution to the optimum development of the child, the physical educator must use *all* opportunities. For example, physical education can be one of the avenues for educational experience in thinking, reasoning, making quick decisions and using long-term memory.

Physical education should be a part of every individual's total education. Vigorous physical activity is a physiological necessity for optimum health and well being, yet it is a need which is often poorly met in our sedentary society. Through physical education a person can and should learn the satisfaction and joy of movement, exercise and activity. The individual can and should acquire adequate physical movement skills so that throughout life that person will seek physical activity and thus maintain muscle tone and cardiovascular efficiency. Physical education participation provides a means to maintain and extend endurance, strength and flexibility. It can be a physically beneficial, socially acceptable means to release tension; but more than that, it can be a social participation in which one can grow to know one's self. An instructional program in physical education with opportunities for some selection of sports, dance, conditioning, outdoor and recreational activities should be a part of the educational curriculum of every individual.

Physical Education Objectives Derived
From Educational Objectives

Physical education as part of the school curriculum must share the function of education. That function is related to helping individuals grow, develop, and adjust to the problems of individual happiness, to competent membership in the family, to constructive citizenship in a democracy, and to appreciative understanding of the ethical values that undergird our world society.

In 1956 B. S. Bloom developed a taxonomy or classification of objectives for education in which he established three broad areas or domains: the psychomotor, cognitive, and affective. In physical education the psychomotor domain is a unique goal which has more specific application than in other areas of education. It is included in any and all listings of physical education objectives as we consider general body coordination, fitness, and development of specific movement skills. The cognitive domain includes knowledge and understanding both of self and human movement, creativity in many physical education activities, and also game rules, strategies, etiquette, etc. The affective domain, including emotional and social development, is an objective which is shared with the rest of education and with the home. This area, sometimes called concomitant learnings, should include planned educational experiences where students can learn to make adjustments to the group and, perhaps even more important, can learn to know and accept themselves as worthwhile and contributing individuals.

As a member of the educational family physical education subscribes to educational objectives and endeavors to make its best contribution to their realization. The only justification for physical education—or any other subject in the school curriculum—is that it contributes in an important way to educational objectives. The criterion applied to every school subject or activity is that it be in harmony with educational goals. Physical education is not peculiar in the objectives it strives to attain but it is unique in the opportunities that its activities provide both because of their nature and the methodology inherent in them.

The Purposes of Education

Over the past half century many writers, committees, and commissions have given expression to statements of educational objectives. By all odds, the best known and most influential were those formulated in 1918 and 1938 and described below. The Commission on the Reorganization of Secondary Education spent three years preparing the *Cardinal Principles of Secondary Education,* which was published in 1918. This publication proposed a set of seven cardinal objectives for the school. These were (1) health, (2) command of the fundamental processes, (3) worthy home membership, (4) vocational competence, (5) effective citizenship, (6) worthy use of leisure, and (7) ethical character. This statement of educational objectives has been extensively used by educators. Even today they are still quoted frequently. It is worth noting in this connection that the Educational Policies Commission,[2] a high-level committee of the National Education Association, had this to say about the *Cardinal Principles of*

Secondary Education: "It is probably the most influential educational document issued in this country."

In 1938 the Educational Policies Commission[3] in its *The Purposes of Education in American Democracy* developed four objectives, each with various subobjectives. These were:

1. The objectives of self-realization.
   a. The inquiring mind.
   b. Speech.
   c. Reading.
   d. Writing.
   e. Number.
   f. Sight and hearing.
   g. Health knowledge.
   h. Health habits.
   i. Public health.
   j. Recreation.
   k. Intellectual interests.
   l. Esthetic interests.
   m. Character.
2. The objectives of human relationship.
   a. Respect for humanity.
   b. Friendships.
   c. Cooperation.
   d. Courtesy.
   e. Appreciation of the home.
   f. Conservation of the home.
   g. Home-making.
   h. Democracy in the home.
3. The objectives of economic efficiency.
   a. Work.
   b. Occupational information.
   c. Occupational choice.
   d. Occupational efficiency.
   e. Occupational adjustment.
   f. Occupational appreciation.
   g. Personal economics.
   h. Consumer judgment.
   i. Efficiency in buying.
   j. Consumer protection.
4. The objectives of civic responsibility.
   a. Social justice.
   b. Social activity.
   c. Social understanding.
   d. Critical judgment.
   e. Tolerance.

    f. Conservation.
    g. Social applications of science.
    h. World citizenship.
    i. Law observance.
    j. Economic literacy.
    k. Political citizenship.
    l. Devotion to democracy.

To a considerable extent these objectives represented a restatement or reclassification of the seven cardinal principles. They have been extensively used and have largely superseded the seven cardinal principles.

In 1961 the Educational Policies Commission listed the development of the rational powers of man as the central purpose of American education. The following quotation contains the Commission's concluding statement:[4]

> Individual freedom and effectiveness and the progress of the society require the development of every citizen's rational powers. Among the many important purposes of American schools the fostering of that development must be central.
>
> Man has already transformed his world by using his mind. As he expands the application of rational methods to problems old and new, and as people in growing numbers are enabled to contribute to such endeavors, man will increase his ability to understand, to act, and to alter his environment. Where these developments will lead cannot be foretold.
>
> Man has before him the possibility of a new level of greatness, a new realization of human dignity and effectiveness. The instrument which will realize this possibility is that kind of education which frees the mind and enables it to contribute to a full and worthy life. To achieve this goal is the high hope of the nation and the central challenge to its schools.

This latest statement by the Educational Policies Commission should not be construed as a rejection of or lack of support for the 1918 and 1938 statements of educational objectives. Rather it represents a reemphasis upon the central purpose of education. This reemphasis does not negate the previous statements of educational objectives. That the seven cardinal principles or the four objectives enunciated by the Educational Policies Commission in 1938 are still valid educational purposes can be seen by the statement from *The Central Purpose of American Education*[5] that "The American school must be concerned with all these objectives if it is to serve all of American life. That there are desirable educational objectives is clear."

In summary, the educational purposes that have had special significance for physical education for the past fifty years still have validity. Such objectives as health, good citizenship, ethical character, wise use of leisure, self-realization, human relationships, and civic responsibility are as important today as they were previously.

The Objectives of Physical Education

There is no dearth of statements of the objectives of physical education. Down through the centuries various authors have given expression to the values which, they believed, were inherent in physical education programs. Despite the fact that the educational philosophy of the time and place does exert an influence upon physical education objectives it is amazing how consistent these statements have been over a span of hundreds of years. Today in scores of textbooks there are found statements of physical education objectives in the context of modern educational philosophy.

Stoodley[6] analyzed the physical education objectives as they are stated by 22 different authors. Altogether 493 different items were listed. These have been summarized under these headings, (1) health, physical, or organic development, (2) mental-emotional development, (3) neuromuscular development, (4) social development, and (5) intellectual development.

In addition to the objectives stated by various authors there are also available the objectives as formulated by professional organizations. Publication of objectives by professional organizations has the advantage of being prepared by a group of carefully selected individuals. They represent the opinion of more than one individual. Because of their influence and value official statements of the objectives of physical education by the American Association (now Alliance) for Health, Physical Education and Recreation will be presented.

At a Professional Preparation Conference of the American Association for Health, Physical Education, and Recreation[7] an overview of physical education was given in the following statement:

> The physical educator is primarily concerned with man's movement, and especially with the following aspects:
>
> 1. *The development of motor skill.* The specialist must understand the roles of the skeletal and the neuromuscular systems in movement. This requires understanding of mechanical laws and of the relationship of inherent patterns of coordination to so-called voluntary movement.
> 2. *The effect of stress.* Exercise and other forms of stress place demands upon the human organism and affect its growth and development. Basic to an

understanding of these demands and their effects is the study of biological and behavioral sciences.

3. *Movement as a means of communication.* Feelings are likely to be expressed in overt movement and in posture. Such expressions have been highly developed in graphic arts, in dramatics, and in dance. Some specialists will concentrate in this phase and will need study in related art forms and in aesthetics.

4. *Preparation for leisure.* The motor skills developed in the physical education program should enable and stimulate the individual to participate in motor activities throughout life. Therefore, the school curriculum should include development of skills which not only are useful in life's daily routine but also constitute leisure activities for all ages in the society in which the individual lives.

5. *Social adjustment through group activities.* Socially acceptable behavior and skill in human relations may be developed in part through participation in games and sports and other physical education activities involving cooperative endeavor and group interaction. Special demonstrations also provide many opportunities for social growth. The study of sociology and other social sciences furnishes an important background for potential leaders.

6. *An avenue for guiding character development.* Experiences involved in sports and athletics, especially those of a highly competitive nature, offer opportunities for guidance which are unusual in many respects. In the emotionalized situation, intensified by the attitude of spectators and by public testing of skill, the performer can learn to concentrate on his obligations and can develop ability to place values related to success and failure in their proper perspective. He can experience the value of preparation involving effort, sacrifice, and drudgery in the satisfaction of utilizing high levels of skill and superb physical condition. In the intensive movements of competition, he may discover that determination to carry on brings forth abilities previously unrecognized.

7. *The need to feel secure, to belong, to love and be loved.* Man receives satisfactions from the approval of his peers and superiors, but he must also respect himself and recognize personal progress toward desirable goals. Physical education is rich in opportunities to meet these needs. Personal improvement may be tested and noted, memberships on teams satisfy the need to belong, and achievement of success at all levels provides incentive for further achievement. Prospective leaders should gain a thorough understanding of behavioral sciences so as to be more effective in guiding human development through the satisfaction of such basic needs.

Physical education division statement. This Is Physical Education,[8] prepared by a committee of the Division and subsequently approved by the

Division, was published in 1965. The objectives of physical education recommended in this statement are:

1. To help children learn to move skillfully and effectively not only in exercises, games, sports, and dances but also in all active life situations.
2. To develop understandings of voluntary movement and the ways in which individuals may organize their own movements to accomplish the significant purposes of their lives.
3. To enrich understandings of space, time, mass-energy relationships, and related concepts.
4. To extend understandings of socially approved patterns of personal behavior with particular reference to the interpersonal interactions of games and sports.
5. To condition the heart, lungs, muscles, and other organic systems to respond to increased demands by imposing progressively greater demands upon them.

Emphases of the Sixties and Early Seventies

Competency-Based Teacher Education (CBTE), also referred to as Performance-Based Teacher Education (PBTE), is a teacher preparation approach intended to aid students in developing specific competencies. This method places great emphasis on objectives and individualization. The approach arose in response to public and parental demand for educational accountability—in view of rising costs, what are the actual results of education? Education's answer was the introduction of specific written behavioral objectives to be used in each teaching-learning experience. With the CBTE educational system and the use of behavioral objectives students can be clearly aware of competencies required. Performance-based teaching requires the development of sound evaluative criteria.

Behavioral or performance objectives should include three parts: (1) the statement of an observable, measurable behavior, (2) the condition under which the behavior is to occur, and (3) criterion for evaluating whether the objective has been achieved. Following are a few examples of performance objectives as they might be used in sports: See Tables 7-1, 7-2.

After reviewing the professional literature since 1950, and grouping and combining statements to avoid repetition, Ted Hunt[9] checked his findings on physical education objectives with twelve men and women who were directors of physical education in Canadian and American universities. With a few minor suggestions for change, all agreed that the list was comprehensive and representative of public school objectives for physical education. The list of twenty statements follows:

A.   The Physical Dimension
  1. Adjustment of correctable body defects. (Overweight, underweight, re-
     laxation of tension, flexibility, spine deformity, athletic injury).
  2. Physical fitness and muscular strength. (Adjustment to increased physi-
     cal demands or emergencies; speed, strength, balance, agility).
  3. Endurance. (Ability to resist fatigue, stamina).

TABLE 7-1. PERFORMANCE OBJECTIVES FOR BADMINTON

Beginning	Intermediate	Advance
Service	Service	Service
Serves 4 out of 5 in service court area.	Server will score 3 out of 5 in quarter circle with 6' radius located on near inside corner of service court.	Server will score 7 out of 10 shots in either quarter circle (6' radius) located on deep outside corner or near inside corner of service court.

	Receiving	
Drop Shot	Drop Shot	Drop Shot
On a teacher controlled volley the student will return 2 out of 5 into area between net and service line from a position at mid court.	On a teacher controlled volley the student will return 3 out of 5 into area between net and front service line from a position at mid court.	On a teacher controlled volley the student will return 4 out of 5 into area between net and front service line from a position at mid court.

TABLE 7-2. PERFORMANCE OBJECTIVES FOR SWIMMING

Beginning	Intermediate	Advance
Knowledge	Knowledge	Knowledge
The student will score 60% or more on a beginning test covering water safety, elementary forms of rescue and the analysis of beginning swimming skills.	The student will score 60% or more on an intermediate knowledge test covering water safety, rescue skills and the analysis of intermediate swimming skills.	The student will score 60% or more on an advanced knowledge test covering water safety, rescue skills, and the analysis of advanced swimming skills.
Skill	Skill	Skill
The student will swim the crawl stroke for a distance of 15 yards, turn over and perform the back float for 1 minute, change direction and swim the crawl stroke to the starting point.	The student will swim each of the following fully coordinated strokes for 100 yards: a. front crawl stroke b. breast stroke c. side stroke	The student will swim each of the following fully coordinated strokes for 100 yards: a. elementary back stroke b. front crawl c. breast stroke d. side stroke e. over-arm side stroke f. back crawl g. trudgen crawl

   4. Cardiovascular efficiency. (Efficient functioning of heart, lungs, blood vessels; strong, slow pulse).
   5. Good posture and pleasing physical appearance. (Muscle tone, grace, rhythm, coordination).
   6. Freedom from disease. (Colds, influenza, tuberculosis).
B. The Psycho-motor Dimension
   1. Proficiency in fundamental skills. (Natural skills of movement developed; walking, running, dodging, lifting, hopping, gauging moving objects, climbing, skipping).
   2. Proficiency in team sports. (General skill in sports of the culture; football, hockey, soccer, basketball, rugby, volleyball).
   3. Proficiency in recreational sports. (General skill in leisure activities; lifetime individual sports; golf, tennis, badminton, dance, skiing, swimming).
   4. Proficiency in health and safety skills. (First aid, swimming, life-saving, boating, artificial resuscitation methods).
C. The Social Dimension
   1. Development of socially desirable attitudes. (Sportsmanship, honesty, fair play, respect for others, loyalty, cooperation).
   2. Development of social skills. (Leadership, followership, democratic procedures, compromise, analysis of human nature).
D. The Personal-Emotional Dimension
   1. A realistic view of physical limitations and capabilities. (Recognition of and adjustment to physical shortcomings).
   2. Mental health and stability. (Courage, perseverance, self-control, self-confidence).
   3. Self-satisfaction through success. (A sense of belonging, pride in achievement).
   4. Fun or amusement. (A joy in participation, joy in movement).
E. The Intellectual-Interpretive Dimension
   1. Aesthetic appreciation. (Love of nature, appreciation of form, rhythm, grace, experiencing movement as an expression of self).
   2. A lifetime appreciation for the benefits of exercise. (A desire for physical activity; favorable attitudes toward physical education).
   3. Understanding of the scientific principles related to physical fitness and to movement. (Stress, force, mass, physics, anatomy, physiology).
   4. Knowledge of strategy, rules, and tactics. (Health regulations, game rules, safety rules, team tactics, game strategy).

Recapitulation

In the review of physical education objectives that has just been made it is apparent that certain variations exist. Some statements include a greater number of objectives than others. Certain objectives are included in some listings but not in others. Such variations should be expected because of differences in terminology and philosophy. Some terms are more inclusive than others. However, the impressive feature is that so much similarity exists in the expressions of objectives. An adequate summary of physical education objectives as formulated by various authors and professional organizations can be listed as, (1) the physical development objective, (2) the motor development objective, (3) the knowledge and understanding objective, and (4) the social and emotional development objective. The recreation objective has not been omitted. Rather, it has been included as part of the motor development objective. Each of the objectives will be considered in some detail.

THE PHYSICAL DEVELOPMENT OBJECTIVE

This objective—also known as physical fitness, physical conditioning, organic development or biological development—is concerned with increasing the capacity of the body for movement. It is involved with such characteristics as strength, stamina, cardiorespiratory endurance, agility, flexibility, and speed. This objective has been basic for physical education for thousands of years. Even in primitive times it was recognized that physical exercise was capable of increasing the physical fitness of individuals. Military leaders particularly were conversant with the role of physical activity in improving the effectiveness of their military personnel.

Plato was among the first to recommend the careful planning of the physical education of youth. In his *Protagoras* of about 350 B.C. he said: ". . . send them to the master of physical training so that the bodies may better minister to the virtuous mind, and that they may not be compelled through bodily weakness to play the coward in war or any other occasion."

Socrates also emphasized the importance of the physical development objective in these words: "No citizen has a right to be an amateur in the matter of physical training . . . what a disgrace it is for a man to grow old without ever seeing the beauty and strength of which his body is capable."[10]

Down through the ages similar expressions have been made. Goethe, for example, said: "Take thought for thy body with steadfast fidelity. This soul must see through these eyes alone, and if they be dim, the whole world is clouded."

Browning expressed similar sentiments in his poem, "Rabbi Ben Ezra": "Thy body at its best. How far can that project thy soul on its lone way!"

Basic to the physical development objective is the optimum development of the vital organs. Today, we are aware of the important role of physical education in the development of organic power. It is a well-known fact that increased physical activity results in increased activity of vital organs. When an individual exercises vigorously the bulk of the muscles involved and the amount of combustion are so great that the demand for oxygen and the need for elimination of waste products stimulates a greatly increased functional activity of the circulatory, respiratory, excretory, and heat-regulating mechanisms, and eventually of the digestive system.

Hetherington[11] points out:

> Although we have, generally speaking, no volitional control over the organic functions, by controlling the intensity and the duration of big-muscle activity we can control indirectly and to a fine degree the heightened functional activity or exercise of the organic mechanisms and nutritive processes. In this way, we control the development of organic power.

Hetherington observes that "activity is the *only source of the development of the latent powers* that are planted in the organism by heredity." Proper sleep, rest, and nutrition are favorable to the proper functioning of the organism but they have no power to develop latent resources. Only physical activity is capable of doing this.

The benefits of vigorous physical activity are not restricted to the vital organs. The skeletal and muscular systems are also improved. Some of the beneficial effects are:[12]

1. Structural development of bones, ligaments, and cartilage by furtherance of ossifications, the toughening of the ligaments, and thickening of articular cartilage.
2. Functional adaptation of all structures in skeletal muscles including muscle fibers, the tendons and related connective tissue and the capillaries.

It is this involvement of the muscular system that leads to the development of strength and muscular endurance, which are such important aspects of physical fitness.

Hetherington[13] also points out that the development of a strong, stable, healthy nervous system depends largely upon much vigorous physical activity during childhood and youth. The optimum development of the nervous system is highly related to the strength, health, and stability of the less complex, larger, and phylogenetically older nerve centers as contrasted with the younger, smaller centers controlling the finer integrations of the fingers, and vocal and sensory mechanisms. The only way that the nerve centers can be reached and developed is by exercising them, by exercising the muscles that they control. Consequently, thorough development of the big, fundamental muscle groups will bring about a corresponding development of the important nerve centers controlling these muscles. As Hetherington puts it: "Natural muscular development is a symbol of nervous development and functional power."

Importance of Physical Development Objective Accentuated by Automation

While the physical development objective always has been highly regarded throughout man's recorded history, events of the past several decades have enormously accentuated its importance. The events alluded to are the rapid development of automation and mechanization. Mechanical equipment has largely eliminated the physical effort involved in most work activities. This, in turn, has had profound effects upon our people.

Automation and mechanization represent the latest stages of the Industrial Revolution. For the past 150 years there has been a steadily increasing replacement of human effort by mechanical devices. Modern Western civilization represents the climax of this development by combining maximum technical perfection of labor-saving gadgets with their maximal mass distribution. These developments are dramatically substantiated by Dewhurst:[14]

TABLE 7-3. SOURCES OF ENERGY IN TOTAL WORK OUTPUT

	1850	1900	1950
Human	13.0%	5.3%	0.9%
Animal	52.4	21.5	0.6
Inanimate	34.6	73.2	98.5

Labor-saving devices have greatly reduced the physical effort involved in work of every conceivable type including housekeeping. Our children have also been relieved of most of the exercise in other aspects of their lives. The running and walking that boys and girls have engaged in for countless generations have been greatly curtailed by our modern modes of transportation. We ride everywhere—even around the block to the store. Extensive television viewing has also played havoc with the exercise practices of our children and youth.

Automation and mechanization, while providing many blessings, have had a disastrous effect upon the physical fitness of our children, youth, and adults. It is clear that our extensive technological developments in America brought widespread sedentarianism, which in turn has resulted in the serious deterioration of the physical fitness of our people. This situation should occasion no surprise because a fundamental biological principle is that disuse results in deterioration. What we do not use we lose. Thousands of years ago Hippocrates, Father of Medicine, said: "That which is used, develops; that which is not used, wastes away."

Values of Physical Fitness

Of what consequence is physical fitness? Why should we be concerned about the declining levels of physical fitness of our children, youth, and adults? In our automated age what need do we have for such qualities as strength, endurance, agility, vitality, and vigor? There are two reasons why the physical erosion of our people is a matter of serious concern. These are that (1) physical fitness increases the functional efficiency of the human organism, and (2) physical fitness is significantly related to health.

Increased functional efficiency. Physical fitness is necessary for a successful and enjoyable life because it increases the functional efficiency of the human organism. People who are physically fit can do more things and do them more efficiently than the physically unfit. The stronger the muscles, the more one can experience with less fatigue. The weaker one's muscles, the more quickly does fatigue discourage activity, whether physical or mental. Fatigue reduces the service one may render. The individual who builds up greater resistance to fatigue comes to the end of the day and the end of the week much less exhausted. He can enjoy life more and his disposition is better. As Montaigne says: "The stronger the body the more it obeys; the weaker, the more it commands."

According to Ruskin: "There is no wealth but life." Yet life without health, energy, stamina, zest, and satisfaction is sterile. The essence of living is action. If people are too weak or too tired to act, they really are not living. Weakness makes us slaves; strength sets us free. What choice shall we make? Emerson, in his "Essay on Education," advises:

> Let us have men whose manhood is only the continuation of their boyhood, natural characters still; such are able for fertile and heroic action; and not that sad spectacle with which we are too often familiar, educated eyes in uneducated bodies.

The following statement by Lee and Wagner emphasizes the importance of physical fitness:

> No matter what the arena of life, physical fitness increases materially the opportunities for living fully. Many people live at a level of fitness far below their capacities, making drudgery both of work and play. Others, although living more nearly at their fitness level, do not experience a rich, full life

through sheer lack of what it takes physically to reach the heights. Those who in the growing years attained the heights of physical capacity and, in later years, have had the determination to maintain those heights experience a fullness of life that is a closed book to the weak of spirit.[15]

Much evidence is available to show the effects of physical fitness on the functional efficiency of individuals. According to Dr. Hollman:[16]

Males, who do not practice any kind of sport, have lost, on an average, one-third of their former performance capacity of heart and circulation by the time they reach the age of 55. On the other hand, physical trained persons between 50 and 60 years old, were as fit as the average person between 20 and 30 who take no physical exercise. Exercises and sports training act as a brake element against biological aging and the resulting decrease in fitness. At the same time, lack of movement activity, for instance, leads to a reduction of an average of 18 per cent of the performance capacity coupled with functional disorders of the circulation, as if a healthy person spends about a week in bed. The same applies in principle also to female persons.

Studies have shown that low physical fitness is often associated with poor academic performance. Coefield and McCollum[17] at the University of Oregon found that seventy-eight male freshmen with lowest Physical Fitness Indices were definitely low in scholastic achievement even though they were above average in scholastic aptitude. Page[18] found that 83 percent of the freshmen male students dismissed from Syracuse University because of academic deficiencies had Physical Fitness Indices of less than 100; 39 percent had PFI's below 85. Jarman[19] investigated the academic achievement of boys at ages nine, twelve, and fifteen years, who had high and low scores on various physical fitness and strength tests. For each age and for each test, the high and low groups were equated by Intelligence Quotients with the means and standard deviations being comparable. Quite generally, the boys with the high scores on the various physical tests had significantly superior grade-point averages in their class work and significantly higher means on standard scholastic achievement tests.

Former President John F. Kennedy's convictions[20] about the relationship between physical fitness and intellectual performance are pertinent:

For physical fitness is not only one of the most important keys to a healthy body; it is the basis of dynamic and creative intellectual activity. The relationship between the soundness of the body and the activities of the mind is subtle and complex. Much is not yet understood. But we do know what the

Greeks knew: that intelligence and skill can only function at the peak of their capacity when the body is healthy and strong; that hardy spirits and tough minds usually inhabit sound bodies.

Physical fitness is highly related to successful participation in play activities. This relationship plays a very important role in the social adjustment of children. A study designed to show the relationship between physical fitness and social acceptance and academic success was made by Popp.[21] He administered the Physical Index test to 100 sophomore boys. The twenty boys with the highest Physical Fitness Indices (102–135) and the twenty boys with the lowest indices (56–79) were chosen for contrast through case studies. All forty boys selected were arranged in a single alphabetical list. Five teachers and administrators without knowledge of the boys' test scores independently chose boys they would most and least like to have for sons. Ten boys were selected by each judge in each of the two categories. Sixteen boys were named by at least one judge in the "desirable" classification. Eleven of these or 69 percent were from the high PFI group and five or 31 percent had low PFI's. Sixteen boys were also chosen in the "undesirable" group. Twelve of these or 75 percent were from the low PFI group. Other comparisons made are shown in Table 7-4. The boys in the high fitness group checked only half as many fatigue problems on the Health Habit Questionnaire as did the boys in the low fitness group.

TABLE 7-4. High-Low PFI

	High Group	Low Group
Overweight	None	10 or 50%
Intelligence Quotient	108.7	104.5
Grade Point Average		
(C = 2; D = 1)	2.22	1.86
Failure to Graduate with Class	1 or 5%	8 or 40%
Rank of Entire Group of 20 in		
Graduating Class of 200	88th	108th
Entered College	8 or 40%	7 or 35%
Number and Percentage Graduating		
from College	8 or 100%	2 or 15%

Contributions of physical fitness to health. The second reason why physical fitness is so important is that it is highly related to health and well-being. The detrimental effects of physical inactivity have reached such alarming proportions that it has been found necessary to coin a term—hypokinetic diseases, i.e., diseases produced by lack of activity—to designate them.

Research demonstrates conclusively the dangers of a sedentary existence to health. Hein and Ryan[22] made an intensive survey of clinical observations and research literature concerning the contributions of physical activity to physical health. The conclusions of the 117 research studies reported were:

1. Regular exercise can play a significant role in the prevention of obesity and thereby influence the greater incidence of degenerative disease and shortened life span associated with this condition.
2. A high level of physical activity throughout life appears to be one of the factors that inhibit the vascular degeneration characteristic of coronary heart disease, the most common cause of death among cardio-vascular disorders.
3. Regular exercise assists in preserving the physical characteristics of youth and delaying the onset of the stigmata of aging and probably exerts a favorable influence upon longevity.
4. Conditioning the body through regular exercise enables the individual to meet emergencies more effectively and so serves in turn to preserve health and to avoid disability and perhaps even death.

Further evidence that emphasizes the significant relationship of physical education to health is the following resolution that was passed by the House of Delegates of the American Medical Association in June, 1960:

Whereas, the medical profession has helped to pioneer physical education in our schools and colleges and thereafter has encouraged and supported sound programs in this field; and

Whereas, there is increasing evidence that proper exercise is a significant factor in the maintenance of health and the prevention of degenerative disease; and

Whereas, advancing automation has reduced the amount of physical activity in daily living, although the need for exercise to foster proper development of our young people remains constant; and

Whereas, there is a growing need for the development of physical skills that can be applied throughout life in the constructive and wholesome use of leisure time; and

Whereas, in an age of mounting tensions, enjoyable physical activity can be helpful in the relief of stress and strain, and consequently in preserving mental health; therefore be it

Resolved, that the American Medical Association through its various divisions and departments and its constituent and component medical societies do everything feasible to encourage effective instruction in physical education in our schools and colleges.[23]

DEVELOPMENT OF MOTOR SKILLS

This objective of physical education is as old and as highly esteemed as the physical development objective. It refers to learning to move skillfully and effectively in all types of situations including games, sports, and dances. The synonym—neuromuscular skills—is frequently used since the mechanisms of behavior involved are muscle-nerve structures.

Very early in life the child begins to combine simple bodily movements into a pattern for some purpose. This process of pattern forming is what is termed motor skill learning. It continues in a sequential hierarchical development with each skill made up of and built on the base of such skills as the individual already possesses.

During the first few years of life the child gradually acquires the skills of crawling, sitting, standing, and walking. Immediate problems are those of postural and balance control and space orientation. After many repetitions these actions become automatic and the child is ready for the more difficult coordinations of running, jumping, kicking, bending, throwing, and climbing. These are all basic, fundamental movements upon which complex motor skills are eventually built.

The degree of the development of motor skill depends upon the variety, amount, and intensity of participation in motor activities during the years of growth. Nature gives the impulses for the proper amount of activity in the repetition of play. A child throws a ball many thousands of times in order to throw it effectively. So it is with each activity. Through infinite repetition the harmonious coordination of the nervous and muscular systems is achieved and motor skill is the result.

At the beginning stages of learning motor skills the child must give attention to the detailed movements. With much practice, however, the skill can be performed automatically. This is of great advantage because the individual can now devote attention to other considerations such as meeting the exigencies and contingencies of the game. Higher brain centers are now free to concentrate on relating personal efforts to those of teammates and on strategic maneuvers. Skilled performance would be impossible if the performer found it necessary to give conscious attention to all the detailed movements.

Neuromuscular skill must be gained through continuous activity during the period of childhood and youth. It is difficult to gain after maturity. In an unpublished report entitled "Motor Learning at the High Skill Level," John Lawther points out:

> This quantitative aspect of early motor learning has been overlooked in much of the motor-learning research. Without an extensive variety of childhood motor experiences as a background, the adolescent and the adult skill learning will be very slow and discouraging; and perhaps will not be

persisted in, until efficient levels are attained. The adult who is the so-called motor illiterate has not the patience, the desire but, more importantly, no longer either the time or the energy to build such motor skill bases as were skipped over because of a childhood of relative inactivity.

Importance of motor skills. The attainment of all of the objectives of physical education depends to a large extent upon the development of a wide variety of motor skills. We know that individuals will not continue to participate in sports, games, or dances unless they possess some reasonable measure of skill. Individuals become frustrated and embarrassed when, after considerable practice and effort, their motor performance is still inept. There is no joy or satisfaction in participating in a physical activity if the result is always failure and defeat.

The attainment of the physical development objective depends heavily upon participation in physical activities in out-of-school hours and throughout the period of adult life. The limited time available in the physical education program will pay much greater dividends insofar as physical fitness is concerned if it is used to develop interest and skill in sports, dance, and other activities in which the individual will participate after school. A high relationship exists between the level of skill developed and future participation in that activity.

High among educational objectives is the development of desirable leisure-time activities. With unprecedented amounts of leisure at our disposal and with the advent and rapid spread of automation the prospects for the future indicate that much more free time will become available to everyone. That this is not an automatic blessing is one of the tragic lessons we have learned from our experience. Because leisure has such great potentialities for enriching or degrading life its proper use has become a major concern of society. As a consequence recreation has assumed increasing significance as an educational goal.

The contributions that physical education is capable of making to wholesome recreation cannot be equaled by any other school subject. Participation in sports is a preferred form of recreation not only during youth but throughout the period of adult life. Sports represent particularly desirable leisure-time activities because they are interesting, wholesome, healthful, adventurous, and truly re-creative. Inherently youth desires physical activity, competition, cooperation, fellowship, and many of the other elements of the physical education program. It is well to note that adequate provision for the leisure time of adolescents is more important than is the preparation for their leisure time when they will be adults. If the problem is adequately handled in youth, there will be little cause for anxiety about it during the time of adult life.

To make a major contribution to the recreational aspects of physical education two conditions must prevail. In the first place activities should be included in the program which have high potentialities for carrying over to present and future leisure. Secondly, at least a fair degree of skill in these activities must be developed. A high relationship exists between the level of skill attained in a sport and the extent of recreational participation in that sport. Many physical educators adhere to the belief that physical education objectives are better served by teaching fewer activities but developing a higher level of skill in them than by offering twice as many activities that would be learned only half as well.

Motor skills play an important role in the social adjustment of children and youth. In play situations the good performer is the hero and the poor performer is pushed into the background. Much of child life is play life, and a large share of it deals with physical skills; whereas, only a small part of adult life is play, and good performance is not stressed so much. If an adult loses at golf or does poorly in a softball game at a picnic, it matters little, for success in those areas is not particularly vital; there are many other things that influence happiness so much more. The child does not have these numerous other phases of endeavor to which to turn for success if failing in physical skills. The child who lacks skill loses status with the group and all too often retreats or vents discontent in unsocial behavior.

Evidence is available to show the impact upon a child who lacks physical skills. Breckenridge and Vincent[24] point out the fact that much social contact evolves from physical skills and activities. "The boy who cannot throw a ball or run fast becomes a group liability. The girl who does not roller skate or ride a bicycle with skill is likely to have a lonely time." Colemen[25] made an extensive study of ten Illinois high schools in 1957–58 and concluded that, regardless of school size, location, or socioeconomic composition, athletics dominated school life. In a 1975 follow-up to Colemen's study Eitzen[26] concluded in his study of fourteen high schools that there is "strong overall support that it (social status of sport) continues to prevail but that other criteria are becoming important in determining one's status among adolescents."

DEVELOPMENT OF KNOWLEDGE AND UNDERSTANDING

The physical educator is concerned with teaching knowledge-type as well as skill-type subject matter. While this objective does not ordinarily receive the emphasis and attention to which it is entitled, it is, nevertheless, a vitally important aspect of physical education.

One type of subject matter that is invariably taught in physical education is the knowledge of rules, techniques, and tactics of the various activities included in the program. This content is indispensable. Much of it is presented in the form of outside reading assignments. There is a great deal of intellectual activity involved in physical education activities and successful performance is directly related to it.

A considerable body of related health information is taught in connection with physical education classes. Such health considerations as warm-up, conditioning procedures, safety measures, desirable sanitary practices, and the like can be effectively covered. Students become acquainted with various physiological factors such as muscle soreness, hypertrophy, and second wind. A wide variety of exercise precautions are naturally presented as a part of physical education instruction.

When the *why* of physical education is included in classes such topics as the following are presented:

1. Physiological aspects of physical activity.
2. Anatomical aspects of physical activity.
3. Psychological aspects of physical activity.
4. Physical fitness evaluation.
5. Relationship of physical activity to physical and mental health.
6. Meeting future physical activity needs.
7. Importance of proper use of leisure.
8. Sociological aspects of exercise and sports.

Another type of knowledge which results from physical education is the understanding of other individuals which it provides. While the physical education teacher does not formally present such materials to the students, the activities of physical education offer an exceptional opportunity to understand human nature. In the close, intimate, face-to-face contacts in physical activities the real person is revealed. Particularly in competitive sports students throw off self-consciousness, formality, artificiality, and restraints and their fundamental character and personality are displayed. Under the pressures, excitement and emotional tension of competition such qualities as honesty, loyalty, teamwork, determination, dependability, resourcefulness, leadership as well as their opposites can be observed. In ordinary relationships in school or out, such insights are rarely possible.

Finally, a valuable part of the knowledge that comes through physical education is not easily expressed in words. Musicians and artists have called the sensory experiences associated with their disciplines as "nonverbal communication." In physical education the sensory perceptions identified with kinesthesia are in the same category. Some of the most valued meanings in the lives of people come from the perceptions identified with movement. This idea is well described in the following state-ment:[27]

> The experiences in the physical education class also provide specialized opportunities for developing ideas about how space is organized, how time is related to space, and how gravity acts on all material objects. These understandings result in many specific concepts about what it means to pull, to push, to lift, to carry, to run, to jump, to swim, to be strong, to exert force, to resist force, to play, to fight, to cooperate, to compete. Dictionary defini-tions of these concepts show how difficult it may be to express their full meanings in words, but they become meaningful within the context of the physical education experiences. The concept of rhythm, for example, can be understood and acted out long before it can be verbalized. Other con-cepts such as balance, equilibrium, motion, up, down, circle, round, parallel, vertical, horizontal, spiral, twist, turn, and juggle can all be demonstrated by moving in appropriate ways. These lists suggest only a few of the complex concepts that may be understood by organizing the sensory data available within the movement-oriented experiences of physical education.

THE SOCIAL AND EMOTIONAL DEVELOPMENT OBJECTIVE

Students acquire social development when they become familiar with the ways of the group, become active members of it, adjust to its stan-dards, accept its rules, and, in turn, become accepted by the group. There is much for the youth to experience, to learn and to incorporate as part of his behavior before he becomes truly socialized. A variety of social habits, attitudes, and ideas must be acquired by one in order to adjust to the family group, peers, classmates, and to the wider social relationships involved in his community, state, nation, and the world.

Character and personality are intrinsic aspects of the social objective. This is so because the behavior of an individual usually affects other people who assess it as good or bad, moral or immoral, socially acceptable or unacceptable. The assessment by others of one's behavior reflects the character of an individual. Character, in turn, is the basis for personality. Since personality is the sum total of an individual's responses to social situations it, likewise, has social implications.

Basic to the development of a strong character and desirable person-ality is a set of values which gives purpose, meaning, and dedication to life. Everything we are and do and say reflects our basic values. Thus it is that character, personality, and values are all involved in the social develop-ment objective. Likewise, citizenship, which is concerned with desirable attitudes and behavior towards organized society and its institutions, is a part of this objective.

Specifically, the social objectives mean that the boy or girl acts in a sportsmanlike manner, works for the common good, and respects the personalities of one's fellows. One enjoys, contributes to, and is at ease while participating now and in the future in physical education activities with those of one's own and the opposite sex. The boy or girl should be able to exercise self-control in activities that are mentally stimulating and often emotionally intense, to react quickly and wisely under pressure, to be courageous and resourceful. He or she should be able to take defeat graciously and without rancor or alibi and victory with modesty and dignity. Students appreciate their obligations and responsibilities as leaders and followers in group situations. They have respect for the rules and properly constituted authority.

In summary, the specific qualities involved in the social objective include sportsmanship, cooperation, teamwork, tolerance, loyalty, courtesy, justice, friendliness, service, unselfishness, integrity, dependability, helpfulness, and thoughtfulness.

Contribution to the Social Development Objective

Physical education is one phase of school work that lends itself particularly to the development of character. Student interest prevails, activity is predominant, and relatively great authority and respect are accorded those in charge. The physical education class provides more than just a place to discuss character education theory; it furnishes a laboratory for actual practice. We develop character much more surely through experience than we do by hearing about what should be done or should not be done. It is one matter to decide upon the correct response to a tense situation when merely looking on, and an entirely different proposition to decide and act correctly when in the midst of heated combat. One contestant may foul another, unnoticed by the official, near the end of a close game and thus prevent an opportunity to score. The player fouled cannot get advice about ensuing action and decide some time later what to do. One must decide at once and provide an immediate answer through action. This splendid educational laboratory demands actual responses to tense situations just as much as life in general does. The whole setup provides real rewards and punishments, which with proper guidance will serve to encourage sportsmanship, cooperation, sociability, self-control, leadership, and other qualities of character and citizenship.

The competitor is an active citizen, not a passive one. It is the acting citizen who receives training. There are laws or rules that must be obeyed as one drives on toward the ambition of winning the contest or performing well. There are penalties imposed immediately upon any infraction of the law. Opportunities to give, to take, to obey, and to cooperate are numerous. Here is the ideal setting for developing the good citizen, the socially adjusted and ethical individual, provided, of course, that the situation is well handled and well regulated. In no school situation are the goals adequately attained if those in charge are incapable or indifferent.

The dominant drive for a winning team or good performance leads to the development of good habits. Sane character habits, such as abstinence from smoking and the use of alcohol, are steps in the direction of good health that can be prompted by athletic competition. In order to be a better player, the youngster will practice these and other habits of good citizenship. In the long run as well as in the immediate situation, clean living builds for success. Habits of clean living and good citizenship tend to carry on just the same as do undesirable habits. Enough good ones crowd out some bad ones. Our personality with its basis of character is, after all, the sum total of our responses to the social situations in which we find ourselves. We establish characteristic reactions to familiar situations. Pursuit of interesting, desirable goals during the period of habit formation will help to develop desirable reaction patterns. All good traits certainly will not carry over completely from one situation to another; but, if there are many, at least a few may be expected to carry over to similar situations. When all other phases of school life contribute their bit toward good citizenship and ethical character, *generalizations* of fairness, sportsmanship, and the like can be built up which will have some carry-over value. The identical elements involved should also carry over to similar home and community situations.

Much research data can be used to demonstrate the important contribution that physical education is capable of making to the social development objective. The value of motor skills was shown. Studies provide convincing evidence that physical education under good leadership is capable of making a major contribution to the education and socialization of the individual.

Obligation of physical education to contribute to social objectives. The fact that physical educators are able to develop such qualities as strength, endurance, agility, and a wide variety of physical skills imposes an obligation upon them to develop in their students a sense of direction and a framework of values consistent with the purpose of the school. When a high level of physical fitness has been developed in an individual, he or she is more effective for good or bad, depending upon attitudes and ideals. It is just as easy to develop a more effective antisocial individual as it is to produce a person who uses superior physical endowments for social benefit. Accordingly, it is essential that physical educators stress the social and moral values of their activities as well as the physical. This point is expressed exceptionally well by Williams:[28]

This emphasis upon the education of the whole person runs the risk that the physical may be neglected because of the pressing demands of the intellectual and because of the high compensation that an industrial society pays for mental skills. Nevertheless, that risk should be run. Force and strength without humane direction are too terrible to contemplate. All persons should know that vigor and vitality of peoples are dependent mainly upon muscular exercise for their development and entirely for their maintenance, and that, aside from the conditioning influences of heredity and favorable nutrition, vigorous physical education is the indispensable means today for national strength. But it should never be forgotten that vitality that is ungenerous, beastly and knavish is no proper objective for any division of education. Let the sponsors of physical education have deep convictions about the tremendous importance of vigor and vitality in peoples; let them assert, time and again, and everywhere, the strategic and imperative role of muscular activity in development, but let them guard against an unworthy exclusiveness that leaves them devoted to strength with no cause to serve, skills with no function to perform, and endurance with nothing worth lasting for.

Most Important Objective in Physical Education

Which of the four objectives, namely, physical development, motor skills, knowledges, and understandings and social adjustment is the most important insofar as the physical educator is concerned? It is immediately apparent that each of these is a highly valid objective, which makes a significant contribution to our educational programs. Over a long period of time each has become recognized as deserving appropriate emphasis in our schools.

From the standpoint of American society, the social objectives are undoubtedly the most important. No one would question that the character, personality, citizenship, and values of our students deserve a higher priority than physical fitness or motor skills. Certainly, qualities such as ideals of justice, truth, duty, personal integrity, self-discipline, sportsmanship, cooperation, and the like, deserve emphasis ahead of strength, endurance, coordination, and game strategy.

However, it must be pointed out that the social objectives are not the sole province of the physical educator. The responsibility for these important outcomes is shared with other areas of education. Every teacher, regardless of teaching specialty, has the responsibility for guiding students into emotionally, socially, and ethically approved behavior.

Moreover, it is necessary to point out that any course of study in the school curriculum must justify its existence in some special way beyond the generalized contribution it might make. Our schools cannot afford the time or expense of school subjects that cannot demonstrate a distinctive contribution to educational purposes.

The unique objectives of physical education are physical development, motor skills and knowledges and understandings about physical education and related activities. If these purposes are not accomplished in physical education, they will not be achieved elsewhere in the school. Consequently, they deserve a high priority insofar as the physical educator is concerned. To give these objectives a priority does not represent an attempt to set up an order of value, but rather an order of approach.

Physical Education, An Integral Part of Education

Physical education is that part of education which proceeds by means of, or predominantly through, movement; it is not some separate, partially related field. This significant means of education furnishes one angle of approach in educating the entire individual, who is composed of many component, interrelated functional units, rather than of several distinctly compartmentalized faculties. The physical, mental, and social aspects must all be considered together. *Physical education, when well taught, can contribute more to the goals of general education than can any other school subject;* not more to each goal than any other subject but more to all goals than any other school subject. This is made possible, in part, by the fact that participation in physical education is very largely on the level at which the youngsters live. They grant their coaches and teachers great authority; the instructors in physical education have less need to demand it than do most other teachers. Opportunity for excellent achievement knocks continually at the door of the physical educator, making physical education one of the keenest-edged tools in the educational kit. With it the physical educator may sculpture beautiful figures or hack to pieces and multilate the already partially shaped raw material. In discussing contributions, we assume that a reasonably skilled teacher is in charge, for even the most perfect system or machine will not function without competent direction.

SELECTED REFERENCES

BARROW, HAROLD M., *Man and His Movement: Principles of His Physical Education.* (2nd ed.) ch. 1,2,3. Philadelphia, Pa.: Lea & Febiger, 1977.
Knowledge and Understanding in Physical Education. Washington, D.C.: AAHPER, 1973.

KRYSPIN, WILLIAM J. and JOHN F. FELDHUSEN, *Writing Behavioral Objectives*, Minneapolis, Minn.: Burgess Publishing Company, 1974.
OBERTEUFFER, DELBERT and CELESTE ULRICH, *Physical Education*. (4th ed.), New York: Harper & Row, Publishers Inc., 1970.
POPHAM, W. JAMES, and EVA L. BAKER, *Establishing Instructional Goals*. Englewood Cliffs, N.J.: Prentice-Hall, Inc., 1970.

NOTES

1. F. Duras, "Some Thoughts About Physical Education," *The Australian Physical Education Journal* (March 1965), p. 3.

2. Educational Policies Commission, *Purposes of Education in American Democracy* (Washington, D.C.: National Education Association, 1938).

3. Educational Policies Comm., Purposes.

4. Educational Policies Commission, *The Central Purpose of American Education* (Washington, D.C.: National Education Association, 1961), p. 21.

5. Educational Policies Commission, *The Central Purpose*, p. 2.

6. Agnes Stoodley, *The Stated Objectives of Physical Education for Women* (Ed.D. dissertation, Stanford University, 1947), p. 37.

7. *Professional Preparation in Health Education, Physical Education, Recreation Education* (Washington, D.C.: AAHPER, 1962), pp. 18–19.

8. Physical Education Division, AAHPER, *This Is Physical Education* (Washington, D.C.: AAHPER, 1965, p. 3.

9. Edmund Arthur Hunt, "Teacher, Parent and Student Differences Concerning Curriculum Objectives: The Physical Education Case" (unpublished Doctoral dissertation, University of British Columbia, 1976).

10. E. N. Gardiner, *Greek Athletic Sports and Festivals* (London: Macmillan & Co. Ltd., 1910), p. 130.

11. Clark W. Hetherington, *School Program in Physical Education* (New York: Harcourt, Brace & World, Inc., 1922), p. 37.

12. The Athletic Institute, *Report of the National Conference on Interpretation of Physical Education* (Chicago: The Athletic Institute, 1961), p. 10.

13. Hetherington, *School Program,* p. 33.

14. Frederick Dewhurst and Associates, *America's Needs and Resources* (New York, The Twentieth Century Fund, 1955), p. 908.

15. Mabel Lee and Miriam Wagner, *Fundamentals of Body Mechanics and Conditioning* (Philadelphia: W. B. Saunders Co., 1949), p. 1.

16. Wildor Hollman, "The 'Hufeland' Prize Essay," *Sport* (Hamburg, West Germany: Broschek and Company, 1964), p. 47.

17. John R. Coefield and Robert H. McCollum, "A Case Study Report of 78 University Freshmen Men With Low Physical Fitness Indices" (Master's thesis, University of Oregon, 1955).

18. C. Getty Page, "Case Studies of College Men with Low Physical Fitness Indices" (Master's thesis, Syracuse University, 1940).

19. Boyd Jarman, "Academic Achievement of Boys Nine, Twelve and Fifteen Years of Age as Related to Physical Performances" (Master's thesis, University of Oregon, 1959).

20. From "The Soft American" by John F. Kennedy, *Sports Illustrated,* December 26, 1960, © 1960 Time Inc.

21. James Popp, "Comparison of Sophomore High School Boys Who Have High and Low Physical Fitness Indices Through Case Study Procedures" (Master's thesis, University of Oregon, 1959).

22. Fred V. Hein and Allan J. Ryan, "The Contributions of Physical Activity to Physical Health," *Research Quarterly* (May 1960), p. 263.

23. Reprinted with the permission of the American Medical Association, Chicago, Illinois.

24. Marian E. Breckenridge and E. Lee Vincent, *Child Development* (Philadelphia: W. B. Saunders Co., 1955), p. 272.

25. James S. Colemen, *The Adolescent Society: The Social Life of the Teenager and Its Impact on Education* (New York: The Free Press of Glencoe, A Division of the Macmillan Company, 1961), p. 306.

26. D. Stanley Eitzen, "Sport and Social Status in American Public Secondary Education," in *Review of Sport and Leisure,* ed. Benjamin Lowe (Governors State University, Park Forest South, Ill.: Vol. 1, Fall 1976), p. 147.

27. Physical Education Division, AAHPER, *This is Physical Education,* p. 5.

28. Jessie Fiering Williams, *Developing Democratic Human Relations,* Section on Physical Education (Washington, D.C.: Association for Health, Physical Education, and Recreation, 1951), pp. 83–84.

8

The School
Physical Education Program

The total physical education program with which all schools are concerned consists of three aspects, namely: the instructional, intramural, and interschool programs. Each phase is important, and no physical education program is complete unless each of these aspects is well developed, coordinated, and integrated. The instructional program (also known as the required program or the activities program) is that which is ordinarily required by state law or local regulation. The classes are scheduled during the school day, and all students are expected to participate unless excused. The emphasis is instructional, and the objective is to provide each student with the minimum essentials of physical education. The intramural program is concerned with the provision of recreational activities and athletic competition for all students within a school. Ordinarily, the competition is in addition to any game competition which occurs in the instructional program. The intramural program is important because it gives all students an opportunity to develop the athletic skills they have been taught in the instructional program. The interschool program is that phase which is concerned with the provision of competition for the most highly proficient students in the various sports with teams from other institutions. This chapter will be devoted to a discussion of the instructional program.

THE INADEQUACY OF PRESENT-DAY PROGRAMS

It is unfortunate that in most communities physical education practice lags far behind current physical education philosophy. The curriculum, especially, has not kept pace with the best thought in the field. From the elementary school through the university, a great many programs are inadequate and haphazard. There are a number of notable exceptions in the more progressive schools, but many programs of physical education are not soundly conceived and well organized.

Evidence of Inadequate Programs

There is a great deal of evidence extending over several decades that our physical education programs have not been particularly successful in achieving their objectives. Data are available from many sources that the record of physical education in accomplishing the physical development objective is far from impressive. One of the major revelations of World War II was the lack of physical fitness of a large percentage of men inducted into the military service. Physical fitness testing programs in the Army, Navy, and Air Force revealed an appalling lack of strength, endurance, agility, and coordination of inductees. Karpovich and Weiss[1] in a study of inductees into the Army Air Forces, found that 48 percent were in poor or very poor condition. Larson[2] discovered that it was necessary to improve the physical fitness status of Army Air Forces personnel as much as 90 percent beyond entrance condition in order to meet minimum physical fitness standards. What is particularly distressing about these data is that they represented the performance of the group of men in America from ages 18 through 38 who were generally considered the most fit.

The President's Council on Physical Fitness and Sports first published a manual in 1961, revised in 1973, titled *Youth Physical Fitness: Suggestions for School Programs.* It is reported in the *Physical Fitness Research Digest*[3]:

> . . . A strong effort was mounted and sustained to stress the need for physical fitness programs in the schools. . . . National normative surveys showed substantial gains; however, while these gains were maintained, the most recent survey did not show additional appreciable progress.
>
> Three motor fitness surveys were conducted in 1958, 1965, and 1975 by Hunsicker and Reiff using comparable scientifically-selected national samples of boys and girls 10–17 years of age. Sizes of the samples varied between 7,800 and 9,200. The items composing the AAHPER Youth Fit-

ness Test were utilized in all surveys. Nearly all test scores for both boys and girls at all ages improved significantly, even dramatically in some instances, between 1958 and 1965. All but one of the averages were higher, nearly all of them significantly so. Unfortunately, however, American boys and girls did not improve in the decade between 1965 and 1975. Girls made some minor gains in endurance and muscular power, but average fitness test scores for the 1974–75 school years were virtually identical to those recorded 10 years earlier.

. . . More than a month prior to announcement of the latest survey, the President's Council on Physical Fitness told President Ford of its concern about a decline in school physical education programs. In the words of the Executive Director: "Physical education has been hit hard by the trend away from required subjects in the schools. I also think physical fitness has suffered because of optional programs. Where students are given wide latitude, they tend to choose activities which require little physical exertion."

PHYSICAL FITNESS CLARIFIED[4]

Before practices and programs can logically be considered, the meaning of physical fitness should be clear and the essential components should be identified. . . . Physical fitness is defined as the ability to carry out daily tasks with vigor and alertness, without undue fatigue, and with ample energy to enjoy leisure-time pursuits and to meet unusual situations and unforeseen emergencies. Thus, physical fitness is the ability to last, to bear up, to withstand stress, and to persevere under difficult circumstances where an unfit person would be ineffective or would quit. The definition implies that physical fitness is more than "not being sick" or merely "being well." It is a positive quality, extending on a continuum from death to abundant life. Thus, living individuals have some degree of physical fitness, which is minimal in the severely ill and maximal in the highly-trained athlete; it varies considerably in different people and in the same person from time to time.

Inasmuch as this physical fitness objective is so general, a breakdown into its underlying components is essential for its measurement and for determining program content in its realization. Assuming a body which is organically sound and free from disease, the components of basic concern to the physical educator are muscular strength, muscular endurance, and circulatory-respiratory endurance. Within the broader concept of motor fitness, other components are recognized, including muscular power, agility, and speed. For those with inadequate trunk-hip flexibility and marked postural deviations, appropriate steps should be taken for their amelioration.

The decision of the physical educator as to the essential components of physical fitness is vital; it should be decisive in the selection of tests to evaluate physical fitness and should form the basis for the selection of physical fitness activities and for the formulation of the physical fitness program to be applied to boys and girls in the schools.

APPROACH TO SCHOOL PHYSICAL FITNESS[5]

Since 1961 a basic tenet of the President's Council on Physical Fitness and Sports has been to provide special programs for boys and girls who are "physically underdeveloped," interpreted here as those below acceptable standards on the basic physical fitness components. The Council also urged that the schools provide special programs for pupils with orthopedic disabilities, postural faults, obesity, malnutrition, perceptual motor difficulties, and other health-related problems. This report is concerned with the development of the three basic physical fitness components of muscular strength, muscular endurance and circulatory-respiratory endurance; stress is placed on those found to be deficient in one or more of these components.

The essential processes proposed for conducting physical fitness programs in schools are as follows: (a) discover boys and girls who are deficient in the basic physical fitness components by use of valid tests; (b) for those with deficiencies, provide appropriate exercise for their improvement; (c) identify the cause or causes of the subfit condition for those who do not improve scores satisfactorily on retests; (d) refer to other specialists, such as physician, guidance personnel, or school nurse when physical defects, organic lesions, personality maladjustments or nutritional disturbances are detected or suspected; (e) conduct maintenance physical fitness activities for those meeting accepted physical fitness standards; and (f) check periodically to determine physical fitness status, so that individual program adjustments may be made when indicated.

In summary, data from World War II and the intervening years have provided convincing evidence that our physical education programs have not made an impressive record in achieving at least two of its objectives, namely, the physical development and the motor skills objectives. Unquestionably, physical education programs have improved appreciably over the past several decades. Personnel are better prepared and facilities are generally better. However, the problem is that the need for physical education has become accentuated. Improvement in programs has not kept pace with the tremendous decrease in physical activity in our daily lives coupled with a growing culture of abundance, ease, and comfort. In other words, the need for physical education has developed more rapidly than has program improvement.

Causes of Inadequate Programs

Inadequate time allotment has been one of the factors which has made it difficult to accomplish the objectives of physical education. Although several states make a daily period mandatory in all elementary and secondary schools, most states do not begin to approach such a requirement.

Another factor that has adversely affected physical education programs is inadequate facilities. Physical education activities, involving as they do vigorous activity, require considerable space, which is usually expensive. In addition, certain activities such as swimming, bowling, golf, racquet ball, handball, and tennis require specialized facilities which are extremely costly. Because of the high expense of many physical education facilities, they are often not provided, and many worthwhile activities cannot be included in the program. Probably more than any other single factor, the limitations imposed by inadequate facilities restrict the type of program that might be offered.

A final reason for the existence of so many inferior programs lies in the fact that educationally sound methods of curriculum construction have not been applied in physical education. The physical educator frequently builds his or her own program. The activities that the instructor teaches will depend upon training and philosophy. Whether the program is good or bad it is usually accepted. School administrators are usually alert to deficiencies in other aspects of the curriculum but may have a lack of critical judgment in regard to physical education, which has led to the acceptance of inadequate instructional programs. This opportunity for physical educators to construct their own programs has often been exploited. If it is desired to build up the varsity athletic teams, the entire program may be shaped toward this end with no consideration for educational outcomes. This has been a fairly common practice. It is an unfortunate fact that too often the physical education program is organized and conducted for purposes other than the best interests of youth.

Technique of Curriculum Development

Until comparatively recently, the development of the physical education program involved only the director or supervisor of physical education. This individual was presumed to be the expert on curriculum building, and he or she planned the course of study which the various instructors were expected to follow. In many cases, particularly in large cities, the course of study was worked out in great detail with each day's lesson prescribed, even to the sequence in which the activities were to be presented and the number of minutes that were to be spent on each. The task of supervision involved comparing the course of study with what the teacher was doing to ascertain whether the lesson was being taught in the prescribed manner.

Curriculum construction and revision today should be done on an entirely different basis. All staff members must be provided ample opportunity to express their views. Modern curriculum development programs are postulated upon the assumption that only as the teacher plays an active and intelligent role in the development of the course of study materials can the curriculum be effectively revised. The same postulate should be applied to students. When students and teachers are involved in planning, selecting, implementing, evaluating and revising the curriculum, the physical education program is more likely to achieve the needs and interest of the participants.

There are other populations who can contribute to development of curriculum and who also should be consulted. The principal or a designated representative, curriculum specialists in the central office of the school district, school board members, and interested parents who have special qualifications also can be valuable contributors.

Citizen advisory groups are a must in a modern physical education program. Program revision is often limited by facilities, equipment and supplies, staffing, and transportation. The citizenry of the community can often help solve these problems, but they are less likely to be interested in trying to help if they are not represented in the development of the curriculum. On the other hand, when they are involved they can be the moving force to implement the seemingly impossible.

Many techniques should be utilized to implement curriculum construction and revision procedures. One which is very effective and widely used is the curriculum committee involving all the populations who have a stake in the education of the consumer. The curriculum committee should be on-going and meet on a regular basis, not only for handling emergencies, but to plan for future needs.

The many populations (parents, students, community) should be surveyed periodically to evaluate interest and needs. Evaluation of the present program by students, faculty and parents provides important feedback in program construction.

Steps Involved in Curriculum Construction

A vast amount of literature on curriculum construction and curriculum revision has become available in recent years. Definite procedures are recommended to be followed in developing a school curriculum or a course of study within the total curriculum. These steps usually involve:

1. Social philosophy. Any consideration of the nature and purposes of physical education must inevitably be based upon the social and educational philosophy of the time and place in which it operates. Physical educators frequently want to start the curriculum construction process with a consideration of the objectives of physical education and the selection of activities which will attain the objectives. However, prior considerations are involved. Since physical education is a part of the

entire system of education, its philosophy and objectives must be consistent with the philosophy that prevails in education. Educational philosophy in turn arises out of the social philosophy of the society in which it functions. Physical education does not exist in a vacuum. It obtains its direction and purpose from the society in which it exists and the educational system of which it is a part.

In America our social philosophy is based upon the belief that the total well-being of each person is a primary and controlling consideration.

The basic tenets of a democracy include:

a. Worth of the individual. Democracy holds that the individual and the society of which he/she is a part have common purposes, namely, bringing about through effective cooperation the highest and fullest development of each individual.

b. Belief in the equality of opportunity for the optimum development of each individual's potentialities.

c. Reciprocal individual and group responsibility for promoting common concerns.

d. The free play of intelligence in the solution of common problems. In a democracy common problems are to be solved through the free play of intelligence rather than through force, appeal to authority, or uncritical acceptance of the value of any one group or individual.

2. Educational philosophy. The basic purpose of education during all periods of civilization, from the primitive to the present, has been and is to enable the individual to become a better citizen of the society in which he lives. No society would tolerate for long a school system whose purposes were not in harmony with the welfare of that society. An educational program is successful only when in all of its aspects it contributes to the purposes of the society in which it lives and has its being. Thus, in America the aim of education is to assist each individual to achieve optimum development in meeting effectively the continuous demands of living in a democratic society and in a closely interdependent world. Educational objectives implement educational philosophy. They are the steps that lead to the aim.

3. Statement of objectives. Objectives express needs as seen by the person or persons who formulate them. Education—and therefore physical education—exists to meet the needs of children. These needs are of two types: individual and societal. Individual and societal needs blend in objectives toward which the school sights are set.

4. The nature of children. Although the needs of children determine the direction of development for which the school shall strive, it is the nature of the child which determines what is appropriate for educa-

tion at each stage of development. The best conceivable forms of adult behavior represent goals toward which the education of the child must proceed, but the steps necessary in moving toward these goals are dictated by the character of the child's interests, urges, and capacities. It is evident that a thorough understanding of the nature of the child is an essential prerequisite for the physical educator when he builds a program.

5. Selection of activities to attain objectives. This is the most difficult of all aspects of curriculum construction. The activities which are of greatest value in meeting the needs of children are obviously the ones that should be given priority. However, certain activities satisfy the needs of children better in one area than others. For example, some activities are outstanding from the standpoint of developing physical fitness but may be of little value from the recreational standpoint. Other activities may contribute appreciably to the recreational needs of students but have little value insofar as physical fitness is concerned. This poses a difficult problem to those who are developing the program.

6. Evaluation of the program. The program needs to be periodically evaluated to determine if it is accomplishing the intended results. If it is not, the proper corrective procedures should be employed. Evaluative procedures are considered in a separate chapter.

Principles for Selection of Activities

In order to select from the many activities of child and adult life those more likely to attain the objectives of physical education, certain guiding principles will be set up. All of the activities of the program will not satisfy all of these criteria, but those that conform to the majority of them are of greatest value. The program based upon the following physiological, psychological, and sociological principles is a practical one, although lack of facilities and inadequate training of teachers may eliminate some of the activities. These practical considerations vary so widely that any modification of the program must be made locally.

Physiological Principles

1. The physical education program should provide ample opportunities for a wide range of movements involving the large muscles.

2. The facts related to the growth and development of children should guide in curriculum construction.

3. Provision should be made in the program for the differences in physical capacities and abilities that are found among students.

4. The physical fitness needs of students must be met by the physical education program.

Psychological Principles

5. The physical education program should consist predominantly of natural play activities.

6. The activities should be selected in the light of the psychological age characteristics of the child as well as the physiological.

7. Activities that are valuable in arousing and expressing emotions should be chosen.

8. In the selection of activities some provision should be made for progression.

9. In the selection and placement of activities sufficient time should be provided so that the skills may be learned reasonably well.

10. Activities that best meet the seasonal drives of the students should be selected.

Sociological Principles

11. The curriculum should be rich in activities adaptable to use in leisure time.

12. Activities should be selected for their possible contributions to the youth's training for citizenship in a democracy.

13. The curriculum should be suited to the ideals of the community as well as its needs.

14. Activities that are particularly rich in possibilities for individual character training are especially desirable.

Inasmuch as these principles form the basis upon which a successful program may be built, the following points concerning each should be noted:

1. The physical education program should provide ample opportunities for a wide range of movements involving the large muscles. Physical education is primarily concerned with big-muscle activities. The big muscles are those of the trunk, shoulders, hips, and neck and are used in running, jumping, throwing, striking, climbing, and pushing and pulling activities, and the small muscles are those of the face, throat, fingers, and toes. The small muscles are used in writing, drawing, typing, piano playing, and other like activities. In man's evolution, the big muscles are the older, fundamental muscles, and the small muscles are the newer accessory ones. Most of the values attributed to physical education arise from the fact that the activities are big-muscle activities. For example, the development of health has already been mentioned as a prominent objective of physical education. There is little development of health by the action of the smaller muscles because very little organic activity is in-

volved. But when the big muscles of the body are used, they burn up more energy, which results in a greatly increased functional activity of the circulatory, respiratory, excretory, and heat-regulating mechanisms and, later, the digestive mechanism. It is this organic activity that develops organic power, vigor, vitality, resistance to fatigue, and health. The only known way to reach and develop the vital organs is through vigorous total body activities.

2. The facts related to the growth and development of children should guide in curriculum construction. In order that the best educational results may be obtained, those activities that are best adapted to the strength, endurance, and coordination of each age group should be selected. From the standpoint of the readiness of the organism to assimilate physical education activities, there is a best time for each activity. There is also an optimum degree of exercise that is beneficial at the various stages of development. This principle is recognized somewhat by the modified playing regulations of junior and senior high school sports as compared with college regulations. But much more needs to be done in interscholastic athletics as well as in physical education classwork.

Growth and development take place according to a definite and continuous pattern that depends upon hereditary and environmental factors. Growth and development do not proceed evenly and do not occur in the same manner in both sexes. The appearance of new teeth, the slow development of the heart, the physiological changes brought on by adolescence, and sex differences are only a few of the factors that can affect the program of physical education.

3. Provision should be made in the program for the differences in physical capacities and abilities that are found among students. Special provision must be made in the physical education program for the great physical differences that exist among students. In order to avoid a program that would make excessive demands upon any individual, it is necessary to know what his physical capacities and abilities are. The medical examination will discover the physical defects that would handicap or prevent students from engaging in the regular program. For these students other activities must be provided. These activities must be within the capacities of each individual and selected with a view to remedying the defect, if possible.

There are also in every group those who are appreciably below normal in coordination, speed, strength, agility, and balance. Rather than to require such students to participate exclusively in the regular activities, a special program should be arranged to give special attention to their deficiencies. When these students have developed a suitable level of physical fitness, they should return to the regular program.

4. The physical fitness needs of students should be met by the

physical education program. Automation, by drastically reducing the vigorous exercise involved in work of all types, has accentuated the importance of physical education's contribution to physical fitness. The physical aspects of fitness of each individual should be periodically assessed, and proper activities to meet individual and group needs should be scheduled.

One aspect of physical fitness in which our youth is particularly lacking is strength of the arm and shoulder girdle. This deficiency is serious because it affects successful performance in so many different sports. Unfortunately, some of these sports are not, in and of themselves, particularly good developers of arm and shoulder girdle strength. For this reason, teachers must be alert to this situation, and if a need exists they should provide appropriate activities. Among the better activities to develop strength in the upper extremities are wrestling, gymnastics, rope climbing, weight training, and selected conditioning exercises.

5. The physical education program should consist predominantly of natural play activities. Natural play activities are those that are based essentially on activities developed thousands of years ago in response to the situations that confronted primitive man. He had to run, jump, throw, strike, chase, flee, pounce upon, dodge, and climb to get food, provide goods, and preserve his life. From time immemorial man has performed these activities so that today there is a powerful inner drive in every individual to do these things. But the twentieth century offers few opportunities for their expression except perhaps through physical education activities. Football, basketball, baseball, in fact all of our popular sports, are popular largely because they are composed of natural activities. It might well be said that the most interesting activities are those that include most of these instinctive drives. Football is extremely popular because it satisfies so many urges, such as running, jumping, throwing, kicking, dodging, chasing, striking, and fleeing. On the other hand, calisthenics and marching have seldom been popular because they include very few of the natural activities. Expression through these natural play activities is inherently satisfying, for each individual is prepared in his or her nervous system to respond in the required way. The program, in order to utilize these inner drives to the fullest extent, should consist predominantly of play activities based on them.

6. The activities should be selected in the light of the psychological age characteristics of the child as well as the physiological. This is one of the most important factors to be considered in constructing a physical education program. There are rather clearly defined age stratifications in regard to play interests, and the content of the curriculum should be in harmony with them. As a general rule, children of nine-to-twelve have developed different play interests from those they had at the six-to-nine-

year level. College students usually have different play interests from those in the junior high school. Most men and women can readily recall their own changing interests in their youth. These changes do not appear and disappear at exactly the same time for all children; nor do the latter all desire to express the same play interest in the same way. Individual differences do exist, but there is a striking similarity in the play interests that children manifest at various ages. The good curriculum will be guided by these natural tendencies that appear at different ages.

The significance of this for the curriculum builder is that the program should contain a variety of activities from which each individual may select those that interest him or her most. Of course, the activities of the program must be in harmony with the age level of the group. A wide variety of play activities should be presented in the elementary school. It is important that students should have the exploratory experience before they are permitted to elect. Unless they are familiar with all the activities available, the privilege of election will be almost meaningless.

7. Activities that are valuable in arousing and expressing emotions should be chosen. The development of the intellectual capacities has so engrossed educators that they have devoted little thought and attention to the emotions, which are the generative forces behind most conduct. Man's behavior has sprung from emotions and instinct for so many thousands of years that we cannot expect our conduct today to be based entirely upon intelligence. What is needed in our schools, as much as anything else, is provision for the education of the emotions.

Physical education occupies a strategic position among the school subjects for guiding and modifying the emotions. Latin, rhetoric, and mathematics neither arouse the emotions nor offer the opportunities for emotional expression that physical education activities do. Mankind craves sports and games that are dramatizations of situations that exercise instincts and emotions. If expression rather than repression were the rule, the mental health of our nation would present a much less serious problem. Emotional stability is only achieved through practice in controlling and modifying the feelings released. Physical education makes a most substantial contribution to education in providing a laboratory setting in which emotional control is practiced. In view of this fact, the curriculum of physical education should include those activities which are particularly valuable in arousing and offering an outlet for emotional expression. Body-contact activities, such as football, basketball, soccer, and wrestling, are very effective in this respect, because they exercise deeper, more powerful emotions than many of the noncontact activities. The contact sports are even of benefit to spectators, who experience them vicariously and give expression to their aroused emotions by cheering.

8. In the selection of activities some provision should be made for progression. The physical education program should show progression

from the kindergarten through the twelfth grade. This requires that the elementary and middle or junior and senior high school physical education programs be carefully integrated. Unfortunately, in many instances, the programs at these different school levels are completely unrelated. This results in overlapping and duplication in certain areas and in complete neglect in others. A program that is well integrated will accomplish significantly more results than one that is not.

Every school system should determine what qualities, skills, and attitudes it desires its high school graduates to possess as a result of their experiences in physical education. These qualities, skills, and attitudes thus become the objectives of the entire school system, and the program at the various grade levels should be developed to accomplish these objectives. All of the activities of the elementary and middle or junior high school should be planned with reference to the senior high school program.

9. In the selection and placement of activities sufficient time should be provided so that the skills may be learned reasonably well. Far better results will be secured from a physical education program that provides a few activities to be learned well than from one that offers many activities that are learned only partially. Everyone enjoys doing that which he or she can do well. There is far more value in acquiring a fair degree of skill in several sports than in becoming a jack of all sports and a master of none.

Under this principle, more time will be provided for the more difficult skills. The backward handspring is a more complex skill than the forward roll, and the "full gainer" is more difficult to perform than a "front header" dive. Similarly, the fundamentals of softball are much less difficult to master than those of baseball. If a skill is worth acquiring, it should be well acquired. This does not necessarily mean that every skill must be thoroughly mastered by every student in the class. It suggests, rather, that sufficient time be allowed in order to enable the average student to perform the activity with a fair degree of skill.

10. Activities that best meet the seasonal drives of the students should be selected. Students have a readiness for seasonal activities. When professional, college, and high school teams are playing football or soccer, students have a desire for these sports. When the football and soccer seasons are over, they anticipate basketball and other indoor activities. The spring of the year is time for baseball, track and field, golf, and tennis. There is far more readiness for indoor activities in disagreeable weather than on warm, sunny days.

11. The curriculum should be rich in activities adaptable to use in leisure time.

The new and growing leisure represents one of America's greatest social problems because of its extent and almost universal possession; because it may be said that his sense of time is the measure of man; because misuse of this gift can destroy health, reduce efficiency, break character and degrade life while wise use can enhance health, increase efficiency, elevate character, and enrich and glorify life. Civilization itself can be advanced or destroyed according to the use of it by people as a whole.[6]

The solution to this great social problem that leisure presents lies with education. Our schools are gradually devoting more attention to the activities with which people occupy their leisure time. This concern is not solely with the leisure-time activities of adults, for children of all ages have been emancipated from many of the chores and duties that diminished their available leisure time.

The increased emphasis on avocational activities in the schools is of considerable significance to physical education. Americans, young and old, spend countless leisure hours either playing or watching sports and games. Preparation for all these leisure hours spent in the realm of sports is one of the major objectives of the program of physical education. The practice of postponing until adulthood the education in golf, tennis, handball, volleyball, swimming, racquet ball, and other big-muscle play activities of adults has always failed and will continue to fail to produce satisfactory results. The vast number of college graduates who have very little or no skill in these sports, and will never develop any, is ample evidence of the weakness of the physical education program of the past. Moreover, in order to produce the most favorable educational results, some preparation for the leisure activities of the child should be provided throughout his school life. It would be a mistake to select the activities entirely on the basis of adult needs. One of the outstanding criticisms directed against education today is that the activities are too far removed from the student's present needs and interests and, therefore, are not significant to him. Although it is doubtful that this criticism would be true for play activities to the extent that it is true of academic activities, nevertheless the program of physical education should be adaptable for use in both present and future leisure time.

12. Activities should be selected for their possible contribution to the youth's training for citizenship in a democracy. One of the most fundamental objectives of our educational system is the development of the civic and social virtues desired in a democratic society. These virtues are best developed by practicing them in natural situations. This is possible in physical education activities. Team sports under capable leadership can develop cooperation, loyalty, leadership, followership, sportsmanship, respect for the rights of others, and other qualities essential in the citizens of a democracy. In athletics, the dominating drive to win stimulates the development of these qualities, for youth soon finds out that they are

necessary for success. Furthermore, provincialism, which is contrary to democratic principles, is reduced by team sports. Regardless of the diverse nationalities that may be represented in a team, the players are teammates, and all barriers between them cease to exist as they cooperate for a common purpose. In team competitions, the only measure of a person is what she or he does as a member of the team—race, creed, wealth, and class are all forgotten. No better training for citizenship in a democracy is available anywhere in the school system.

13. The curriculum should be suited to the ideals of the community as well as its needs. What may be a perfect physical education program in one community might prove to be an utter failure in another. Social dancing is a physical education activity that is readily accepted in certain schools, but which in others would not be tolerated by the community. Communities with a large foreign population often prefer soccer to all other activities. Thus, the ideals of the community are powerful factors to be considered in the selection of the content of the program. Likewise, the needs of the community must be reckoned with. In the northern states winter outdoor activities can hold a prominent position on the program, but they may be utterly out of place in the south.

When the physical educator finds himself in a community that is hostile to certain valuable activities, he should hold them in abeyance until public opinion has become favorable to them. Nothing is gained by attempting to force a physical education program that is unacceptable. The best procedure is to change gradually the attitude of the students and public in favor of the new activities.

14. Activities that are particularly rich in possibilities for individual character training are especially desirable. The development of character as an objective of physical education has already been discussed. Because physical education activities exercise the most fundamental emotions and instinctive tendencies, they are powerful factors in developing good character. The skilled teacher, by teaching, by suggestions, and by example, will utilize the possibilities inherent in sports and games for developing desirable traits of character that will operate in these activities and may even carry over into other life situations.

COEDUCATIONAL CLASSES

By mandate of Title IX of the Educational Amendments of 1972 sex discrimination is prohibited in education in all programs and activities receiving or benefiting from federal financial assistance.

A course which would deny participation of either sex cannot be scheduled in school districts and post-secondary institutions as a result of the Title IX regulation. Elementary schools had to comply with the regulation by July 1976 and secondary and post-secondary level institutions had to implement and fully comply by July 1978.

Title IX does not prohibit grouping of students in physical education classes and activities by ability as assessed by objective standards of individual performance developed and applied without regard to sex. An additional provision allows separation of students by sex within physical education classes or activities during participation in wrestling, boxing, rugby, ice hockey, football, basketball and other sports the purpose or major activity of which involves bodily contact.

Further, where use of a single standard of measuring skill or progress in a physical education class has an adverse effect on members of one sex, the recipient shall use appropriate standards which do not have such effect.[7]

The effects of Title IX have many implications for districts and institutions both philosophically and practically. Physical educators must provide equal opportunity for participation in all activities to both sexes and cannot segregate classes by sex. Segregation of students by ability can be used to group students homogeneously within a class. The range of ability in any one class may be greater than it has ever been before, thus requiring the physical educator to organize the classes more effectively so that better teaching takes place.

Fewer girls will be in the high ability groups because they are lower in strength, endurance and speed. The disparity in these attributes will diminish as the girls have more opportunity to participate in more rigorous activities.

Time Allotment

The matter of time allotment is of great importance because no program of activities can operate successfully unless a proper amount of time is allotted to it. Unfortunately, the time required by most state physical education laws is totally inadequate for a well-balanced program. The minimum requirement for the different states, based on a survey updated in 1971, is shown in Table 8-1.

The amount of time which should be devoted to physical education in the various grades depends upon the needs of children for physical activity. Under the present circumstances the meager time allotted to physical education is best utilized by devoting it predominantly to instructional purposes, with the hope that there will be sufficient carryover in the leisure-time activities of children to satisfy their needs for big-muscle activity. Physical education leaders believe that approximately an hour a day would be a desirable allotment of time, but few schools ever realize

TABLE 8-1. TIME AND GRADE REQUIREMENTS FOR PHYSICAL EDUCATION IN ELEMENTARY AND SECONDARY SCHOOLS—STATES AND POSSESSIONS*

State	Required by Law or Regulation	Time Requirement	Grade Requirement
Alabama	Yes	1-6—30 m/day; 7-8—daily; 9-12—1 credit	1 through 12
Alaska	No	(Schools which offer PE must meet minimum requirements for issuing of credits).	
Arizona	No	Recommended only; 1-3—10% of day; 4-8—14% of day; 9-12 not specified	None
Arkansas	Yes	1-8 required but no time specified; 9-12—1 credit	1 through 12; secondary 1 credit required
California	Yes	1-6—200 m/2 wks; 7-12—400 m/2 wks	1 through 12
Colorado	No	None (Physical education in grades 1 through 12 is required for state accreditation)	Non-regulatory state
Connecticut	Yes	Not specified	Required by law in elementary and secondary schools; grade level optional
Delaware	Yes	1-6—suggested 200-250 m/wk; 7-8—2 periods/wk; 9-10—2 periods/wk one semester, 3 periods/wk adjacent semester; 11-12 elective	1 through 10; 11-12 elective (effective April 1970)
District of Columbia	Yes	Grade 1—150 m/wk; 2-6—125 m/wk (combined with health); 7-9—90 m/wk; 10-11—3 periods/wk; 12 elective	1 through 12

*Grieve, Andrew, "State Legal Requirements for Physical Education," *Journal of Health, Physical Education Recreation,* April 1971, pp. 19–21 (updated by author).

State	Required by law or Regulation	Time Requirement	Grade Requirement
Florida	Yes	1-6—daily period; 7-8—90 periods/yr (2 55-m periods/wk); 9-12—2 credits	1 through 8; 9-12—2 credits
Georgia	Yes	1-8—30 m/day (combined HE & PE)	1 through 8
Hawaii	Yes	K-6—90 m/wk; 7-10—½ credit/yr	K through 10
Idaho	Yes	1-8 not required; 9-12—1 credit	9-12—1 credit
Illinois	Yes	1-12 daily period equal in length to other subject periods	1 through 12
Indiana	Yes	1-6—10% of day recommended; 7-8—15% of day recommended; 9-12—1 credit	9 through 12—1 credit required
Iowa	Yes	50 m/wk minimum	1 through 12
Kansas	Yes	9-12—55 m/day	1 through 8 recommended only; 9-12 required
Kentucky	Yes	1-8—120 m/wk; 9-12—1 semester (suggested in 9 or 10)	1 through 8; 9 through 12—1 semester or ½ credit for graduation
Louisiana	Yes	1-8—120 m/wk; 9-12—150 m/wk minimum, 300 m/wk maximum	1 through 12
Maine	Yes	1-11—2 periods/wk for all pupils in public schools	1 through 11
Maryland	Yes	1-6 required but no time specified; 7-8 daily period; 9 daily where possible, 9-12—1 credit	1 through 12; 9-12—1 credit
Massachusetts	Yes	1-6—90 m/wk; 7-12—120 m/wk	1 through 12
Michigan	Yes	Not specified	Not specified

State	Required by Law or Regulation	Time Requirement	Grade Requirement
Minnesota	Yes	1-6—30 m/day; 7-10—2 55-min periods/wk	1 through 10
Mississippi	Yes	1-6—20 to 30 m/day	1 through 6
Missouri	Yes (use voluntary classification plan)	1-6—2 30-min periods/wk; 7-12 required but no time specified	1 through 12
Montana	Yes	1-3—15 m/day; 4-6—20 m/day; 7-8—30 m/day; 9-10—3 periods/wk	1 through 10
Nebraska	No	None by law; for accreditation— elementary 150 m/wk; secondary 2 55-m periods/wk	Can get accreditation for meeting indicated requirements
Nevada	Yes	1-8 not specified; 9-12—3 years 5 daily periods/wk	9 through 12— 3 years required
New Hampshire	No	None	Recommended for elementary schools
New Jersey	Yes	1-12—150 m/wk	1 through 12 (includes some health education)
New Mexico	Yes	1-3—125 m/wk; 4-6—150 m/wk; 7-8 equivalent of 1 period/day for 1 year; 9-12 equivalent of 1 period/day for 1 year	1 through 6; 7-8 equivalent of 1 period/day for 1 year; 9-12 equivalent of 1 period/day for 1 year
New York	Yes	1-6—120 m/wk; 7-12—300 m/wk	1 through 12
North Carolina	Yes	1-8—150 m/wk; 9 daily period (combined with health)	1 through 9
North Dakota	Yes	Daily instruction for all	1 through 12

State	Required by Law or Regulation	Time Requirement	Grade Requirement
Ohio	Yes	1-8—100 m/wk; 9-12—2 periods/wk for 2 years	1 through 12 (dependent upon fulfillment of 2 yr. requirement)
Oklahoma	No	None	None
Oregon	Yes	K-3—10% of school day; 4-6—15% of school day; 7-8—35-45 m/day; 9-10—45-60 m/day; 11-12 optional	K through 10; 11-12 optional but strongly recommended
Pennsylvania	Yes	1-6 daily but no time specified; 7-12—2 periods/wk but no time specified	1 through 12
Rhode Island	Yes	1-12 average of 20 m/day (combined with health)	1 through 12
South Carolina	Yes	1-6 daily period; 7-8—2 or 3 periods/wk; 9-12—1 credit	1 through 8; 9 through 12—1 credit required for graduation (may apply 2 credits toward graduation)
South Dakota	Yes	1-9—90 m/wk	1 through 9
Tennessee	Yes	1-6—30 m/day; 7-8—1 hr twice weekly or 45 m alternate days or 30 m/day; 9-12—1 credit	1 through 12; 9 through 12—1 credit required
Texas	Yes	1-6 required but no time specified; 7-8—130 clock hrs/yr (minimum); 9-12—1½ credits (240 clock hrs)	1 through 12; 9 through 12—1½ credits required
Utah	Yes	1-6—30 m/day recommended; 7-9—1 semester; 10-12—1 semester in 2 of 3 grades	7 through 12 (time requirements indicated)

State	Required by Law or Regulation	Time Requirement	Grade Requirement
Vermont	Yes	1-8 no time specified; 9-12—1 credit	1 through 12
Virginia	Yes	1-8 no time specified; 9-12—3 credits required of combined health & physical education	1 through 12
Washington	Yes	1-8—20 m/day; 9-12—90 m/wk	1 through 12
West Virginia	Yes	1-6—30 m/day; 7-8—1 period/day; 9-12—minimum of 2 periods/wk	1 through 12
Wisconsin	Yes	1-6 daily period; 7-12—3 periods/wk	1 through 12
Wyoming	Yes	1-8 required but no time specified	1 through 8
		POSSESSIONS	
Canal Zone	Yes	1-6—30 m/day; 7-12—55 m/day	1 through 12
Guam	Yes	1-6 no time specified; 7 and 9—1 period/day; 10 and 11—1 period/day	1 through 6; 7 and 9; 10 and 11
Puerto Rico	Yes	1-6—80 m/wk; 7-9—50 m/wk; 10-12—250 m/wk elective	1 through 9; 10 through 12 elective
Virgin Islands	Yes	1-6—45 m/wk; 7-10—180 m/wk	1 through 10

this ideal. Several states require a daily program, but the large majority require only two or three periods per week.

What portion of the allotted time should be devoted to each of the activities in the program must also be carefully considered. The program should be systematically organized and graded in order that the limited time may be used to the best advantage. The practice of devoting the bulk of the time year after year to the same activities is indefensible and reflects an outworn philosophy of physical education. Even the best activity becomes relatively less valuable after several years of regular exposure to it. To offer basketball for three years in the senior high school physical education program to the exclusion of other important activities is as unjustifiable as to offer the same students the identical course in ancient history for three years. Of course, the more important and complicated activities require greater time than some of the simpler, less important ones. The first appearance of an activity in the program should call for instruction in the fundamentals; later appearances of the same activity call for instruction in the more complicated skills and strategic maneuvers.

THE ELEMENTARY SCHOOL PROGRAM

In addition to the general objectives of education each division of the school has a purpose that is peculiar to itself. The unique function of the elementary school is to provide preparation for the child in the tools of education or, as expressed in the seven cardinal principles, "command of the fundamental processes." It is the place where the child acquires the basic knowledge, skills, habits, and the ideals of thought, feeling, and action that are essential for everyone.

Importance of Physical Education in the Elementary Schools

Unquestionably, the weakest aspect of physical education is the program in the elementary schools. This period is likewise more important than any other similar span of time because this is when a strong foundation for physical and motor fitness must be established. The basis must be laid for the development of such factors as strength, endurance, agility, coordination, balance, flexibility, power, and skill in a wide variety of motor activities. In fact, if the proper beginnings are not made during this period, adequate adjustment may be almost impossible at a later date. Unquestionably, the elementary school years represent "the golden years" from the standpoint of developing the physical and motor potentialities of our people.

The accumulation of evidence concerning the alarming lack of physical fitness of the American people and the consequent results upon their effectiveness, health, and well-being has given rise to much speculation about what must be done to solve the problem. Many proposals have been made and it is almost unanimously agreed that the *single most important consideration is the improvement of the elementary school physical education programs*. The facts are that the manner in which physical education is conducted in most of our elementary schools does not even begin to approach adequacy.

Time allotment for physical education in elementary schools. The two most vulnerable aspects of elementary physical education are time allotment and leadership. Concerning time allotment, a daily period of thirty minutes is the standard recommended by the American Alliance for Health, Physical Education, and Recreation, as well as by many other professional organizations. Fifteen to thirty minutes per day may have been enough in the past but this amount does not suffice in our highly mechanized, automated existence. The amount of physical activity which the boy and girl from six to twelve partakes in outside of school does not remotely compare to that which children fifty and even twenty-five years ago had. The work activities and chores that formerly provided the vitally needed physical development have been virtually eliminated.

These changed living circumstances greatly accentuate the importance of physical education in our schools. We must now rely almost solely on our school physical education programs to provide the physical activity that is essential to the well-being of our children. However, if physical education is to compensate for the effects of automation and technology and particularly the automobile and television, it must be at its best. More time and attention must be devoted to it. Elementary school physical education is incapable of meeting its greatly increased responsibilities with the traditional allocation of time. No less than sixty minutes per day from first grade through sixth grade is necessary.

Leadership for physical education in elementary schools. Classroom teachers are seldom capable of producing high quality programs when teaching elementary school physical education classes. They have a very superficial professional preparation for such an assignment if they have any at all. Further, many of them are not interested in assuming the responsibility for this program. A major reason for their attitude is that they do not feel properly qualified for such teaching. Certainly, they cannot begin to approach the performance of a professionally prepared physical education teacher.

The time has arrived when a truly professional performance is necessary in the physical education program of the elementary schools. When life outside of school was meeting some of the exercise needs of children, the quality of leadership was not as crucial as it is today. We can no longer afford the myth that a nonprofessionally prepared teacher can do a professional job. Physical education has now become so important in our schools, it is so significantly related to the health, adjustment, happiness, and attitudes of children that it can no longer be relegated to untrained leaders.

It is an interesting fact that in most of the countries that have long-standing, well-established educational systems, specialists are used for the physical education program in the elementary schools. For example, in most of the European countries it is considered so essential to get elementary school children started properly that specialists teach the physical education classes. The attitude prevails that physical education in the elementary schools is much more important than it is in the secondary schools and should be given priority.

THE PHYSICAL EDUCATION PROGRAM IN THE PRIMARY GRADES

Characteristics of Primary Grade Children

Before the activities for the physical education program in the primary grades are selected it is necessary to know the nature of the child physically, psychologically, and socially. The child is usually five or six years of age when she or he starts in the elementary school. Preschool years have been spent mainly in getting control of the fundamental movements of the body and in familiarizing the child with his and her environment. Chief characteristics are:

Physical Characteristics
(Ages 6–8)

1. Stature: in the period of slow but steady increase.
2. Weight: in the period of steady growth.
3. Health: susceptibility to disease is somewhat higher than it was before the child started school. The child does not have many antibodies in the blood when entering school because he or she has not come into daily contact with large groups of other children.
4. Pulse rate: higher than in adults.
5. Blood pressure: lower than in adults.
6. Red blood cells: fewer in number; 4,000,000 per cc. of blood is normal for children of this age group, and 4,500,000 to 5,000,000 per cc. is normal for adults.
7. Oxygen debt: the child can accumulate less oxygen debt than adults.
8. Hemoglobin: 85 percent is normal for adults, and 70 percent is normal for children of this age group.

9. Heart: smallest in comparison to body size of any age. The heart at the age of seven is one-third adult size, but it must supply a body that is nearly one-half adult size.

10. Endurance: poor, as would be expected from the red blood cell count, small heart, and hemoglobin content of blood.

11. Strength: not well developed at this period. Arm and shoulder girdle strength are particularly lacking.

12. Eyes: not sufficiently developed to focus on fast-moving, small objects.

13. Coordination: child is just getting control of gross movements; not much skill in fine movements yet; kinesthetic control improving.

14. Skeleton: bones are soft and easily deformed. Postural emphasis is needed in the grades because it is difficult to remedy poor posture after the ossification of bones has occurred.

15. Reaction time: not well developed.

Much data are available to show that children of elementary school ages today are taller, heavier, and more mature than their counterparts of several decades ago. Hale[8] reports:

> Since 1880, a period of only 75 years, the average 14-year-old boy has gained five inches in height and 24 pounds in weight. In weight alone this represents a 25 per cent increase. In the same period, the average 10-year-old girl has gained four inches in height and 14 pounds in weight. In the last 25 years, the average 12-year-old boy and girl has gained three inches in height and 15 pounds in weight, and the average 14-year-old boy of today has grown to the size of the 16-year-old.

The accelerated rate of maturation of children is due to advances in medicine, nutrition, and control of our environment. Antibiotics and vaccines have eliminated or lessened many childhood diseases. Vitamin-fortified and balanced diets provide for more optimum growth.

Psychological Characteristics

1. Imitation is strongest characteristic.

2. The child has hunger and drive for exercise and activity.

3. Short interest span. The child needs a considerable number and variety of activities rather than a few.

4. The child is egocentric; not interested in team games.

5. Curiosity is a strong characteristic.

6. The child is very assertive.

7. Interest in activity is for its own sake rather than any future outcome of it. The child does not like to drill on a skill.

8. The child does not demonstrate leadership qualities.

9. Interest is chiefly in large-muscle rather than small-muscle activity.

10. Approval of adults is more important than that of peers.

11. Interest is great in stories, rhythms, swimming, chasing, being chased, hiding and finding, and hunting games.

Implications for the Physical Education Program in the Primary Grades

The elementary school program should provide the students with the opportunity of exploring a great variety of movement activities, of discovering new and pleasurable movement patterns, as well as developing efficiency and control of their own bodies in structured activities. The elementary program must provide an environment in which an individual student can think, move, and learn while having an enjoyable experience in activity. As with all other areas of the elementary school instructional program, the basis of future learnings, activities, thoughts, and attitudes are either nurtured or destroyed in the early formative years. The elementary physical education programs have been ignored or non-existent until recent years. Even now far more is spent in most school districts on high school athletic programs than on the whole of the elementary instructional program.

Probably no single area of public school instruction has changed as much as elementary physical education in the past decade. It has become a thinking, moving, learning laboratory rather than an imitative sports skills program. The curriculum content and the methods of teaching have become more humanistic and individual in nature. With the development of the "exploratory" and "active learning" approach to teaching young students results have been more positive, and future generations of adults should view physical education as a part of the school curriculum differently from present day adults.

Although a daily period of thirty or more minutes of vigorous activity is recommended for all elementary school students, when teaching and learning are sacrificed to very large numbers in the learning laboratory five days a week, one must re-assess this recommendation. When we find many children at the third grade level who still cannot perform basic locomotor activities because the teachers have had so many students in classes that it has been impossible to determine who can and who cannot skip, for example, we must re-evaluate the daily period concept. This level is so critical to the student's present and future motor learning that the smallest size classes should be at this level so the teacher can do a good job of analyzing and assisting in correction of basic movement skills. If classes of over twenty-five students are necessary they should be at the upper grade levels, but large classes are undesirable at any level if the teacher is expected to function effectively in a teaching/learning environment rather than to simply act as a traffic cop.

The teacher of students in the elementary school must have some unique qualities not necessarily required at the high school level. The teacher must be able to relate to young students on their own level and with a genuine and sincere manner of interest and concern. The teacher must present an enthusiasm which will instill in students an anticipation and expectation of enjoyment toward learning in physical education. The teacher must also be able to effectively teach the curriculum to all of the various ability levels within any given group of students. The effectiveness of the teacher to meet individual needs will require patient, dedicated involvement in the communication processes between student and teacher. The ability to organize and plan for the maximum amount of activity and learning during each class period is critical to providing a meaningful experience for students. The teacher must further be able to utilize and effectively put into practice both exploratory and analytical methods to best meet the needs of students in today's schools.

Planning the program of instruction for young students demands that the teacher have some understanding of the nature, interests, and abilities of the children involved as well as basic knowledge of physical growth and the means of acquiring motor skills. If young students are to profit from their experiences in elementary and middle or junior high school physical education, they must be exposed to a wide variety of activities. These experiences should be available to them on a vertical basis from simple to more complex, from low organized games to modified or actual team games, from forward rolls to hand springs, and from creative movement activities to square dance type activities.

The process of programming begins with the teacher planning the general scope and sequence of instruction for the school year. Unit plans and specific lesson plans are developed during the school year as the time approaches when actual instruction is to occur.

Physical Education Program for Primary Level (K, 1,2,3)

The nature of the primary age child is one that can best be described by one word—"active", mentally, physically and socially. Even though most children in this age group appear to be in a slow physical growth period, many are entering the accelerated growth spurt by the second and third grades. Most of those students evidencing acceleration in physical growth and changes in secondary sex characteristics will be girls, however some boys may also be found to be growing rapidly.

Students at these ages are eager to learn, providing expectations are set within their individual challenge levels and not too far beyond them or too demeaning. Also, they are actively experimenting with acceptable and non-acceptable behavior in their attempts to learn how to get along with others socially.

The physical education program should be one which will help these children learn to know their own bodies and what they can do with a reasonable amount of success. Body awareness, and positive self-concepts should be basic competencies resulting from the physical education program.

TABLE 8-2

Time Allotments Recomended for K,1,2,3	Percentage of Physical Education Instructional Time
Efficiency of Movement	10%
Games and Sports Skills:	
Ball Handling Activities	10%
Low Organized Games	20%
Developmental Activities	15-20%
Rhythms and Dance	35-40%
Individual and Dual Activities	5%

Primary Level Program Content.

A. Efficiency of movement.
   locomotor and non-locomotor activities.
   posture and body mechanics.
   body awareness—self concept activities.
   relaxation.
B. Games and sports skills.
   ball handling skills.
   basic play skills.
   beginning sports skills.
   low organized games.
      with balls.
      without balls.
C. Development activities.
   playground apparatus.
   stunts and beginning tumbling skills.
   small apparatus.
   exposure to heavy apparatus.
   exposure to track type activities.

D. Rhythms and dance.
   expressive and creative activities.
   singing games.
   simple folk dance.
   basic rhythm work and marching.
E. Individual and dual activities.
   rope jumping activities.
   playground games.
   swimming.

THE PHYSICAL EDUCATION PROGRAM IN THE MIDDLE OR JUNIOR HIGH LEVELS

These students are "skill-hungry" and their desire to participate in sports and games is a dominant one. If good leadership is available they will make extremely rapid progress. Those students who are unfortunate in not having a good program during this period will fall so far behind in their development that it will be exceedingly difficult to catch up.

The consequences of children falling appreciably behind their group in strength, coordination and skills in the popular activities are serious. Play is the major concern of these students and repeated failure in this important realm produces social and emotional disturbances that often have detrimental and unfortunate results in later years. Children attach great importance to their peer group and if they do not perform well in physical activities their peers will reject them. Eventually this results in the withdrawal of the weak, awkward child from the group.

Characteristics of Middle Grade Children

The chief characteristics of students in these grades are indicated below. It is necessary to point out that children do not suddenly change when they reach a certain age. The fact is that considerable individual differences exist in children at all school levels. In the fourth grade there will be those who are as advanced as some sixth graders physically and psychologically. The converse is also true.

Physical Characteristics
(Ages 9–11)

1. Height and weight: there is a steady increase in height and weight.
2. Skeleton: the bones are still soft, but ossification is progressing.
3. Endurance: quite improved.

4. Heart: the child is stronger and better able to undergo considerable hard work.

5. Eyes: children can now focus better on fast-moving objects.

6. Coordination: many skills are now automatic. The child no longer needs to devote higher brain powers to body movements and can now think of the play and strategic measures that he or she might employ to effect activities.

7. Health: excellent; resistance to illness is high.

8. Strength: improved; but the child is still surprisingly weak, particularly in the upper extremities.

9. Reaction time: excellent.

10. Children have boundless energy. They are very active.

Psychological Characteristics

1. Beginning of gregarious spirit—teams, clubs.

2. Cooperation and teamwork are more developed.

3. The child is less individualistic and self-assertive.

4. Interest in competitive and fighting activities is developing.

5. Interest span is gradually lengthening, and fewer activities are engaged in.

6. There is love of excitement and adventure. The child likes to dare.

7. Interested in practicing to develop skills.

8. Children are ready to assume leadership responsibilities at the end of this period.

9. Girls are interested in rhythms, but boys may lose interest unless the teacher is very skillful.

10. In the latter part of this period the standards and approval of the peer group become of paramount importance.

11. Children like to imitate sport heroes and heroines.

12. There is a marked interest in the popular American sports.

Children from ten to twelve years of age are predominantly preadolescents. This stage of development is distinguished by two outstanding characteristics. The first of these involves an emancipation of the child from primary identification with adults. Up to this time he or she has lived in submission and obedience to adults. The dependence upon adults now gives way to a developing individuality with its normal desire for self-direction. The child, in the latter part of this school level, exhibits a growing independence and self-reliance. An attitude of hostility to parental and adult standards frequently develops. The child demands the right to make his and her own choices.

Secondly, as the child begins to loosen ties with adults he and she must turn elsewhere for the security that is so essential for healthy development. They find this in the peer group. This is a difficult but essential adjustment to make. This is where the boy and girl obtain important lessons in getting along with others, in give and take, in modifying their desires and actions in terms of other persons. This is also where they acquire another code of behavior—the peer code. Unfortunately, all too often this code is diametrically opposed to that of adult society. Adults must realize that the child is undergoing inner conflicts as a result of efforts to live up to the standards of both parents and peers.

THE MIDDLE OR JUNIOR HIGH SCHOOL PROGRAM

This period is one in which all the students are undergoing marked changes physically, psychologically, and socially. At no other age level do such profound changes occur and such wide individual differences exist as during this period.

Characteristics of Middle or Junior High School Students

It is obvious that the physical education program for boys and girls of this age level must be geared to accommodate these radical adolescent changes. Before one can successfully set up a program adapted to the needs of these boys and girls, the curriculum planner must be familiar with their various physical and psychological characteristics.

Physical Characteristics (Ages 12-14)

1. Puberty: reached first by girls from one to two years in advance of boys. A small percentage of girls have their first menstruation between ten and eleven years of age; the typical girl starts in her thirteenth year; about 10 percent do not start until after their fifteenth birthday.

2. Anatomical age: the union of the epiphyses of the metacarpal bones and phalanges of the female hand is completed at the age of sixteen. In the majority of boys this union occurs between eighteen and nineteen, indicating a sex difference in anatomical age of from two to three years.

3. Skeleton: bones grow rapidly, especially the long bones of the

arms and legs. This causes posture to become poor unless an effort is made to prevent it.

4. Height and weight: the most rapid acceleration in rate of growth of height and weight is at the age of twelve for girls and fourteen and a half for boys. Prepubescent boys grow 1.8 inches and increase in weight 7.6 pounds in one year. Postpubescent boys grow 3.3 inches and gain 16.6 pounds in one year. Great differences exist among pupils. Some are as much as five years apart physiologically.

5. Strength: develops rapidly after puberty begins in boys. However, the greatest acceleration takes place *after* the rapid increase in height.

6. Motor ability: continues to improve but at a slower rate. Some boys appear to have a lower motor-ability score during the most rapid increase in growth. Awkwardness is more likely to accompany the rather sudden beginnings of growth than the later and more rapid growth.

7. Circulatory system: the heart increases greatly in size and volume.

8. Endurance: reduced during the junior high school period.

Psychological Characteristics

1. Age of loyalty—of teams, clubs.
2. The peer group assumes great importance.
3. Increasing power of attention. Narrowed interest to fewer games.
4. Power of abstract reasoning developing.
5. Desire for excitement and adventure.
6. Hero worship and susceptibility to adult leadership.
7. Fighting tendency strong in boys.
8. Great interest in dancing by girls, but possibly a loss of interest by boys.
9. Desire of both sexes for competitive activities.
10. Interest in personal appearance.
11. Confidence in oneself frequently lacking.
12. Tendency to become moody and unstable.

Implications for the Physical Education Program for Middle or Junior High Levels

Educators have experimented with almost every possible combination of grade and age levels between fourth and ninth grades in an effort to find some combination of groupings which function better than others. The most frequently used combination has been to combine grades 4, 5 and 6 as an intermediate grouping and grades 7, 8 and 9 as a junior high school. More recently a middle school concept has gained popularity. The middle school may be almost any combination of grades between fourth and ninth, the most common being sixth through eighth grades. The inability of any such groupings to be completely satisfactory undoubtedly relates to the tremendous ranges of individual differences found among these ages. At any one age level within these years we find at least a five year range of normal physical growth. Some students are well into the accelerated period, others have almost reached termination of this growth spurt, and still others have not yet begun. These broad ranges of development could apply as well to the mental and social development of students in these years.

The program of instruction for these middle school age levels must be one in which the student can feel comfortable with a changing body and yet provide an opportunity for the student to be exposed to types of activities different than those experienced in the early elementary program. The student must be allowed some opportunity for independent choice of activities to be learned and pursued.

The program of instruction at these levels should be broadening the basic background of the student and building on the basic skills foundation established in the elementary program. The program should provide students with a greater repertoire from which to make choices as they progress into high school.

TABLE 8-3

Time Allotments Recommended	Percentage of Physical Education Instructional Time
Efficiency of Movement	5%
Games and Sports Skills	25–30%
Developmental Activities	20–25%
Rhythms and Dance	25–30%
Individual and Dual Activities	20–25%

Middle and Junior High Program Content
A. Efficiency of movement.
   posture and body mechanics.
   integrate movement principle with skill instruction.
B. Games and sports skills.
   specific sports skills: seasonal activities.
   modified and actual team games.
      position play.
      team play—exposure.
      strategy.
   low organized active games.

C. Developmental activities.
   tumbling.
   beginning gymnastics—small and heavy apparatus.
   track and field.
   wrestling.
   self defense activities.
D. Rhythms and dance.
   creative activities.
   native dance.
   international folk dance.
   square dance.
E. Individual and dual activities.
   outdoor education activities.
   boating. rock climbing.
   fishing. hiking.
   swimming.
   target games—exposure to: bowling, golf, badminton, archery, etc.
   net games.
   skating.
   skiing.
   bicycling.

THE SENIOR HIGH SCHOOL PROGRAM

The senior high school years, grades 9 or 10 through 12, are those in which most students reach maturity. However, there is still a wide range in rate of maturation. Senior high school students continue to mature physically, mentally, emotionally and socially. Their needs and concerns are different than those of the junior high students. Many of the junior high student needs and concerns are accentuated; others lessened or eliminated at the senior high level. Peer behavior and performance standards are probably the most influential characteristics of this age.

Characteristics of Senior High School Students

Characteristics that will influence the physical education program planned for the young people of this group are as follows:

Physical Characteristics

1. Height and weight: the girl has passed through the period of rapid growth. Her height remains comparatively constant, although she will increase in weight. Some boys are pubescent and in the period of most rapid growth. Others are postpubescent and will increase little in height. Boys increase rapidly in weight.

2. Strength: increases greatly in boys during this period, although arms and shoulder girdle strength is deficient. The strength of girls reaches its peak at the age of sixteen and declines or remains stationary after this age.

3. Coordination: gradual improvement.

4. Skeleton: well calcified, but posture is poor.

5. Circulatory system: at age sixteen it is 82 percent of adult efficiency. At seventeen it is 90 percent of adult efficiency. At eighteen it is 98.5 percent of adult efficiency. Thus, from age sixteen the heart is capable of strenuous activities.

6. Endurance: endurance is better than at any previous age. With proper conditioning, endurance no longer represents a problem except, perhaps, in a few pubescents who are still in the stage of very rapid growth.

7. Reaction time: better than it has ever been.

8. Motor ability: rate of motor learning increases; greater ability to handle the body. Pupils are eager to perfect skills.

Psychological Characteristics

1. Further narrowing of interests and trend toward specialization.

2. Still an age of loyalty and cooperation, but the desire to belong is tempered by consideration of personal interests and advantages. Still an age of team games.

3. Marked development of self-confidence.

4. Greater powers of attention and reasoning. Increase in ability to participate in group planning and problem solving.

5. Strong interest in grooming and personal appearance by both sexes and interest in their physical development.

6. Hero and heroine worship is still a strong influence.

7. Fighting tendency is strong in boys. They are highly competitive.

8. Some girls have an inclination to be attracted by passive social activities.

9. Strong interest in opposite sex.

10. Increased interest and ability in leading.

Implications for the Senior High School Program

Students at the senior high school need to be more involved in the decision making process for planning their physical education curricula. If the programs in the elementary, middle and junior high schools have been broadbased programs, the students are now ready for more selective programs. Provisions for selective physical education opportunities in team and life time sports, dance, and developmental activities are needed. At least 50 percent if not all of the senior high school years should be elective in nature. Many high schools provide several alternatives from which the students may make a choice and the following are examples of the activities which may be included.

Senior High School
A. Dance.
   Jazz, Folk, Social, Square and Modern.
B. Development Activities.
   Gymnastics—tumbling and apparatus.
   Track and Field.
   Wrestling.
   Self-defense activities.
   Weight training.
   Conditioning exercises.
   Jogging and Running.
   Swim conditioning.
C. Team Sports.
   Soccer and variations.
   Touch Football and variations.
   Basketball.
   Volleyball.
   Hockey.
   Field Hockey.
   Softball and variations.
D. Life Time Sports.
   Bowling.
   Badminton.
   Tennis.
   Golf.
   Handball.
   Racquetball.
   Archery.
   Table Tennis.
   Skiing—downhill, cross country.
   Mountaineering Activities.
   Bicycling.
   Water Skills.
   Hiking.

The Physically Educated High School Graduate

The elementary and secondary school physical education programs should be articulated to produce the best results. The objective should be to attain to the maximum extent the objectives of physical education. At the National Conference on Fitness of Secondary School Youth[9] the attributes of the physically educated high school senior at graduation were spelled out. These were:

Attitudes:

1. A strong desire to be healthy.
2. Acceptance of the need to exercise daily to maintain physical fitness.
3. An awareness of the value of safety procedures in and on the water.
4. Appreciation of "change of pace" from work to recreational activities (an essential part of healthy living).
5. A desire to achieve a high degree of excellence in skills to enjoy participation.
6. Appreciation of one's strengths and limitations.
7. Acceptance of the concept of one's role as a member of a team.
8. Positive attitudes and desire for personal cleanliness and safe practices in physical activities.
9. Appreciation of wholesome intergroup relationships and respect for the rights of others.
10. Appreciation of the values in good sportsmanship and of its fullest application to total living.
11. Appreciation of the value of the creative aspects of correct body movements.

Knowledge:

1. Knowledge of what constitutes body mechanics (acceptable posture) and how this relates to good health.
2. Knowledge of the proper functioning of the body and of their responsibility to maintain personal fitness.
3. Knowledge of the rules of water safety (swimming, rescue, artificial respiration, boating, etc).
4. Understanding of the nature and importance of physical fitness and knowledge of how to develop and maintain it throughout life.
5. Understanding of the rules, strategies, backgrounds, and values of sports and other physical activities.
6. Knowledge of proper selection and care of school and personal athletic equipment.
7. Understanding and appreciation of the role of physical education in the total education program.
8. Knowledge of the proper mechanics of sports and activities.
9. Understanding of the importance and the role of physical fitness in successful academic achievement (sound mind, fit body).
10. Knowledge of the scientific and health reasons for proper hygiene and safety practices as applied in physical activities.

11. Understanding of one's physical capacities and limitations.
12. Knowledge enabling them to be intelligent spectators of the popular American sports.
13. The ability to distinguish between sound and unsound commercial health and exercise practices and programs.

Skills:

1. Ability to assume good posture and maintain it while sitting, standing, walking.
2. Development of skills in at least four seasonal team sports, the level of skill attained being such that there is enjoyment in participation.
3. Ability to swim well enough to feel at home in the water (involves mastery of the different strokes and survival skills).
4. Development of skills in at least four indoor and outdoor single or dual sports, the level of skill being such that there is enjoyment in participation.
5. Development of proper rhythmic response to music, including basic skills in folk, square, modern, and/or social dance.
6. Development of skill in one combative activity (boxing excluded), the level of skill being such that there is enjoyment in participation.
7. Ability to apply skills in fundamental body movements—in running, throwing, jumping, lifting, carrying, etc.—to other physical activities.
8. Achievement of an adequate level of skill in self-testing activities such as track and field, calisthenics, tumbling, apparatus, etc.
9. Good habits of cleanliness, personal appearance, and safety practices in all physical activities.

The Block Program

In junior and senior high school the use of the block program of scheduling physical education activities is recommended. In the block program the time allotment for an activity is concentrated rather than distributed. For example, if it were determined that thirty periods were to be allotted to basketball in the senior high school program this entire period of time would be utilized in a block. Thus, if physical education were scheduled daily, basketball would be scheduled for six consecutive weeks before another activity were scheduled. The most popular block of time is four weeks. Blocks of three, five, and six weeks are also extensively used.

A widespread practice is to schedule the same program each year without change. In this type of program, each student repeats in the eleventh and twelfth grades what he had in the tenth grade. This procedure is defended on the basis that students have a readiness for seasonal activities and that they should have them when their interest is so great. This is contrary to the block program.

The use of the block system is preferred for several reasons. In the first place, there is no educational justification in repeating the same activities in the same way, year after year. New material should be presented each class period (excepting, of course, an occasional period during which an examination is given or the previous material is reviewed), just as it is in the class meetings for every other subject. The expectation prevails that in an educational institution, the children will grow in understanding, skills, and attitudes. The instructor is expected to start where the instruction terminated the previous period and to carry on from that point.

Secondly, the block program is favored because it facilitates learning. If the time allotment for an activity is spread out over a considerable period of time, with other activities intervening, students will forget what they have been taught in previous lessons. Finally, students are better able to develop the skills and the physical condition for a particular activity when the instruction is concentrated. If thirty-six periods are allocated to wrestling for the three years of the junior high school, more skill, understanding, and physical fitness will be developed if all the periods are concentrated during one year than if twelve periods are scheduled for each of three years. Eighteen periods for each of two years is preferable to twelve periods each year.

An advanced course in an activity is very much to be desired if it is really advanced. The elementary course should definitely be a prerequisite to the advanced course. In reply to the contention that students want seasonal activities, this is certainly a fact but there are a variety of seasonal activities. Wrestling, gymnastics, badminton, and volleyball are just as seasonal during the winter months as basketball. Also, when students want additional participation in a sport, they may obtain it in the intramural program. For example, if an adequate unit on basketball were provided in the tenth grade, students could participate further in this sport in the eleventh and twelfth grades in the intramural program.

Modular Scheduling

By modular or flexible scheduling is meant that the classes will be of varying lengths and sizes and will not necessarily meet on a daily basis. Flexible scheduling is contrasted with the traditional set schedule in which all classes were of the same length and size and usually met on a daily basis. This new approach to scheduling is more applicable to secondary schools because elementary schools and colleges and universities have always had more variation and flexibility in the length, size, and number of periods per week.

The pattern of modular scheduling most frequently found involves fewer periods per week but of greater length. As an example, a school which previously had allotted a daily 45-minute period for physical education changed to two double periods and one single period per week. This really benefits physical education because more time will be available for activity. Assuming that 20 minutes per period were needed for changing and showering the daily period would provide 125 minutes per week for instruction and participation. On the other hand, each double period would permit 70 minutes for physical education. Thus, two double periods and one single period would provide 165 minutes of actual class time contrasted to 125 minutes in the daily program. If three double periods per week replaced the daily schedule—as is done in some schools—the advantage would be even greater.

The longer periods have an additional advantage. In many secondary schools it is necessary at times to use facilities that are located at some distance from the school. Such facilities may be athletic fields, swimming pools, tennis courts, bowling alleys, and golf courses. Double periods greatly facilitate the use of such facilities. In fact, double periods are advantageous for classes held at the school. Physical educators have complained for years about the difficulty of accomplishing their objectives in a 25- to 30-minute activity period. To have 70 or 80 minutes available for instruction, practice, and participation would seem a more favorable situation.

In addition to varying the number and length of the class meetings each week, modular scheduling also involves variations in class size. The students from three or four classes may be combined on regular occasions. Such an arrangement is advantageous when it is desired to present the same material to the students in several classes. It may be that the same lecture or film is planned. The economy of staff time under this system is apparent. Such an arrangement also facilitates the use of visiting speakers.

Modular scheduling in secondary schools is still in its early stages. It seems safe to predict that virtually all schools will adopt some of these procedures. What the ultimate effect will be on health education and physical education programs is difficult to forecast. At the present time the advantages seem to bulk larger than the disadvantages. The chief disadvantage appears to be the reduction in number of class meetings per week. However, if this is offset by *more minutes of activity* per week it does not appear to be a serious disadvantage.

Substitutions for Physical Education

In some school systems the substitution of band or ROTC for physical education is permissible. This practice is based on the assumption that physical activity is involved in military drill and in the marching band. It is immediately obvious that this is not a valid justification and that it should be resisted by the physical education administrator as strenuously as possible. A proper substitution occurs when the outcomes of the different programs are approximately identical. The results of band practice and ROTC are worthwhile, but they are different from those in physical education. The small amount of vigorous exercise involved in these activities would never develop organic vigor, vitality, strength, and stamina. Nor would band practice or military drill develop the neuromuscular skills in motor activities or the social and moral values that can be achieved through physical education.

Still another type of substitution is found in many secondary schools. This involves the acceptance of participation on an interschool squad in lieu of participation in the instructional program. This practice is based upon the assumption that the values of interschool athletics are synonymous with those of the instructional program. Proponents of this system point out that the physiological outcomes of athletics are greater than those found in the instructional program. Also, the social and character values are at least equivalent. In addition, it is argued that members of varsity squads, if they also participate in the required physical education program, will get more physical activity than is good for them. Moreover, these athletes could make valuable use of the period normally devoted to physical education classes for study purposes.

The opponents of this point of view point out that instruction is given in a wide variety of activities and that varsity squad members will miss important units of activity if they are excused. It is clear that to excuse those on the football squad from instruction in swimming, lifesaving, tennis, dancing, golf, and the like is to deprive them of exceedingly valuable instruction. These opponents are also skeptical of the claim that participation in the instructional program will overly fatigue varsity candidates. For these reasons, leaders do not recommend the substitution of the varsity program for the instructional class activities.

A middle ground is taken by those who recommend that interschool squad members be excused from the instructional program when that course is identical to or closely related to the varsity sport in which they are participating. Thus, members of the football squad might be excused from the instructional program when a touch football unit was being covered. They would not be excused from any other activity. Members of the basketball squad might be excused from participating in basketball instructional classes.

Preparation of Curriculum Outline

It is a standard practice in secondary schools (and in colleges and universities) to require each instructor of academic subjects to prepare a curriculum outline for all the courses for which he or she is responsible. This outline is ordinarily prepared in accordance with specifications that have been established in the particular school. A copy of the curriculum outline is filed in the principal's or superintendent's office.

Such a practice is recommended for physical education. The advantages of this procedure have been proved over the years. Yet, in many schools, the physical educator is not required or expected to provide a curriculum outline. Relatively few school administrators have such outlines from the physical education department on file. This is unfortunate and casts a reflection upon the quality of the physical education program and the training and ability of the physical education administrator.

Summer Session Physical Education Programs

One of the most recent and promising trends is the provision of physical education programs for elementary and secondary students during the summer. These may be designed for several objectives. One purpose is remedial. This program could be particularly beneficial to the students who are poorly skilled or are in the low fitness category. Another purpose is to provide activities such as tennis, golf, and swimming, which cannot be made available during the academic year.

THE COLLEGE PROGRAM

When high school graduates enter a college or university in America they frequently discover that like English composition a certain amount of physical education is required for graduation. Although the number of years or terms of the requirement, the hours required per week, and the nature of the program may vary, many college students must register for some physical education. This practice of requiring physical education is of many years' standing. It originated nearly a hundred years ago because college administrators and faculty members considered that a certain amount of participation in physical education activities was essential to the health and well-being of students and, accordingly, should be required.

Should Physical Education be Required?

In recent years the validity of the requirement has been debated in many institutions. The arguments in favor of the requirement can be summarized as follows:

1. The health and well-being of the students, both now and in the future, is dependent upon regular exercise. Such activity is a health practice universally endorsed by the medical profession.

2. Unless physical education is required, those who need it most will evade it. The weak, flabby, poorly coordinated students have little desire to engage in activities that are difficult for them and in which they were previously unsuccessful. No one enjoys participating in an activity in which he or she appears to poor advantage.

3. Most high schools provide such poor programs that their graduates are not adequately prepared to elect activities in college. To elect intelligently requires a knowledge of the alternatives.

4. A certain amount of regular physical activity is necessary in a college or university to provide respite from the academic pursuits. Students cannot study advantageously all the time. After several hours of concentrated intellectual effort any individual will be refreshed after a period of vigorous, enjoyable physical activity.

5. College and university students also need a certain amount of recreation to balance their intellectual regimen. It is to their benefit when their recreation is obtained in wholesome activities, such as sports and games.

6. The physical education requirement does not limit the student to a specific activity but to a field or area of activities. The university requires a certain number of hours for graduation. Practically all of these hours must be intellectual activities. But a small part of this total requirement is to be in the area of movement.

The common arguments against the requirement are:

1. It encourages poor teaching. The students are required to attend; thus the instructor finds little incentive to be a superior teacher.

2. College students are sufficiently mature that they can be depended upon to do the things that are best for them. They will take physical education voluntarily if they need it.

3. College students resent requirement. As a consequence they are not likely to continue participation after the requirement has been fulfilled.

4. The requirement is undemocratic. It provides a "captive audience," which defeats the very objectives of the program.

5. The requiring of participation is the wrong approach to get people to participate voluntarily throughout their adult life.

The elective program has little chance of operating successfully unless the following essential conditions prevail:

1. Strong, effective physical education programs in the public schools are experienced by all high school graduates. In other words, an elective program would be feasible if all the students who enter colleges and universities came with the knowledge, skills, and attitudes that are the results of excellent public school physical education.

2. Adequate numbers of superior physical education teachers are available.

3. Superior facilities and equipment exist in the institutions of higher learning.

4. The entering students are, in some way, made aware of the opportunities that are available to them in the physical education department. To accomplish this all faculty members in the institution must understand the physical education program and publicize its advantages among their students. An alternative would be to require each freshman to consult with a member of the physical education department who could explain the opportunities the program offers.

Even in those states where physical education is most advanced, public school physical education is far from ideal. By the same token, only a very small percentage of the institutions of higher learning meet the above stipulations.

Proficiency Requirement

Some colleges and universities make extensive use of proficiency or achievement tests. By passing such a test, which is equivalent to the final examination in a service course, the student is relieved of one term or one semester of the requirement. In other words, if he or she possesses the skill and knowledge that the average student possesses at the end of a service course, part of the requirement is waived. No credit is granted. In some institutions a skilled, versatile student might be able to pass enough achievement tests to have the entire service requirement waived.

Orientation Programs[10]

Some colleges and universities make use of orientation programs. Such programs are predicated on the conviction that physical education should have purposes over and beyond the development of physical fitness and motor skills. Proponents of orientation courses argue that college students need to know something about the philosophy of physical education, its importance in modern life, why it is part of the curriculum, the outcomes that may be expected. They emphasize the value of understanding the origin, backgrounds, development, and significance of sports in our society. Many other areas of knowledge are important, such as sports etiquette, the laws of training and conditioning, safety precautions, physiology of exercise, first aid, purchase of athletic equipment, and the nature and significance of sportsmanship. Certainly, from the standpoint of public relations, the accomplishment of these intellectual objectives would be invaluable.

There are three types of orientation programs. The first type is generally conducted during the freshmen orientation week. This usually involves only one period during which all freshmen are given pertinent information, which they need to relate themselves properly to the physical education, intramural, and intercollegiate athletic programs offered by the institution.

The second type of orientation program is a part of the regular instructional program. Part of the time is devoted to lectures, movies, discussions, and demonstrations pertaining to related material. This may be done at regular or irregular intervals. For example, one period per week in which the students meet in an academic classroom may be devoted to orientation materials. In some instances outside reading assignments are required.

The third type is an entirely separate academic course. This may be an elective course or it might count as part of the physical education requirement. A textbook is employed which is specifically designed to give the students an understanding and appreciation of physical education.

Survey Course in Activities

In some institutions the physical education program during the first term or first year is devoted to giving all freshmen students an opportunity to participate in a wide variety of activities. For example, ten or twelve activities may be surveyed, with from six to ten periods devoted to each.

The purpose is to familiarize students with the most important activities so that their subsequent choices will be made intelligently.

Waiver of the Physical Education Requirement

In the majority of schools, both World War II and Korean War veterans have been routinely excused from physical education. In addition, in other schools ROTC is accepted in lieu of physical education. In 1949 the College Committee on Physical Education and Athletics,[11] representing the College Physical Education Association, the National Collegiate Athletic Association, and the American Association for Health, Physical Education, and Recreation, issued the following statement in regard to this matter:

1. It should be clear to all in college physical education and in colleges generally that military science and physical education are not synonymous. They are two different programs employing different techniques, seeking different outcomes, and existing for different purposes. Leaders in both areas recognize these differences. One seeks preparation for defense through military skills and techniques, the other seeks adjustment to democratic ways through recreational skills taught to secure outcomes in total personal development. Confusion remains only in the minds of those who believe that physical fitness is the sole, or at least the principal, outcome of both. Obviously, both military science and physical education (including athletics) have a place in twentieth century society. They are not, however, mutually inclusive.

2. On campuses where both programs are offered there should be developed a spirit of cordiality and cooperation without infringement, precedence, or domination of one over the other.

3. The College Committee fully subscribes to the recommendation of many other groups to the effect that a course in military science is not a proper substitution for physical education.

4. Likewise, the College Committee strongly urges faculties to establish the principle of equivalence when accrediting military experience with reference to physical education. This problem loomed large following VJ Day, and the Committee feels that some considerable injustice was done many veterans by eliminating them from recreational or therapeutic physical education so necessary to their continuing adjustment to the college or community environment. The best results were obtained on those campuses where credit was given for physical education as it was for other areas of learning; that is, on the basis of experience in the services equivalent to the kind and quality of instruction receivable on the campus. The Committee recommends that where blanket or indiscriminate credit for physical education was given just because the student was in military service, the practice be now discontinued and ex-

perience in physical education from any future military service be evaluated for quality the same as experience in other fields.

The Program of Activities

If boys and girls have been given the proper physical education program in their precollege careers, they will be prepared to continue in several activities in which they have some skill and which they have learned to enjoy before entering college. They will now be more concerned with their future leisure-time recreational activities than they have been heretofore, and, consequently, there will be an increased interest in adult play activities. This preparation for leisure is in harmony with the purpose of the college, which is to prepare students for their adult life. Unfortunately, however, very few students enter college with an adequate background in physical education, and in the past far too many have graduated from college with the same disadvantage. The wide difference in the secondary school preparation of college students presents a problem in setting up the physical education curriculum. It necessitates as extensive a program of activities as it is possible to provide with existing facilities.

It is desirable to stress recreational activities in the college instructional program. Some provision should be made to insure that each college student has some activities that he or she can use in later life. Certainly activities such as golf, tennis, swimming, dancing, racquetball, handball, bowling, badminton, archery, skiing, and fly casting, which will provide recreation and enjoyment for thirty or forty years to come, are essential to all college students. Moreover, all students should be equipped with activities that they can use at home to maintain their health and vigor.

The list of activities in Table 8-4 is based on the interests and needs of college students. Beginning courses in all of these activities are necessary for those students who lack fundamental training in the sports that interest them. Likewise, advanced courses should be offered for those with an adequate background who desire to go further.

PHYSICAL EDUCATION FOR THE HANDICAPPED CHILD

The Education for All Handicapped Children Act of 1975 (Public Law 94-142) provides for an administrative and financial commitment on the part of the federal government to assure that all handicapped chil-

TABLE 8-4. PROGRAM FOR COLLEGE STUDENTS

Adapted Area	Physical Fitness Area	Gymnastic Area
Adapted Sports	Conditioning	Olympic Gymnastics
Exercise Program	Circuit Training	Recreational Gymnastics
Corrective Program	Jogging	Tumbling
Wheelchair Sports	Weight Training	Trampoline
	Yoga	

Outdoor Area	Team Area	Aquatic Area
Bait/Fly/Spin Casting	Basketball	Swimming-Beg., Int., Adv.
Bicycle Touring	Baseball	Diving-Springboard
Cross Country Skiing	Field Hockey	Life Saving
Downhill Skiing	Flag Football	Water Safety Instruction
Canoeing	Touch Football	Water Polo
Camping	Ice Hockey	Synchronized Swimming
Hiking	Flickerball	Skin Diving
Ice Skating	Lacrosse	Scuba Diving
Horseback Riding	Rugby	Surfing
and Jumping	Softball	
Crew (rowing)	Soccer	
Kayaking	Speedball	
Mountaineering	Volleyball	
Winter Mountaineering		
Orienteering		
Sky Diving		
River Running		
Sailing		
Water Skiing		

Combatives Area	Dance Area	Recreational Area
Wrestling	Folk	Archery
Fencing	Square	Tennis
Judo	Ballroom	Golf
Self-Defense	Modern	Handball
Karate	Clog and Tap	Racquetball
	Jazz	Badminton
	Ballet	Squash
		Bowling
		Table Tennis
		Horseshoes and Quoits

dren have a "free appropriate public education" which emphasizes special education designed to meet their unique needs. Of particular importance is the fact that physical education is specifically identified in the law as a necessary and guaranteed course of study within the total curriculum for these students.

Public Law 94-142 specifically stipulates that state educational agencies must guarantee that physical education is available to all handicapped children as an integral part of their education and that provisions are made for handicapped populations to participate in the regular physical education program available to non-handicapped children.

This concept of integration, referred to as "mainstreaming" in many educational spheres, is represented in the law by the term "least restrictive environment." It is required that each state, in order to qualify for federal funds, establish procedures to assure that, to the maximum extent appropriate, handicapped children, including children in public and private institutions or other care facilities, are educated with children who are not handicapped.

The implications of P. L. 94-142 for physical education professional preparation at the pre-service and in-service levels seem manifest. The thrust of the law charges the physical educator with evaluative and prescriptive responsibilities in the areas of motor fitness, motor skills, body mechanics, individual and group games and sports, movement education, and the concomitant development of affective, social, and cognitive learning.

Physical education professional preparation programs must evaluate their undergraduate and graduate curricula with respect to P. L. 94-142 and initiate specific educational experiences that will enhance the physical educator's ability to effectively educate these special students. The provision for special physical education in the "least restrictive environment" places the responsibility for integrated programs directly with the physical education teacher. Many physical educators have had no direct experience with mentally and physically handicapped students. Therefore, it is essential that pre-service and in-service professional preparation programs provide extensive academic and practical educational experiences oriented toward exceptional populations.

Just as the public schools will in the future have more programs designed to meet the special needs of the handicapped, the professional preparation programs in physical education must provide opportunities for present and future teachers to achieve competence in educating this special population.

SELECTED REFERENCES

College Physical Education—The General Program. Washington, D.C.: AAHPER, 1973.

CORBIN, CHARLES B., *Becoming Physically Educated in the Elementary School* (2nd ed.), Philadelphia: Lea & Febiger, 1976.

Ideas for Secondary School Physical Education. Washington, D.C.: AAHPER, 1976.

MILLER, ARTHUR G., JOHN T. F. CHEFFERS, and VIRGINIA WHITCOMB, *Physical Education: Teaching Human Movement in the Elementary Schools* (3rd. ed.), Englewood Cliffs, N.J.: Prentice-Hall, Inc., 1974.

SINGER, ROBERT N., and WALTER DICK, *Teaching Physical Education—A Systems Approach.* Palo Alto: Houghton Mifflin Company, 1974.

VANNIER, MARYHELEN, and HOLLIS F. FAIT, *Teaching Physical Education in Secondary Schools.* Philadelphia: W. B. Saunders Co., 1975.

NOTES

1. Peter V. Karpovich and Raymond A. Weiss, "Physical Fitness of Men Entering the Army Air Forces," *Research Quarterly* (October 1946), p. 186.

2. Leonard A. Larson, "Some Findings Resulting from the Army Air Forces Physical Training Program," *Research Quarterly* (May 1946), pp. 144–146.

3. H. Harrison Clarke, ed., "Physical Fitness Practices and Programs for Elementary and Secondary Schools," *Physical Fitness Research Digest* (President's Council on Physical Fitness and Sports, Oct. 1976), p. 1.

4. Clarke, "Physical Fitness Practices," pp. 4–5.

5. Clarke, "Physical Fitness Practices," p. 5.

6. Eugene T. Lies, "The New Leisure Challenges the School," *Journal of Health, Physical Education, Recreation* (November 1934), p. 18.

7. Federal Register, Vol. 40, No. 108—Wednesday, June 4, 1975. Section 86.34, Access to Course Offerings.

8. Creighton Hale, "Changing Growth Patterns of the American Child," *Education* (April 1958), p. 467.

9. Report of the National Conference on Fitness of Secondary School Youth, *Youth and Fitness* (Washington, D.C., American Association for Health, Physical Education, and Recreation, 1959), pp. 28–29.

10. The material in this section has been adapted from Hubert McCormick, *Enriching the Physical Education Service Program* (New York, Teachers College Bureau of Publications, 1942), pp. 58–101.

11. The College Committee on Physical Education and Athletics, "College Physical Education for Peace and Defense," *Fifty-second Annual Proceedings of the College Physical Education Association* (Chapel Hill, N.C., 1949), p. 134.

9

School Health Education

Many people regard health education and physical education as synonymous or one as being part of the other. This is an entirely erroneous impression. Health education and physical education are separate and distinct, though closely allied, fields. Physical education is that phase of education which comes about through or in connection with vigorous muscular activities. Health education, on the other hand, comprises all of the experiences that contribute in any way to the individual's health knowledge, health habits, and health attitudes. Health education differs from physical education in subject matter, methods, and in some purposes.

Physical education has important contributions to make to health education, and vice versa. Inherent in physical education are exceptional opportunities to develop health knowledge, health habits, and health attitudes. On the other hand, the emphasis in health education on such areas as exercise, nutrition, recreation, rest, and desirable health practices has important implications for physical education. However, a lecture in health education or a trip to the local dairy is not physical education; nor is a unit in basketball or wrestling health education.

HEALTH EDUCATION RESPONSIBILITIES

Many physical educators in secondary schools and colleges and universities have equally important responsibilities in the school health education program.

However, this situation occurs less frequently now than in the past. If health education courses are taught by a physical educator, the teacher should have at least dual certification in health and physical education. More schools are now employing health education specialists who have separate health education certification.

All physical education teachers have the responsibility in their physical education classes for teaching health habits, health attitudes, and health knowledge whenever a favorable opportunity presents itself. Because of their good background, many physical educators serve as health counselors, particularly in the smaller schools. Finally, physical education and health education are combined into one department in many schools with the physical education director having the responsibility for administering both programs. Because of these important and varied relationships to the health education program, the physical educator must be familiar with health education. This is particularly true for the administrator in physical education who may bear the responsibility for implementing all of the health education obligations of the department. Unfortunately, many administrators have not done justice to these responsibilities because of lack of preparation or interest or both.

CHANGING OUTLOOK ON HEALTH

Schools have broadened the scope of their programs considerably in the last half century. Modern philosophy considers that an educational institution is concerned with more than the intellectual development and vocational preparation of youth. Experience has clearly shown the inadequacy of an education that has been limited to only these objectives. Health has come to be considered one of the most important objectives of education. In fact among the total spectrum of health jobs, this profession ranks among the top three as a source of employment in the United States today.

Health is too important to be trusted to individual or family initiative alone. Educators realized that whatever other objectives were sought, health aided in progress toward them. Health is basic to learning, to happiness, to success, to effective citizenship, and to worthwhile living. Without health, the individual is less effective and is handicapped in everything he or she does. Some persons with poor health have made significant contributions to society, but these contributions have come in spite of their handicaps.

World War II greatly increased the importance of the health objective. The lack of health and physical fitness of American men and women was one of the major revelations of the war. The selective service medical examinations revealed all too clearly that insufficient attention had been given to health. Public opinion was aroused, and all health agencies accelerated and expanded their activities. The schools responded to the challenge and are now emphasizing health to a degree never before approached.

The World Health Organization defines health as a "state of complete physical, mental and social well-being." This means a state of positive good health rather than simply the absence of disease. To promote health the school health program must offer a safe, comfortable, healthful environment, health services, and health education.

ADMINISTRATIVE PRACTICES FOR THE SCHOOL HEALTH PROGRAM

The aim of the school health program is the development of optimum physical, mental, emotional, and social health among all pupils. A checklist of administrative practices which can serve as a guide to the administrator in the accomplishment of this aim is outlined by Anderson and Creswell:[1]

1. Recognize health as a basic objective of education.

2. Secure and budget adequate funds for the health program.

3. Keep parents informed of the health program.

4. Establish an appropriate cooperative relationship with community health agencies.

5. Maintain communication with community organizations.

6. Employ qualified school health service personnel.

7. Become informed about health problems of the school-age group.

8. Arrange the school day in accord with sound health practice.

9. Establish an effective system for keeping health records.

10. Establish a policy on school health examinations.

11. Provide for health observations by the teachers.

12. Establish a systematic referral program.

13. Promote measures to ensure corrections for every child.

14. Establish program policies aimed at control of communicable diseases.

15. Procure necessary materials, facilities, and equipment for health instruction.

16. Provide time and facilities for health instruction in the secondary school.

17. Appoint only qualified teachers for health instruction.

18. Provide a healthful physical environment.

19. Provide a mentally hygienic environment.

20. Establish a school safety program.

21. Provide facilities, personnel, and an established plan to meet emergencies.

22. Provide health services for professional personnel.

23. Provide in-service health education for teachers.

24. Provide for faculty sick leave.

Anderson and Creswell add that "this checklist does not include all of the health responsibilities of the administrator, but by specifying the essential minimum practices, it serves as a practical, realistic measure of the administration's contribution to the school health program."[2]

ORGANIZATION OF THE SCHOOL HEALTH PROGRAM

It is important that supervision and control of the school health program be centered in the board of trustees or board of education. In the past many communities placed the responsibility for the public health work in the board of health. The board of health has the machinery for the control of communicable disease and can administer this phase of the program better than the board of education. However, considering the educational aspects of the school health education program, the control should reside in the board of education with cooperation among all local groups interested and concerned with health.

The best way of bringing about school and community coordination and cooperation in matters relating to the health of the school population is through a community health council. This council should be composed of representatives of the schools, the local board of health, the county medical and dental associations, and all other public and private agencies concerned with health. The community health council concerns itself with broad policies and problems and mobilizes all the health resources of the community behind the school health program.

The organizational-administrative structure of the school health program is depicted in Figure 9-1 from Anderson and Creswell[3]:

A health council or health committee should be organized, where possible, in each school. The function of the health council is to give guidance and leadership to the health education program within the school and to cooperate with the community health council through duly appointed representatives. Membership on the health council

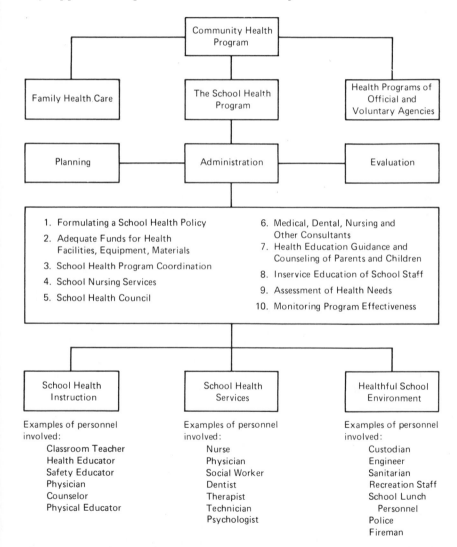

Figure 9-1. Organizational and administrative interrelationships of the school health program. (From Anderson, C. L. and Creswell, William H., Jr. School Health Practices, ed. 6, St. Louis, 1976, The C.V. Mosby Co.).

should include the principal, the school medical adviser, the health coordinator, various teachers, and student and parent representatives. If a school psychologist, nurse, nutritionist, and dentist are available, they should also be included.

Every school must have a physician who will function as a school medical adviser. Small schools will be unable to afford a full-time medical adviser, but it will be possible for them to obtain one on a part-time basis. It is essential that every school have recourse to a physician to advise upon the many health problems that require medical judgment. In many communities where the school is unable to afford a paid medical adviser, the county medical society will frequently cooperate by contributing the part-time services of several physicians without charge.

There must be someone in each school who has a definite responsibility for the total school health program. This individual is known as the health counselor or health coordinator. There is an increasing trend toward use of an administrative position, that of District Health Coordinator, to be given to a person professionally trained with a major in health education. In the smaller schools and colleges the coordinator may be any instructor, head of department, or, in the case of high schools, the principal or superintendent. Regardless of the size of the institution, the best qualified individual should be in charge of the health program. The director of physical education is frequently the health coordinator. Educators have associated physical education closely with health values and objectives. Unless the physical educator is well trained for health education there is no justification for placing that person in charge of the health education program. If well prepared, however, the physical educator is in a strategic position to perform excellent service. Students usually esteem highly and grant great authority to the physical educator, particularly if that individual is also the coach. The coach and the physical education teacher come into close informal contact with the students and thus can gain understanding of their health problems and needs. Innumerable opportunities occur in the physical education classes and intramural and interscholastic sports to protect, promote, and teach health. In the smaller institutions the physical examination is usually conducted by the physical education department. For these reasons the physical educator makes a good health coordinator in the small schools if he or she is well trained.

The Health Coordinator

The success of the school health program depends to a great extent upon the health coordinator. This person should have the following qualifications and training:

1. A strong basic science background, including physics or chemistry, biology, physiology, and bacteriology.

2. A strong preparation in education, including educational psychology, principles of education, educational methods, curriculum construction, and tests and measurements.

3. Thorough preparation in the field of health, including personal health, nutrition, mental hygiene, first aid, health and physical diagnosis, and communicable disease control.

4. An understanding of the purpose and functions of all health agencies in the community, particularly the local public health organization.

5. An understanding of the nature and functions of the total school health program.

6. An appreciation of the potential contribution of all subject-matter fields and all other phases of school life to the total health program.

7. Training in special skills required in health education, including the methods and materials in health education, the evaluation of sources of material and information, the nature, preparation, and use of visual aids, public relations and publicity methods and techniques, and the nature of the printing and duplicating processes and their use.

The duties of the school health coordinator usually involve the following activities:

1. To assume the responsibility for developing and supervising the total school health program.

2. To coordinate the school health program with all pertinent agencies and individuals, including parents, public health agencies, family physicians, and the local medical society.

3. To interpret to teachers the results of physical, medical, dental, and psychological examinations of their students.

4. To assume the responsibility of the follow-up of medical and dental examinations.

5. To ascertain that the school physician's recommendations for special programs for certain students are implemented.

6. To help secure the most effective utilization of the school physician's time.

7. To see that students needing special attention are referred to the school physician.

8. To assist teachers who have pupils or advisees with health problems.

9. To determine that students who participate in extracurricular activities can do so without adverse effects upon their health.

10. To check students who return to school after illness or injury and to assist in their readjustment.

11. To assume the responsibility for checking the sanitary environment of the school.

12. To analyze the health factors involved in truancy and excessive absence and to take appropriate action.

13. To maintain all health records of students.

14. To make arrangements early in the school year for screening tests for vision, hearing, and posture.

15. To secure publicity for the school health program and to see that all staff members are aware of the services available to them.

16. To give leadership to the health instruction program. This involves curriculum revision with all those who teach special health courses; preparation of syllabi; assistance in obtaining films, books, and health instruction materials; and provision of in-service training where necessary. It also means coordinating the efforts of all teachers whose courses offer excellent possibilities for correlating instruction.

17. To work out detailed procedures to be followed when accidents occur.

18. To assume the responsibility for the school safety program.

19. To set up procedures for the evaluation of the school health program.

Personnel. Health cannot be effectively taught in two or three periods a week. The entire staff of the school must protect, promote, and teach health every day in every way if a genuine contribution to the health of the child is to be made. A health-conscious staff is essential to a successful program.

The health personnel may include physicians, dentists, dental hygienists, psychologists, psychiatrists, nurses, oculists, nutritionists, other specialists, and visiting teachers. There are no accepted standards as to the size of the staff, although physicians, dentists, and nurses are considered necessary. The size of the staff is dependent upon what the school board and the community want and are willing to pay for. It is desirable that all of the health staff have some educational training in order that they may have an educational viewpoint.

The Scope of the School Health Program

The major phases of the total health program are: (1) healthful school living, (2) health service, and (3) health instruction. Although each of these major areas is discussed separately, it should be emphasized that all are so closely related as to form parts of one coordinated whole, and only by such coordination can be a worthwhile program be developed. The relationships can readily be perceived in Figure 9-2.

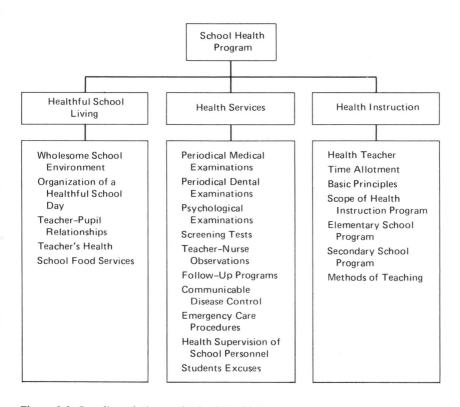

Figure 9-2. Coordinated Phases of School Health Program.

HEALTHFUL SCHOOL LIVING

Meaning

Healthful school living is a more inclusive term, to be preferred to those that formerly designated this phase of school health education. This term refers to the entire environment that surrounds the pupil. It not only involves safe and sanitary facilities but also includes careful planning of the school day for study, play, and rest. Since teachers are also part of the school environment, the establishment of healthful teacher-pupil relationships is an important aspect of healthful school living.

Wholesome School Environment

Every school is obligated to surround its students with a healthful environment: physical, social, and emotional. Intelligently planned, hygienically arranged, well-equipped school plants kept in a sanitary and safe condition are essential in the development and protection of child health. Construction and maintenance of the school building should be in accordance with standards established by law and by official building and health regulations. Adequate and well-arranged lighting and seating, properly functioning heating and ventilating systems, reliable equipment for fire protection, approved plumbing, suitable acoustics, adequate toilet facilities, and sanitary drinking fountains are some commonly recognized requirements for a healthful school environment. Furthermore, adequate handwashing facilities, hot and cold water, liquid or powder soap, and paper towels are all necessary for pupils as well as for teachers.

Standards for school sanitary facilities are established in building codes of state education departments and sanitary regulations of state health departments. These standards were determined by experts, and if they are up to date and adhered to within a school, the proper physical environment for children will be assured. The responsibility for sanitary inspections may be that of the school nurse, school doctor, health officer, or sanitary inspector, principal or superintendent. In smaller schools, the health coordinator or superintendent may make the inspections.

The Organization of a Healthful School Day

The health educator has more control over the organization of a healthful school day than over the environmental conditions of the children. Any organization of the school day must be considered unhygienic if it overtaxes school children mentally or physically. Some of the factors that must be regarded by the health counselor are these:

1. The length of the school day.
2. The number and the length of the periods.
3. The student load.
4. The number and kind of study periods.
5. The placement of the activities.
6. The amount and kind of homework and the importance attached to it.
7. The number, length, and kind of rest and relaxation periods.
8. Extracurricular activities.

More high school and college students have had their health affected adversely by poor organization of the school day and unsatisfactory teacher-pupil relationships than by unhygienic surroundings. High school and college students need guidance in the scholastic load they are carrying. They are frequently prone to undertake a heavy extracurricular load as well as other outside work. Some supervision is necessary to prevent them from undertaking too much. The extracurricular participation may be restricted, the scholastic schedule may be lightened, or, if possible, the outside work may be reduced if the student demonstrates that he or she is carrying too great a load.

The daily schedules of high school and college students should be such as to establish a regular program of work and insure sufficient time for meals, sleep, rest, exercise, and recreation. The college scholastic work should be limited to approximately eight hours per day or forty hours per week. The scholastic load should be about six hours per day in the high school.

School Food Services

An important feature of healthful school living is the school food service program. This program has two objectives: (1) to improve the health of children through serving more nutritious, well-balanced meals at minimum cost, and (2) to use the lunch period as an educational experience.

The food service program really cuts across all aspects of the total school health program. The provision of good nutrition is a part of healthful school living. Nutrition education belongs in the area of health instruction. The supervision of the diets of students who are suffering from malnutrition is an aspect of the school health services program.

The principal and ultimately the superintendent of schools is responsible for the total food services program. Whenever possible this responsibility is delegated to a qualified director of food service.

Teacher-Pupil Relationships

Every teacher in the school has a contribution to make to the health of the pupil. In addition to instructing and supervising the health of the students, the teacher can do much to promote health by his teaching methods. The latter are particularly important from the standpoint of mental hygiene. Too much stress should not be placed upon term examinations as a basis for promotion or final grades. The policy of rewards and punishments should be considered carefully. Imprudent disciplinary measures may have serious mental hygiene implications. The instructor should use fear only as a last resort to motivate desirable attitudes and conduct. Insofar as possible classes should be conducted so that fear of failure, ridicule, sarcasm, or embarrassment may not result. It must be recognized that constant failure invariably causes poor mental hygiene. The instructor is confronted with many different personalities and cannot treat them all alike. Teachers who understand the principles of mental hygiene and put them into daily practice make an indispensable contribution to the health education program.

The Teacher's Health

The highest attainable health of the body, the mind, and the personality of every school child is the aim of the health education program. Such an aim could hardly be attained by unhealthy teachers. For years teachers were assumed to be healthy when, in reality, many were not. The school has as much right to expect physical fitness from its teachers as intellectual and moral fitness. Not only is it incompatible for a teacher in poor health to teach, but such an individual may even prove a source of contagion to the students. An unhealthy instructor is a health liability to an educational institution.

High schools and colleges have been giving more and more attention to the matter of the health of the instructional staff. In the past, the school itself was responsible for many of the factors that impaired the teacher's physical fitness. The heavy teaching load, the unhygienic lighting and ventilation of the school room, inadequate salaries, lack of rest rooms and rest periods, and dogmatic, destructive criticism were factors unfavorable to health. Other causes of ill health include hurried eating, insufficient recreation, poor living conditions, and lack of exercise.

The teacher's health may be promoted and safeguarded in a number of ways. Following are some recommended procedures for maintaining and improving teacher health:

1. Periodic physical examination, including a tuberculin test and a chest X-ray for positive reactors.
2. Health qualifications for new teachers.
3. A reasonable teaching load.
4. Rest periods and rest rooms.
5. Recreational facilities for teachers.
6. Adequate salaries.
7. Insurance of salaries during illness.
8. Sanitary and healthful teaching environment.

9. Medical and hospital care for teachers.
10. Desirable, healthful living quarters for teachers.
11. Provision for health instruction for teaching staff.
12. Retirement fund for teachers.
13. Health insurance.
14. Teacher tenure.

SCHOOL HEALTH SERVICES

Nature and Scope of Health Services

This service program embraces the various protective measures assumed by the school to conserve and improve the health of children. The highest attainable physical, mental, and emotional health of every school child is the goal of the school health services program. The health services vary considerably in different institutions, but the minimum essentials of a good program include the following activities:

1. Health appraisal:
   a. The periodic medical examination.
   b. The periodic dental examination.
   c. Psychological examinations.
   d. Screening tests.
   e. Teacher-nurse observations.
2. The follow-up program.
3. Communicable disease control.
4. Emergency care procedure.
5. Health supervision of school personnel.
6. Student excuses.

The scope of the school health services is limited in the curative and remedial field because of the noneducational aspects of this type of activity.

Health Appraisal

The total assessment of the health status of the school child is called *health appraisal.* Health appraisal is defined as "the process of determining the total health status of a child through such means as health histories, teacher and nurse observations, screening tests, and medical, dental, and psychological examinations."[4] Not only do the physician, dentist, and nurse play a part in the health appraisal but the parent, teacher, and psychologist are also involved. The term *health appraisal* is a broader and more comprehensive one than physical examination, health examination, or medical examination.

The periodic medical examination. The medical examination is that phase of health appraisal which is performed by the physician. A periodic medical examination is the very foundation of the entire health program, as health protection, health instruction, and health promotion are all dependent upon it. By determining the health status of every student, the medical examination may be used as the basis on which to plan the student's curricular and extracurricular activities or as a yardstick to measure improvement in health and to guard against impairment of health. Cases of communicable disease must be discovered in order that their transmission may be checked and treatment obtained.

The ideal program is one in which the examination is done by the family physician and the results reported to the school. The parents and pupils are thus taught that medical care and supervision are their responsibilities and not those of the community. In addition, the family physician is better acquainted with the pupil, and more time and opportunity are available for a thorough examination. Then if any therapy is needed it can be done immediately. Family physicians should employ the same examination record form that the school system uses.

The students who are not regularly given an examination by their family physicians should receive one from the physician serving the school. If a school physician is not available there are usually some local agencies, such as a welfare or health department clinic, which can arrange to take care of children from underprivileged homes.

The recommended standard for the number of medical examinations includes one that is a preliminary to entrance to the kindergarten or first grade, one in the intermediate grades, one in the junior high school, and one before leaving school. Additional examinations should be arranged whenever there are suspicious indications. Previously, the recommended standard was an annual examination. Experience has shown that this standard was impractical. Those schools that were attempting to meet this standard were often providing such a superficial examination as to invalidate the procedure. Less frequent but more thorough examinations produce better results.

When examinations are given at school, qualified physicians and nurses should give them, although the faculty and reliable students may assist in some of the routine details, such as weighing and measuring. The time of the physician should be devoted as much as possible to those aspects of the examination which cannot be done by anyone else. A satisfactory examination requires from twenty to thirty minutes for each student. A minimum of fifteen to twenty minutes of the physician's time should be given to each individual. The child should be stripped to the waist or clothed in a slipover. Privacy is essential if the fullest confidence of the student is to be secured.

Preliminary to the examination, all available health records of the student should be brought up to date and reviewed. Each pupil should have a cumulative health record throughout his or her school career. Excellent forms have been developed for this purpose. In addition to the data from the periodic medical and dental examinations, the cumulative record should include the family health history, the health history of the individual, health habits and complaints, symptoms and signs of health disturbances that he or she reports, teachers' and nurses' observations of health, attendance record, and the results of all psychological tests.

The medical examination should be quite complete. If a blood test or urinalysis is needed, it should be done privately. Both tests are too expensive for most schools to provide routinely. Some provision should be made for detecting tuberculosis. Many schools administer the tuberculin test and X-ray the positive reactors. Schools can obtain specialized assistance from local, state, and national organizations devoted to tuberculosis control.

Participation in interscholastic or intercollegiate athletics should be contingent upon passing an adequate medical examination. The recommended standard is an examination of the participants prior to the beginning of each sport. The minimum standard is an examination once each year with a reexamination for those who have suffered a disabling injury or illness. The general examination that is ordinarily given to students is not thorough enough for athletes. The medical examination of athletes should include an examination of the heart, pulse, and blood pressure before and after exercise, the lungs, bones, joints, and the inguinal and umbilical region for hernia. A urinalysis is strongly recommended. A tuberculin test, followed by an X-ray for the positive reactors, should be required.

The periodic dental examination. The periodic dental examination is another essential aspect of the health appraisal program. The fact that dental decay is the most prevalent physical defect among school children emphasizes the necessity of providing such a program. The great majority of school children experience some dental decay, which could readily be prevented by the application of proper procedures.

Basic to the accomplishment of the objectives of the dental health program is an annual visit to the dentist for an examination and correction of defects that are found. This procedure will enable the dentist to discover and correct conditions before they become serious.

The school's responsibility in regard to dental health involves the encouragement of children and their parents to see their dentist at regular intervals. Every parent should be made aware of the child's dental defects and the possible consequences if not corrected. It also includes, in many communities, the conduct of dental inspections. A dental inspection is not as complete as a regular dental examination in the dentist's office, but it does serve the purpose of discovering dental conditions that require correction. Many schools routinely provide dental inspections, but others do not. Dental hygienists often administer the dental inspections. The trend is definitely to place the responsibility for dental treatment upon the parents. Special arrangements are usually possible for the children of destitute families.

Psychological examinations. Another important aspect of health appraisals is related to the mental and emotional health of the pupils. This is a significant aspect of health and one that must not be neglected. Tests of intelligence, reading, social adjustment, personality, and attitudes towards school and other children are very helpful in providing additional data that relate to the health of children. In addition, the classroom teacher is able to report anecdotes, particularly of those children who deviate from the normal. The school administrator, psychologist (if one is available), counselor, guidance teacher, social worker, health educator, physician, and nurse may have valuable data to add to the cumulative health record in regard to the mental and emotional aspects of health.

The mental health program is concerned with the discovery and prevention of mental and emotional illness. In the discovery of such conditions the classroom teacher plays a vital role. Close association with students throughout the school year gives the teacher an exceptional opportunity to understand them. The teacher who has a good preparation in child growth and development and understands child behavior will be able to detect children who depart from the normal. A knowledge of the factors that lead to mental and emotional illness is important in the prevention program. One of the most important considerations is that the child experience some success in school activities. Constant failure is damaging to anyone's mental and emotional health. Providing an opportunity for each pupil to be creative in ways natural to that child is another important factor. Satisfying relationships with classmates are also indispensable for the well-adjusted child.

Screening tests. Screening tests are so-called because they "screen out" pupils who may be in need of further examination and diagnosis by specialized health service personnel. Such tests are utilized particularly for height, weight, vision, and hearing. The screening process is usually done by the classroom teacher or nonmedical personnel, thus saving the valuable time of the school physician or nurse.

The classroom teacher should measure the height and weight of pupils at stipulated intervals, preferably at the beginning, middle, and end of each school year. The weighing and measuring should be done under constant conditions. Children who lose weight, show no gain, or gain excessively over a period of three months, should be examined by a physician to determine the reason.

The Snellen test is the most extensively used screening test for vision in the schools. Whichever test is used, it should be administered by the classroom teacher. It should be given annually to all elementary and secondary school pupils and more frequently when visual defects are suspected. A screening test for color deficiency should also be administered once in the upper elementary grades.

The screening test for hearing should be administered annually in the elementary schools and every two years in the secondary schools. The audiometer is used for this test. It should be administered by a technician, nurse, or the classroom teacher. The teacher who does it should have special training.

Teacher-nurse observations. Teacher-nurse observations are also an important part of health appraisal. The teacher, particularly, comes into constant contact with the students and may, therefore, readily observe changes in their behavior or appearance. Frequently, teachers are not qualified to detect deviations that may be significant but they may easily be prepared to do this. Teachers may be taught what to look for by the school nurse, health coordinator, or physician.

Among the conditions that the teacher should note in observing pupils are the following:[5]

1. Eyes:
   a. Sties or crusted lids.
   b. Inflamed eyes.
   c. Crossed eyes.
   d. Repeated headaches.
   e. Squinting, frowning.
   f. Protruding eyes.
   g. Watery eyes.
   h. Rubbing of eyes.
   i. Excessive blinking.
   j. Twitching of the lids.
   k. Holding head to one side.

2. Ears:
   a. Discharge from ears.
   b. Earache.
   c. Failure to hear questions.
   d. Picking at the ears.
   e. Turning the head to hear.
   f. Talking in a monotone.
   g. Inattention.
   h. Anxious expression.
   i. Excessive noisiness of child.

3. Nose and throat:
   a. Persistent mouth breathing.
   b. Frequent sore throat.
   c. Recurrent colds.
   d. Chronic nasal discharge.
   e. Frequent nose bleeding.
   f. Nasal speech.
   g. Frequent tonsilitis.

4. Skin and scalp:
   a. Nits on the hair.
   b. Unusual pallor of face.
   c. Eruptions or rashes.
   d. Habitual scratching of scalp or skin.
   e. State of cleanliness.
   f. Excessive redness of skin.

5. Teeth and mouth:
   a. State of cleanliness.
   b. Gross caries.
   c. Irregular teeth.
   d. Stained teeth.
   e. Gum boils.
   f. Offensive breath.
   g. Mouth habits such as thumb sucking.

6. General condition and appearance:
   a. Underweight—very thin.
   b. Overweight—very obese.
   c. Does not appear well.
   d. Tires easily
   e. Chronic fatigue.
   f. Nausea or vomiting.
   g. Faintness or dizziness.

7. Growth:
   a. Failure to gain regularly over 6-month period.
   b. Unexplained loss in weight.
   c. Unexplained rapid gain in weight.

8. Glands:
   a. Enlarged glands at side of neck.
   b. Enlarged thyroid.
9. Heart:
   a. Excessive breathlessness.
   b. Tires easily.
   c. Any history of "growing pains."
   d. Bluish lips.
   e. Excessive pallor.
10. Posture and musculature:
    a. Alignment of shoulders and hips.
    b. Peculiarity of gait.
    c. Obvious deformities of any type.
    d. Alignment of spine on "standing tall."
    e. Muscular development.
    f. Coordination.
    g. Muscle tone.
    h. Use of the feet in standing and walking.
11. Behavior:
    a. Overstudious, docile, and withdrawing.
    b. Bullying, overaggressive, and domineering.
    c. Unhappy and depressed.
    d. Overexcitable, uncontrollable emotions.
    e. Stuttering or other forms of speech difficulty.
    f. Lack of confidence, self-denying, and self-censure.
    g. Poor accomplishment in comparison with ability.
    h. Lying (imaginative or defensive).
    i. Lack of appreciation of property rights (stealing).
    j. Abnormal sex behavior.
    k. Antagonistic, negativistic, continually quarreling.

If the teacher observes some signs of disease or health defect, the student should be taken to the school physician, the school nurse, or the principal. Every school should have some individual who can make a more thorough examination of the suspected cases and authorize them to be sent home or to remain in school. The teacher should never be expected to make the decision of whether or not the pupil should be excluded from school. When the individual is sent home from school, the parents should be notified of the reason. They should be urged to secure medical attention, and the nurse or visiting teacher should ascertain whether the services of a physician have been obtained. When the student is able to return to school, a certificate to that effect should be brought from the doctor. It is recommended that the students be examined also by the school physician or nurse before being readmitted to class. The control of communicable disease is made more difficult in schools where undue emphasis is placed upon perfect attendance. The real tribute belongs to the child who protects his classmates by staying home when not feeling well.

The Follow-up Program

The value of a medical examination depends in a large measure on the follow-up program. In too many institutions the results of the examinations are recorded, filed, and forgotten. The number of defects which are corrected after the examination is far more important than the number of defects discovered by the examination. Concerning the correction of defects there are two principles that must be recognized: (1) no school health service must take away the fundamental responsibility of the parent; and (2) any corrective work must be made an educational procedure.

The school is an educational institution, not a hospital or clinic. The school is not prepared for curative or remedial services and should minimize its activities in this field. The responsibility for the treatment of defects and disease rests upon the family. The school staff should render first aid in emergencies and then call for the services of the family physician if further attention is needed. The only corrective work to be undertaken by the school must be educational in nature. Adapted or corrective physical education falls into this category. The department of physical education provides corrective classes in which those individuals with physical defects and organic disturbances that are amenable to correction by physical modalities are given certain exercises or activities to remedy their condition. Instruction and practice in various recreative activities in keeping with the individual's defect are also given.

If the parents are unable to be present at the medical and dental examinations, they should be notified by letter of the findings, and suggestions should be made concerning future examinations, treatment, and care. It is advisable to invite the parents to visit the school and confer with the school physician or nurse on the examination results. Instead of sending a letter, the school nurse may visit the home and report and interpret the results of the examination and the recommendations of the examiner. At school, the results should be interpreted to the students and their individual needs pointed out.

The teachers should be informed of the health status of their pupils and the steps that should be taken to remedy the defects. Teacher-nurse conferences should be regularly scheduled. They are usually most valuable if devoted largely to review and exchange of information regarding specific cases of children who seem to be in serious need of medical care, follow-up, or special study. The fully informed teacher can be most helpful both in adjusting the classroom program to the student's needs and influencing the student and parents to obtain correction of the remediable conditions as recommended by the family or school physician.

The correction of all remediable defects found on the medical and dental examinations is the chief purpose of the follow-up program. When the family cannot or will not assume the responsibility for correcting the defects, the school should bring the fact to the attention of public health authorities and social agencies. All agencies contributing to child health should be coordinated and their services brought to the attention of those families that are unable to pay for the attention of a physician. The school nurse or the visiting teacher is usually in the best position to make the arrangements between the family and the welfare organization.

Communicable Disease Control

The local health officer is the legal representative of the state board of health, which has full power in the control of communicable disease. The health officer consults with the private physician when the illness affects the community or school and informs the schools concerning the current rules, regulations, and policies for the control of communicable disease. The health officer also plans jointly with the school administrator for the immunization and testing program in cooperation with the private physicians in the community, and advises school officials concerning the exclusion from school of pupils or teachers because of exposure to or presence of communicable disease.

The superintendent or principal is responsible for giving the school staff adequate interpretation of the most recent public health practices and for developing for their guidance procedures that are based on these practices. Written and printed instructions with reference to the teacher's role in communicable disease control should be placed in the hands of every teacher in the school. The school administrator collaborates with the private physicians and public health officials in formulating plans for the schools and should also keep parents informed about the school's policies and procedures, usually by letter and group meetings.

One of the most important considerations in communicable disease control is the immunization procedures that are employed. It is a recognized fact that artificial immunization through vaccination is highly effective against smallpox, diphtheria, tetanus, measles, whooping cough, and polio. Despite this fact, a large portion of the school population is unprotected against these diseases. If the immunization program operated as it should in the preschool years and in the elementary schools, the problem of immunization in high school and college would be reduced considerably.

Parents should be encouraged by every means possible to have their children immunized by their family physician in their preschool years. It is recommended that the smallpox vaccination be administered to children before their first birthday. The diphtheria, whooping cough, and tetanus immunization is recommended for children from three to six months of age. This can be done at one time by means of the triple antigen, which provides protection against all three diseases simultaneously.

The practice of postponing these protective procedures until the children enter elementary school should be strongly discouraged. The public must be educated to the value of artificial immunization and the necessity of having it done early. The real facts should be placed before the public through the newspapers, school publications, letters, visits by the school nurse, and parent-teacher meetings. Religious objections and ignorance are the chief foes to be combated. The schools should cooperate with the public health program of promoting immunization.

As each child enters the elementary school his needs for immunization should be determined. The necessary information is obtained from the family physician on a form that is sent to the parents. Some children will not have had any previous immunization. Those children who have been previously immunized will require booster injections. Whatever the needs of the children, follow-up procedures will be necessary for proper immunization. Parents are expected to assume this responsibility through their family physician. When the family cannot afford this expense public health or social agencies are available to handle it. Some colleges and universities give vaccinations as part of the service for the student health fee. Others make no charge for it and vaccinate those who need it as part of the entrance examination. During epidemics the public health agencies or the school usually furnish emergency inoculations.

The common cold. The common cold is a communicable disease that presents special problems. No difficulty is presented when the student actually has a severe cold. Such a student should be excluded from school. Also, when it becomes clear that a severe cold is impending, the student should be discouraged from remaining in school. However, it would not be feasible to exclude from school all students who manifest symptoms of a cold. Often the student has an allergy rather than a cold. Probably the best procedure is to delay action until the evidence justifies exclusion from school.

Emergency Care Procedures

All schools should be prepared to render first-aid treatment in the emergency situations that occur so often. The school doctor should prepare detailed instructions and standing orders for the guidance of the teachers and nurse with reference to the procedure in handling common school emergencies. The school doctor or nurse should administer first aid if it is needed. If they are not available, first aid should be given by some member of the teaching staff who is qualified to do it. All teachers of physical education, shop, health, driver-training, and safety education classes should be certified in Red Cross first-aid training. In the event of a serious accident, the school doctor or any other physician easily and quickly obtainable should be called immediately. The names, addresses, and telephone numbers of nearby physicians who may be called in emergencies should be posted in the principal's office.

After first aid has been given, the parents should be tactfully notified of the child's accident. The parent should indicate the hospital, physician, or home address to which the sick or injured child should be taken if the parent cannot promptly call for the child. The sick or injured child should never be sent home unaccompanied by a responsible person. If the parents cannot be reached, the family physician should be called. There should be on file in the school the name of each pupil's family physician, whose notification in case of emergency has been authorized by the child's parent. The best-qualified individual should be prepared to help an uncertain parent decide what is to be done next for the child. All school personnel should clearly understand that they should not go beyond first-aid treatment of an accident or illness. They should not diagnose or administer medication of any kind unless prescribed by a physician.

Excuses

The problem of excuses arises chiefly in connection with physical education classes. A written excuse by a physician should be the customary method of excusing students from classes. Whenever possible, the school physician should be the only individual authorized to grant excuses. Many unjustifiable excuses have been requested by family physicians. In order to reduce unwarranted excuses to a minimum, the family physician should be requested to write out the reasons why the students should be excused. The school physician should then review the validity of the excuse and in case of doubt request justification by the family physician. When family physicians know that their excuses are subject to the approval of the school physician, they will hesitate to grant unjustifiable excuses. Whenever excuses are granted, their duration should be indicated.

When the problem of excuses develops, the cause may be that the program is so poor that it does not deserve the support of the physician.

Another reason may be that many physicians do not understand the nature and purposes of the program. If this situation prevails it should be rectified. The physicians can be readily approached through the local medical society. The orientation of the physicians should preferably be made by the school medical adviser if one is available.

HEALTH INSTRUCTION

Meaning and Purpose of Health Instruction

The third phase of the school health program is health instruction. Students learn a great deal about health from the health service and healthful school living phases of health education, but the term *health instruction* is used to define the effort to promote understanding of health and the observance of desirable health practices. The fundamental purpose of health instruction is to equip the student with sufficient knowledge about health to enable him to attain and maintain, both in attitude and practice, the highest possible level of health.

Importance of Health Instruction

Health instruction is an important means of bringing about healthful behavior among all people. A healthful environment and excellent health service in themselves will not solve all our health problems. Every individual must make countless decisions that affect not only his own health but the health of others about him. Many health objectives depend upon the understanding cooperation of all people. Thus, every individual should be capable of intelligent self-direction in matters related to personal and community health. As far as possible everyone should possess a scientific attitude toward health and conduct himself in accordance with recognized scientific knowledge.

Ignorance, indifference, and prejudice need to be combated as vigorously as sickness and disease. The outstanding problem in the prevention of disease at the present time is not the accumulation of more knowledge about disease but the putting into practice of the now available knowledge of disease prevention and control. The failure of many people to employ immunization procedures is an example. Many physical defects developing during childhood, such as those involving hearing, sight, posture, nutrition, and dental decay, could be prevented in large part by intelligent health behavior. A scientific attitude toward health is needed to break down superstitions and fads and to counteract the misleading advertisements in newspapers, in magazines, and over radio and television.

Sliepcevich[6] has aptly summarized the importance of health instruction in the following:

> In the schools is found an age group in its developmental stages of growth and maturity and habit forming years. Given the necessary climate for learning, health instruction can provide young people with scientific evidence so they can think critically about health problems, weigh alternate choices and make sound decisions, achieve self-direction and self-discipline for their own health, and acquire a sense of responsibility for health problems of the immediate and worldwide community. In what better place and at what better time can an individual acquire these skills and attitudes than within the framework of our educational system? The solution of health problems confronts every individual throughout his lifetime. Every day he must make choices that may adversely or favorably affect his health. No one can escape these decisions.

The Health Teacher

According to the definition given of health instruction, this term is to be used to define that time and effort given in class to promote an understanding of health and the practice of health habits. Obviously, in a broader sense, the child learns of health through other classes. In this sense, health instruction is a responsibility of the entire faculty.

Health instruction in the elementary school grades is usually considered as best left with the classroom teacher. The teacher should be as well prepared for this task as for arithmetic, social studies, reading, or any other subject taught. This is rarely the case. In some states certification requirements insure some preparation but they are minimal. In larger school districts supervisory assistance is usually provided. Under present circumstances supervisory assistance is indispensable because the background in health education of elementary school teachers is unequal to the responsibility.

The predominance of physical educators as health education teachers raises the question of their qualifications. Many physical education teachers—probably most—are not adequately prepared to teach health education. While the great majority have had some preparation in health education, it usually consists of two or three courses which, at best, provide a very superficial background.

There is a growing dissatisfaction with the quality of health instruction in our elementary and secondary schools. The performance of inadequately prepared, disinterested physical educators is particularly criticized. Many health educators are insisting that only fully certified health education teachers teach this subject. Oregon and the State of New York are in the process of accomplishing such an objective.

There can be no argument that health education must be taught by well-prepared teachers who are enthusiastic about this area. Our entire educational system is predicated upon this concept. If physical educators are to teach health education they should have a double major or at least a minor in health education and should be deeply committed about the importance of health education. Many physical educators have greatly strengthened their preparation in health education in their graduate work or via in-service training.

Our schools still need well-qualified physical educators to help in our health instruction program. Physical educators continue to be needed to help with this program. However, unless they are professionally qualified and committed they cannot be considered assets.

Time Allotment

In the first three grades the teaching of health is carried out largely through a correlation of health with the other subjects in the curriculum. However, an average of at least two periods per week should definitely be devoted to health instruction. In the upper elementary grades this correlation is continued but, in addition, three periods a week should be devoted specifically to this subject. (The State of Oregon currently requires fifteen minutes per day of health education instruction from kindergarten through grade three and twenty-five minutes per day for grades four through six.) Specific health courses should be required in the secondary schools with a minimum time allotment of a daily period for one semester either in the ninth or tenth grade and a similar amount of time in the eleventh or twelfth grade. The minimum time devoted to health in colleges and universities should not be less than two or three semester hours. Most institutions of higher education require such a course.

Many schools are not giving proper emphasis to health instruction. One of the most pernicious practices is to use part of the time allotted to physical education for health instruction. This is sometimes done when inclement weather prevents outdoor physical education activities. In some schools one period per week of the physical education time is given over to health instruction. Other schools do not have a specific time allotment but attempt to teach this subject entirely through the use of special speakers. The speakers used are mostly physicians, dentists, nurses, or public health personnel. Although these talks may have value, health instruction, if it is to take its rightful place in the school program, should be made part of the regular curriculum with a specially prepared teacher in charge.

Basic Principles of Health Instruction

Anderson and Creswell[7] recommended the following basic principles, which are recognized as fundamental to sound, effective health instruction.

1. Emphasis is on the positive aspect of health, not the negative aspects. That is, the aim is to build up and maintain as high a level of health as possible in each child.
2. Health is an end to be gained, not an academic subject.
3. Instruction is directed to the well, or normal, child. Children temporarily below par will be benefited by the health practices acquired by the whole class.
4. Throughout school life, health promotion should be one of the objectives of the whole school program.
5. Learning experiences must be adapted to the physiological, psychological, and social development of the children.
6. Instruction must be based on the child's interests, needs, abilities, and backgrounds.
7. Learning results from experience, and opportunities must be provided for experience through participation, doing things, and reacting to situations.
8. Problem solving provides the most effective learning situation but only when the problems are real and meaningful to the learner.
9. The objectives of any activity must be specified in terms of learner outcomes and must be recognized as personal goals by the child if learning is to be effective.
10. Instructional activities must always be related to the actual experiences of the learners.
11. Learning experiences are most effective when the child sees the relationship of one experience to the whole of experience.
12. Learners should be helped in making generalizations and in applying these generalizations to various new experiences.
13. Integrated learning is most effective, and only as it becomes unified will learning be lasting. Both fragmented learning and isolated facts are ineffective and soon forgotten.
14. Repetition, or drill, is justified when the learning must be precise and is useful as a tool or skill.
15. Each child is unique, learns at his own rate and in his own way, and thus a variety of activities and materials is essential.
16. Accompanying, incidental learning always takes place, and teachers should be alert for opportunities to make each learning experience yield greater returns in learning.

17. Health work in the school cannot be fully effective unless integrated with the life of the home and the community and the forces in which both can contribute to the child's education.

Scope of Health Instruction Program

The health instruction program should not be thought of as being limited to the formal health course. Two other aspects of health instruction are recognized as important. These are the incidental instruction and the correlated teaching. The incidental health instruction is that which arises naturally in various contacts with students. In such associations situations develop which enable the instructor to give guidance relative to health matters. The student may come to the physical educator with a personal health problem and solicit advice. As a result of close, informal relationships with students the physical education teacher frequently discovers students who need health advice. The report of each student's medical examination provides an exceptionally good opportunity for incidental health instruction.

Interest can be aroused and health habits motivated by the ways in which health is taught. In addition to being taught in a definite course devoted to the subject, health can be presented in many other school subjects. The practice of teaching various aspects of health in other school subjects has been long advocated by leaders in the field of health education. If the faculty member directly responsible for the health program is well trained and is given proper cooperation by the entire teaching staff, a large amount of factual health knowledge can be presented through established subjects in the curriculum. Health instruction is to be looked upon not as a responsibility of the health teachers alone but as a joint responsibility of the entire faculty. Too many times no practical application to the field of health is made by the other teachers. The health coordinator is usually responsible for the direct instruction, if there is a separate time allotment, and for the integration of health with the other subjects in the curriculum. The health coordinator should be able to show the other members of the faculty how integration of health instruction with their subject can be made in a perfectly normal way, and the program should be worked out so that duplication of factual material is minimized as far as possible.

The health course. On the junior and senior high school levels and in colleges and universities formal courses in health are essential. Even though some health may be effectively taught through incidental and correlated instruction, invariably important areas will be omitted. In addition, such a course is needed to provide students with a unified, integrated presentation of the health materials that are related to their needs.

Health instruction in the elementary schools. In the elementary grades, health instruction is the responsibility of the classroom teacher. In the primary grades a daily period of health instruction is not eseential, but a minimal time allotment would be two 30-minute periods per week. In the intermediate grades three periods of substantial length are needed. It should be stressed that incidental and correlated instruction, of which there is a good deal in the elementary grades, should be over and beyond this time allotment. Another important consideration is that when teachable moments arise the teacher may spend considerably more time on health instruction than usual.

In the elementary grades, the emphasis is placed upon the development of desirable habits and attitudes toward healthful living. The scientific facts upon which habits and attitudes are based should not be stressed. The instruction should be informal and should grow out of the daily experiences of the children. In the upper elementary grades the development of health practices and attitudes should continue, but the children need to know reasons for acceptable health behavior. They are interested in factual information and are eager to discover answers for themselves.

A number of studies have provided insight into the health needs and interests of elementary school children. These indicate that the major emphasis in the primary grades should be given to such aspects as developing habits of personal cleanliness, caring for teeth, eyes, ears, and nose, proper eating habits and choice of foods, developing proper attitudes toward physical and dental examinations, preventing colds, skin disease, and other infections, wearing appropriate clothing, and acquiring habits of safety. In the intermediate grades instruction can be continued on many of the above items but on a more advanced level. Other aspects that may be covered include prevention of infections, nutrition, fire prevention, traffic safety, safety measures in school, home, and playground, rest, getting along with adults, simple first-aid procedures, and purification of water and milk.

The importance of the health coordinator has been previously discussed. Such a person is particularly needed in the elementary schools because the teachers are not as well prepared for their health education responsibilities as they are on the secondary school level. Someone must plan a program with sequential, steadily more advanced learning experiences at each succeeding grade. Teachers need assistance in articulating what they teach with what has been taught before and with what will be taught later. In planning what is to be taught in the separate health class, the health content that has been taught through other subjects and incidental teaching must be taken into consideration. It is apparent that without such coordination the elementary school health education program will be conducted on a hit-or-miss basis, which will inevitably result in needless repetition of content on the one hand and omission of essential material on the other.

Health instruction in the secondary schools. In the secondary schools, an increasing emphasis should be given to health knowledge. The development of proper health habits, attitudes, and knowledge should proceed concurrently. Experience has clearly shown that the relationship between health knowledge and health behavior is not high. Most people with unhealthy habits really know better. The problem is one of proper attitudes. The correct feelings and emotions must be taught along with the health facts. This means that the cognitive, affective and psycho-motor domains must all be considered in health education with more emphasis placed on mental health.

Three important considerations involved in determining the content of the secondary school health instruction program are: (1) health interests of students, (2) strengths and weaknesses in health content areas, and (3) needs of students as revealed by research. Community mores differ; but we know that children are maturing earlier than in the past. Thus there is need for local acceptance and for determining when to teach such subject matter as drug information and human sexuality.

Ruth Engs[8] wrote about the health concerns of college students. On a 50 item health Concern Questionnaire 285 students in Personal Health classes cited 4 items, listed in rank order as follows, as those with which they were "very concerned": (1) air pollution, (2) water pollution, (3) population explosion, and (4) birth control. Thus, the leading health concerns of these students were environmental issues. For example, they were more concerned about air pollution, which they ranked as number 1, than poor teeth or decay which was ranked 27th.

The Conceptual Approach

This approach to the health education curriculum grew out of the School Health Education Study.[9] What is known as "the conceptual approach" has been designed to solve such problems as the needless repetition of subject matter and memorization of facts, the failure to produce behavioral change, and the difficulty of selecting what to teach out of the extraordinary amount of knowledge that has developed in recent years. The conceptual approach emphasizes concepts or generalizations about related data rather than facts. This approach has been undertaken in other curriculum areas.

Health education really has no alternative but to employ the conceptual approach. The accumulation of facts about the physical, mental, and social dimensions of health is so enormous and changes so rapidly that it would be virtually impossible for students to absorb and retain this information. With the conceptual approach students acquire generalizations about related data rather than try to master the vast number of specific items of information. The teacher of health education would do well to use the conceptual approach because no other method has a chance for success.

The conceptual approach involves setting up a framework for health education from kindergarten through the twelfth grade. This framework includes:

1. Three key concepts which are the unifying threads that characterize the process underlying health. These concepts are:
   a. Growing and developing.
   b. Interacting.
   c. Decision-making.

2. Ten concepts emerge from the key concepts and are viewed as the major organizing elements of the curriculum or indicators for the direction of the learning experience. These are:
   a. Growth and development influences and is influenced by the structure and functioning of the individual.
   b. Growing and developing follows a predictable sequence, yet is unique for each individual.
   c. Protection and promotion of health is an individual, community, and international responsibility.
   d. The potential for hazards and accidents exists, whatever the environment.
   e. There are reciprocal relationships involving man, disease and environment.
   f. The family serves to perpetuate man and to fulfill certain health needs.
   g. Personal health practices are affected by a complexity of forces, often conflicting.
   h. Utilization of health information, products, and services is guided by values and perceptions.
   i. Use of substances that modify mood and behavior arises from a variety of motivations.
   j. Food selection and eating patterns are determined by physical, social, mental, economic and cultural factors.

3. Thirty-one substantive elements, which serve as guides to select and order the substances of health education in its physical, mental and social dimensions.

4. A set of long-range student *goals* categorized under three domains; cognitive, affective and action.[10]

Human Sexuality

Sex education has been a highly controversial subject in many communities. Many parents and religious groups believe that this issue should not be dealt with by the schools. Because it is such an explosive area, this topic needs to be handled wisely.

The approach to sex education should not be on the basis of a separate course taught with that title. There are important aspects of this subject which should be covered in other courses in the curriculum. In addition, various aspects should be covered in an orderly, sequential way throughout the entire K-12 health education curriculum. The proper information can best be presented to students as a part of a comprehensive health education program.

Another important consideration is the qualifications of the instructor. A competent teacher knows how to approach this subject in a way which avoids sensationalism and public opposition. The teacher should also seek the support and involvement of parent groups and other pertinent community agencies and would be wise to consider the team teaching approach for certain parts of the instruction.

Methods of Teaching Health

One of the most common criticisms of health teaching is that the subject lacks interest. This criticism has been made by elementary and junior and senior high school groups, as well as by freshmen in college. It has been due, no doubt, in the past in large part to insufficient preparation of the health instructor and too much duplication of teaching material. Many school principals, superintendents, and other faculty members still think of health in terms of washing the hands before eating, brushing the teeth three times a day, and drinking six or eight glasses of water daily. Although some of these facts have some value, one can hardly expect interest if they are taught in the elementary grades and again in the junior and senior high school and college. If the health course is to appeal to students, their interests and needs must be considered in the selection of subject matter. These needs and interests are constantly changing; and unless the health instruction is modified and adapted to them at the different school levels, this subject will always prove distasteful and uninteresting. There is also the tendency to base the instruction predominantly on adult needs and interests. While these are important, it is extremely difficult to interest students in health problems that are thirty to forty years away. The best procedure is to follow the middle path and to consider both present and future needs and interests.

In the past the lecture method was used predominantly in health education courses, but the trend is now a combination of the lecture and textbook method along with audiovisual materials. The use of the textbook is a highly desirable method of teaching health education, for it results in greater student activity and application. One of the drawbacks to using a textbook has been the scarcity in the past of good publications in this field. Health texts not only must be well written, interesting, and nontechnical, but they must include the latest developments in all phases of health. There are constant changes occurring in the subject matter covered in health education. Fortunately, there are now available a number of excellent publications, and with the increased interest in this field it appears likely that there will be no lack of good health textbooks in the future.

The use of group discussion in conjunction with the lecture method is strongly recommended; students find it more enjoyable and they are more highly motivated to adopt desirable health practices. In addition, studies have substantiated that students felt that when opportunities for discussion were provided learning was more effective.

Through the use of well-selected health films, slides, and posters a health course may be made interesting and certainly much more valuable. There are health films available for elementary, junior, and senior high schools presenting material in an interesting way and including material that many times would be impossible or at least very difficult to present by ordinary class methods. Health films and slides, however, are not to be looked upon as a teaching method but as a teaching aid. Most state boards of health have extensive film libraries. At very little cost schools from the state may procure these films. Slides are available from the same source. The teacher sufficiently interested, with a small amount of training and very little material, should be able to make his or her own collection of slides. Posters are available from most of the national associations, such as the National Safety Council, the National Tuberculosis Association, the National Society for the Prevention of Blindness, or the National Society for the Control of Cancer. The materials presented by these associations are authentic, and the teacher should not neglect these sources.

The use of class demonstrations is a very effective means of presenting health facts. The teacher should have received sufficient training in health to be able to carry out various simple experiments. The growth requirements of bacteria, their wide distribution, the effects of drying, sunlight, boiling, and pasteurization on them can be easily demonstrated. A comparison can be made of the bacterial count of raw milk with that of pasteurized milk or of river water with tap water. The size and the shape of various types of bacteria can be shown easily by the staining of these organisms and by the use of the microscope. Simple feeding experiments carried out as a class project would be an interesting and worthwhile method of presenting certain facts in this field. There are many other simple, inexpensive demonstrations that may be made. There are on the market various health workbooks and laboratory guides that should be of value to the teacher for class demonstrations.

In every community there are various class trips that can be taken which should add interest and value to health instruction. A visit to the sewage-disposal and water plants will create more interest in municipal health problems than will ordinary classroom instruction. A visit to some good dairy to show modern sanitary methods of processing milk and to a farm where precautions are not taken should be interesting and valuable. The health teacher should take every opportunity of utilizing those facilities available in the community.

Graphic materials, such as wall charts, are great aids in teaching health. Some universities and colleges are able to use human cadavers and specimens to facilitate instruction. Many departments use health habit inventory charts as a means of bringing the desirable and undesirable habits before the students. In junior and senior high schools an excellent device is to put on a health exhibit.

Teaching by television is being used increasingly. It has been frequently employed to teach health education. Research has shown that television instruction is as effective as or significantly more effective than conventional methods of teaching. Evidence is also available to show that television is a valuable teaching aid when used in conjunction with other methods of teaching.

The behavioral approach is being developed and used in health education as it is in other fields of education. In this approach the teacher determines concepts to be developed from principles. Then to evaluate student concepts, behavioral objectives or competencies are developed. As part of the curriculum planning process the State of Oregon[11] suggests, for example, that in the area of mental health the student should progress from knowing, to understanding, to evaluating, to being able to demonstrate activities to show the relationship between mental health and each of the following: physical health, community health and safety. Suggested topics for developing course goals, performance indicators and/or learning activities are identified:

Physical Health.
Physical expressions of ideas.   Tension release.
Physical coordination.   Meeting physical challenges.
Physical condition.   Health habits.
Physical activities.   Sustained emotional conflict.
Physical appearance.   Physical disability or disease.

Community Health.

Community pride.

Available quality services.

Community involvement.

Feeling of community.

Concern for others.

Safety.

Emergency services.

Available quality services.

Concern for others.

Occupational safety.

Hazards.

Personal emergency care skills.

In summary, it is apparent that the health education teacher has a variety of teaching methods at his disposal. The considerable research that has been done to evaluate the different procedures indicates that no one method is clearly superior for all situations. A variety of methods is preferable to the exclusive use of one method. The teacher must consider the age and background of his students, class size, student interests and goals, and the nature of his subject matter in determining the method he will finally select.

SELECTED REFERENCES

ANDERSON, C. L. and WILLIAM H. CRESWELL, JR., *School Health Practice*, (6th ed.), Saint Louis, Mo.: C. V. Mosby Co., 1976.

FASSBENDER, WILLIAM V., *You and Your Health*. New York: John Wiley & Sons, Inc., 1977.

JENNE, FRANK H. and WALTER H. GREENE, *Turner's School Health* and *Health Education*. (7th ed.), Saint Louis, Mo.: C. V. Mosby Co., 1976.

KIME, ROBERT E., RICHARD G. SCHLAADT and LEONARD A. TRITSCH, *Health Instruction; An Action Approach*. Englewood Cliffs, N.J., Prentice-Hall, Inc. 1977.

NEMIR, ALMA and WARREN E. SCHALLER, *The School Health Program*. Philadelphia, Pa.: W. B. Saunders Co., 1975.

READ, DONALD A. and WALTER H. GREENE, *Creative Teaching in Health*. (2nd ed.), N.Y., N.Y.: Macmillan Publishing Co., Inc., 1975.

NOTES

1. C. L. Anderson and William H. Creswell, Jr., *School Health Practice*, 6th ed. (St. Louis: The C. V. Mosby Company, 1976), p. 380.

2. Anderson and Creswell, *School Health Practice*, p. 380.

3. Anderson and Creswell, *School Health Practice*, p. 96.

4. National Education Association and American Medical Association Joint Committee on Health Problems in Education, *School Health Services* (Washington, D.C., and Chicago, 1953), p. 7.

5. Joint Committee on Health Problems in Education of NEA and AMA *Health Appraisal of School Children* (National Education Association, Washington, D.C., 1957), pp. 13–15.

6. Elena Sliepcevich, *School Health Education Study: A Summary Report* (Washington, D.C.: School Health Education Study, 1964), p. 12.

7. Anderson and Cresswell, *School Practice,* p. 224.

8. Engs, Ruth C., "The Health Concerns of College Students Enrolled in the Spring Term, 1970 Personal Health Course at the University of Oregon" (unpublished Master's thesis, University of Oregon, 1970).

9. The materials relating to the School Health Education Study have been abstracted from: School Health Education Study, *Health Education: A Conceptual Approach* (Washington, D.C.: School Health Education Study, 1965).

10. The School Health Education Study. *Health Education a Conceptual Approach to Curriculum Design.* (Washington, D.C.: 3M Education Press, 1967) p. 15-20.

11. Oregon Department of Education, Salem, Oregon (Pre-publication draft of *Health Education Guide*).

10

Intramural/Recreational Programs

DEVELOPMENT OF
INTRAMURAL/RECREATIONAL PROGRAMS

Translated literally, intramural means "within the walls." Intramural/recreational programs, therefore, may be defined as activities carried on within the walls of an institution. Intramurals appeared in the schools long before anyone even thought of physical education and inter-school athletics. The desire to play is universal, and some form of it has always existed. It seems inconceivable that this powerful urge could have been entirely suppressed in our first educational institutions. The beginnings of intramurals can undoubtedly be traced to the informal sports and games that were indulged in by our first students in their leisure moments. This type of play, within the walls of the institution, may properly be considered intramurals, although it does not exactly resemble our intramural programs of today.

There is ample evidence that boys participated in various sports in our early American schools despite the obstacles in the form of hostile teachers and the Puritan philosophy of the sinfulness and foolishness of play. As educational institutions multiplied and the school population increased, informal play activities among students expanded. The haphazard nature of these activities gradually gave way to better organization. Competition was organized between societies, fraternities, dormitories, and classes. The students conducted their activities by themselves. The faculty was indifferent. In 1859, the Yale undergraduate body was divided into twelve intramural boating clubs of twenty men each. These contests continued for nine years before giving way to a system of interclass crews. Baseball was organized as an intramural sport at Princeton in 1864. Field days for track and field sports were conducted on an intramural basis at Yale and Princeton about this time.

As the intramural program developed, students looked beyond the confines of their own institutions for competition. It is interesting that interschool athletics arose from intramural sports. But the development of interschool athletics had no deleterious effect on intramurals. The students continued to play among themselves with no faculty guidance or interference. The fact that these activities continued with unabated interest in the face of the bitter interschool rivalries is ample testimony to the vitality of intramural athletics. Those students who were not good enough to represent their school against other schools expressed their natural desire for play and competition against their fellow students. Intramural athletics, discovered by students and promoted by students, continued to expand and develop.

About the beginning of the twentieth century, some progressive physical educators began to take an interest in these intramural programs. They saw in these activities unusual opportunities to broaden the scope of physical education. From 1907 to 1912 it became increasingly apparent that some authorized individual was needed to control and regulate these expanding activities. The athletic associations at Michigan and Ohio State made provision for departments of intramural athletics in 1913. Other schools soon followed their example. World War I gave a tremendous impetus to intramural sports. Athletic departments were always favorably disposed, because they saw in intramural athletics a training ground for varsity material. In high schools the movement to include intramural activities was evident by 1925 and became firmly established in the 1930s. Intramural development was considerably slower in the secondary schools than in colleges and universities where intramural athletics had a steady growth up to World War II. Because so many college men were drawn into the armed services, the intramural programs were greatly curtailed during the war.

As the previous war had done, World War II exerted a profound effect upon intramural programs. The war had clearly demonstrated the values of sports, and a general conviction prevailed that intramurals must be made available to all who were unable to make the institutional varsity teams. A determined effort was made to provide more intramural services to more students. Programs were expanded, chiefly by including additional activities. While the ideal "athletics for all" was not attained in most institutions, it was more nearly approximated than ever before.

Women's intramural programs did not experience the rapid growth that characterized programs for men even though many women physical educators strongly supported intramural type programs rather than varsity competition. It was not until the 1960s that girls and women on all educational levels began to have the intramural opportunities that were provided for boys and men. Title IX of the Education Amendments of 1972 finally provided equal opportunities for girls and women in terms of scope of program, equipment, use of facilities and financial resources to support all aspects of an intramural program.

Comprehensive intramural programs provide men's activities, women's activities and coeducational activities. The coeducational aspect of intramural/recreational programs has received increased emphasis since 1972 and such programs have been highly successful. Equalizing opportunities for women and men and the development of strong coeducational programs are beneficial outgrowths of the Title IX legislation.

Intramural programs have been extended to include elementary students. The benefits that were received by secondary age students provided an impetus to expand programs to reach younger children in our school systems also. This has been primarily due to a broadened concept of intramurals encompassing varied recreational activities that are appropriate for the elementary age child. Increased emphasis and steady growth in the number and quality of elementary and secondary school intramural programs has been noted since 1970.

Intramurals initially took the form of athletic competition. In the early years of intramurals the programs were titled intramural athletics. This term is no longer appropriate and the term intramural/recreational activities more accurately describes the type of program that has developed in our schools at all levels. A broad span of activities ranging from the highly competitive to informal recreation will be found in current intramural/recreational programs. Factors such as age, expressed interests of students, opportunity to participate on varsity teams, and the geographical area of the country influence the type of activities that are available in intramural/recreational programs.

PHILOSOPHY OF
INTRAMURAL/RECREATIONAL PROGRAMS

Physical educators have frequently viewed intramurals as an extension of the instructional physical education program. In many schools this is still a legitimate philosophical position. Intramurals do provide an opportunity for students to use skills learned in class and a close relationship between class work and intramurals can be of value to the total physical education program. However, the broadened concept of intramural/recreational programs requires a more comprehensive view of the objectives and values of intramural/recreational programs and, to provide for all student needs, a program must be much more than merely an extension of a physical education instructional program.

Enjoyment should be a high priority objective in every intramural/recreational program. The fun that students have when participating in an event, activity or contest is reason enough to establish an intramural program. Release of tension associated with the pressures of school life is another important objective and participation serves to enhance mental and emotional health. Even the most intense competition can provide a means to relax from the physical and psychological stress of the school day. Intramural/recreational activities provide an important carry-over value. Interests and skills developed in these programs will positively influence the future leisure time activities of the students. Skill development is an important outcome for many participants. Through intramural/recreational activities students can attain a higher level of skill which will be of value to them throughout their lives and assist them in enjoying activities more. They also have the opportunity to participate in activities that might not be available to them from any other source.

Vigorous activities assist students in attaining and maintaining satisfactory levels of physical fitness. For many students, intramurals are one part of their personal physical fitness program. Intramurals also satisfy the desire of students for competition. A good program will provide non-competitive as well as competitive experiences. However, intramural/recreational programs traditionally place a strong emphasis on competition for the senior high school and above. This type of competition is healthy if the program is properly administered.

Socialization and teamwork experiences are two additional goals that are reached through an intramural/recreational program. A chance is provided for students to meet and interact with other students in an enjoyable and meaningful manner.

Intramural activities were once considered to be extracurricular because they were originally initiated and conducted by students and carried on outside of regular school hours on a voluntary, noncredit basis. However, when the concept of the curriculum was broadened to encompass all the activities conducted under school auspices, intramurals came to be considered a legitimate curricular activity. Today, the intramural/recreational program is an integral part of the educational program and justifies the expenditures and attention given to it.

Intramurals are to be available for everyone. This means that programs must provide for a wide range of abilities as well as interests. The superior athlete should have a place in the interschool athletic program. However, many highly skilled athletes are unable to participate on school teams because the provision is made for only a small percentage of those who would profit from such an experience. Work demands and lack of interest in putting in the time and effort required of interschool athletic performers also creates a pool of skilled students in many high schools, colleges and universities who desire a high level competitive experience. All levels of ability must be considered when administering an intramural program since there are more educational values derived when competing against opponents of similar ability. The needs of students can best be met through a comprehensive, integrated physical education program, including the instructional, intramural/recreational and interschool activities. Each of these phases of the total program should aid and supplement the others. Intramural athletics must not be conducted as a training ground for varsity athletics. There can be no objection, however, if, out of the intramural activities, students are able to develop skills which will permit them to participate on varsity teams.

ORGANIZATION OF THE INTRAMURAL/RECREATIONAL DEPARTMENT

There are a number of different ways that an intramural program can be organized. The educational level, size of the school, school philosophy, and emphasis placed on intramurals are all influencing factors. At the elementary and secondary level most intramural/recreational programs are directed by the physical education department. At the college and university level there are varied organizational relationships. Some intramural/recreational programs are organized to function as departments in schools or colleges of physical education. Others are organizationally attached to the office of the Dean of Students or Vice-President of Student Affairs. In some colleges and universities, intramural/recreational programs operate as separate entities. A few programs are still part of the athletic department, but this has proven to be an unsatisfactory arrangement for intramurals.

Figures 10-1 through 10-4 give examples of organizational relationships in intramural/recreational activities in an elementary school, a small high school, a large high school and in a college or university.

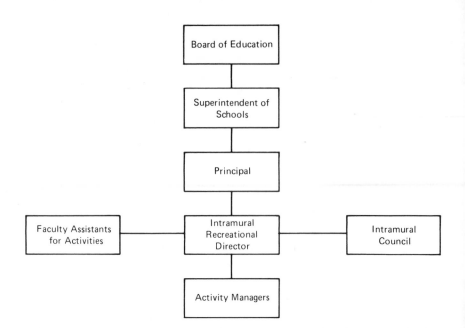

Figure 10-1. Organization of Intramural/Recreation Program for Elementary Schools.

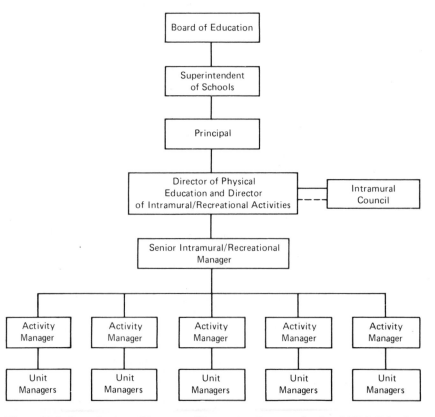

Figure 10-2. Organization of Intramural/Recreation Program for Small High Schools.

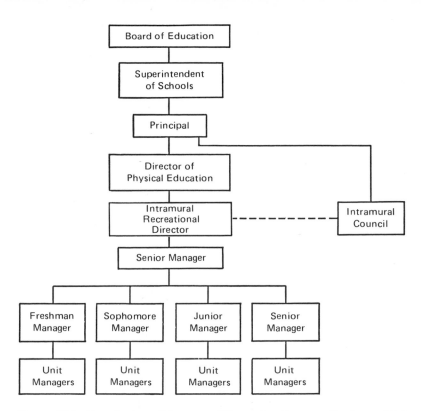

Figure 10-3. Organization of Intramural/Recreation Program for Large High Schools.

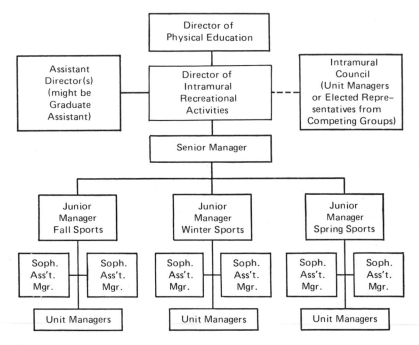

Figure 10-4. Organization of Intramural/Recreation Program for Colleges and Universities.

ELEMENTARY SCHOOL
INTRAMURAL/RECREATIONAL PROGRAMS

Elementary school programs were slow to develop. This was due in part to the inadequate number of professionally prepared physical educators in the elementary schools. Recess activities and sporadically scheduled half days devoted to games were the most common examples of intramural/recreational programs found in elementary schools. The improved quality and scope of elementary physical education programs has led to the implementation of strong intramural/recreational programs also. These programs provide an opportunity for the students to use and improve the skills learned in class. A strong emphasis is placed on fun activities with a limited amount of stress placed on highly-organized contests and league structure.

The Intramural Director

The intramural director should be a physical educator who is adequately compensated by the school district for administering the program. The director will frequently utilize the skills and competencies of other faculty members in the operation of the program. However, it is the director's responsibility to organize the over all program and to see that appropriate administrative procedures are followed.

Student Involvement in Administration

Students should be involved in as many leadership roles as possible. They can serve as recordkeepers, managers, scorekeepers, equipment supervisors, officials and team captains. Responsibilities should be rotated frequently to allow many students to gain this type of experience.

An intramural council should be formed to assist in planning and conducting the program. This is a valuable leadership development opportunity for the students and such a council assists the director in providing a program that will be of interest to the students. The council is normally composed of representatives chosen by the classes or other units of competition. Additional representation can also be obtained from the captains of the various teams.

Students are used as managers for each activity that is offered. They assist in preparing for an activity and cooperate with the director in administering and supervising the activity.

Finances

A relatively small amount of money is needed to operate an elementary school intramural/recreational program. The best procedure is to use physical education class equipment. This additional use must be considered when preparing the physical education equipment budget. Funds to cover administrative costs, publicity, awards, specialized equipment and other expenses should be included in the school's operating budget.

Units of Competition

Good units of competition contribute a great deal to the success of the intramural program. Selection of competing units is not a problem in the individual sports, for each individual is a separate unit. Strong units for team sports are necessary, however, inasmuch as teams tend to break up after several defeats. This is not a major problem at the elementary level since there is not as much of an emphasis placed on high level competition and the sport seasons are usually of a shorter duration.

The individual classroom has been found to be a good unit. Where appropriate, two teams can be organized from one classroom. This unit is particularly good when there are three or four classes in each grade level. Age can also be used as a basis for grouping. This grouping permits the teams to be equalized when there are participants of different ages. For some activities it may be desirable to group on the basis of height-weight as well as age.

Some schools have found that the most effective way to group for teams is to have the intramural director and/or physical education teachers place students on teams in as equitable a manner as possible. Performance tests can also be used to make certain varying skill levels are present on all teams. In the interest of equal competition and encouraging all students to participate, the procedure of having students form their own teams is not recommended.

Program of Activities

A program of activities as varied as the intramural director and the intramural council can devise should be provided. The sports taught in physical education classes form a foundation on which an imaginative director can build. Such things as novelty relays, stunts, rope-jumping, yo-yo contests, marble competition and bicycle contests are examples of activities that can be included.

Time Periods

Finding a time can be the most difficult part of establishing an elementary intramural/recreational program. If students are bused, there are logistic problems that must be overcome when scheduling activities before or after school hours. Parental permission should always be obtained and arrangements made for transportation to ensure student safety. Weekends have also been used effectively and family evening recreational hours can add an important dimension to the program. An activity period scheduled during the school day is an ideal time to schedule activities. The lunch hour can also be used for some types of intramurals. It should be pointed out that the intramural activities will frequently need to be modified to fit into the time frame that is available.

Other Considerations for Elementary School Intramurals

Many of the problems associated with secondary and college intramural problems do not exist or are minimal at the elementary level. Eligibility rules are not needed as every student should be permitted to participate. School or family insurance should be required. Regular school physical examinations are sufficient for participation in intramurals unless the student has a physical condition that requires medical approval prior to participating in some activities. Few officials are needed and physical education teachers and other faculty can usually handle the activities that require officials.

Publicity about activities can be distributed through physical education classes and the classroom teacher. Bulletin boards can also be used effectively. Awards are of minimal significance at this level and should have limited monetary value. Ribbons or homemade awards which provide desired recognition are satisfactory for elementary participants. Having a traveling trophy when the classroom is the unit of competition can also be used effectively to promote intramurals.

SECONDARY SCHOOL INTRAMURAL/RECREATIONAL PROGRAMS

The intramural/recreational program should be an integral part of the physical education program. As such, it is considered a part of the school's educational program and should derive its financial support from regular school funds.

214

The Intramural Director

The intramural/recreational program should be headed by one individual, known as the director of intramural/recreational activities. The plan of placing one physical educator in full charge of intramurals is the most effective way of organizing and coordinating all activities. Some schools attempt to have different people responsible for different seasons of the year or for different sports. This procedure fails to provide for a comprehensive program and the lack of organizational and administrative uniformity frequently causes confusion and results in only a minimal program. The intramural director should not be a coach or have other administrative responsibilities and the salary should be consistent with that received by coaches.

An essential criterion of the intramural director is enthusiasm. Regardless of other desirable qualifications, the director will not be successful in overcoming the encountered difficulties and problems without providing dedicated and resourceful leadership to the program. A desultory, disinterested attitude on the part of the director toward intramurals explains many weak programs.

Organizational ability is a prerequisite to success. Professional preparation in the organization and administration of intramural/recreational activities is invaluable. The director must have an understanding of the relationship between the physical education service program and intramurals.

The most readily available individual will not always be a successful director. Neither will an intramural department function properly when the various coaches of the different sports combine to administer the program. Nothing will do more harm to an intramural program than fluctuating leadership throughout the year. This is a weak administrative setup and should be avoided at all cost.

The custom of having coaches assist in the intramural department has been criticized on the grounds that the coaches are primarily interested in developing candidates for their respective teams and that this interest dominates their intramural duties. If coaches have adequate physical education backgrounds, there should be little objection to their work in intramurals. The intramural director requires assistance, and the coaches can be of great help in their various specialties or in their off seasons.

Intramural Councils

Many secondary schools make use of intramural boards, councils, or committees to help administer the program. It is usually made up of the intramural director, senior manager, representatives of the participating groups, a member from the student council, and interested faculty members. The functions of these boards include formulating policies, making eligibility rules and modifying the rules of various sports to meet local conditions, acting upon protests, deciding forfeits, and approving the budget.

Such a board is of great assistance to the intramural director. In addition, it provides an exceptional opportunity for students to exercise leadership. The democratic process also gives the program more vitality and appeal because the students are a part of it.

Student Managers

The student managers perform much of the work of the intramural department. They assist in making out schedules, notifying teams of their games and assignments, promoting activities, assembling data on contests and providing general supervision of the program. Their many responsibilities and duties offer exceptional practical training in leadership and executive development.

Team Managers

Each unit participating in the intramural program should be represented by a manager. This individual serves as the contact person between the intramural department and the unit and usually acts in this capacity for the school year. Responsibilities include the submitting of entries, eligibility lists, protests, and announcing scheduled contests. This person is also responsible for seeing that the team is in the proper place at the correct time. Some individual must assume the responsibility of the team when an intramural contest is being played. This may be the team manager, the coach or the captain.

Intramural Finances

The per pupil cost for intramurals is very low even when the salary of the director is included. Money is expended upon awards, office supplies, labor, equipment, intramural handbooks, and salaries. Officials in high schools are rarely paid. Intramural departments, as a rule, require the players to supply their personal equipment. Footballs, basketballs, soccerballs, nets, bases and the like are generally provided. This equipment is usually part of the physical education department inventory. In some school districts a charge is assessed against the intramural program for use of this equipment to aid in cost accounting when planning budgets. Most intramural departments receive their funds from the physical education budget. It should not be necessary to resort to money raising schemes to support intramural activities. The regular physical education facilities are used.

Units of Competition

Homerooms serve as a good basis for intramural competition. It is easy to reach the teams and communication difficulties are reduced to a minimum. Physical education classes are also used as are arbitrarily assigned teams. Interest groups, self-formed groups, clubs, and teams formed by randomly assigning students who have signed up for an activity are other techniques that are used to form teams. Arbitrarily or randomly assigned teams sometimes lack the cohesiveness found when students compete with friends or as part of an on-going group. Arbitrarily assigning groups does make it possible to better equalize the skill levels of the various teams.

The Program of Activities

The intramural programs will naturally vary in different localities, just as the physical education programs will. Winter sports are extremely popular in the northern states, but they would be impossible in the south. In certain areas, soccer is more popular than any other fall sport. In other localities wrestling is more enthusiastically received than basketball. There are, however, certain activities that seem to be in demand everywhere. Basketball, touch football, softball, volleyball, tennis, track and field are almost invariably successful intramural activities. Countrywide, basketball is undoubtedly the most popular intramural activity. Practically all students are familiar with and enjoy the game. The number of players is small and can be readily assembled. Very little equipment is needed, and the game does not consume an inordinate amount of time. Sports that are familiar, that do not need much time and equipment, and are free from long, arduous training periods are the most preferred intramural activities. Students engage in intramural sports for the joy and recreation that they receive and thus, for the most part, are unwilling to undergo hard work and punishment.

The range of activities naturally varies with the size of the school. Something for everyone all the time should be the goal of the intramural department. In order to provide for individual differences, several different activities should be available at all times. Sports in which little interest is demonstrated should be eliminated from the program after they have had a fair trial. There is a danger in having too many activities, but that is to be preferred to too few activities. The size of the school, the availability of facilities, and time will determine the number of activities that can be offered concurrently.

Activities should be provided for all levels of ability. The special education student will receive as much benefit and enjoyment from intramural participation as will the highly skilled athlete. Varying levels of competition and non-competitive recreational activities should be included in every intramural program so that the low skilled and inexperienced student will want to participate and not be intimidated by the highly skilled student. There should be a good mix of team, individual, and group activities. Activities should be offered for girls, for boys, and on a coeducational basis. Each student should have equal access to programs, facilities, and equipment.

Examples of activities for the intramural/recreational program are listed in Table 10-1.

TABLE 10-1. ACTIVITIES FOR SECONDARY AND COLLEGE STUDENTS.

Archery	Fly or Bait Casting	Paddle Ball
Backpacking	Football Field Meet	Paddle Tennis
Badminton	Free Throw Shooting	Roller Skating
Baseball	Golf	Scuba Diving
Basketball	Gymnastics	Shuffleboard
Bowling	Handball	Skiing
Camping	Hiking	Snowshoeing
Canoeing	Horseback Riding	Soccer
Card Games	Horseshoes	Softball
Checkers	Ice Hockey	Speedball
Chess	Ice Skating	Squash
Crafts	Indoor Track	Swimming
Cross Country	Judo	Table Tennis
Curling	Karate	Tennis
Cycling	Lacrosse	Touch Football
Dance (folk, modern,	Mountaineering	Track & Field
square, social)	Music Activities	Turkey Trot
Deck Tennis	Novelty Events	Volleyball
Dramatics	Open Recreation	Water Basketball
Fencing	Orienteering	Water Polo
Field Hockey	Outings	Wrestling
Fishing		

Eligibility for Intramural Competition

The opinion prevails that a student who is permitted to remain in school should be allowed to participate in intramural athletics, regardless of scholarship attainment. Little is gained by barring players from intramural competition because of scholastic deficiencies. The intramural department is more interested in encouraging students to participate than in setting up barriers to their participation. Eligibility rules usually specify participation on only one team in the same sport in the same season and do not permit switching of teams during the season. Interscholastic team members should be restricted from participation in their sport during the duration of the season.

Medical Examinations and Accident Insurance

The regular school medical examinations can be used as a basis for permitting intramural participation. For some strenuous activities it is a good policy to require a medical examination prior to participation. The participants should be required to have either family or school accident insurance.

Preliminary Training Periods

In order to further safeguard the health of the intramural contestants, preliminary training periods are advocated. The instances where students have entered swimming and track meets and other strenuous sports, such as wrestling, speedball, soccer, basketball, and water polo, without a day of preliminary practice are far too numerous. The intramural department should make it impossible for a participant to engage in strenuous activities without an adequate conditioning program.

Time Periods

The best time for intramural contests is in the afternoon after the classes are over. Students prefer it, as do their parents. Faculty supervision is easier to obtain. For these reasons intramural contests should be scheduled at this time if it is at all possible. The major problem is the conflict with interschool squads regarding the use of facilities. This is usually more acute during the indoor season than in the fall or spring. A partial solution is to play intramural contests on the afternoons when the varsity basketball teams play night games. Some schools arrange to practice the varsity teams at night or in the morning in order to provide opportunity for intramurals in the afternoon. In certain schools a period is provided for intramural competition before varsity practice starts. The practice of scheduling intramural contests during the regular physical education classes cannot be condoned.

The noon-hour period is extensively used in high schools. In some situations it is possible to play off contests before the participants eat.

Many intramural activities of a somewhat less strenuous type such as volleyball, softball, table tennis, horseshoes, and foul shooting, may be conducted after lunch. If the activity causes the participants to perspire, they should be encouraged to shower and change clothes afterward.

The time before classes begin in the morning can be used for some types of activities. Some schools also schedule activity periods during the day and when space and staff resources permit, provision can be made for recreational activities during students' free periods.

Because of the lack of space, it is frequently necessary to arrange intramural competition at night. Transportation should be provided and care should be taken when scheduling so students will have sufficient time for completing their homework. A rule of thumb would be no more than one night per week for any student. There are some situations where more extensive evening scheduling will work to the advantage of the students. An excellent time for intramurals is on Saturday morning and, frequently, on Saturday afternoons. The physical education facilities are not being used, and the majority of students are unoccupied at these times. When outside facilities are used, the times that they are available will determine when the intramural/recreational activity can be scheduled.

Officials

Faculty members and varsity players are the most frequently used officials in high schools. Volunteer students are also usually available. They should be closely supervised and training programs provided to develop their officiating skills.

Protests and Forfeits

Policies should be established to handle protests and forfeits. Protests should be kept to an absolute minimum and the intramural director can alleviate many problems by settling disputes at the time of the contest.

Intramural Publicity

In order to arouse and maintain interest in the intramural/recreational program, the students should be kept informed constantly about the activities of the program. Continuous publicity will do much to stimulate additional students to enter into activities and, at the same time, will serve as an added incentive to those who have been participating. Good publicity will also enable the intramural department to operate much more efficiently, as the students will be better informed of playing dates, playing locations, changes in schedules, entry dates, league standings, playoffs, and many other facts that should be known.

The best source of intramural publicity is the student newspaper. Space is usually easy to obtain, and if the intramural director makes effective use of it, great interest can be stimulated in the program. Items of unusual interest, noteworthy achievements, unique program features, league standings, schedules, and daily results should be publicized. The local newspaper has also been found to be effective in publicizing the intramural program.

The bulletin board is an excellent means of informing the student body of the intramural program. Every intramural department should have at least one bulletin board. In some schools several boards are used to good advantage. The bulletin board should be strategically located so that the greatest number of students will see it. It should be well lighted and well maintained, with eye-catching, up-to-date announcements, posters, and schedules.

Announcements at student gatherings and in physical education classes are a frequently used method of conveying information to students. Homeroom announcements are very helpful. Mailing information bulletins to students has been effectively used in some schools. A recommended procedure is to gather all entering freshmen and new students together and explain the program to them. Such a meeting may well be a part of the orientation sessions that many schools provide new students. At this occasion intramural handbooks can be distributed and interest-finding questionnaires secured from all students.

Intramural handbooks should be available to all students if they can be afforded. Many departments furnish handbooks and feel that the expense is well justified. Intramural handbooks give the student a clear picture of the intramural department, its organization, its administration, its rules and regulations, its leaders, the program of activities, the point systems, and additional facts with which the students should be familiar. The intramural director and managers will find that the handbook will save them many explanations and interpretations of the rules. The students will find that the handbook will give them a much clearer understanding of the operation of the intramural department and enable them to conduct their activities more intelligently.

Intramural Coaching

Coaching is usually done by team members. The intramural director, physical education staff and coaches should be available as resource people to assist the students.

Intramural Awards

Those who advocate the discontinuance of awards are attacking a universal practice. Awards are granted in all walks of life, and if a reform is desired, more would be accomplished by starting the proper training in infancy. Crusading physical educators would produce few worthwhile results if awards were abolished only in physical education and in no other lines of endeavor. The use of awards as incentives to intramural participation can be defended as long as they remain inexpensive.

The winners of competition can be awarded medals, cups, school insignia or ribbons. Team trophies have little value unless the competitive units are homerooms. In this case a traveling trophy might be appropriate.

Intramural Statistics

Records of intramural participation should be kept to evaluate the effectiveness of the program. Information of this type will assist in making changes and improvements to better meet the needs of the students.

COLLEGE AND UNIVERSITY
INTRAMURAL/RECREATIONAL PROGRAMS

College and university intramural/recreational programs fill an important role. More students are reached by these programs than any other aspect of campus life. The values received in terms of enjoyment, development of group cohesiveness and emotional and physical health make this program a high priority item on every campus.

The Intramural Director

An intramural/recreational specialist is needed to administer and develop quality programs. Educational preparation in physical education and/or recreation and experience working with intramurals are prime requisites for a person who desires an intramural position. Many individuals develop an interest in intramurals and gain experience by assisting with their school's program while undergraduates. The director must be able to work effectively with many people and be proficient in record keeping and administering a multi-faceted program. Budgetary skills and the ability to utilize the skills of assistants (undergraduates, graduate assistants, and faculty members) are other attributes that a successful intramural/recreational director must have.

Supervision of activities is an important responsibility of an intramural director. The direct supervision will be delegated to an assistant in large programs, but the ultimate responsibility rests with the director. Supervisory responsibilities include safety checks, following established first aid procedures, site organization, seeing that record keeping procedures are practiced, enforcement of appropriate participant behavior, and making provision for care and return of equipment. Graduate assistants and undergraduate intramural managers commonly serve as supervisors. Some activities, such as tennis and golf, that have minimal potential problems are run by the participants themselves.

Intramural Councils, Student Managers, and Team Managers

The well-run intramural/recreational program will involve students in all aspects of the program. An effective council is critically important if students are going to support the administrative procedures and policies that are needed. Much of the work involved in intramurals must be done by students.

Intramural Finances

The major expenditures are for awards, office supplies, postage, officiating, intramural handbooks, secretarial assistance, equipment and salaries. Financial support comes from several sources at most colleges and universities. Student activity fees are a major source of funds. The institution frequently provides support in terms of salary, equipment and facilities. Some intramural/recreational programs are supported as part of the physical education budget and intercollegiate athletics provide support at other institutions. Entry fees are also used in some programs.

The intramural director is responsible for preparing and administering the budget.

Units of Competition

Fraternities and sororities are the most effective units for intramural competition. Dormitories are also strong units, particularly if they are not too large. Dividing students into smaller dormitory groups makes better competitive units. Sorority, fraternity, and dormitory students develop strong group solidarity, and they are easily organized for intramural competition.

In the past, class units, that is, freshmen, sophomores, juniors and seniors, have been extensively employed. Interclass competition is especially successful in the smaller colleges. Divisions within the college or university, such as liberal arts, engineering, and education, are natural groups that might be used as bases of competition. In larger institutions, the various colleges can be divided into their different departments, such as civil engineering and mechanical engineering and further subdivided into freshman, sophomore, junior, and senior engineering. Other competitive groups may be military units (where ROTC programs are in operation), sports clubs, literary societies, and eating and boarding clubs.

The biggest problem of most intramural directors is to obtain sufficient participation of the unorganized, independent students. These students will participate satisfactorily in single and dual sports, particularly if the tournaments are well publicized and energetically promoted. The real difficulty is to secure participation in team sports. The independent students are not permanent and they have no basis for loyalty. They are hard to contact. The crucial factor is the leadership of these groups of students. All methods of motivating and promoting participation must be consistently and effectively employed to get a substantial percentage of independent students into the program.

A number of schools have discovered that the best way to organize the independents is to divide the entire student residential area into districts or zones. The zones are carefully worked out so that each contains approximately the same number of independent students. Each zone operates under the leadership of an athletic manager who makes every effort to organize the students within the area for intramural athletics. In most larger schools the independents compete among themselves, but the winners meet the intrafraternity and dormitory winners for the championship of each sport.

A system of organization which can work out well in a small institution is to assign all students by lot to a team. New students are assigned to the team having the fewest members on its roster. Once assigned to a team, a student remains a member as long as he or she attends the college or university.

Program of Activities

Activities that can be included in an intramural/recreational program are listed in Table 10-1. Many other events can be added to the list and will be successful if properly promoted.

Eligibility for Intramural Competition

Scholastic requirements are not used as a basis for eligibility. Some of the common regulations are:

1. Varsity squad members are ineligible for all intramural activities during the varsity season. Any player who is dropped for ineligibility may not compete in that sport in the intramural program.

2. Letter winners are ineligible to compete in the intramural sport in which they won their letter.

3. Freshmen squad members may not compete in intramural sports at the same time that they are on a freshmen squad.

4. A student who is barred from a varsity or freshman team because of professionalism is not permitted to compete in intramurals in the sport in which he or she is a professional.

5. A student may play on only one team during a given season.

6. After playing in one contest with a given team, a player may not transfer to another team in that sport.

7. Any special student or any student taking less than half the normal work shall be ineligible for intramural competition.

8. Any student who is on probation for disciplinary reasons may not participate in intramural activities.

9. Any team using an ineligible player shall forfeit the contest or contests in which that player participated.

10. Any player who is guilty of unsportsmanlike conduct may be declared ineligible to compete in intramural sports.

Medical examinations, accident insurance and preliminary training periods. Policies relating to these areas are covered in the secondary school section of this chapter.

Time Periods

Nights and late afternoons are the most used times for intramural/ recreational activities. At universities and colleges with large resident populations, weekends are also effectively used for activities. Facilities for recreational use as well as informal activities should be scheduled throughout the day as well as night. Many of the individual sport participants compete whenever they have free time if facilities are available. Challenge tournaments as well as some elimination tournaments can be run whenever two contestants are free to meet each other.

Officials

Specially attired and trained officials are an important ingredient in the success of an intramural program. Paying officials is a desirable practice and contributes to the upgrading of the quality of officiating.

The problem of intramural officiating is facilitated in those colleges and universities that have a professional physical education program. Physical education majors make excellent officials. In many institutions a course in officiating is required, and the laboratory part of the course consists of officiating in intramural contests.

Intramural officials' associations have proven effective in raising the standard of intramural officiating in many colleges and universities. The objectives of such associations are to promote a higher degree of sportsmanship and fair play in all intramural sports, to control serious injuries through competent officiating, and to make the games more interesting and enjoyable to both participant and spectator. In one institution the intramural officials' association meets three days a week throughout the season. Rating cards are sent in concerning each official's performance after each game. In many institutions the intramural officials' association conducts sports clinics for various intramural sports. Such clinics are scheduled prior to the start of competition and include rules, interpretations, and discussion of ground rules. Sports' clinics have the effect of facilitating officiating.

Protests

The customary ruling in regard to protests is that they be made in writing within twenty-four hours after the contests in question, accompanied by a small fee, which is returned if the protest is granted but kept if it is not. This gives the students time to cool off and reconsider their protest. Protests will be reduced if the intramural department has someone available at the various games to settle disputes. The protests that are filed with the intramural department are usually acted upon by the intramural council. No consideration should be given protests that involve mistakes in judgment by the officials. Legitimate protests are those based upon the question of ineligibility of players and mistakes involving interpretation of the rules.

Forfeits

Forfeits are the bane of the intramural director's existence. They present a problem for all intramural departments, although the better-organized departments are less troubled in this respect than the poorly-organized ones. If the students and organizations regard their intramural participation as a privilege, there will be fewer forfeits. Some departments place a heavy penalty upon forfeits, and this appears to reduce them. This penalty usually involves the loss of intramural points, although some departments deprive the forfeiting organization of all intramural privileges for the remainder of the year. This seems to be a heavy penalty, but it has worked to reduce forfeits. The cause of forfeits, in most cases, is discouragement following repeated defeats. If the competition is equalized to a reasonable extent, some of these forfeits can be prevented. The number of forfeits is appreciably diminished where the weaker organizations compete among themselves.

Intramural Publicity

The publicity techniques that are used in a secondary school are applicable to colleges and universities also. All types of literature and promotional techniques should be used to reach the students.

Intramural Awards

The winners of individual competition may be awarded medals, cups, class insignia, or ribbons. Group competition is usually divided into leagues comprising the permanent groups, such as fraternities and dormitories, and the temporary groups, such as independents. The winning teams of the permanent group are awarded pennants, shields, plaques, or cups. The winning temporary groups would have no use for team trophies; so they are usually given emblems or medals. A larger, more pretentious cup is awarded to the permanent group and to the individual for the best all-year performance. Some institutions purchase the awards before the competition for them commences. This procedure is to be recommended, as the students have the opportunity to see the awards for which they are competing, and it ensures prompt distribution of the awards after they have been won. An award that is granted six months after it has been won has lost much of its value to the student.

Intramural Statistics

The intramural department ought to have careful records of student participation in the activities of the program. In order to have a true picture of the intramural participation, the director will want to discover (1) the total number of students who have been reached by at least one activity, (2) the average number of sports in which each student participated, and (3) the average number of games played in each sport by each student or the participation hours of each student. The participation hours of every student in the separate activities is extremely valuable information to have, but more difficulty is involved in securing it. It is quite necessary that all of the above be compiled every year. The values of these participation records are as follows:

1. The gain or loss in intramural participation over the previous year can readily be ascertained.

2. The proportion of the entire student body participating in intramural sports will be discovered.

3. Whether the students are taking advantage of the intramural program throughout the year or are only participating sporadically will be disclosed.

4. The popular and unpopular activities will be discovered. The gain or loss in interest in the various activities from year to year will be evident.

5. The most successful units of competition can be ascertained.

6. The statistics may be used to show the need of greater financial assistance.

7. The success or failure of various administrative procedures may be checked.

In compiling participation statistics, a separate card should be kept for each individual. This card should give a complete picture of the intramural participation of the student. Only the actual games in which the student engages should be recorded. A record of the informal, unorganized play of each individual would be highly desirable, but practical considerations make it unfeasible.

Point Systems

Intramural point systems are used to determine the group of individuals who performed most or best or both throughout the entire year. Such scoring plans are very valuable in stimulating and maintaining interest in intramural activities for the entire year. Many organizations and individuals are inclined to enter only those activities in which they are proficient. A point system, however, encourages them to engage in a wide variety of activities. The group influences all its members to participate, and, incidentally, those who most need big-muscle play activity are persuaded to enter into various sports. Many students get their first experience with different activities in this manner. With individual and group point systems operating, the whole participation in the program becomes less haphazard and sporadic. Scoring plans will function effectively in both college and high school intramurals.

Group Point Systems

There are many different types of group scoring plans. Teams usually receive participation points and place points. Different activities have different point totals. The point totals are determined by the number of teams competing, the number of players on a team and the type of tournament that is used. Additional points are sometimes awarded for each win.

Individual Point Systems

Individual point systems are similar to group scoring plans. Every student has the opportunity of competing for individual honors. The total points accumulated during the year will be used to determine individual honors at the end of the year. It should be pointed out that a problem exists in regard to individual point systems. The record keeping, particularly in programs that have large student participation, is extensive. It is for this reason that many intramural departments do not make provisions for an individual point system.

CHARACTERISTICS OF INTRAMURAL/RECREATIONAL PROGRAMS

A broad concept of intramurals characterizes present programs. A wide variety of events ranging from the highly competitive to informal recreational activities to outdoor education activities are included in good programs. Many different sports are incorporated and programs are adjusted to meet changing student interests. Coeducational activities are an important part of intramural/recreational programs.

Many different clubs are included under the intramural/recreational umbrella at colleges and universities. These include sport clubs and special interest groups such as hiking, outing, and orienteering clubs.

Intramural directors also provide the opportunity for spontaneous informal athletic competition when facilitities permit. There are always students who are anxious to play when the facilities and equipment are available. By setting facilities aside for such competition and publicizing the opportunity, many more students are brought into such competition. Intramural departments extend this program by providing a matchmaking service for all sports. The amount of participation and the number of participants justifies the effort of the intramural department to promote this informal competition.

SELECTED REFERENCES

MUELLER, PAT, *Intramurals: Programming and Administration* (4th ed.), New York: The Ronald Press Company, 1971.

PETERSEN, JAMES A., ed., *Intramural Administration—Theory and Practice.* Englewood Cliffs, N.J.: Prentice-Hall, Inc., 1976.

ROKOSZ, FRANCIS, *Structured Intramurals,* Philadelphia: W. B. Saunders Company, 1975.

11

Interschool Athletics

As far back as anthropologists can go in man's history they find evidences of participation in sports and games. But despite the fact that man has always wanted to play, and has played when possible, only recently has mankind ventured to play in the schools. The traditional philosophy of education, with its emphasis on scholarship and intellectual development, could conceive of no place for play in an educational institution. Naturally, this powerful urge could not be entirely throttled, and despite the unsympathetic and frequently hostile attitude of the faculty, the students indulged in various sports and games in their leisure moments. It was not until the nineteenth century that students dared form teams for interschool contests. Organized athletics appeared in England as early as 1822 when the first Eton-Harrow cricket match was played. Oxford and Cambridge met for the first time in 1827. In the United States, the first interschool contest was a rowing race between Yale and Harvard in 1852. In 1859 the first baseball game was played between Williams and Amherst.

Despite these sporadic contests prior to the Civil War, the real development came afterward. Up to this time the impromptu type of play on campus predominated. But the war, as all wars since have done, greatly stimulated interest in sports. This fact, plus the greatly expanded enrollments, gave such impetus to athletics that the informal, intramural type of program developed a new facet, namely, men's interinstitutional competition. The better teams within institutions began to challenge similar teams in nearby schools. This form of extramural competition proved immediately popular. Participants and student bodies were extremely enthusiastic and supported this new development wholeheartedly. Faculty members were undoubtedly aware of these student activities but took no action to control or curtail them.

At first, the captain was the coach of the team. As interest in intercollegiate athletics increased, it became obvious that more experienced leadership was necessary. The practice developed of employing on a seasonal basis an alumnus who had been an outstanding performer. Alumni coaches eventually gave way to professional coaches. In the days before gate receipts, coaches were paid by the students, alumni, or friends of the institution. Since colleges and universities had no facilities for athletics, it was necessary for students to obtain, prepare, and maintain the playing areas. Originally, all the playing equipment and uniforms were furnished by the players, but as the importance of the contests grew, parents, alumni, or friends contributed to their purchase.

For a number of years after the Civil War this student-initiated and -conducted program flourished. But as it grew many problems developed. In the first place, the amount of work which was necessary to conduct a program of athletics became too much for students who were expected to carry a normal academic load. Secondly, the constantly changing student population prevented any stability in leadership and continuity in policy. Thirdly, due to both of these factors many undesirable practices occurred. Business matters were not efficiently handled, and financial irregularities resulted. A fierce struggle was waged within the institution when the different sports competed with each other for players, financial support, and facilities. Many questionable practices were engaged in to recruit athletes. Eligibility rules were nonexistent; travel was unrestrained. Students with injuries did not receive proper medical care. Student leadership proved incapable of meeting the many problems that developed.

When it became clear that the leadership left much to be desired, college administrators came to the conclusion that the only way to conduct intercollegiate athletics along educational lines was to appoint a faculty member to administer them. The most logical person in the majority of institutions was the director of physical education or some member of the staff. These individuals were already concerned with the physical phase of the student's life. Many had participated in intercollegiate athletics and had coaching experience. When increasing numbers of these individuals received professional preparation in physical education, they were well qualified to direct the athletic program. Along with this change in organizational setup colleges and universities accepted the financial responsibility of the program. The great majority of institutions provided and maintained the facilities and employed the personnel from the institutional budgets. Generally, the intercollegiate program was expected to be self-supporting insofar as the current operating expenses were concerned.

With these developments athletics, at long last, were accepted as an integral part of the educational programs. Even though they were partially self-supporting and still included some type of athletic committee setup, they were organizationally and philosophically a legitimate phase of the educational life of the institution. To be sure there were exceptions, primarily among the larger institutions, where the graduate-manager and student-athletic-association type of organization persisted. But in the smaller colleges and universities and some of the larger ones the athletic program had evolved through the stages of the impromptu intrainstitutional competition, the student-sponsored and conducted programs, and the graduate-manager and athletic-association setup to the place where it was regarded as within, rather than without, the institutional curriculum.

INTERSCHOLASTIC ATHLETICS

The development of interscholastic athletics followed and paralleled that of intercollegiate athletics in many respects. It is quite likely that many features of high school athletics were copied from the intercollegiate patterns. The interscholastic movement began ten or fifteen years after the Civil War, when athletics in institutions of higher learning were already well underway. Like intercollegiate athletics, high school athletics were initiated by students without the support and sympathy of school administrators and faculty members. The students received more encouragement and assistance from the community than from the school. The early physical educators were uncooperative and, in many cases, hostile to the program because it was contrary to their philosophy and practice. Just as in colleges and universities, many problems and uneducational practices developed under student sponsorship and leadership. When conditions became intolerable, school administrators were forced to assume control. This led eventually to the acceptance of interscholastic athletics as an essential part of the school curriculum.

THE RELATIONSHIP OF ATHLETICS TO
PHYSICAL EDUCATION

While athletics were springing up without the encouragement or guidance of school authorities, physical education classwork was being increasingly emphasized in the schools. The growing number of students with nervous breakdowns and otherwise impaired health finally forced school administrators to recognize that steps must be taken to safeguard the health of students. Confronted with this problem, educators turned to Europe again and borrowed the most popular systems of physical education then in vogue, which, together with hygiene, were added to the curriculum to assist in the digestion of the already heavy intellectual diet. In colleges, physicians, because of their medical background, were placed in charge of the hygiene and physical education classes. Physical education usually consisted of American modifications of German or Swedish formal gymnastics. This form of physical education was unpopular with both high school and college students, who endured it only because it was required. At the same time, the students in their leisure moments were vigorously and enthusiastically promoting various sports and contests among themselves and with students of other schools.

When school administrators decided to accept interschool athletics and introduce it into the school curriculum, they logically located it in the physical education department. It proved to be an unwelcome guest. Physical educators viewed this foundling with suspicion and reluctantly accepted it as a necessary evil. A bitter struggle was waged for the leadership of the combined department. Little harmony and cooperation existed between athletics and physical education, and considerable jealousy and antagonism developed. This was to be expected, because, at that time, the two areas were so far apart in philosophy, activities, and methodology that they could never be harmoniously reconciled.

A new philosophy of education, emerging about the beginning of the twentieth century, had profound implications for physical education. This new philosophy exploded the ancient theory of the dualism of the mind and the body and accepted the concept of the unity of the human organism. It also conceived of the function of the school as that of directing children and youth in learning the activities that constitute socially efficient conduct. No longer was the purpose of the school the development of the mental capacities only. No longer was the classroom the "brain factory" and the gymnasium the "muscle factory." The structural, analytical concept of education, which dismembered the child into his mental, physical, social, and moral attributes and then attempted to develop each independently, was rejected. The school existed for the purpose of preparing each child for the finest kind of living possible for him to achieve, given his capacities.

Out of this new philosophy of education a new philosophy of physical education evolved gradually. It conceived of physical education as education by means of the physical rather than education of the physical. In other words, fine living became the aim of physical education just as it became the aim of every phase of school life. The emphasis shifted from the purely physical to the mental and social as well. This new conception revolutionized traditional practices in physical education. In 1910, because of the influence of Wood and Hetherington, a new era of physical education began. They advocated the elimination of the formal systems of gymnastics and the substitution of natural play activities. This new movement gathered impetus, and today it is accepted as the American system of physical education. It has largely replaced the German and Swedish systems and their variations, which were not acceptable to American youth.

The broadened educational philosophy also gave athletics a new significance in the educational setup. Here were great potentialities for developing in youth desirable knowledge, skills, habits, and attitudes. It was found that athletics, under proper guidance and leadership, could become a powerful educational force, particularly in the development of social and moral, as well as physical, qualities. The dramatic nature of interschool athletics made them even more valuable in some respects than the physical education activities of the curriculum. But the regrettable fact remained that the administration of interinstitutional athletics left much to be desired. Although the conduct of athletics has been improved immeasurably since their inclusion within the school program, certain practices still exist which can hardly be called educational in nature.

OBJECTIVES OF ATHLETICS

The objectives of interschool athletics should be identical with those of physical education. The opinion is well established in educational circles that the only justification for interscholastic and intercollegiate athletics is their contribution to educational and physical educational objectives. The great majority of school administrators and faculty members still evaluate athletics upon this basis, although the programs in some schools are conducted for purposes that could never be construed as educational.

Coaches of interschool teams have the opportuntiy to achieve physical education objectives to a greater extent than the leaders of service and intramural activities. They have significant advantages in the greater time and better facilities that are available. In addition, they are concerned with a smaller number of students, all of whom are highly motivated. Under the circumstances, participants in interschool competition attain a greater measure of physical fitness and motor skills than is possible in the service and intramural programs. Insofar as the mental, emotional, and social objectives are concerned, the potentialities for developing them are greater in the interschool program, but the extent to which these opportunities are realized depends upon the leadership.

Standards in Athletics in Secondary Schools

Interscholastic athletics have been conducted in America for over one hundred years. In this long period of time many valuable lessons have been learned. Gradually, desirable standards for the conduct of athletics have evolved. Such standards have done much to improve interscholastic athletics. They represent ideal practices and policies, which, if extensively adhered to, would raise the quality of athletic programs.

CONTROL OF ATHLETICS

Control of Intercollegiate Athletics

Once school administrators arrived at the stage where they endeavored to control and supervise athletics, they soon found that however well one school might conduct its own program, other schools did not necessarily do likewise. The need for some organized body to direct and control intercollegiate athletic competition was soon felt, and this gave birth to our present athletic associations and conferences.

Another factor was also involved in the development of athletic conferences. In the early days of intercollegiate athletics, administrators who wanted to raise standards found it very difficult to do so alone because of the pressures of alumni, students, supporters, and townspeople who did not always have the best interests of the institution and participants in mind. They found, however, that this objective was much easier to accomplish with a group of like-minded administrators. Pressure groups had difficulty in opposing the new standards because each institution in a league or conference had to comply or lose its natural rivals.

Control on a National Level

The National Collegiate Athletic Association (NCAA) is a national organization, which has as its primary purpose "the regulation and supervision of college athletics throughout the United States in order that the athletic activities of the colleges and universities may be maintained on an ethical plane in keeping with the dignity and high purpose of education." Membership in the NCAA, originally organized in 1905 as the Inter-Collegiate Athletic Association, is open to all colleges and universities in the United States.

Membership in the NCAA is voluntary. In 1977 over 850 institutions were members. Dues are based upon the size of the institutions. Each member institution is entitled to one faculty representative. Thus, the association represents faculty control on a national level.

Until 1947, the NCAA had never attempted to force compliance to its regulations and standards. Prior to this time it had attempted to control intercollegiate athletics by persuasion and appeal to reason. In 1948 legislation was adopted to curb the rapidly developing abuses and evils. This legislation, which became known as the "Sanity Code," made the NCAA an accrediting association, which forced compliance to its regulations under pain of expulsion from the organization. The controversy over this new role was so great that the "Sanity Code" was rescinded in 1951. In 1952, however, enforcement machinery was established to implement the Association's regulations. Since that time the legislation of the Association, particularly in regard to illegal recruiting, has been enforced.

Regional Control of Intercollegiate Athletics

Athletic conferences have assumed much responsibility for controlling the athletic programs of member institutions. Most colleges and universities belong to some type of conference. Institutions of similar types, curriculum, philosophy, entrance requirements, size, and financial resources tend to join together in athletic conferences. Sometimes these institutions are all within one state, but frequently they are located on a regional basis.

These conferences exist for the purpose of regulating athletic competition between like-minded institutions. The member institutions want to compete with schools that have similar standards. The NCAA necessarily must be general in its rules and regulations and allow the conferences to equalize competitive opportunities on a state or regional basis.

The athletic conferences are controlled by faculty representatives of member institutions. The athletic directors, coaches of various sports, and publicity directors have separate organizations of their own which ordinarily meet at the same time as the faculty representatives. These different groups may make recommendations to the faculty representatives, but in the last analysis, the latter group establishes the policies, rules, and regulations of intercollegiate competition of member institutions.

A number of the larger athletic conferences employ a full-time commissioner who discharges stipulated duties. Usually, these duties involve the enforcement of the conference regulations, particularly those relating to eligibility, subsidization, and recruiting. Institutions that are found to violate conference regulations may be fined, obliged to forfeit contests, placed on probation, or expelled from the conference.

Local Control of Intercollegiate Athletics

The third and final phase of controlling intercollegiate athletics resides within each institution itself. This form of control complements those of the NCAA and the athletic conferences. Although each level of control is important and has its unique functions, the most important form of control is undoubtedly that on the local level. No outside agency can adequately control an institution that endeavors to employ devious practices to win games. The ideal in intercollegiate athletics is to have each individual college and university conduct its athletic affairs on such a high level that no outside regulation becomes necessary.

Over the years, the methods of administering athletics have gradually changed. Today, two major issues are involved in the institutional control of intercollegiate athletics. The first of these is concerned with the matter of whether intercollegiate athletics will be administered as an integral part of the overall physical education program or as a separate athletic department. The second issue involves the question of whether or not an athletic committee consisting primarily of faculty should be employed and, if so, what its relationship to the athletic program should be.

Athletics as part of the physical education program. In many colleges and universities, particularly the smaller ones, the program of intercollegiate athletics is a part of the overall physical education program. The director of physical education has the ultimate responsibility for the entire athletic program. The policies for the athletic program may be developed either by the general faculty or the physical education staff. The athletic director is responsible to the director of physical education, who, in turn, is responsible to the president. The cost of the athletic program is included in the physical education budget. Any income is purely incidental and goes into the institutional treasury. Coaching duties are carried on by various physical education staff members.

Athletics as a separate department. This type of administrative pattern is one in which a separate athletic department is headed by a director who is directly responsible to the president or athletic committee. This type of organization is found more frequently in large institutions. Such a method of administering intercollegiate athletics was not possible in the early days because well-trained administrators were not available. However, over the years a vast body of material relating to the administration of athletics has been built up. Today, many directors are available who have acquired the techniques and understanding necessary to administer an athletic program.

The advantage of a separate department is more obvious in a large institution. The size of the operation and the amount of money involved are factors that favor separation from the physical education department. It is admittedly more expensive to operate, but big-time intercollegiate athletics usually have the funds for separate facilities and personnel. In many of the larger institutions arrangements are worked out where certain personnel and facilities are shared with the physical education department. When athletic personnel are used in the physical education department, they should be scheduled during the terms when they are not under heavy coaching pressures.

Athletic committees. The second issue referred to above in administering intercollegiate athletics relates to the use of athletic committees. Practices are so varied in colleges and universities that it is difficult to describe a trend. Some institutions make no use whatsoever of such committees. In other colleges and universities these committees have complete administrative authority over intercollegiate athletics. This latter method of controlling athletics predominated when institutions first took over the conduct of the athletic program. In recent years it has been largely discarded because of its inherent defects. A committee is a poor administrative unit because it is constantly changing. The alumni and student members cannot profit from the experience because their terms are usually only one year in length. Moreover, the committee may ignore all the experience and training of the director.

The advisory athletic committee is probably the most extensively employed and popular type of such plans in use today. The person responsible for athletics possesses complete authority, but the advisory athletic committee recommends policies. Students, alumni, and faculty are usually represented on such committees. The advantage of an advisory committee is that all interested groups have a channel through which they can express their convictions about the program to the director. The director possesses complete power, but it is helpful to know the reactions of undergraduates, alumni, and faculty to the conduct of the athletic program. Such an advisory committee is objected to on the basis that other departments in the institution do not have them.

Control of Interscholastic Athletics

Interscholastic athletics, like intercollegiate athletics, are controlled on three different levels, namely, the national, state, and local levels. All of these different aspects of control are closely interrelated and complement each other. Each will be discussed in turn.

Control on the National Level

Interscholastic athletics are administered nationally by the National Federation of State High School Associations. This national organization was developed out of the state athletic associations. The beginning was made in 1920, when representatives of five nearby state associations met in Chicago to discuss problems that had resulted from high school athletic contests that were organized by colleges and universities or other promoters. The need was evident for a national organization that could operate in areas beyond the scope of the state athletic associations. In 1921, four states—Illinois, Iowa, Michigan, and Wisconsin—formally started the national organization. They were charter members, and the future development of the organization was due in large part to their leadership.

In 1922 representatives of eleven states attended the Chicago meeting. Since that time the National Federation has grown rapidly. By 1940 a national office with a full-time executive staff was established.

The purpose of the National Federation[1] is stated in its Constitution:

> The object of this Federation shall be to protect and supervise the interstate athletic interests of the high schools belonging to the state associations, to assist in those activities of the state associations which can best be operated on a nationwide scale, to sponsor meetings, publications, and activities which will permit each state association to profit by the experience of all other member associations, and to co-ordinate the work so that waste effort and unnecessary duplication will be avoided.

Control of Interscholastic Athletics by State High School Associations

The history of interscholastic athletics is a story of a long, difficult struggle to place these activities on a sound educational basis. So many vicious, undesirable practices developed around the high school athletic competition that school administrators were forced to take steps to control them in order to preserve their educational values. School superintendents and principals organized state high school athletic associations to control interscholastic athletics because they were unable to solve the problems individually. These organizations deserve most of the credit for the present high plane on which interscholastic athletics are conducted.

The first state high school athletic association was formed in Wisconsin in 1896. Indiana followed in 1903, and Ohio in 1904. Today, every state has an organization to administer interscholastic athletics. Membership in these associations is usually permitted to any accredited public high school, although in some states any high school that meets the standards for membership is permitted to belong. For each member school the principal must be the responsible spokesman.

It should be noted that some of these state organizations are known as "school activities associations" rather than "athletic associations." This designation is used because in some of these state organizations responsibility for nonathletic activities comes under their jurisdiction. Supervision of contests in musical, dramatic, speech and other nonathletic activities is provided.

These associations are conducted by boards of control which range in size from three to sixteen members. Membership on the board of control is confined in most states to school administrators, but in some states teachers, coaches, school board members, and university professors are eligible for membership. The duties of the boards of control are usually to determine the general policies of the association, to decide the rules of eligibility, and to settle disputes referred to them by various districts or sections of the state into which the association is divided. Every state has an athletic commissioner or executive secretary who has full charge of the clerical, financial, and executive work of the association. Most states have full-time executive secretaries; the remainder have part-time executive secretaries. The executive secretary conducts tournaments and meets, keeps detailed accounts of the competition, handles the finances, receives the scholastic records of the competing students, disseminates publicity, and performs other duties. The administrative authority, however, is usually vested in the board of control.

State athletic associations are classified into three types: (1) the voluntary, independent associations, (2) the associations affiliated with state departments of education, and (3) those affiliated with state universities. Approximately two-thirds of the associations are of the voluntary type. In the associations affiliated with state departments of education, the control resides with the department of education. In the voluntary associations, school administrators control the program. It is a common practice in these associations for the state director of physical education to be represented on the executive committee.

Functions of state athletic associations. State high school athletic associations vary in the functions they perform. The following functions are carried on by most state associations:

1. Sponsoring athletic-injury benefit programs
2. Conducting tournaments and meets
3. Establishing standards for interscholastic athletics
4. Registering and classifying officials
5. Sponsoring coaching clinics
6. Publishing bulletins and newsletters
7. Interpreting playing rules
8. Promoting summer athletic programs
9. Establishing contest regulations
10. Adjudicating disputes
11. Arranging and supervising competition in various nonathletic activities

Financing state athletic associations. A variety of sources of income is available to support state athletic associations. Most states have annual membership fees, with the majority assessing the fee on the basis of school size. Receipts from state tournaments and meets are the largest source of revenue in the great majority of states. Entry fees and fees for registration of officials are negligible from the standpoint of income production.

Local Administration of Interscholastic Athletics

In the final analysis the activities of the National Federation and the state athletic associations are translated to local high schools. The efforts of the state and national organizations are designed to come to fruition in each individual school. However, what happens in the local schools depends to a large extent upon how the program is conducted. The standards which the state and national associations endorse can be defeated by poor local administration.

The superintendent of schools. The superintendent of schools is the individual ultimately responsible for the type of athletic program which is in operation in the schools. Although the school board has the final responsibility for all that happens in the schools, it is the superintendent who recommends policies to them. The superintendent should take the initiative in establishing a desirable athletic policy for the local schools.

The principal. The principal is more directly concerned with the actual operation of the program and is held accountable by the superintendent for the conduct of interscholastic athletics in accord with the stipulated policies. In schools that have athletic committees the principal is invariably a member, frequently the chairperson, and possesses veto power over the actions of the committee.

The relationship of school administrators to the interscholastic athletic program requires that they be prepared to cope with the problems that develop. The principal and superintendent will make many costly mistakes in their relationships to the athletic programs unless they are familiar with the philosophy, principles, policies, and standards that should prevail. It is an unfortunate fact that few school administrators ever receive proper professional preparation in this important area.

The director of athletics. The director of athletics administers the details of the athletic program and is responsible to the principal for the conduct of the athletic program in accord with the policies of the school and the state athletic association.

The athletic committee. Athletic committees constitute an important factor in the administration of athletics in many high schools. The larger schools tend to make greater use of athletic committees than smaller schools. The individuals generally serving on such committees are the principal, athletic director, coaches, faculty members, and students. In some schools the dean of students, superintendent, and a member of the school board may serve. The faculty members, in most cases, are appointed by the principal. The student members are elected by the general student body of each class or appointed by the student council.

MEDICAL SUPERVISION OF ATHLETICS

Protecting the Health of Athletes

In citing the values of athletics, coaches invariably mention the contribution that is made to health. There can be no doubt that athletics, if well conducted, will make a significant contribution to the health of the players. Unfortunately, however, in many schools the health of the athlete is not given the consideration it merits. Outside of a few universities, colleges, and high schools, the method of conducting athletics from the health standpoint leaves much to be desired.

The medical examination. The medical examination is the first and most important measure to be considered in the proper health supervision of athletics. All athletic aspirants should be examined to determine their physical fitness for participation in athletics in general and also in any one sport in particular. The examination should be made by a physician who has the time and facilities to do the task properly.

Treatment of athletic injuries. The team physician is the key person in the treatment and care of the injured athletes. It is preferable to have as team physician an individual who has had specialized training in orthopedics. Knowledge of athletic contests and their demands is also an important prerequisite. However, smaller institutions with limited funds are often forced to use the doctor they can afford. Many doctors volunteer or accept very small token payments for treating injured athletes because of their interest in the program.

Many schools have a trainer who serves as an adjunct to the team physician. He performs many valuable services, such as taping, bandaging, massaging, supervising the use of various therapeutic equipment, like the whirlpool bath and infrared lamp, administering first aid, and supervising special exercises which have been prescribed by the physician. The National Athletic Trainers Association is very actively encouraging state licensure and wants a trainer in every school that has interscholastic athletics.

The coach can play an important role in the reduction of injuries by emphasis upon physical conditioning. Although three weeks of practice before the first football or basketball game has become an accepted practice, players should be well-conditioned when they report for practice. More and more football coaches are prescribing a conditioning program for all squad members during the month preceding the opening practice. To insure the accomplishment of this objective many coaches hold a mile run on the first day of practice.

The use of weight training has grown rapidly not only from the standpoint of strength development but also to prevent injuries. Research has revealed that a properly designed and conducted weight-training program is capable of reducing the incidence of injuries.

The football coach must exercise appropriate precautions to prevent heat cramps, heat exhaustion, and heat stroke. These conditions must be anticipated during the early weeks of the football season when high temperatures and high humidity are frequently encountered.

Another cause of injuries is overmatching. A small institution with a limited squad should never schedule a football game with an institution that has a squad of such size that they will be physically overpowered. Likewise, individuals should not be matched against each other in contact sports if they vary appreciably in size, strength, ability, and experience. Courts have found coaches liable for negligence when injuries have occurred because of extreme mismatching.

The coach should insist upon equipment that provides a high degree of protection for the participants in body-contact sports. Much research has been done in order to develop equipment that will reduce the incidence of injuries. As a result of this research significant improvements have been made. The protection of the player should be the paramount concern as the purchase of equipment, particularly football equipment, is contemplated. Proper fitting of equipment is also an important consideration.

The many health implications of interschool athletics emphasize the importance of the professional preparation of the coach. The best preparation for coaching is found in physical education. The professional preparation of the physical education major is designed to prepare the individual to safeguard the health of the students in the many ramifications that occur in physical education and interschool athletics. The coach whose preparation has been as an academic teacher is not qualified for the responsibilities in safeguarding and promoting the health of team members.

Athletic Accident Benefit Plans

Colleges and universities assume the cost of most of the athletic injuries that members of intercollegiate squads sustain.[2] A few of the larger high schools do likewise, but most schools assume no responsibility for the injuries incurred in interscholastic athletics. Within recent years state high school athletic associations have developed athletic accident benefit plans to reduce the financial burden upon the parents of the injured participant that the treatment of athletic injuries may impose. These athletic benefit plans have proven so successful that the efforts of the state associations in this regard are generally considered among their most significant undertakings.

In each athletic accident benefit plan coverage is provided for supervised practices and regularly scheduled interscholastic contests. Many plans provide coverage for injuries sustained in intramural competition. Compulsory physical education classes are or can also be covered in many plans. Injuries received during transportation to and from contests and practices are often covered by plans if the transportation is school provided or school approved and under the supervision of qualified school personnel. Many plans pay benefits for locker and shower room accidents. Some of the plans provide for the inclusion of coaches in the coverage offered. In Wisconsin the coverage includes elementary school students and students in supervised athletic programs conducted during the summer months. All of the plans pay medical, dental, and X-ray benefits for injuries suffered under conditions outlined by the terms of the plans. Almost all of the plans provide hospitalization benefits.

ELIGIBILITY REQUIREMENTS

Importance of Eligibility Requirements

Athletic associations and conferences have always been concerned with the eligibility requirements of those who take part in interschool competition. This problem was instrumental in the formation of these groups and is today one of their chief concerns. Standardization of eligibility requirements was necessary to equalize athletic competition. Our entire structure of interschool athletics is based upon uniform eligibility requirements. Equitable competition and educational outcomes would be impossible without common standards.

The Amateur Rule

The most frequently stipulated eligibility requirement is that each individual must be an amateur in order to compete against other schools. An amateur is defined by the National Collegiate Athletic Association as one who engages in sports solely for the physical, mental, or social benefits he derives therefrom and to whom the sport is nothing more than an avocation.

Amateur standing may be lost by:

1. Playing under an assumed name
2. Using knowledge for gain (officiating, coaching, tutoring)
3. Receiving money or board for playing
4. Competing with professionals
5. Competing for prizes
6. Selling prizes
7. Betting on competition
8. Issuing a challenge to compete for money
9. Playing on an outside team where admission is charged
10. Receiving money in excess of actual expenses
11. Signing a professional contract and/or negotiating with a professional agent in the sport in which the athlete is participating
12. Receiving consideration for connecting oneself with any athletic organization

Many heated debates have been precipitated on the subject of amateurism in school athletics. The amateur code is claimed to have come to us from England, where it originated to preserve sports for the aristocracy by keeping out of competition those who had to work for a living. Such a code is out of place in a democracy, many people aver. These opponents also point out that the amateur rule does not operate for the other school subjects, such as music, art, speech, or literature.

As a result of the amateur rule, much subterfuge has been resorted to for the purpose of evading it, in spirit if not in letter. The purpose of the rule, ostensibly, is to prevent the individual who has sufficient skill to command a price for the skill from competing against others who do not have this degree of skill. The opponents of the rule advocate more modern and educationally sound means of classifying players and equalizing competition. In a recent major rule change the NCAA now allows athletes to participate as amateurs in sports other than the one in which the individual athlete signed as a professional.

High School Eligibility Regulations

In addition to the rule on amateurism other eligibility regulations for interscholastic athletic competition are:

Age. The trend in high schools is definitely in the direction of reducing the upper age limits at which students may participate in interscholastic athletics. Not many years ago the upper age limit in most states was twenty-one years of age. The upper age limit in most states is now nineteen years.

Attendance. Most states limit the amount of competition by any student in any sport to four years. All states consider the student ineligible after attending a four-year high school eight semesters or a senior high school six semesters. Attendance of fifteen days is regarded as a semester.

Entrance dates. In the great majority of states the period of enrollment ranges from ten days to three weeks after the opening of school, after which no student may enter and be eligible during that semester.

Residence and migration. All states rule that the student becomes ineligible for a year or one semester when changing from one school to another, unless there is a bona fide change of residence. When the family actually moves into the new school district, the student usually becomes eligible immediately, providing that student was in good standing at the original school. An exception to this occurs when evidence becomes available that undue influence was used to bring about the change in residence. This has become a problem of sufficient magnitude to cause some state associations to establish regulations against it.

Participation on nonschool teams. The great majority of state athletic associations have regulations that forbid a member of a school athletic squad to compete on a nonschool team during the season. Several states have the regulation that outside competition may be permitted if approved by the school principal. However, such permission would be granted only rarely.

Physician's examination. Most states require a physician's certificate stating that the student is physically fit to participate in interscholastic athletics. It is surprising that such an essential and universally recognized practice is not mandatory in all schools.

Scholastic requirements. The great majority of states require that the student must have completed with a satisfactory grade a designated number of courses—usually three—during the preceding semester. Nearly all states also require that the student be doing passing work in three full-credit subjects during the current semester. This eligibility regulation is based on the assumption that satisfactory achievement in the various academic courses is the primary purpose of the secondary school. Students are prevented from participating in other school activities until they can demonstrate adequate accomplishment in these essential courses. Participation in athletics is thus a reward for successful scholastic attainment. Students who fail to do passing work obviously need to spend more time and effort in study. Because athletics are time-consuming and strenuous, participation in them should be denied to those who cannot carry both programs successfully.

In 1938 New York eliminated the scholastic eligibility requirement on the ground that interscholastic athletics are an integral part of the physical education program and no student should be prevented from gaining the benefits of participating in them. This move eliminated in this state the distinction between curricular and extracurricular activities. In effect, it gave athletics equal status with the academic subject. It eliminated the questionable practice of employing scholastic eligibility as a disciplinary measure. It recognized that athletic participation is just as important for a poor student as for a good one.

Undue influence. Some states have regulations that declare a student ineligible if it is proven that undue influence has been used to get the student to enroll in a particular school.

Parents' consent. Some states report that it is necessary for the student to obtain the consent of parents in writing before becoming eligible for participation in interscholastic athletic contests. Most states using this rule provide a special form for the student to take home for the parents' signature.

College and University Eligibility Regulations

The eligibility rules for intercollegiate competitions are much the same as those for high schools. In some conferences, the freshmen rule is observed, and some schools have interschool contests for freshmen while others do not. Participation must be completed within a period of five consecutive years. Certain entrance requirements are maintained. There is not the uniformity of scholastic requirements in colleges that there is in the secondary schools. Most institutions require passing work in two-thirds to three-fourths of the normal student load in both the previous and the present semesters. Normal progress toward the degree is required. Outside competition on teams not representing the institution is quite uniformly prohibited.

AWARDS

Value of Awards

The practice of granting awards to those who compete in interscholastic and intercollegiate athletics is found in practically all schools. The custom is in accord with the universal practice of honoring successful or outstanding performance. In the schools, it corresponds to the honors, keys, pins, emblems, insignia, and the like, which are granted for meritorious achievement or service in either curricular or extracurricular activities. This practice has received considerable condemnation on the ground that the student should engage in an activity for itself rather than for any outside rewards. However, when the awards are intrinsically rather than extrinsically valuable, the objection to them is not so justifiable. When an award has only a sentimental value attached to it instead of a monetary or utilitarian value, it is unlikely that the award will become the sole goal of the activity. As an incentive to engage in worthwhile activities, it seems that an inexpensive award is justifiable.

The school letter has replaced the laurel wreath of the ancient Greeks as the award for athletic performance. In high schools the letter constitutes the customary form of award, although some schools also award a sweater with the letter. The majority of states follow the rule of the National Federation of State High School Associations and limit the cost of their awards. In colleges a sweater and letter are usually presented to the person who qualifies. Some schools grant a sweater and letter for each achievement; others merely present the sweater and letter for the first award in a sport and only the letter in subsequent qualifications. Some universities and colleges permit a choice between a sweater and letter and a blanket carrying the school letter for the school award in the same sport. Many high schools having freshmen and class teams reward the qualifying players with class numerals. Numerals and sweaters are usually awarded to freshmen in institutions having the freshmen rule.

THE ATHLETIC DIRECTOR

In colleges and universities the director of athletics administers the athletic program. In large institutions this is usually a full-time position, but in many schools the director will have other duties as well. In fact, some physical education directors also direct the athletic program. In small colleges the athletic director generally has coaching or teaching duties. In most secondary schools an athletic director administers the athletic program. Not uncommonly, however, a separate member of the faculty designated "Faculty Manager of Athletics" assumes the direction of the athletic program.

Responsibilities of the Athletic Director

The administrator of the interschool athletic programs is generally involved with the following duties:

1. Purchase and care of equipment
2. Preparation of budgets
3. Ticket sales and finances
4. Public relations
5. Preparation of facilities
6. Scheduling
7. Game contracts
8. Preparation of eligibility lists
9. Securing officials
10. Arranging team travel
11. Student manager system
12. Arrangments for scouting
13. Supervision of coaching staff
14. Administration of home athletic contests

A number of the above duties are considered in other chapters. The remainder will be discussed below.

Scheduling. The responsibility for scheduling falls upon the athletic director. In arranging schedules, close consultation with the head coaches of the various sports is necessary. Although it is not always possible to do so, the schedules should meet the approval of the coaching staff. In addition, the schedule should be approved by the athletic council or board. The school administrator—usually the principal, but in some schools the superintendent—gives final approval. In making schedules, the athletic director is guided by institutional policies and by league or conference regulations. The total number of games in each sport is determined in part by school policy and in part by conference or state athletic association regulations. Ordinarily, one half of the contests are played at home. Ideally, the home games and the games away from home are alternated. High school schedules are generally made a year in advance, but colleges and universities frequently arrange their schedules five or six years ahead. Schools that are in leagues or conferences have most of their schedules automatically filled. They may be able to play only one or two outside teams.

Athletic directors are expected to arrange schedules that will not conflict appreciably with school work. For this reason the weekends are preferred. Care must be observed in arranging team trips so that absence from classes will be held to a minimum. The schedule should not conflict with important school events that are held regularly. It is advisable for the athletic director to consult with the school administrator and the student council because many major events such as Homecoming, Dad's Day, and the like are built around the athletic schedule.

Game contracts. The great majority of interscholastic and intercollegiate athletic contests are confirmed by means of contracts. Most state high school athletic associations have standard forms, which the high schools in the state are expected or required to use. Each school has a signed copy of the contract, which specifies the date, time, place, and financial arrangements for the contest. It may also state the manner in which officials will be selected. The principal as well as the athletic director is supposed to sign the contracts for high school games.

Preparation of eligibility lists. A standard procedure in interscholastic athletics is for the competing schools to exchange eligibility lists prior to the game. This is required by most state associations. This list, which is certified by the principal, is usually exchanged about one week prior to the contest. The required data concerning each player varies from state to state. In some states merely the names of the eligible athletes are indicated. Others go into considerable detail and include such data as date of birth, year in school, number of semesters in athletics, and number of subjects passed the previous semester and passing the current semester. Most state athletic associations also require member institutions to submit an eligibility list to the association office.

Much the same procedure is followed in most colleges and universities. In some of the larger conferences the eligibility lists are sent to the conference commissioner, who checks the status of all players on the list.

Securing officials. Poor officiating cannot be condoned. There are so many capable officials, that there is no justification for securing poor ones. The practice of "trading games" has led to much poor officiating. Instead of being selected on the basis of his ability, an official is chosen on the basis of his willingness to reciprocate. Furthermore, the practice of trading games leads to suspicions of favoritism. For the sake of the players and the game, good officials should be obtained.

The usual practice in selecting officials is for the two schools to agree upon certain individuals. The athletic director of the home institution initiates the matter by sending a list of approved officials to the athletic director of the visiting school. As soon as agreement has been reached, contracts should be sent to the chosen officials. Such contracts usually specify the date, time, place, assignment, and financial arrangements. The athletic council of the school should finally approve all officials selected. It is recommended that negotiations for officials begin early. The better officials are engaged many months in advance of the opening of the season.

To promote uniformity in the interpretation of playing rules, as well as to give school administrators the assurance that only qualified persons are in control of their contests, many states have established plans for the registration and classification of all persons who desire to become officials. Only officials who meet these standards are permitted to officiate in interschool competition. As a result the players, the schools, and the spectators benefit from a more efficiently handled contest.

Some colleges and universities secure their officials through the office of the conference commissioner, who makes the assignments from the list of approved officials. To get on the approved list the officials must pass rule examinations and demonstrate a satisfactory degree of competence in trial officiating. The larger conferences conduct rules interpretation meetings and carefully supervise the work of the officials. In many small colleges it is necessary to resort to the procedure of submitting a list of officials to the other institutions and deciding upon mutually satisfactory individuals.

Arranging team travel. The athletic director must take care of a variety of details in connection with team trips and should consult with the head coach on some of the important details, such as the menu, the time of arrival and return, the hotel, and the like. Many directors permit the team managers to handle most of these details, but the responsibility still remains with the athletic director.

The squad should leave together, stay together after they arrive, and return home together. It is standard procedure not to permit players to return home with any other individuals except their parents. It goes without saying that the coach should always accompany the squad.

All details of the trip should be arranged in advance. All the players should know who is on the traveling squad and the time and place of departure. The hotel, transportation, and eating arrangements should be prepared well ahead of time.

Money should not be given to the players for expenses. It is better for the coach or manager to handle the funds on trips and defray all the expenses that are incurred. Sufficient cash should be available to meet all the expected expenses of the trip, and receipts should be procured for all funds expended. Ordinarily, the hotel and transportation costs are billed to the school.

It is standard procedure that the players assume responsibility for their personal equipment. Duffle bags are usually provided for this purpose. The remaining equipment, such as balls, first-aid supplies, helmets, and blankets, is the responsibility of the student managers. They also need to check the players carefully to see that they do not forget their personal equipment.

If the trip can be made in several hours it is preferable to make it on the day of the game. Not only is this policy less expensive but it is better for the players. They eat and sleep better at home and are more relaxed when they are in familiar surroundings.

Student manager system. Student managers render invaluable services to athletic directors and coaches. Practically all high schools and colleges and universities use student managers. A good manager is a joy to both the coach and athletic director because the manager relieves the coach of many responsibilities.

The work of student managers is hard and time-consuming. In addition, it frequently appears to be thankless. However, the student stands to benefit from it in a variety of ways. In many schools the head managership is considered one of the most coveted positions. The manager learns how to work with a variety of people and benefits from the responsibility carried and from the lessons learned by doing the job.

The manager is generally appointed by the athletic director or coach of the sport concerned. Usually, the coach and athletic director have reached an agreement on the candidate beforehand. Frequently, the selection is made on a merit basis. This last method is preferred in the larger institutions where a number of candidates are available. It operates by having a number of sophomore managers from whom two junior managers are selected. One of the junior managers is then selected as senior manager. In smaller schools the athletic director and coach consider themselves fortunate if they have any volunteers.

Student managers perform a wide variety of duties. Some of the common ones are:

1. Recording the daily attendance
2. Bringing all the equipment to and from the practice field
3. Caring for the equipment during practice
4. Keeping a list of the addresses, phone numbers, locker numbers and combinations, and class schedules of all squad members
5. Officiating practice games
6. Checking on players' eligibility
7. Arranging for trips, meals, and hotels
8. Rendering a report of all expenditures after a trip
9. Packing various items of equipment for trips and making sure that the equipment is available
10. Checking that all players have their personal equipment on trips
11. Supervising the work of the assistants
12. Meeting visiting teams and rendering whatever assistance is needed
13. Meeting officials and taking care of their needs
14. Recommending his successor to the athletic director
15. Being available to assist the coaches and athletic director in any way they request

Arrangements for scouting. Scouting is accepted today as an essential part of interschool football and basketball. It is no longer regarded as spying and unethical but is approved and regulated. The scout, usually an assistant coach, calls for tickets at the athletic department office and makes his or her presence known to the team being scouted. The scout is provided with seats in the press box and is shown every courtesy. The purpose of scouting is to discover the basic offensive and defensive formations, the trick plays, and the abilities and peculiarities of the team. Some coaches exchange formations or films with each other in order to dispense with scouting. However, scouting, as it is conducted today, is the best assurance against suspicion. Most of the no-scouting agreements have been abrogated because of the difficulty incurred in preventing information concerning an opponent from reaching the coach and the players.

The chief problem with scouting today is to regulate it. There is a trend to scout each opposing team not more than twice. A further limitation is to permit only two representatives to scout a game at one time. Many coaches consider it unethical for coaches to make scouting reports, game films, and coaches' analyses of games available to other schools.

Supervision of coaching staff. The athletic director has the responsibility of conducting the athletic program in accordance with the policies of the institution and the regulations of the conference or league to which the school belongs. In addition, compliance with state and national athletic association regulations is required. The athletic director must be alert to the many policies and requirements and observe them in spirit as well as in letter. This involves, among other things, the supervision of the various members of the coaching staff.

The majority of state associations permit only certified teachers to coach in secondary schools. Most colleges and universities follow the same practice. Experience has demonstrated that it is easier to control athletics when the coaches are bona fide faculty members. Their professional preparation is such that they understand and appreciate the purposes of the school and the necessity for the various regulations to govern athletics.

The quality of the athletic program is determined more by the caliber of the coaches than by any other consideration. This fact makes their selection a vitally important matter. Unfortunately, coaches are too often chosen on the basis of their technical competence. The character and ideals of candidates receive too little attention. Ideally, the coach should understand the sport thoroughly and should know boys and girls and be an effective leader. The coach needs to be a skilled teacher, with the ability to develop sound fundamentals and well-coordinated offensive and defensive team play. He or she must realize that athletics are a part of school experiences and they must therefore be conducted to achieve educational objectives. The coach must appreciate that sports exist for the education and development of students rather than that students exist for the winning of games.

Administration of Athletic Contests

One of the most important responsibilities of many athletic directors is the management of home athletic contests. This task must be done well because the public, students, and visiting team will resent and be critical of inefficient management. Poor administration of athletic contests will eventually result in reduced income from gate receipts.

The efficient management of a home game is dependent upon careful planning. Well-managed athletic contests do not happen accidentally—they are as efficiently managed as they are planned. The chief difficulty in the administration of contests is to handle the multitude of details which is involved. These details are known but it is easy to forget or to overlook some of them. For this reason some athletic directors employ a check list. Such a check list includes all the details that must be handled in the management of a contest. After a detail has been discharged a check is made to indicate the fact. Such a scheme should eliminate inefficiency in athletic contest management.

PROBLEMS OF INTERSCHOOL ATHLETICS

There are numerous problems facing interschool athletics. The most serious of these are emphasis on false values, bad athletic practices, championships and tournaments, player control, proselyting and subsidization, junior high school athletics, interschool athletics for girls and women, the academic teacher versus the physical educator as coach, overemphasis, and public pressures. Each will be discussed in turn.

Emphasis on false values. After an exhaustive study, the Education Policies Commission has indicated that the emphasis upon false values is one of the major problems that mar interscholastic athletics in American schools today. Their four main topics are: overemphasis on winning, glorifying star athletes, disparaging the nonathlete, and school games as public spectacles. The Commission also lists as bad athletic practices: overemphasis on the varsity, distortions in the educational program, coaches under pressure, financial woes, farm teams, recruiting of players, neglecting the girls, and recruiting by colleges.

Championships and tournaments. For many decades there has been much opposition to championships and tournaments. This opposition is not found as much in institutions of higher education because the problems are not as acute. The participants are more mature, and since they usually travel by plane there is less interference with the academic program. Likewise, there is little criticism of league or conference championships being awarded on the basis of percentage points. The prime targets have been high school state championship meets and tournaments. Particularly condemned were the state tournaments extending over three or four days preceded by regional, district, and sectional tournaments, each also spread over several days. It was not at all uncommon for a team to play 5 or 6 games over a three-day period.

The advocates of reform of championships base their objection on the following points:

1. Championships rather than the game itself become the objects of play

2. The schools involved become disrupted

3. Participants lose much time from classes

4. The importance of winning is overemphasized

5. Tournaments are physically and emotionally harmful to participants

6. The expense of engaging in tournaments is too heavy in some schools

7. Communities expect too much of their teams.

In defense of state play-offs it should be pointed out that state athletic associations derive most of their income from this source. In addition, in some states the participating schools receive part of their tournament expenses from this income. Further, certain values have been attributed to championships, such as the benefits of travel, the crystallization of school spirit, increased community interest and pride, and the social values to the players. Finally, it should be recognized that if the schools did not provide such play-offs other agencies probably would. It is unquestionably better that schools conduct championship competition rather than private or commercial agencies.

Over the years the conduct of tournaments and meets, particularly at the high school level, has improved to such an extent that much of the criticism has abated. The credit for this improvement belongs primarily to the state athletic associations and the school administrators who direct them. These people have been very conscious of the undesirable features of state championships and they have made every effort to eliminate them. They have stopped the national championships. The three or four tournament stages preceding the final competition have been reduced or eliminated. Very helpful has been the creation of tournaments for schools according to their size. When the schools of the state are divided up into three or four separate tournaments the length of tournament structure is reduced and the number of games to be played by each school is sharply curtailed. As a consequence the schedule can be arranged to avoid the necessity of any team playing more than one game per day. In addition this arrangement is more equitable to the small schools.

Player control. On October 20, 1927, the Central Committee of the New York State Public School Athletic Association passed the famous "Regulation One," which was modified on December 27, 1927. In substance, this regulation recommended that after the contest began, the two coaches should sit together and permit the respective captains to direct the teams. The coach might attend to the physical injuries of the team, and could order the withdrawal of a player from the game; but that was the extent of his authority. When a player was withdrawn, that player was unable to reenter the game. A substitute was selected by the captain, who made substitutions as he or she chose. It was suggested that each coach send a representative to the other team's dressing room in order to prevent accusation of bad faith. The intention of the rule was to give every opportunity for the development of responsibility and resourcefulness on the part of the captain and of responsiveness to team-mate control, true loyalty, and team play on the part of the players.

There immediately arose a storm of favorable and unfavorable criticism concerning this radical departure from the traditional method of conducting athletic contests. Those who endorsed this reform felt that it was in harmony with the best educational philosophy. Ability to solve problems is best attained by practice in problem solving; leadership is best attained by practicing it. The domination of the coach during the contests destroyed the richest educational values of leadership, responsibility, and resourcefulness. There were some who believed that the pressure on the coach to win would be reduced with the players themselves in control of the games. There is no doubt that the standard of performance would be lowered, but both teams would be equally affected.

The opposition to this proposal was very strong, particularly among the coaches. The opponents of the reform felt that it was idealistic but impractical. They pointed to the early history of interschool sports when the faculty was forced to regulate these activities because of student mismanagement. Why abolish the coaches who have raised the standards of athletics from their poor position before the advent of the twentieth century? The coach is far better qualified to conduct athletics on a high plane than the coaches of the past have been. Another argument used against player control was that many schools, particularly the small high schools, had no student leaders who were qualified to handle this difficult assignment. Even with the coach on the bench, it is frequently difficult for the captain or team leader to control the team. Athletic contests are filled with intense emotional situations, and the responsibility upon the captain in control would be tremendous. Mistakes would be magnified by team mates, and hard feelings would be sure to result. The captain would be accused of playing friends. It is doubtful whether the captain could be entrusted with the physical welfare of team mates, although the coach or a physician on the bench could manage this.

The sentiment in favor of "Regulation One" has practically disappeared. Few, if any, schools adhere to the recommendations of this regulation today. The unlimited substitution rule in college and high school football and the rule in basketball which permits the coach to talk to the players during a time out are steps in the opposite direction. However, even though present regulations increase coach control, good coaches will continue to make every attempt to develop leadership and resourcefulness in their athletes. There never was a good team without a good leader. By developing better leaders and thinkers, the good coach is building a better team. The coach is unable to dominate every situation that occurs during the game, and with better developed player initiative and leadership, the better will these situations be met. Furthermore, the interval between halves presents the coach with a most favorable educational opportunity to inculcate the valuable lessons that can arise out of athletic competition.

Proselyting and subsidization. This is the most serious problem confronting intercollegiate athletics. Proselyting and subsidization do exist in high schools, but nowhere to the same extent as in colleges and universities. High schools are publicly supported local institutions, and the expense of attending them is very little. Furthermore, in many cities where there is more than one high school, the district in which the student lives determines the school he or she must attend. The state high school athletic associations have vigorously combated proselyting and subsidizing by passing regulations against them. But this does not mean to imply these evils do not exist in secondary schools. Financial aid is sometimes given to students who would not otherwise be able to attend high school. Considerations of various kinds are used occasionally to persuade parents to move to another community in order that their child might participate in athletics in a certain school. On the whole, however, this problem is minor in comparison to what it is in colleges and universities.

The effort to control proselyting and subsidizing of star athletes in institutions of higher learning has a long history. College administrators have opposed it for many years. College athletic conferences and associations have attempted unsuccessfully to halt the practices. The Carnegie Foundation investigation of college athletics, which culminated in its 1929 report (Bulletin No. 23), revealed a shocking disregard for the athletic codes and educational standards. However, despite this revelation the flagrant abuses have continued.

The evidence is clear that intercollegiate athletics in many institutions are permeated with hypocrisy, dishonesty, and deceit. Agreements that institutions have pledged to honor have been deliberately broken. Lack of respect for rules may be traced to an attitude of studied evasion, which amounts to a philosophy of the calculated risk. Institutional personnel, as well as alumni, have been involved in these sordid schemes against the regulations. The amazing feature about the matter is that colleges and universities are dedicated to truth, justice, honor, integrity, and other lofty virtues. Among the mottoes of American universities the word "truth" or its Latin equivalent *veritas* appears more than any other. This inconsistency in what the school is aiming to achieve and what is actually happening in athletics must be eliminated.

Three groups of individuals are primarily involved in this problem. The first is comprised of the college and university administrators. In the last analysis, the president of the institution is responsible for what happens to it. If the president has the power and is determined to have the athletic program in the school conducted in accord with the established regulations, it will be done. Many instances are available where this has been done. However, many presidents do not have the power, desire, or courage to cope with the situation. Alumni pressures, particularly, make it difficult for them to maintain desirable standards.

The coach is placed in an untenable position in many institutions. Uncertain tenure makes it imperative for the coach to win. The alumni constantly clamor for winning teams, and they are willing in many instances to supply the necessary financial assistance. The heavy financial obligations that many athletic departments have represent an additional pressure. In order to solve these problems good athletic material from high schools or junior colleges is a necessity. In this situation it is difficult for the coach not to succumb to the temptation of violating the regulations governing recruiting.

The alumni have proved the source of most of the difficulties in intercollegiate athletics. Their insistence upon winning teams has led to most of the evils which beset this program. They have been willing to spend much time and money to go after the prospects that the coaches have designated they want. Their activities have been almost impossible to control. They feel they are rendering a service to their alma mater and, at the same time, helping deserving students who could not otherwise afford to attend college. Perhaps the reason why they cannot see the wrong in violating athletic regulations is that little effort has ever been made to develop the proper attitudes among them.

Since the close of World War II the trend has been to liberalize the financial assistance given to athletes. A number of athletic conferences provide a full athletic scholarship—tuition, board, room, books, and a small amount for incidental expenses. However, with current budgetary restrictions, there is a trend toward limiting the number of athletic scholarships.

Junior High School Athletics

Perhaps the most valid argument against junior high school interscholastic athletics is that in regard to the adequacy of the resources for the instructional and intramural programs as well as the interschool program. The needs of the majority of students should be met before a varsity program is initiated.

The opponents of junior high school athletics claim that the main motivation for such teams is to prepare material for high school teams. This is an adult exploitation of the interest of students and produces unfortunate results. At the same time a program does not produce a wealth of varsity material to the same extent as a comprehensive intramural program. The limitation of squads will automatically eliminate some students who would later develop into varsity players. The phenomenon of puberty produces many amazing results, and the small, unimpressive student in the seventh grade may be an outstanding athletic prospect in the senior high school. If strong varsity teams are desired for the senior high schools, the best way to attain them is to provide a comprehensive intramural program in the junior high schools.

The proponents of junior high school athletics argue that many of the criticisms of this program are unfounded. They point out that practices are shorter, fewer games are played, and the length of games is reduced to bring the competition within the capacities of the players.

Insofar as the educational argument that the junior high school period is too early to specialize in one sport is concerned, supporters of the program point out that students have the opportunity to become acquainted with a variety of activities in the physical education class program. They also contend that only a small number of players participate in the varsity program in more than one sport.

To justify the varsity program in junior high schools it is pointed out that unless the school provides a program for the superior performers various agencies within the community will do so. Ordinarily, these agencies will not conduct the program on as high a level as the school will. It is a fact that many students participate on several different teams during the same season. The possibility of deleterious consequences of this type of competition are decidedly greater than that involved with school teams.

The academic teacher versus the physical educator as coach. The question of whether it is better to have an academic teacher rather than the physical educator do the coaching of varsity teams has been extensively debated. It is argued that if the physical educator teaches classes as he or she should, they may be devoid of the energy and the enthusiasm the coach should have. A much more serious disadvantage is the neglect on the part of physical educators of their duties in the instructional program. Because of the pressure to win and the inordinate demand upon their time, some physical educators who serve as coaches become "ball tossers" in order to devote more time to preparation for their practices.

On the other hand, the major advantage of the physical education teacher as a coach is that he or she is specifically prepared for this responsibility. There are three separate aspects of this preparation: (1)

can better appreciate the place and purposes of athletics in the total school program because of a background of the philosophy and objectives of physical education, (2) possess the physiological, anatomical, and health background necessary to protect and safeguard the health and welfare of the participants, and (3) has a much broader and more diversified preparation for the actual coaching.

The academic teacher has several advantages. Being confined to the classroom all day, this person can find a wholesome diversion that will not interfere with teaching responsibilities. The informal relationship with the students helps the academic teacher understand the students in a setting not otherwise available. It is beneficial to the morale of the school to have a number of academic teachers interested in and cooperating with the students in athletics.

The only serious disadvantage of academic teachers as coaches is that ordinarily they do not have special preparation for this assignment. To play on a varsity team in college does not constitute adequate preparation for coaching. If the school administrator were fortunate to have some academic teachers with major or minor preparation in physical education, this disadvantage would not pertain.

Several considerations are involved in providing a solution to this problem. In the first place, most administrators must use a combination of physical education and academic teachers to meet the requirement of coaches. Considering the number of sports in which competition is conducted, the necessity of having second, or junior, varsity and perhaps even freshman teams, and the desirability of having more than one coach per team in certain sports, the school administrator is hard put to provide the necessary leadership and has no other recourse but to use academic teachers.

Reducing overemphasis. Overemphasis in interschool competition is commonly seen in the heavy schedules and the overly long seasons of some teams. To reduce such overemphasis, many state athletic associations restrict both the number of games which can be scheduled in a sport and the length of the sports season. Many states set definite dates for the beginning and end of the various sports seasons. Because of the varying climatic conditions, the dates of beginning and ending of the sports seasons will differ. In most states, the football season begins on the first day of September and terminates on the Saturday after Thanksgiving. The basketball season commonly extends from the first day of December to the last day of the state basketball tournament.

Public pressures. Public pressures of various kinds are exerted upon educational administrators on both the secondary school and college and university levels when dissatisfcation develops about the interschool athletic program. Webber[3] identifies these pressure groups as:

1. Booster or Quarterback Clubs
2. Parents. In this group are those parents who are dissatisfied with the won–lost record of the team; those who have sons they feel should be playing more; and those who desire to exploit their sons' athletic ability.
3. Sports writers and announcers
4. Promoters of special events

These groups frequently assist the athletic program in a variety of ways. They may purchase and erect scoreboards, obtain additional seating capacity, provide funds for the purchase of needed athletic equipment, procure jackets for players and coaches, and arrange postseason banquets. However, Webber[4] points out some of the undesirable results of such pressure groups.

1. Overemphasis on winning
2. Public criticism of the coach
3. The use of key athletes, regardless of physical condition
4. Participation in championships or all-star games
5. Presentation of special awards to winning teams, outstanding players and successful coaches
6. Extensive publicity concentrated on a few athletes
7. Overemphasis on spectator sports

The solution to the problem of undesirable pressure groups has several facets. One of the most important of these is a clear, concise statement of athletic philosophy and the policies that will guide the conduct of the athletic program. This statement should be read annually at the first meeting of these pressure groups.

A second important consideration is the selection of the right type of coach. The coach who is selfishly interested in making a name for himself will make use of pressure groups in unacceptable ways. He can create serious problems for the institution and the athletic director by soliciting undesirable forms of assistance from outside groups. The preferred type of coach is one who is interested in the educational objectives of athletics and who subscribes completely to the athletic philosophy and policies of the school.

The athletic director and the educational administrator must stand behind the coach when criticisms come from pressure groups. Mistakes and defeats are inevitable but the solid support of the coach by his superiors will not only maintain the morale of the players and the coaching staff but will counter the undeserved judgments of critics.

The final measure to employ in dealing with pressure groups is to take the initiative in guiding their activities. They cannot be ignored. Rather than to become involved in controversy it has been found necessary to maintain good public relations with them. Meetings should be held and philosophy and policies explained. If proper rapport can be established with them such groups can become an asset rather than a liability to the athletic program.

DESIRABLE TRENDS IN ATHLETICS

There are definite trends in intercollegiate and interscholastic athletics. Athletics, as they are conducted today, are far more acceptable educationally than they were forty years ago. Some of the trends toward more educationally significant goals are pointed out below.

Increasing power of athletic associations and conferences. The state associations have gradually expanded their powers and assumed more and more control of interscholastic athletics within their jurisdiction. Their original concern was eligibility, but now their functions have broadened to include athletic insurance, officials, awards, athletic equipment, the conduct of meets and tournaments, the classification of schools, and the development of high school standards for high school students. This expansion of the powers and functions of the state associations is undoubtedly a step in the right direction. There can be no more effective agency in the state for raising the plane of interscholastic athletics to the high level upon which it should be conducted. College and high school athletic conferences may also become powerful forces for improving the standards of interschool athletics. Progress can be made only through the medium of well-organized groups.

Classifying schools and players. There is a trend toward classifying schools and players. Instead of having one state championship, a number of states are conducting tournaments for two or three types of schools, depending upon their size. This is a much more equitable method of conducting tournaments, and it has proved extremely popular. The small schools have an equal opportunity under this setup, and athletics have been stimulated in these schools. The practice of having "B" teams and lightweight teams is also an advancement over the single heavyweight team. Not only does this plan give more students an opportunity to engage in interschool athletics, but the lighter students who would have no chance to make the heavyweight team are able to obtain the benefits of competition. Educationally, the classification of schools and players is sound procedure.

Interschool athletics for all. There are many more students today who are given the advantages of intercollegiate and interscholastic athletics than ever before. In the decade of the thirties there was a trend to schedule competition in many more sports. This trend has continued for presently the National Federation of State High School Associations lists twenty-three sports in which some kind of state championship is determined in many states and thirty-six sports in which students may participate in some schools.

Increase in benefit and protection plans. State high school athletic associations have continued to improve their programs to take care of athletes who become injured in athletic competition. These plans have been so successful that they are gradually expanding in a number of ways. Not only are they providing more and better coverage to varsity athletes but they are now embracing students injured in the service and intramural programs.

Wider distribution of honors. The tendency for teams to elect co-captains and for the coach to appoint captains for different games is in contrast to the practice in the past. This is a healthy sign that the opportunities for leadership are being distributed more liberally than heretofore. Another indication of the same tendency is the large number of awards that are granted to all teams. Substitutions are made much more frequently than they have been in the past. With "B" and lightweight teams, with limitation of participation, with more frequent substitution, and with a wider variety of sports, the ideal of "athletics for all" may more nearly be approached.

Reduction in school time lost. Much greater consideration is given today to the time lost from school by athletes. Long trips are things of the past for most high schools. Intersectional games were frequent a decade ago, but they are quite exceptional today in high schools. Most state associations have adopted the policy of prohibiting postseason games of any nature. Schools are competing within their conferences and against local opponents. Emphasis on national championships has been eliminated, and there is considerable question as to the advisability of state championships.

Extra pay for coaches. The practice of paying high school coaches an additional stipend for their coaching duties developed during World War II. Agitation for extra pay arose during the war when many other teachers were able to supplement their incomes by various types of employment in the afternoons after their school duties were over. Coaches felt they were entitled to additional remuneration because in most cases the time devoted to their coaching duties was over and above a full teaching load. The great majority of interscholastic coaches are now recipients of extra pay for their coaching duties, and teachers' unions now often negotiate for extra pay for all extracurricular responsibilities assumed by teachers.

Certification of coaches. Sentiment in favor of requiring coaches to be better prepared professionally for these duties has increased rapidly. Many states require high school coaches to be certified teachers; more and more are also imposing special professional requirements. While a majority of coaches are physical education majors or minors a substantial percentage have had no preparation whatsoever for such responsibilities. It is this latter group that presents the problem. They clearly lack most of the professional qualifications for coaching.

ATHLETICS FOR GIRLS AND WOMEN

Historical Perspective

Until the latter part of the nineteenth century women's sports and athletics consisted almost exclusively of gymnastic exercise. The trend toward sports participation became apparent as several colleges instituted physical training programs involving tennis, crew, archery, croquet, bowling, track and field and basketball. The formal beginning of athletic competition for girls and women in this country came near the turn of the century. At the 1899 Conference on Physical Training, a committee was appointed to make an extensive study of the many versions of basketball played by women. The committee published "girls' rules" for basketball with special stress on standards safeguarding the health of the participants.

Basketball and field hockey were the principal sports in which intercollegiate competition was held prior to World War I. Field hockey was introduced to this country in 1901 by Constance Applebee, a player-coach from England. Individual and team merit were recognized with letters, chevrons, sweaters and trophies. However, Coffey[5] made the following point:

> As enthusiasm for girls[sic] sports spread, leadership was not always of the highest. In many cases health examinations were ignored. Thus the first seed was planted for the ever-present controversy regarding the extent of sports competition for women.

A summary of Lee's 1930 survey of intercollegiate athletics for women[6] included these two disadvantages as well as thirteen other disadvantages to participants:

> They would be apt to get more "physical straining than physical training," showing the most perhaps in nerve fatigue. . . . A question which should not be ignored is that raised by certain members of the medical profession as to the bad effect of intense athletic participation on child bearing.

In 1923 the National Amateur Athletic Federation was formed to promote physical education in educational institutions, encourage standardization of rules, facilitate the participation of United States athletes in the Olympic Games, and to foster the highest ideals of amateur sports. Mrs. Herbert Hoover assumed leadership in the girls and women's division of the Federation. This Women's Division disapproved of highly intense specialized competition. Some of their reports included concerns that men scouts were "buying up" girls for teams and that girls were fainting in basketball games from heart attacks or overstrain. The mission of this well-organized group was to encourage the promotion of sports and games for all girls and women and to establish such ideals and principles that sports and games were wisely chosen, wisely promoted and wisely supervised.

There was virtual elimination of championship competition for women in the schools in the early thirties. Lee[7] observed that, increasingly, the vast majority of physical education department directors, staff members and Women's Athletic Associations were opposed to interinstitutional competition.

During the period from 1930–1960 there was a predominance of service and intramural programs in the schools. Women physical educators used the term *extramural* to refer to competition with one or more other schools or organizations. Included in this category were (1) play days and sports days, (2) telegraphic meets, (3) invitational meets, and (4) interscholastic or intercollegiate meets. Play days and sports days represented the type of athletic competition that women developed as a substitute for intercollegiate and interscholastic sports. The women wished to avoid the abuses and defects that have characterized men's interschool competition.

A play day is defined as a day when girls from several schools or colleges meet and play with, rather than against, each other. They come together at the invitation of one of the institutions. The girls are divided into teams, each team representing no one school but a combination of all. The emphasis is on "sport for sport's sake" and "play with us and not against us." The sports day is a variation of the play day. In this type of competition, several schools meet for the day; but the teams remain intact, and the players are not interchanged as in the play day. One or more sports may be included in the program. The advantages of these two types of events are obvious. They offer opportunities for social contacts. A large number of girls can engage in a wide variety of recreational activities.

The question of interschool athletics for secondary school girls and college women has been a controversial one. Up until the last two decades most women physical educators and the women's professional organizations were united in their opposition to such competition. However, objection to vigorous exercise for women is rarely heard today, nor has scientific evidence been produced to suggest limitations.

In the late fifties it was a common opinion among school administrators and people in general that the Division for Girls and Women's Sports was opposed to competition. The 1958 revision of their standards made it clear that this was not true. Evidence suggested that the philosophy of the Division had been misinterpreted and this had limited the development of programs for the highly skilled. Ley[8] stated: ". . . in an effort to do the greatest good for the greatest number, we have emphasized intramural competition but in the process we have not provided competition of sufficient quality and quantity to satisfy the highly skilled girl."

In 1962, the Executive Council of the Division for Girls and Women's Sports committed itself to the belief that the highly skilled girl must have opportunities for competition that would satisfy her desire to excel. Careful distinctions were made between the forms of competition that were intramural in nature and those that were extramural in nature. Standards were developed for the different kinds of competition for different grade levels. According to Clifton, it was at this time that competition for the highly skilled girl was endorsed and wholeheartedly encouraged. She stated, "We have reached the point of 'no return'! Never again will our concept of girls sports be the same. Nor will it remain as we envision it today or tomorrow."[9]

Current Trends

In 1974 the Division for Girls and Women's Sports became the National Association for Girls and Women in Sports. This professional association along with its institutional membership organization, the Association for Intercollegiate Athletics for Women, and the National Federation of State High School Associations provided the framework for competitive programs for all school girls and college women. These groups develop standards and policies for competition as well as developing rules under which various sports are played.

There are three major factors which greatly affect the current revolution of sports programs for girls and women. The first is the increased knowledge of the effects of strenuous activity upon the female. Research has failed to substantiate the claims that the "weaker sex" can not withstand the strains of highly competitive athletics. Secondly, the woman has been emancipated from her role of homemaker and mother. The modern woman of today has demanded freedom from stereotyped sex roles and equal opportunity in all avenues of endeavor. The fact that longstanding myths regarding harmful effects of physical exertion have been disproved and the fact that the women's liberation movement has taken hold, together have caused an unprecedented change in the attitudes toward female participation in sports. However, the third and probably most influential factor is that federal legislation has been enacted which enhances athletic programs for girls and women in almost every school across the nation.

The document of federal legislation is Title IX of the Education Amendments Act of 1972. The basic provision of Title IX reads:[10]

> No person in the United States shall, on the basis of sex, be excluded from participation, be denied the benefits of, or be subjected to discrimination under any education program or activity receiving federal financial assistance.

This provision affects almost all educational institutions. The Department of Health, Education, and Welfare drew up guidelines for implementation of Title IX and is responsible for seeing that the guidelines are followed.

The amount of money allocated for women's athletics at some universities was multiplied ten times between the academic years of 1973–74 and 1974–75. Increasing the monies available for the women's program is the first step toward providing equal opportunity in sport. Similar actions have occurred in the secondary schools. The National Federation of State High School Associations recognized that attitudes toward girls' sports have changed. It has been acknowledged that girls demanding equal funds may modify the big budget, "win-at-any-cost" programs existing in some places for boys.

The future will bring many changes for girls' and women's sports programs. Athletic administrators will be challenged to meet the demands inherent in rapid change. The next decade will be an exciting time as young girls and women reap the benefits of sound competitive experiences which they have previously been denied. It will also be a time of change for existing programs for boys and men since cooperative efforts will be necessary to provide equal opportunities for all participants regardless of sex.

CONTROL OF WOMEN'S INTERCOLLEGIATE ATHLETICS

Control on a National Level

The Association for Intercollegiate Athletics for Women is a national organization which was formed in 1971. It is the recognized controlling body which sponsors national championships for college women. The purposes of this organization are:[11]

1. To foster broad programs of women's intercollegiate athletics which are consistent with the educational aims and objectives of the member schools and in accordance with the philosophy and standards of the DGWS.

2. To assist member schools in extending and enriching their programs of intercollegiate athletics for women based upon the needs, interests, and capacities of the individual student.

3. To stimulate the development of quality leadership for women's intercollegiate athletic programs.

4. To foster programs which will encourage excellence in performance of participants in women's intercollegiate athletics.

5. To maintain the spirit of play within competitive sport events so that the concomitant education values of such an experience are emphasized.

6. To increase public understanding and appreciation of the importance and value of sports and athletics as they contribute to the enrichment of the life of the woman.

7. To encourage and facilitate research on the effects of intercollegiate athletic competition on women and to disseminate the findings.

8. To further the continual evaluation of standards and policies for participants and programs.

9. To produce and distribute such materials as will be of assistance to persons in the development and improvement of intercollegiate programs.

10. To hold national championships and to sponsor conferences, institutes, and meetings which will meet the needs of individuals in member schools.

11. To cooperate with other professional groups of similar interests for the ultimate development of sports programs and opportunities for women.

270

12. To provide direction and maintain a relationship with AIAW regional organizations.

13. To conduct such other activities as shall be approved by the governing body of the association.

The rapid expansion of women's athletics is evidenced by the unbelievable growth of this organization. Membership in the Association for Intercollegiate Athletics is voluntary, however an institution must belong to be eligible for national championships. In 1976 a total of 826 institutions were members. During this same year a junior college division was created and the development of a small college division was being considered.

The Executive Board is made up of the following officers: Presidents (Past, Present and Elect), Treasurer, Chairperson of Ethics and Eligibility, Commissioner of Four Year National Championships, and Commissioner of Two Year National Championships as well as representatives from the nine geographical regions of the association, the Junior College Division and the National Association for Girls and Women in Sports.

The Delegate Assembly, which is composed of one voting faculty representative from each member institution, is the legislative body of the association. This group meets annually to respond to the business of the association and to act on recommendations presented by the Executive Board.

In just the short period of its existence, the Association for Intercollegiate Athletics for Women has done a great deal to enhance quality athletic competition for the college woman. Currently it sponsors championships in badminton, basketball, golf, gymnastics, swimming and diving, track and field, and volleyball. There are both small college (under 3,000) and junior college/community college championships in several sports. Major efforts have been made toward establishing regulations for awarding financial aid and toward approving eligibility requirements for member institutions.

Through participation in Association for Intercollegiate Athletics for Women's (AIAW) National Championships, outstanding women athletes are considered for possible participation in international competition, in particular, for the World University Games. There are AIAW representatives who serve on committees of the United States Collegiate Sports Council and assist at selection and training camps. The AIAW holds a powerful political position since it is the only organization sponsoring national collegiate championships for women.

The purpose of the AIAW Code of Ethics, adopted in 1974, is to provide a means of assisting personnel and students to identify ethical conduct in intercollegiate sports and to encourage those involved to pursue actions which are appropriate. There are separate codes for coaches, players, administrators, officials and spectators. The codes serve to act as guides for acceptable behavior rather than enforceable rules of conduct.

During the first two years of AIAW, the organization did not allow athletic scholarships. The major reason for this ruling was that the founders of the association deplored the evils of pressure recruiting and performer exploitation which frequently accompany the administration of financial aid for athletes. Under pressure from pending legal action, the ruling was changed by a vote of the membership. A very strict document defining the regulations for awarding financial aid was adopted in 1974. Some of the practices currently followed in men's athletics such as paid recruiters, subsidized visits of prospective athletes and funds for books and tutoring services are not allowed by the women.

Regional Control of Women's Athletics

Each of the nine geographical regions of the Association for Intercollegiate Athletics for Women has its own executive and legislative bodies. The regions function independently of one another. Two regions were well-structured before the national association came into existence. However, most regions have developed under the guidance of the AIAW in order to meet national requirements for participation in championships.

The structural pattern of regional organizations varies considerably. Some regions have state associations within them while others do not. In one region an institution must first join the state organization and then the entire state joins the regional association. Within some regions there are established conferences for regulating competition between like-minded institutions.

Regional qualifying events are held in basketball, gymnastics and volleyball in order to determine teams for the national championship. In order to participate in these qualifying events an institution must belong to both the regional organization and the AIAW. However, national membership is not required before joining the regional organization. Most regions support a variety of activities which are not related to national championships.

Local Control of Women's Athletics

What has been written previously in this chapter regarding local control of intercollegiate athletics certainly is relevant to women's athletics. The most important control rests within the institution itself. The organizational patterns which exist number almost as many as there are institutions. The explosion of women's athletics on college and university campuses has been so rapid that there has been little time to develop standard organizational patterns which have been proven effective in various institutions.

Administratively, the Women's Intercollegiate Athletic program may be housed in the Physical Education Department, the Intramural Department, the former "Men's" Athletic Department or in any other unit which may be appropriate for the individual institution. The University committee which originally was charged with advising the President on matters pertaining to men's intercollegiate athletics may now have the additional concern of women's athletics. Some institutions have created a women's athletic board or advisory council to serve as the policy-making body on matters pertinent to women's athletics.

These committees may include coaches assigned to the women's program and the athletic administrator. At the present time, the majority of coaches have faculty status which is not true of most coaches in men's athletics. Some institutions have student-athlete representatives as well as faculty members not involved in the athletic program on their decision-making body. The kind of committee, its purposes and responsibilities, varies from institution to institution.

CONTROL OF INTERSCHOLASTIC ATHLETICS FOR GIRLS

Control on the National Level

Much of what has been written previously in this chapter related to control of interscholastic athletics applies to both the boys' and girls' programs. The National Federation of State High School Associations administers all programs on the national level. This group regulates interstate competitive events, recommends minimum eligibility requirements and publishes rules for interscholastic sports. Until the National Federation began publishing rules for girls in 1970, the major source of rules was the Division for Girls and Women's Sports.

Control of Interscholastic Athletics by State High School Athletic Associations

Interscholastic athletics for girls has not been under the control of state high school athletic associations for very many years. Most of the competitive programs for secondary school girls developed out of interest from women physical educators within the state and thus became the concern of the state's physical education professional association and its Division for Girls and Women's Sports. This state organization had committees to direct girls' sports programs. It followed existing guidelines developed by the national Division for Girls and Women's Sports; however, the state group had little power to enforce guidelines or establish rules and regulations. In most states, the first state tournaments were completely under the direction of the Division for Girls and Women's Sports rather than the state high school athletic association.

More recently, with the growing surge of competitive programs for girls, many of these programs have come under the auspices of the state athletic association. Thus only one structure sets policies, makes decisions, and controls interscholastics at the state level. The functions and financing of state associations are clearly defined earlier in this chapter. In some states there is direct input from the Division for Girls' and Women's Sports into the board of control for the state association.

Perhaps the biggest issue affecting state control of girls' programs is the decision as to which set of rules shall be used in competitive events. Some states follow the directive from the National Federation that their rules are to be used, while other states have allowed the women leaders in the state physical education association to decide which rules would be best for the participants. Many states use Division for Girls and Women's Sports rules until state tournaments come into existence. Then the state high school athletic association dictates that federation rules must be used. The battles over differing sets of rules have caused much concern throughout the country. Hopefully the differences of opinions will not hinder the quality of programs available for girls.

Local Administration of Interscholastic Athletics for Girls

The athletic programs for boys and girls fall under the same administration at the local level. Superintendents, principals, and athletic directors provide the leadership which guides the competitive programs. It is the athletic director who ensures that policies established by the state association and the National Federation are followed. The director is immediately responsible to the principal for the entire conduct of the interscholastic program. Women coaches follow administrative policies that men coaches have used for many years.

SELECTED REFERENCES

Administration of Athletics in Colleges and Universities. Washington, D.C.: AAHPER, 1971.

COOK, TIFF E., and CATHARINE L. BROWN, *Organizational and Administrative Problems in Physical Education, Intramurals and Athletics.* Dubuque, Iowa: Kendall/Hunt Publishing Company, 1972.

DEATHERAGE, DOROTHY and C. PATRICIA REID, *Administration of Women's Competitive Sports.* Dubuque, Iowa: Wm. C. Brown Company Publishers, 1977.

FORSYTHE, CHARLES E., and IRVIN A. KELLER, *Administration of High School Athletics*, 6th ed. Englewood Cliffs, N.J.: Prentice-Hall, Inc., 1977.

HUNSICKER, PAUL, ed., *Administrative Theory and Practice in Athletics and Physical Education.* Chicago, Ill.: The Athletic Institute, 1973.

NOTES

1. National Federation of State High School Associations, *Handbook: 1976–77* (Elgin, Ill.), p. 9.

2. The National Collegiate Athletic Association administers a group insurance program whereby member colleges can provide catastrophe medical coverage for athletes injured in practice, play, or transport. This plan provides coverage only for very serious injuries which require unusually heavy medical expense.

3. Robert Webber, "Public Pressures and Their Effect on Athletes," *Bulletin of the National Association of Secondary School Principals,* Vol. 44, No. 256 (May, 1960).

4. Webber, "Public Pressures."

5. Margaret A. Coffey, "The Sportswomen, Then and Now," *Journal of Health, Physical Education and Recreation,* (February 1965), p. 39.

6. Mabel Lee, "The Case For and Against Intercollegiate Athletics for Women and the Situation Since 1923", *Research Quarterly* (May 1931), pp. 96–97.

7. Lee, "The Case."

8. Katherine Ley, "Interscholastic Athletics for Girls", (Paper presented at the National Conference on Secondary School Athletic Administration, December, 1962, Washington, D.C.), p. 10.

9. Marguerite Clifton, "Expanding Horizons in DGWS," (paper presented at the Northwest Association for Health, Physical Education and Recreation Convention, March 1964, Spokane, Washington), p. 1.

10. Office of the Federal Registrar, Department of Health, Education and Welfare, "Summary Statement for Nondiscrimination on the Basis of Sex Under Education Programs and Activities Receiving or Benefiting from Federal Financial Assistance" (Washington, D.C., June 18, 1974), p. 2.

11. Judith R. Holland, editor. *AIAW Handbook of Policies and Operating Procedures 1974–75* (Washington, D.C., American Alliance for Health, Physical Education, and Recreation, 1974), pp. 8–9.

12

Related Programs

A close relationship exists between physical education and numerous other fields. Some programs, such as health education and recreation education, were at one time considered to be part of the discipline called physical education. As these fields developed a unique body of knowledge and required specially prepared professionals, they separated from physical education organizationally and became separate disciplines. This was an important step as each program requires unique skills. There remains a close relationship between health education and physical education even though the two fields are separate. This relationship is succinctly presented in Chapter 9. Recreation maintains a similar close relationship with physical education. Skills learned in physical education are used in all forms of recreation and the attitudinal and social objectives of both fields are complementary. Recreation, whether it be classified therapeutic, community, industrial, commercial, urban, or outdoor, makes use of physical education competencies and serves as another channel for attaining the intellectual, emotional, social, and physical goals shared by these two disciplines.

The distinctiveness of the field of recreation is manifest through its uniqueness of purpose in providing innumerable creative and constructive forms that will provide meaningful leisure activities for people of all ages.

Physical education also relates to many other disciplines. Joint efforts with teachers of different subjects have proved to be mutually beneficial. Motor development is an important ingredient in reading and writing readiness. Mathematical and spelling skills can be taught through movement education. Significant learning experiences occur when combining movement with music activities. Physical education dances can be used in history and social studies units covering different cultures. A biology unit on exercise can be effectively related to what occurs in a physical education class. The alert physical education teacher will be able to correlate physical education activities at some time or other with almost every other subject in the school. This is one of the strengths of physical education and serves a twofold purpose. It helps other people to better understand physical education and by using a correlated educational program provides a better learning atmosphere for the students.

There are numerous other programs related to physical education. Sometimes these programs are found under the physical education umbrella in our schools and at other times they are organizationally separate or are found in the community.

OUTDOOR EDUCATION

Outdoor education is not a separate discipline. It is a vehicle for learning. Through outdoor settings and experiences children are able to learn better than when being limited to the indoors. Outdoor education makes use of the natural environment to assist in learning and emphasizes first hand experiences. Outdoor education does not supplant classroom experiences, but cultivates and complements the indoor educational experiences. Certain aspects of every subject can be taught more effectively by using the out-of-doors.

Outdoor education takes many forms. One form is available to almost every teacher. This is the out-of-doors that exists just outside the school door. A good teacher will make use of the school yard, a nearby park or other recreational area on a regular basis to enrich the lessons that are being taught. An outdoor setting can provide a laboratory situation for most curricular areas and is ideally suited for the study of natural sciences and social studies. School sites should be designed with outdoor education in mind. A well-designed school site is pictured in Figure 12-1. It should be remembered that components of this excellent outdoor education setting are present or can be developed on many existing school sites.

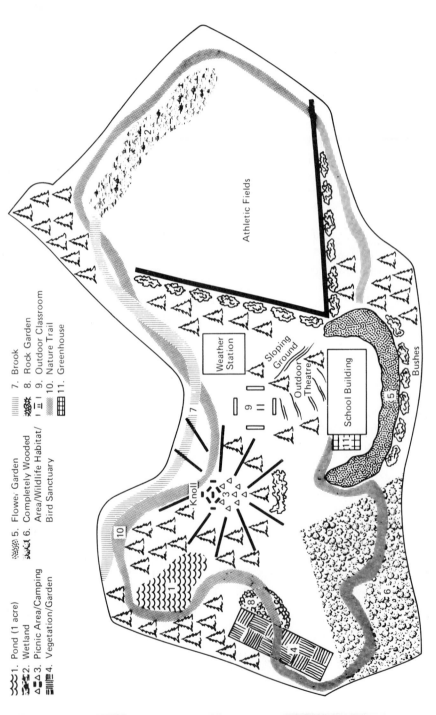

1. Pond (1 acre)
2. Wetland
3. Picnic Area/Camping
4. Vegetation/Garden
5. Flower Garden
6. Completely Wooded Area/Wildlife Habitat/ Bird Sanctuary
7. Brook
8. Rock Garden
9. Outdoor Classroom
10. Nature Trail
11. Greenhouse

Athletic Fields

Weather Station

Sloping Ground

Outdoor Theatre

School Building

Bushes

Knoll

Figure 12-1. School Site Designed for Outdoor Education. (Designed by Elizabeth Wishna and Joyce Lykes.)

Possible Uses of the Outdoor Education School Site Diagrammed in Figure 12-1.

1. School building—basic school work, laboratories, places to store materials found and used in the outdoors.

2. 3. Water areas—including a pond and wetlands. To acquaint students with waterlife, pollution, and to teach swimming and boating skills.

4. Camping area and picnic sites—for overnight camping experiences to learn the art of outdoor cooking and living.

5. Athletic fields—crafts, sports and recreational activities.

6. 7. Horticultural areas—(gardens, lawns, vegetation and shrubs). Develop skills and knowledge related to home gardens, soil problems, seeds, fertilization, plants and plant families, etc.

8. Wooded areas—principles of tree growth, identification of trees, animals, birds, and insects (a wildlife habitat and bird sanctuary), survival techniques, edible foods and plants, compass and map work.

9. Brook—provides information about origin, flow and problems of rivers. Opportunity to study plant and animal life found in streams.

10. Weather station—study weather, atmosphere, wind direction, temperature, astronomy, etc.

11. Rock garden—identification of rocks and minerals.

12. Outdoor classroom—study of outdoors as related to classroom activities.

13. Outdoor theater.

14. Nature trail—throughout the entire site—to observe and develop an appreciation for the wonders of nature.

15. Greenhouse—observe seedlings, germination, growth of plants inside.

Day trips are also used effectively for outdoor education puposes. In some communities these might be walking trips. It is more common to use buses to travel to some site that is related to the subject that is being taught. The site might be a geological formation, a forest area, a historical setting, a waterfront or any number of other types of areas that will make the classroom instruction come alive.

Residential camping is another form of outdoor education that has been enthusiastically endorsed by schools where it has been integrated into a comprehensive outdoor education program. In the typical residential camp, children have the opportunity to live for an extended period of time (usually one or two weeks) in an outdoor environment. Students and teachers share learning experiences related to many areas of the curriculum. The camp experience serves as a focal point for school activities both before and after the time spent at the camp. In addition to the results directly related to the curriculum, residential camping establishes a significant personal relationship between teacher and pupil. Valuable concepts and understandings associated with our natural resources and living in the out of doors become a part of the children's lives. The incidental learnings are as important a feature of residential camping as is the planned instruction.

Some school districts own their own camps and children are sent to the camp on a rotating basis throughout the year. Failure to own a camp should not prevent a school district from implementing a residential camping program. Many federal, state, and regional facilities are available to schools at a nominal cost and private camp facilities can be rented. Private organizations have come into existence as a result of the growth of outdoor education programs. These organizations provide outdoor education experiences for students on a fee basis. They usually have a variety of offerings and will come to the school or provide an outdoor education experience through a residential camp or tent camping. The length of time devoted to these experiences depends on the desired outcomes and the types of experiences that are provided for the students.

Outward Bound

The first Outward Bound school was established in England in 1941. Since that time it has expanded to other countries and has found acceptance by people from many walks of life. The emphasis of this program is on character training and is based on the premise that putting a person in a challenging situation will positively affect reactions to subsequent situations that are encountered. Each Outward Bound school in the United States provides a unique type of physical challenge. Some aspect of the environment, whether it be a climatic condition or geography of the area, is used to provide a personal challenge to the participants. Emphasis is placed on such skills as mountaineering, rock climbing, white water canoeing and snow camping.

Several programs patterned after Outward Bound have come into existence. Their aims are similar. Participants are expected to gain a greater understanding of themselves by experiencing challenging situations that they must overcome individually or as a member of a group. Group work and problem solving are heavily emphasized. The intent is to develop not only personal skills but a spirit of cooperativeness with others. Many problems that are presented can be solved only by joint efforts.

Personal growth and social awareness are additional objectives of these programs. Participants find out that they are capable of doing much more than they thought they could do. Increased self-confidence and the ability to relate positively to others are important outcomes.

Orienteering

This activity had its origin in Sweden. Due to its success there, it soon became a favorite activity in Norway and Finland also. It is now popular in many European countries and has spread to North America. Orienteering has been incorporated into some outdoor education programs on this continent, particularly the residential camping aspect of these programs. The potential for orienteering is enormous and it is anticipated that it will dramatically increase in popularity.

Orienteering was started to encourage young people to make use of forests for physical and mental enjoyment. The intent was to use the natural environment to stimulate youth to do more running. Courses were established through whatever terrain was available and by the use of a map and compass, participants traversed the course.

Orienteering has become very competitive and yet it provides an opportunity for all ages and all levels of ability. The length of the course and the choice of terrain can be changed to provide a challenging activity for everyone, regardless of their competence. Age group competition and divisions based on skill equalizes competition in orienteering events. There is a personal challenge present which allows a person to enjoy orienteering even though the individual times of competitors might vary considerably.

Orienteering puts a premium on map and compass reading. There are usually six to ten control points which must be passed in a designated order. In addition to the challenge of correctly determining the location of the control points, the competitors should search out the best route to reach the control points. Sometimes this will be a direct route. At other times a detour to miss obstacles such as a swamp or a steep hill will be the best procedure to follow. The route to follow will differ from person to person. A fast runner might choose a longer path which has more open area in which to run whereas a slower contestant might use a more direct route which will allow better use of other talents such as the ability to negotiate rock outcroppings.

Orienteering provides a mental as well as a physical challenge. Its adaptability to all ages and skill levels has made it a very popular activity for those who have experienced the exhilaration provided by the physical demands of the sport. An important added dimension is the premium that is placed on the map reading and compass skills that are required to be successful.

Athletic Training

During the early years of interschool athletics, all athletic training was handled by the coaches. This was not a satisfactory arrangement for several reasons. Coaching responsibilities interfered with the time that was needed to properly care for injuries. In many cases insufficient attention was paid to the preventative aspects of athletic injuries. An added concern was the lack of preparation of many coaches to properly handle athletic training responsibilities. The athletic training field developed in response to the obvious need for well-prepared people who could devote their full attention to the safety aspects of interschool competition.

Athletic trainers have been an integral part of college and university athletic programs for many years. Secondary schools have just as great a need for qualified trainers and, although provision for athletic trainers has been slow in developing in many areas of the country, there are numerous schools that do employ qualified athletic trainers. It is encouraging to note that there is a strong effort throughout the physical education and athletic profession to meet the goal of having a qualified athletic trainer in every school that has an interschool athletic program.

The National Athletic Trainers' Association (NATA) has assumed an important leadership role in establishing standards for certification as an athletic trainer. The general requirements include the following:

1. Minimum of a bachelor's degree.

2. Work experience in athletic training.

3. Minimum of one year's membership in the National Athletic Trainers' Association.

4. Letters of recommendation from a NATA certified athletic trainer and acting team physician.

5. Successful completion of a written, oral and practical examination.

6. Proof of certification in Standard First Aid and CPR (or equivalent).

The work experience can be obtained through an approved athletic training curriculum available at various colleges and universities. A minimum of two years of experience under the direct supervision of NATA-approved supervisors is required in these curricula. Other work experience alternatives are an apprenticeship of 1800 hours or five years of athletic training experience or two years' experience in athletic training for a physical therapy graduate.

A strong feature of this certification program is a continuing education requirement for continued certification.

Physical Therapy

Physical therapy is a branch of medical science and is related to several areas of physical education. Good developmental physical education programs make extensive use of the skills of physical therapists. Physical therapy is also used for rehabilitation following athletic injuries. Physical therapy uses therapeutic exercise, massage, ultrasound, water, light, electricity, heat and cold in the treatment of disabilities.

Schools of physical therapy are part of either universities or hospitals and have affiliations with health care facilities to provide practical experience. Students desirous of entering a school of physical therapy after completing their bachelor's degree should request materials from the physical therapy schools to which they plan to apply. They will then know the courses that are required for entrance and can include them in their undergraduate program. A few educational institutions have programs that permit students to major in physical therapy as an undergraduate.

School/Community Recreation

One of the integral aspects of the community school concept has been joint endeavors by the school and community to provide recreational opportunities for community residents. Combined efforts in providing recreational activities have traditionally been present in communities even when other phases of a community school such as educational and social services have received only minimal attention. A major advantage of this approach is the reduction of program and administrative overlap and duplication. Better use is made of facilities since school facilities can be used for community recreation during times when they would otherwise be idle. The tax dollar can be stretched further and thereby provide better recreational services for the community.

Improved facilities for both school and community use are possible because construction funds can be allocated where they are most needed and will not be spent for facilities that will have duplicating functions. More effective use of the available facilities is also a strength of school/community recreation programs.

School/community recreation has the potential to provide broad recreational programs that will be more comprehensive than would be possible if the community recreation department operates as a separate entity. Better use is made of staff and administrative resources and concentration can be placed on developing superior physical education and recreation programs that support and complement each other.

Whether the community's recreation program is administered separately or as part of a school board's responsibility, a close working agreement should be established to mutually benefit both the recreation department and the school system. Milwaukee, Wisconsin is an outstanding example of the latter administrative arrangement. The Division of Municipal Recreation and Adult Education is responsible to the Board of Education. This recreation program has gained world wide recognition and provides ample evidence that school/community recreation programs can be an important factor in improving the "quality of life" of the members of the community.

SELECTED REFERENCES

BENNETT, IAN C., "A Model for Planning and Operating Physical Education/ recreation Facilities Based upon Community Education Ideology," unpublished Ph.D. dissertation, University of Oregon, 1975.

DISLEY, JOHN, *Orienteering*. Harrisburg, Pa.: Stackpole Books, 1973.

SMITH, JULIAN W., *Outdoor Education*. Englewood Cliffs, N.J.: Prentice-Hall, Inc., 1972.

three

Administrative Responsibilities

13

The Physical Education Plant

NEED FOR FAMILIARITY WITH THE PROBLEM

There are very few principles of physical education administration that have been less adequately applied than have those which deal with the planning and construction of buildings to house the program. The large number of inadequate physical education buildings, even on university campuses, is material evidence of this fact. Several factors have contributed to this condition. One of the most significant has been the practice of copying a building in a neighboring city or state, mistakes and good points alike. This practice has been employed because it has proved to be temporarily less troublesome than making a survey of local conditions, studying trends and innovations in building construction, and evaluating the effect of different types of construction on the educational goals of the community before starting to build. Another factor has been a change in educational philosophy and a consequent shift in emphasis from a formal program to a program which encompasses community needs as well as varied school activities. This type of program requires extensive building flexibility which tends to make many of our present facilities obsolete. In some situations there has been an unwillingness on the part of those in authority to seek and utilize the advice of informed staff members, and in other circumstances physical education people have been unable to advise judiciously when consulted.

Wise and efficient planning and construction of a physical education plant can prevent many administrative, financial, and functional difficulties. Elimination of permanent seats in the gymnasium will increase space insofar as the physical education program is concerned; well-placed activity rooms will make supervision relatively easy; properly recessed radiators will reduce the number of accidents; reduction of unnecessary hall space will save money; properly placed drinking fountains and lavatories will make the building a more efficient service unit; properly sloped cement floors will be easier to clean; a sloping roof will shed water much better than a flat one; louver-type windows will provide good ventilation, even in rainy weather; cement locker bases will make the cleaning of the locker room easier, and the concentration of shower, lavatories, and drinking fountains in a comparatively small area will reduce the plumbing bill. Any effort spent in planning will pay large dividends in the future to those who are responsible for the physical education unit. It is not satisfactory to leave all matters of arrangment to the architect who will not have the background of a competent physical educator. Architects have been much maligned for physical education construction errors and inadequacies. This is frequently unfair since reputable architects request information to guide them in planning a facility. They want to know the educational goals, the activities that will be included to attain the goals, the number of teaching stations that will be needed and other information that will assist them in designing a functional building. Problems do occur when sufficient guidance is not provided. This frequently happens when the school board, board of trustees or appointed administrative officers do not establish a construction plan that permits sufficient input from the physical education faculty or designated committee. Unfortunately, the fault sometimes lies with the physical education faculty when they fail to thoroughly determine needs and do not provide information in sufficient depth to adequately guide the architect. It is erroneous to assume that architects and engineers are in a position to keep abreast of all new concepts, designs and materials relative to physical education facilities. The physical education faculty must share in this responsiblity.

It is the responsiblity of the physical education administrator to make sure that adequate planning is done for the new facility. Due to the magnitude of this task, all staff members should be involved in the planning. The needs and requirements of the department must be projected for the life of the building. The building plan should include a detailed listing of the various areas required—gymnasiums, special activity areas, classrooms, conference rooms, swimming pool, offices, locker and shower areas, home and visiting team rooms, supply room, training room, storage facilities, and the like—with their dimensions and desirable features indicated.

It is particularly important that the administrator be familiar with the up-to-date literature relating to the specific facility being contemplated: there are many instances where administrators have been very influential in getting a better facility because of their knowledge. When a major new facility is being planned the administrator should visit outstanding facilities, preferably accompanied by the architect, with the aim of getting ideas for the best facility for the available funds.

The planning process is of critical importance. As a first step, the need for a new facility must be clearly established. The need must be based on factors such as departmental philosophy, educational goals, student interests, community use and future projections. The community must be involved in the planning, and the physical education facility must be an integral part of the school or campus master plan. Selection of the project architect is a critical step and should follow guidelines established by the administrative unit that is responsible for the building. As a minimum, the architect's professional status should be determined, examples of previously designed buildings should be inspected, areas of specialization analyzed and references from previous clients required. It is also important to determine the architect's interest and experience in designing a physical education facility.

The physical education faculty should be actively involved in providing pertinent information during the architectural design stages. Input during the pre-design planning provides the basic information needed by the architect to design the building. Careful analyses and suggestions must continue during the schematic design and design development stages which lead to the construction documents. These final documents should also be viewed carefully for possible errors.

Importance of Teaching Stations

For nearly a century physical education has been plagued by the lack of facilites which has led to the curtailment of the physical education program in a variety of ways. The shortage of teaching stations has resulted in a time allotment of two or three days per week instead of daily, and in a reduction of the number of years that a student enrolls in physical education. Programs of intramural/recreational activities and inter-scholastic programs have also frequently been inadequate mainly because sufficient facilites are unavailable.

The total number of teaching stations required depends upon:

1. Number of students
2. Number of days per week the program is required

3. Number of years program is required
4. Class size
5. Nature of the program
6. Number of periods in the school day
7. The climate in the area
8. The requirements of the intramural and interschool programs

The number of teaching stations required in a school can readily be determined by the following formula:

$$\frac{N \times p}{P \times n} = \text{Teaching Stations}$$

N = Total number of students enrolled at the institution
p = Number of required class meetings per week
P = Total number of periods per week that each teaching station is available
n = Number of students per class

As an example, 12 teaching stations would be needed if a high school had a student enrollment of 2400 students, each student had physical education five days per week, the average class size was 30, and there were 35 periods per week when each teaching station was available.

$$\frac{N \times p}{P \times n} = \frac{2400 \times 5}{35 \times 30} = \frac{12,000}{1,050} = 11.4$$

It should be remembered that the above formula does not provide for future growth when current enrollment figures are used nor does it accurately depict intramural/recreational activity or interscholastic athletic needs. The formula provides the minimum number of teaching stations that are needed. More will be needed if specialized teaching stations such as a fencing room and gymnastic areas are not used for all class periods during the week. Scheduling flexibility also necessitates more than the absolute minimum number of teaching stations. Outdoor teaching stations should not be included in the calculations unless the school is located in a geographical area where outdoor stations can be used the year around. In a majority of schools in the country the total number of teaching stations required must be provided in the indoor facilities because the outdoor teaching stations cannot be used during the winter months. If the outdoor facilities can be used throughout the year a smaller number of indoor teaching stations are required.

Sufficient space must be provided for intramural and inter-scholastic/intercollegiate programs during the peak after school and evening hours. The scope of the program will determine the number of stations that are needed to provide practice and game facilities for athletics and areas for intramural/recreational activities. A location will be needed for each activity that will be using the facility during the highest usage period.

INDOOR PHYSICAL EDUCATION FACILITIES

The trend in the construction of indoor physical education facilities is to provide a large area that can be used for a variety of activities. Synthetic surfaces, improved acoustical engineering and technological advances in designing movable and retractable bleachers and equipment have been important factors in making this a desirable approach. In some situations it has been found best to have specialized teaching stations for activities such as combatives, gymnastics, weight training, dance, correctives and fencing. The flexibility of a large central activities area makes it possible for these types of activities to also be included in the multi-purpose design if that is desired. Swimming pools, bowling lanes, four wall handball, squash, and paddleball courts are examples of teaching stations that must be designed as a separate entity. Flexibility and multi-purpose use are key considerations in facility designs for physical education facilities that will meet changing needs during the life of the building and provide the best return for the money that is expended.

Field House-Arena-Activity Center

These are all terms that are used to describe physical education buildings that are characterized by a large central activity center designed to provide for multi-use. Multiple markings on the floor surface, easily moveable equipment and bleachers and retractable nets are examples of features that make it possible to use facilities such as these for classes, intramurals, athletics, recreation, and a variety of community functions. The size of the facility will be determined by the number of classes and kinds of activities that will be using it.

The Main Gymnasium

Some facilities are designed using the main gymnasium concept. The number and kind of teaching stations that are needed determine the size of the gymnasium. Consideration must also be given to the number of seats that will be needed for spectator events. This type of building does not provide the flexibility that is found in buildings that have large central activity areas. However, the incorporation of synthetic surfaces, folding bleachers, swing up basketball backboards, and similar innovations permits much more flexiblity and can make this type of construction satisfactory for a physical education program.

Courts for badminton and volleyball are invariably laid out in the main gymnasium in addition to those for basketball. It is desirable to plan for sufficient courts to handle a class of appropriate size. An instructor can handle 36 students adequately on three volleyball courts. If there are only two courts for 24 students it is obvious that the instructional cost is appreciably greater.

It may be necessary to conduct fencing, dancing, wrestling, and gymnastics in the main gymnasium. However, separate areas for these activities are preferable. This is particularly true of gymnastics and wrestling, which require specialized equipment that must be moved both before and after class. If separate rooms are not provided for these activities storage space for the equipment must be provided in the main gymnasium.

There is a difference of opinion in the profession about the need for folding partitions to divide a large area into two or more separate teaching stations. For some activities and in some teaching situations partitions are valuable. The improvement in acoustical engineering, the use of the gymnasium for activities requiring many different dimensions, and the fact that there is no longer a "girls' side" and "boys' side" of the gymnasium have made partitions much less important. Nets have also been used effectively for partitions and provide desired safety by preventing loose equipment from going into other teaching stations. If folding partitions are used, they should extend from floor to ceiling and move on an overhead track. The partitions should be electrically operated with an automatic shut-off feature if anyone or anything contacts the moving partition. They should be recessed when closed and should be insulated in order that sound is not transmitted from teaching station to teaching station. The doors should be sturdy enough so that balls may be thrown against them by students practicing various skills.

Some schools have combined a gymnasium with an auditorium or cafeteria. This practice never works out satisfactorily. Conflicts in the use of the area inevitably occur. The combination appears attractive from the standpoint of economy, but over a period of years more satisfactory results are obtained from a separate gymnasium.

Auxiliary Gymnasium

A large number of high schools and colleges and universities find it necessary to construct an auxiliary gymnasium when they construct only a main gymnasium. This is a multi-purpose area and can be used for a variety of activites such as fencing, dancing, calisthenics, games of low organization, tumbling, badminton, and volleyball. Such a facility is frequently used for intramural and recreational activities when the main gymnasium is occupied by the varsity squads.

Wrestling Room

This room should be a minimum of 40′ × 80′ which will provide space for two 40′ × 40′ wrestling mats. The walls should be matted to a height of 6 feet. Proper ventilation is of prime importance. Direct access through double doors should be provided to the area where wrestling meets will be held if bleachers are not available in the wrestling area.

Gymnastic Room

This activity probably requires more equipment than any other phase of the physical education or athletic program. It is highly desirable to have a permanent area available for gymnastics so equipment will not continually have to be put up and taken down. This not only is important from the standpoint of time, but the longevity of the equipment and the safety of the participants is increased when equipment can be left in one position.

If possible, bleachers should be available in the gymnastic area so the equipment will not have to be moved for competition. The equipment should be placed so that it is possible to have women's and men's teams practice simultaneously and even have gymnastic meets scheduled at the same time if this is desired.

Dance Studio

It is difficult to develop a first class dance program without a specialized dance facility. The studio should be approximately 60′ × 100′ for class purposes. The floor should have appropriate resiliency, be non-slippery and constructed for easy cleaning. Specialized equipment such as mirrors, ballet barres, lighting for performances, and sound equipment should be designed expressly for the dance studio.

Other Specialized Areas

Available funds and activities emphasized in a particular community will often determine whether other specialized areas will be provided. The administrator should utilize faculty and community experts, recommendations found in the literature, and follow established standards when making recommendations for the design of a specialized facility.

Storage

Storage space must be planned just as thoroughly as teaching stations since faculty effectiveness is influenced significantly by the size and organization of storage areas. A central storage area for small equipment is recommended for tight control and efficiency in issuing equipment. Larger storage rooms should be located adjacent to teaching stations that have specialized equipment which must be stored after class or at the end of each day. Much teacher and student time will be wasted when storage areas are inadequate and/or poorly planned.

Location of Building

Accessibility for students and community members must be considered when constructing a physical education facility. The facility should be an integral part of the school design and yet be placed so it can be used without disrupting other parts of the academic program. Specialized areas should be available without opening the entire facility or school building.

The concept of integrating physical education into the overall educational plan is innovatively done at Brookdale Community College in Lincroft, New Jersey. The campus design provides a fitness center, open 12 hours per day, situated in the academic complex to encourage students to view physical activity as an integral part of their life. This concept is worthy of emulation by schools at all levels.

The deciding factor in the location of many elementary and secondary schools is the accessibility to outdoor physical education facilities. In recent years the trend has been for school districts and community recreation departments to work out arrangements for joint use of facilities. Such arrangements have resulted in many more physical education areas than would otherwise have been possible. Likewise, the school facilities are available for use by recreation departments during the after-school hours. Such joint planning benefits everyone in the community. Availability of parking space must also be considered when athletic events catering to spectators are to be scheduled in the facilities.

Room Dimensions

The size, shape, and height of rooms will vary according to the purposes for which they will be used; consequently, it is not possible to determine the optimum dimensions without knowing the local conditions that will affect them. Too large a room is proportionately more expensive in terms of the service it can render per unit cost. An idle, enclosed space represents an unwarranted financial burden. Then, too, more teaching stations can be provided if the enclosed space is broken into smaller units. Odd-shaped, many-sided rooms with projections are costly to construct and are limited in their uses; consequently, they should be eliminated as much as possible in the planning.

Each room should have sufficient height of ceiling to accommodate the activities that are to take place in it. Any additional height is unnecessary and costly, and any reduction in desirable height cramps the activity program. The recommended standards for gymnasium ceiling heights are: elementary schools, 20 feet (if the gymnasium is to be used by the recreation department the ceiling height should be raised to 22 feet), junior high schools, 22 feet; senior high schools, 22 to 24 feet. Locker, shower, and classrooms need not be more than 10 to 12 feet in height.

Traffic Control

One of the common mistakes in gymnasium construction is the failure to make adequate provisions for the circulation of the various individuals who will use the facilities. The main objectives in planning for traffic circulation are:[1]

1. Providing for minimum travel distances.
2. Reducing travel congestion.
3. Minimizing the disturbance of classwork.
4. Increasing the comfort and safety of occupants.
5. Providing ease of supervision and desirable separation.
6. Providing for connections to future additions.

In planning for traffic control a flow chart should be prepared to show the movement of all the different types of individuals who will be involved with the facility. While students will be the main users, consideration must also be given to spectators at athletic contests and intramural events, as well as to various groups under the auspices of the recreation department who will use the facilities in the evenings and during the summer months. In addition, consideration must be given to personnel who deliver supplies, equipment, and laundry.

Materials and Construction

The funds available, the materials at hand, the use to which the constructed part is to be put, the attitude of the community toward types of construction and materials, and the work force available at the time will largely determine the quality and type of material and construction that will contribute to each finished unit in the building. If funds are ample and the community desires to use them, there can be relatively great freedom of choice in materials and construction. However, most communities must build economically, if at all, and they consequently wish to select serviceable, reasonably priced materials and put them together in a comparatively inexpensive but substantial manner. In economizing, it is best to use materials of a good standard grade; it is false economy to use cheap materials. All materials must meet fire code standards and, whenever possible, fireproof material should be used.

Indoor Surface Materials

Floors. Most physical education facilities will have several types of floor surfaces. The activity areas will usually be high grade maple or a synthetic surface; the classrooms hardwood, tile or carpet; locker rooms tile, concrete or synthetic carpeting; the dance studio maple; and the offices carpet, hardwood or tile. Cost will be a determining factor for many schools. There are many other factors that should also be considered, particularly when deciding on the surface for the activity area. Initial cost must be compared with the anticipated life of the material. Maintenance, durability, acoustical quality, attractiveness, and adaptability to multiple use are also critical considerations. Material should be carefully analyzed before a decision is made.

Synthetic surfaces are being used extensively in new construction. The versatility of this type of surface makes it very appealing. It can be used for many different sports as well as for other student activities. The two most common types are polyvinyl chloride (PVC), which is usually manufactured in wide strips and applied to concrete flooring with adhesive; and polyurethanes, which can be obtained in strips or poured in place. There is a wide variance in the quality of synthetic surfaces manufactured by different companies. Before deciding on a specific product it is imperative that the school thoroughly investigate the performance of the synthetic surface that it wants to use. Will it maintain its present characteristics over a period of years? Can it be easily maintained? Does it have satisfactory resiliency and will it be safe for participants? Will the company provide the necessary service and is the company capable of backing up the guarantee?

The synthetic surfaces have been an important development in physical education construction. However, high-grade maple remains an excellent choice of floor surface for many schools. This type of flooring has stood the test of time and hard use. Maple is a dense, strong, heavy, remarkably hard, and exceptionally durable wood. It is free from slivering and splintering, extremely resilient, polishes under friction, thus increasing its wear resistance, and because of its close grain is very sanitary. Standard lengths are recommended in preference to the special long lengths. The long lengths are much more expensive, without compensating benefits.

Walls

Concerning the walls of the gymnasium a variety of factors should be considered. These are:

1. It is decidedly advantageous to have the walls smooth up to 12 feet in order to have them serve as rebounding surfaces for balls.

2. No wall should constitute a hazard because of its rough or uneven surface.

3. The lower portion of the walls should be able to take hard usage and should be resistant to marking and scarring.

4. The lower walls should be finished with materials that can easily be cleaned without affecting the finish.

5. Light-colored walls reflect light better and provide a more cheerful atmosphere.

6. Fastenings for equipment and apparatus should be placed in the wall before the finished surface is applied.

7. There should be no projections from the walls into the playing area. Roll-away bleachers should be recessed. Drinking fountains should not be located in the gymnasium area.

8. Above the 12 foot level acoustical materials should be emphasized.

9. A dead air space between the inner and outer walls will provide insulation against sound, cold, and heat.

Ceilings

Ceiling materials vary considerably according to the room. For offices, standard classrooms, and high gymnasium rooms, acoustical tile is recommended. If apparatus is to be fastened to the ceiling, all necessary clamps and fasteners should be installed before the ceiling is finished. To prevent condensation of moisture, ceilings should be insulated. A light ceiling will have the same general lighting advantages as light walls.

Doors

Wood, glass, reinforcing wire, copper, brass, and iron or steel are commonly combined to make satisfactory doors for any part of the physical education building. The specific purpose to be served will dictate the proper combination of the above materials.

Other significant points to consider in selecting and installing satisfactory doors are these:

1. All exit doors should open outward and be equipped with panic bolts, so that crowds will not be trapped by a locked or blocked door.

2. Door stops should be provided to keep doors from being "banged" to pieces.

3. Strong, efficient locks should be provided for doors that need to be kept closed.

4. Large doors should be provided to gym areas for use by visitors or spectators and for use in moving apparatus and materials in and out.

5. Doors should be placed in the most convenient locations to facilitate circulation of traffic within the building.

Lighting

Lighting in physical education areas is provided by natural and artificial means. Natural lighting is that which comes through windows. When windows are used they should be elevated from 10 to 14 feet above the floor on the two long sides of the gymnasium. If windows are used in dressing rooms they should be located above the lockers and as high as possible. The amount of window space should be equivalent to 20 to 25 percent of the total floor area.

When natural light is available it should be combined with artificial lighting. The intensity of artificial light in any part of the area can be regulated by adjusting the intensity of the source and by placing light bulbs and reflectors correctly. Semi-direct light causes less glare and eyestrain. Satisfactory intensity for general physical education activity is from 20 to 30 foot candles: for more exact vision greater intensity is desirable. A foot candle is a measurement of illumination equivalent to that produced by a standard candle at a distance of one foot.

There are basically three types of lighting that are used in physical education facilities. The properties of each should be investigated before deciding on the type that would be best for your building. The incandescent, fluorescent and high intensity (sodium, mercury vapor, or metal halide) lights each have features that make them appropriate for areas in a physical education building.

Careful consideration should be given to energy conservation when choosing a lighting system. Key operated switches and light control by rows from different switches are examples of features that should be incorporated into a lighting system.

Emergency lights must be provided throughout the building. This is particularly important in an area such as the swimming pool and in areas where large crowds gather.

Cooling and Ventilation Systems

A satisfactory cooling system is needed just as much in a physical education facility as in other educational buildings. A dual duct system which provides a proper mixture of cold and warm air is ideal, although expensive, since it keeps room temperatures at a desired level during changing indoor or outdoor conditions. Regardless of the system that is used, room temperatures must be maintained at a level conducive for learning. When large crowds use portions of the building it is also critical that an appropriate cooling system be in operation.

Mechanical ventilation is essential in swimming pools, wrestling rooms, and locker and shower areas if an appropriate system is not provided for the entire building. It is also highly desirable in other teaching stations to remove odors and heat and reduce humidity. In general, ventilation in physical education areas is largely provided by a mechanical fan system with exhausts. Ventilation aims to produce four changes of air per hour without creating drafts.

Plumbing

In selecting plumbing equipment it is wise to purchase good standard materials from a reliable dealer. Durability, strength, simplicity of design, and a good finish are the marks of satisfactory equipment.

All pipes for water, heat, gas, or other purposes and all sewage and drain pipes should be laid before the walls and the foundation are built. Care should be taken to mend the damp-proofing in the event that pipes are laid after the walls are in. Toilets, showers, lavatories, cuspidors, and drinking fountains should be placed conveniently, of course, but in such position that a minimum of approach and disposal pipes are necessary. That is, if some of these service units must appear in each fourth of the building, it is more economical to place them near each other thus

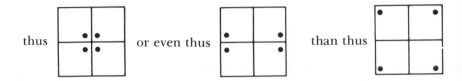

thus   or even thus   than thus

This cannot be arranged in all cases, but it can in many. Girls' showers, for instance, might as well be on the opposite side of the walls from boys' showers as in some other corner of the room or section of the building. Fewer pipes need be used, too, if the unit on the floor above is directly above the unit on the floor below. Hot and cold water pipes should be far enough apart so that the cold water remains cold, especially at the drinking fountains. The cleaning problem is simplified, the appearance is improved, and the danger of accident is reduced if pipes are enclosed in the walls. Those factors sufficiently outweigh the increased cost of installation and the greater difficulty of getting at pipes when something goes wrong, so that enclosing in the walls is recommended if provision is made for access when necessary.

Specific suggestions for each of the following service units are presented under the unit concerned.

1. Heating:
   (a) Sufficient radiation should be provided to furnish adequate heat on cold days—about 60° F. for the activity rooms, about 70° F. for the locker rooms, and about 80° F. for the shower and swimming pool rooms.
   (b) Proportionately fewer heating units are needed to heat large rooms than to heat small ones, because as rooms get larger the volume increases more rapidly than the area of exposed outer surface through which heat passes off.
   (c) Heat pipes should be insulated to conserve heat, to prevent burns, and to prevent overheating of some rooms and halls.
   (d) Heat sources should be distributed so that they provide a comparatively even temperature throughout the room.
2. Showers:
   (a) Sufficient showers to care for the peak load should be provided. The recommended ratio for class purposes is one shower per four students.
   (b) Placing a post shower with mutiple heads in the center of the room

has many advantages over wall showers. This plan also permits use of shower barriers rather than solid walls around the room and affords easy supervision.

(c) Shower heads should be designed to permit water to be discharged diagonally downward so that those who use them may avoid getting their heads wet.

(d) An in-wall liquid soap dispensing system is recommended although a bar soap procedure with recessed soap dishes is preferred by many.

(e) Individual control of showers is advocated. Although central control is more economical, individual control under supervision is not particularly expensive and is much more satisfactory to the shower takers. For economy purposes, a master control can be used to shut off the water when showers are not in use.

(f) The shower heads should be stationary, easy to maintain and replace, and provide a satisfactory spray. They should be self-cleaning and non-clogging.

(g) The recommended light for a shower room is 20 foot candles.

3. Drying rooms:

(a) The drying room should be located between the shower and locker rooms, with entrances to each.

(b) The drying room should be approximately the same size as the shower room.

(c) The floor and the walls (up to 6 feet) should be similar to those in the shower rooms.

(d) Towel racks adequate to accommodate the peak load should be installed.

(e) Foot drying ledges, approximately 18 inches high and 12 inches wide, should be around the wall. They should be constructed of the same material as the wall, be enclosed and have rounded edges.

4. Lavatories:

(a) Lavatories should be near the toilet room.

(b) White porcelain finish is preferred to colored finish.

(c) Paper towels and liquid soap should be provided near the lavatories.

(d) Faucets that turn off automatically when left on are practical.

5. Toilets:

(a) Enough toilets to take care of peak load classes should be provided—approximately one urinal for twenty boys and one stool for fifteen girls, and one stool for twenty boys.

(b) The type of toilet that flushes readily with a small amount of water is practical.

(c) Floor length urinals are preferred.

6. Cuspidors:

(a) The type of cuspidor that will flush easily with a little water is practical.

(b) The foot flush type is preferable.

(c) At least one cuspidor should be placed in the main gym room, recessed in the wall with bars to keep balls out of it. This is essential since some players must expectorate during activity periods, and if a proper place is not provided the floor or wall will have to suffice.

(d) To facilitate cleaning, the bars should be removable or should swing back.

(e) The finish should be a different color from that of the drinking fountain.

7. Drinking fountains:

(a) There should be one drinking fountain just outside the main activity room and another in the locker room. Drinking of water should be encouraged by providing a convenient supply; consequently, additional fountains may be necessary.

(b) Refrigerated water should be provided.

8. Locker rooms:

(a) The locker room should be large enough to provide 20 square feet for each occupant during the peak load.

(b) The recommended standard for lighting is 20 foot candles.

(c) The recommended temperature is 70° F.

(d) Adequate ventilation and acoustical treatment are vitally important.

(e) Locker rooms should be designed with supervision in mind.

(f) Large locker rooms for class participants with team rooms and smaller rooms that can be used for visiting teams should be included in a physical education facility design. Visiting teams should have the privacy of a separate dressing room.

(g) Cement bases or pedestal mounted dressing benches should be provided for lockers.

(h) Aisles 5 feet wide should be provided between lockers on pedestals. Thirty inches should be allowed between lockers and floor mounted benches when cement bases are used.

(i) Forced air ventilation through lockers is highly desirable.

9. Team rooms:

(a) Full-length lockers large enough to permit storage of practice equipment should be available for all squad members.

(b) It is desirable to locate lockers around walls in order to leave center area open for squad meetings if a separate meeting room is not provided.

(c) The team room should be available to squads in season.

(d) A bulletin board and a chalk board should be installed.

(e) The training room should be adjacent to the team room.

10. Custodial facilities:

(a) Custodial closets should be located appropriately to facilitate custodial operations.

(b) A storage area for custodial supplies is necessary.

(c) A service sink in or adjacent to the custodial closets is a necessity.

Locker Unit

Lockers and baskets vary greatly in size, materials used in construction, and methods of handling. The wire type allows clothes to dry much better than the metal louver type but admits more dust and presents more security problems. Larger, full-length (60 or 72 inch) lockers are more convenient and adequate than the smaller 12 by 12 by 36-inch type but are also more expensive. The problem, then, is to provide the combination of lockers and baskets that most adequately meets the needs of the various groups concerned without entailing too great expense.

It is generally agreed that the varsity athletes should have individual lockers placed in the varsity locker room. Full-length lockers are recommended, but if funds will not permit them, half-length lockers can be used. (Additional storage areas must then be provided for some sports.) Each locker should have a good strong lock on it. The master-key-combination type is recommended. The inside of the door should be painted white to improve visibility.

A combination of storage lockers and full length (dressing) lockers is best for most schools. Full length lockers are provided to care for peak load. The peak load will include class members, recreational activity people and intramural competitors who will be needing a locker during the same period of time. Sufficient storage (box) lockers must be available for each student who uses the locker room. Storage lockers range in size but a common size is $12'' \times 12''$ with depth the same as the full length locker. Most systems incorporate 5, 6, or 7 storage lockers per dressing locker which may be full or half length. Students store their equipment in a storage locker when not in class and then transfer their lock to a dressing locker to secure their street clothes and unused equipment while in class. Baskets are sometimes used in place of storage lockers, particularly if an attendant is available to issue the baskets.

When purchasing lockers, literature from locker manufacturers should be examined carefully to make certain lockers meet desired construction standards. Metal and finish quality and assembly techniques are extremely important. Different sizes and unique features provided by different locker manufacturers should be evaluated in light of the particular locker needs. Bright colored lockers should be used in an overall plan to bring warmth and life to locker rooms.

The following locker room accessories are desirable:

1. Benches for all lockers. Either long benches fastened to the floor by steel posts or benches mounted on concrete pedestals with lockers installed on them.

2. A bulletin board near the entrance to the locker room or rooms.
3. Hair dryers and mirrors for all locker rooms.

Apparatus

Apparatus should be selected on the basis of its prospective usefulness in furthering a modern physical education program. Rugged, simple, standard pieces should be chosen. Even though the original cost may be greater, the difference will be compensated for in reduced repair bills. Since shipping costs for heavy pieces are relatively high, it may be more economical to purchase from some dealer close at hand.

Mobile pieces that can be fastened to the floor or wall catches or removed from rollers by means of a lever are recommended. When the apparatus has been used, it can then be swung back against the wall, raised to the ceiling, or rolled off to the apparatus room, leaving the main floor available for other activities. Mats and smaller pieces that require no fastening should be stored out of the way on a platform on wheels and in boxes on wheels.

ELEMENTARY SCHOOL GYMNASIUM

There are some special factors that should be considered when constructing an elementary school gymnasium. Too often these facilities are used for lunchroom purposes or other activities that conflict with physical education classes. Providing sufficient teaching stations is just as critical at the elementary level as at the secondary level. Spectator seating will be needed only if the facility is used by the community for evening and weekend activities. Walls should be as uncluttered as possible so they can be used for physical education activities. A bright, cheery atmosphere will establish a good learning environment and the facility should be activity oriented with ropes, a cargo net, multiple designs on the floor, and varied pieces of equipment available for student use. Basketball baskets should be adjustable to different heights. The gymnasium should be designed for the needs and interest of an elementary age child and not be a scaled down version of a college or secondary school gymnasium.

THE SWIMMING POOL

The swimming pool is a very important physical education facility. Swimming contributes to all of the commonly accepted physical education objectives and it is an ideal recreational activity for people of all ages. Swimming is usually one of the most popular activities in the curriculum, and parents are usually eager to have their children learn to swim for its safety aspects as well as for the recreational opportunities it affords. The ability to swim opens the door to many other aquatic activities such as water skiing, scuba diving, boating, canoeing, fishing, and sailing.

All of these factors justify an important place for swimming in the physical education curriculum. The problem in the public schools is to obtain the facilities. The majority of colleges and universities have swimming pools but secondary schools do not. In elementary and junior and senior high schools swimming is frequently taught in pools that belong to other agencies. School boards are now much more amenable to granting approval for the construction of swimming pools, but it will still be a long time before the majority of secondary schools have one. In many communities, the tax payers are not willing to vote for construction bond issues which include the added expense of a swimming pool. Many secondary schools have been able to acquire such facilities by making them available for total community use in the evenings, on weekends, and during the summer months. It is far more difficult to sell the idea of a pool that will be used exclusively by a school.

Indoor Versus Outdoor Pool

Because the outdoor pool is much less expensive than the indoor one, many communities have built outdoor swimming pools. Unfortunately, this restricts the use of the pool largely to the summer months in most communities. From the standpoint of a school facility, an indoor pool is far more preferable. While some people are not enthusiastic about swimming indoors during the summer months the other advantages decidedly favor the construction of an indoor pool that can be used as part of the physical education program of a school.

The dilemma of whether to build an indoor or an outdoor pool has been solved in recent years by the construction of combination indoor-outdoor pools. In the most basic design, sliding doors are installed and can be opened during the summer months. More sophisticated techniques are now popular and used in many locations. Sliding or removable panels, inflatable roofs that can be rolled up and stored on one side of the frame during the summer and retractable roofs are examples of these techniques. Also, there is increasing use of plastic covers over outdoor pools in order to permit swimming for most of the year.

Preliminary Planning Considerations

Knowledge and experience must be involved in the planning of swimming pools. Throughout the country examples of poorly designed and constructed facilities are easy to find. New concepts, materials, and processes have develped so rapidly in swimming pool construction that it would be a mistake to undertake the construction of aquatic facilities without consulting a knowledgeable individual. If the architect is not an experienced, up-to-date pool builder an expert should be consulted. A consultant is very frequently engaged when a large facility is being contemplated. The guidance of specialists in heating and ventilation, acoustics, plumbing, water purification, and lighting is necessary. Finally, those who will conduct the various programs in the pool should be involved in the planning.

In planning a new pool the various uses that will be made of it are a prime consideration. School pools are used for more than instructing nonswimmers. They include programs for water safety instruction, intramural and interschool competition, synchronized swimming, pageants, water polo, scuba diving, recreational swimming, and hydrotherapy. The requirements for each of these activities must be incorporated in the planning.

Virtually every State Department of Public Health has regulations pertaining to swimming pools. Compliance with these regulations is a must. These laws usually cover such factors as water circulation, filtration, water treatment practices, sanitary standards, and safety features.

Design. Because of construction costs, most indoor pools have been rectangular in shape. A few schools have constructed L, T or Z shaped pools, which have signficant advantages. In such pools the divers are separated from the swimmers; this not only reduces accidents but makes swimming more enjoyable. In addition, since a larger shallow area is made possible an increased number of beginning swimmers can be handled.

The ultimate in swimming pool facilities is to have separate pools for instruction, competiton and diving. The instructional pool only needs to be large enough to handle the beginning swimming classes and should be shallow (3 to 4 feet). The competitive pool should be at least 7 feet deep so it can be used for water polo also. The diving well is provided exclusively for diving. This eliminates the diving boards in the main pool and contributes to safety as well as accommodating more swimmers. The ceiling should be 15 feet above the highest board and the water depth should be 10 feet for one meter boards and 14 to 16 feet for three meter boards.

Since practically all pools are used for competition, a regulation competitive course should be incorporated into the pool design. Most schools currently use the 25 yard race so the pool must be 75 feet and 1 inch in length. The 50 meter Olympic course should be provided if funds are available since there is a trend toward this length. It is possible to provide for both of these lengths by having a pool 50 meters in length and 25 yards in width. The use of a moveable bulkhead should also be considered as this makes it possible to vary the length of a pool for many different purposes. Eight lanes are recommended for competitive purposes and this width provides good flexibility for teaching. Lanes should be a minimum of 7 feet in width with an additional 1½ feet in the outside lanes since this contributes to smoother water for competitive swimmers.

Hydraulic floors have been pioneered in Europe and contribute significantly to multi-purpose use when a school has a single pool. If hydraulic floors are not feasible, the pool depth should range from 3½ feet at the shallow end to a depth at the deep end which will be determined by the diving boards. If a separate diving well is provided, the depth at the deep end should be 7 feet. The slope from the shallow end should not exceed a one foot drop every 20 feet.

The decks of the pool should provide sufficient space for land drills, lifesaving activities, and physical conditioning. At least 6 feet should be provided on one side and 12 feet or more on the other side. The width of the deck at the shallow end should not be less than 10 feet and it should not be less than 15 feet at the deep end. It is a recommended minimum standard that the total amount of deck space be equivalent to the water surface area.

The number of occupants of the pool depends upon the nature of the activity. Recommended standards are given in Table 13-1.

TABLE 13-1. MINIMUM RECOMMENDED
OCCUPANCY DESIGN FACTORS

Activity	Indoor Pools	Outdoor Pools
Shallow-Water Area (Under 5'-0")		
Recreational Swimming	14 sq. ft./capita	15 sq. ft./capita
Advanced Swimming Instruction	20 sq. ft./capita	15 sq. ft./capita
Beginning Swimming Instruction	40 sq. ft./capita	15 sq. ft./capita
Deep-Water Area (Over 5'-0")		
Recreational Swimming	20 sq. ft./capita	25 sq. ft./capita
Advanced Swimming	25 sq. ft./capita	30 sq. ft./capita
Diving (based on area within 20 ft. of deep-end diving wall)	175 sq. ft./capita	200 sq. ft./capita
Minimum Walk Width*	6 ft.	12 ft.
Sum of walk dimensions*, on either side of the pool length or width, shall not be less than	18 ft.	30 ft.

*Walk dimensions shall be horizontal clear deck width, not including any portion of the coping or interior gutter sections.

Source: *Planning Facilities for Athletics, Physical Education and Recreation.* (North Palm Beach, Florida: The Athletic Institute, 1974), p. 185.

Spectator seating should be provided in a controlled area where the spectators can see the nearest edge of the pool from end to end. Retractable seating is preferred so the area can be used for other purposes when the seats are not being used.

When designing pools, appropriate scholastic, NCAA or AAU swimming rule books should be consulted. This is extremely important since pool markings, standards for recessed receptacles, and construction requirements are sometimes changed by these organizations.

Location. An indoor pool can be constructed anywhere in the building but the preferred location is on the ground level. This location is not only the most economical form of construction but it also provides ready access from the outside. In the past the location of the pool directly underneath the gymnasium created serious problems. It is difficult to control the moisture from the pool, which may, of course, damage the gymnasium floor.

The pool should be accessible from both the girls' and boys' locker rooms. The pool should be located so that spectators at swimming events have direct access to the seating area. People using the pool for recreational purposes should be able to reach the appropriate locker and shower areas for the swimming pool without going through other parts of the building.

Materials. A wide variety of materials are used for the construction of the swimming pool shell. Steel, plastic, aluminum, and fiberglass are used, but concrete in various forms is utilized most extensively. The decks, sides, and basin of the pool are usually constructed of reinforced, form-poured concrete. Precast, prestressed concrete or concrete block may be used for the pool walls. Pneumatically applied concrete (Gunite) may also be employed for the entire pool shell.

Tile is the favored swimming pool finish. The advantages of tile are that it can be readily cleaned, slipping is rendered less likely, it is durable and attractive in appearance. Its disadvantage is its cost although over a period of years this factor is not excessive. Abrasive tile is usually used at the ends of the pool to reduce slipping on turns in competitive swimming. The lanes, which are marked on the pool floor, are made of black tile.

A wide variety of other pool finishes are available. Rubber-base paint is the least expensive. Water-resistant oil vehicle paints are much more costly, but they are more serviceable. Various chemical coatings have been developed. Plaster finishes have some advantages. Precast-stone terrazzo construction has been used successfully.

Circuit Breakers. Circuit breakers should be on all electrical outlets in the pool area with no electrical outlets being located within nine feet of the water.

Ladders. Ladders should be available at each corner of the pool. They should be recessed into the side walls.

Coping. The coping is a slightly elevated area from 12 to 18 inches wide which extends around the entire pool. It prevents the return of water from the deck to the pool. The coping also facilitates cleaning the deck without getting dirty water in the pool. It also serves as a slightly elevated platform that swimmers use to dive into the pool.

The coping is usually made from precast-concrete sections. It is essential that it not be slippery when wet.

Overflow systems. Most state boards of health require overflow systems for sanitary reasons. They serve a useful purpose in carrying waste materials and debris off the surface of the water. They also aid in regulating water level and in reducing wave action. The recessed overflow systems also serve as a handhold for swimmers. The "roll-out" and "deck-level" systems which permit the water to come over the pool wall and enter a shallow covered trench, have been used in many pools. The newest system is called the "rim-flow" system and is designed to handle almost immediately all water going over the pool walls. The recommended standard is that overflow systems extend completely around the pool.

Markings. Water depth markings should be located at critical points on the deck. They should be permanent, preferably set in tile. For swimming competition, distances should be marked in 5-yard or meter increments. These markings should be permanent both on the face of the pool and the deck.

Acoustics. Noise will be a problem in indoor pools unless provisions are made to counteract it. Any indoor area with smooth, hard walls and ceiling will be noisy. Moisture-proof acoustical material on the ceiling and on at least two of the side walls will solve the problem.

Heating. The water temperature for instructional classes should be 80° F.; for competitive swimming it should range from 74° F. to 76° F. The air temperature should be 5° F. warmer than the water temperature. Radiant heating in the deck has proven successful in controlling air temperature. The unit heater with attached blower also serves the purpose well. Air temperature should be thermostatically controlled.

Ventilation. Ventilation is important in order to reduce humidity and condensation. It is best provided by a mechanically operated ventilation system. The most important consideration is the location of air intakes. They must be high enough to avoid drafts for those using the pool. The comfort of both swimmers and spectators depends upon temperature and ventilation.

Lighting. Much sentiment exists for completely artificial lighting. If a good system is available uniformity of lighting is assured: glare and shadows are eliminated, and the growth of algae inhibited. Another advantage is that with the elimination of outside windows it is easier to maintain proper air temperature, humidity, and ventilation.

Some natural lighting is available in many pools. Sunlight is desirable if the rays do not cause interference to the swimmers or spectators. This can be controlled by the proper location of windows and the use of glass block or tinted fiberglass.

The recommended standard for lighting is 50 foot candles at the surface of the water or at deck level.

Underwater lighting. Underwater lighting is a desirable feature even though it adds to the expense of construction. Such lighting is invaluable for pageants and water shows but it also facilitates cleaning and promotes safety. Lights are not recommended at the shallow end of the pool. At the deep end the recommended location is halfway between the surface and the bottom. The sidewall lights should be 2 feet below the surface at the shallow end and gradually lower as the pool depth increases.

Access tunnel. An access tunnel around the outside of the pool basin, while not absolutely necessary, is a desirable feature of a pool. Such a tunnel makes it much simpler to inspect and repair much of the plumbing. Underwater lighting is facilitated, and windows for viewing and taking films can be readily provided together with a microphone and two way communication system to the deck.

Water Circulation and Treatment. The purposes of water circulation and treatment are to keep it clear, clean, and pure. The size of the filters and the capacity of the pump should be such as to recirculate the water four times every 24 hours. In this manner the various processes through which the water passes can be accomplished. Filtration, pH control, alkalinity control and disinfection are the four factors involved in water treatment. Appropriate treatment will provide water that (1) has maximum visibility, (2) provides maximum protection against disease and (3) eliminates the factors that cause discomfort to swimmers.

OUTDOOR ACTIVITY AREAS

A significant percentage of the total physical education program in public schools and colleges and universities takes place on outdoor facilities. Consequently it is necessary that these facilities be as carefully planned and designed as the indoor activity areas. Ordinarily, these areas in elementary and secondary schools are planned as part of the total school facility.

A major error in the past was the failure to provide sufficient space. Unfortunately, this mistake cannot be rectified when the area surrounding the school is built up. To prevent such errors, school planners today are giving much more consideration to the total area available when new schools are being contemplated. Many standards have been proposed to serve as guides when planning outdoor facilities. These standards are useful but must be modified according to local conditions and be revised when concepts change.

A major factor that has contributed to school boards and administrators endeavoring to acquire more land for school sites is the expectation on the part of the people of the community that the facilities would be available to other groups when not required for school use. The trend is definitely in the direction of joint use by the school and community. In particular, the recreation department can take advantage of outdoor play areas. In this way the public receives maximum returns from the money expended.

Recommended minimum standards for total acreage for different types of schools are as follows:[2]

1. Elementary schools—ten to thirty acres
2. Junior high schools—twenty-five to forty acres
3. Senior high schools—forty to sixty acres

Site Selection

When sites for schools are being considered the area to be used for athletic fields should be analyzed from the standpoint of suitability. Such considerations as drainage, subsurface water conditions, need for fill or rock excavation should be reviewed. It is desirable that the outdoor areas be close to the locker rooms but not so close that noise will interfere with indoor classes. It is generally accepted that students should not be required to cross a street to get to the play areas.

Activity Areas for Secondary Schools

Sufficient outdoor activity areas are needed to accommodate service classes, intramurals, and interscholastic athletics for all the students. The number of outdoor teaching stations will be determined by the number of students in the school, the number of required class meetings per week and the maximum percentage of the students who will be using outdoor facilities at any class period during the school year. The number of fields that are needed for intramurals and interscholastic athletics will be determined by the student population of the school and the scope of the programs. Sufficient space should be provided for each intramural activity and interscholastic athletic team during the prime after school hours. It is apparent that several outdoor athletic fields are needed. In addition, a battery of tennis courts to be used for instruction, intramurals, varsity teams, and community recreation should be provided.

Extensive facilities for spectators for athletic contests will probably not be needed in most junior high schools. To avoid the expense of constructing expensive facilities for spectators at each senior high school many communities have provided one stadium where the competitive sports of all schools can be played. If possible it is desirable to hold football practice on a field other than the one on which the games are played if the game field has natural turf. The game field can be used for classes and intramural activities.

Junior and senior high schools need athletic fields that can accommodate football, touch football, soccer, baseball, softball, track and field, field hockey, speedball, lacrosse, and archery. A hard-surfaced area, which can be used for outdoor basketball and volleyball, is an asset. The recommended dimensions for game areas are indicated in Appendix B.

Activity Areas for Elementary Schools

Several types of activity areas are needed for elementary schools. The area should be designed so that the lower grades (K, 1, 2, and 3) will be able to use space without conflicting with activities of students in the upper grades or having older students walk through their areas. A hard surface area with painted lines and circles should be provided for young children. An apparatus area with challenging and innovative equipment constitutes another segment of the playground. A grassy area, large enough for basic lead up sports and movement exploration, should also be included. A larger hard surface and grassy area will be needed for the upper grades for games and activities appropriate for those ages.

General Features

Drainage. This is an important consideration on unpaved areas. With adequate drainage athletic fields dry out more rapidly after periods of wet weather and thus permit more usage. There are two types of drainage, namely, surface and subsurface.

Surface drainage is accomplished by grading in such a way that the middle of the activity area is slightly elevated, thus resulting in a slope toward the sides of the field. The recommended slope is 2 percent, i.e., 2 feet in every 100 feet. The water drains off the field into catch basins or natural water collectors. Drain tiles that convey the water to a storm sewer or other outlet is the most common type of subsurface drainage system. More complex systems are also available and are incorporated into natural turf systems such as those described later in the chapter.

Surfacing. The criteria for surfaces of physical education activity areas outlined at the Third Facilites Conference are:[3]

1. All-year usage
2. Multiplicity of use
3. Dustless and stainless
4. Nonabrasiveness
5. Pleasing appearance
6. Durability
7. Resiliency
8. Low maintenance cost
9. Reasonable initial cost
10. Ease of maintenance

No surface is ideal for every type of activity area. Natural turf comes the closest to being the best all-around surface. However, it does not hold up well under heavy use and it is somewhat expensive to maintain properly. Likewise, problems are created in wet weather. It is because of these disadvantages that extensive research has been conducted to develop other surfaces that would meet the varying outdoor surface needs for physical education and athletics. There are two types of surfaces that are needed. One is the court or hard surface and the other is the field or turf surface.

1. Hard surface areas:
   a. Bituminous or blacktop. This type of surface has greatly increased in popularity in public schools and colleges and universities. An up-to-date assessment of this type of surface was reported at the Third National Facilities Conference:[4]

   The common bituminous surface has many of the advantages which are sought in any surfacing material. It provides a durable surface which can be used on a year-round schedule. The maintenance of bituminous surface is comparatively easy and inexpensive. Such a surface can also be used for many different activities. When properly installed, the surface is dust-free and drains quickly. Asphalt surfaces can be marked easily and with a relatively high degree of permanence. Asphalt also provides a neat-appearing, no-glare surface that will blend well with the landscape. The disadvantages of bituminous surfaces are their relatively-high installation costs and lack of resiliency as compared to some other types of surfaces. However, the high installation cost will be offset by low maintenance costs. Bituminous surfaces will vary as to firmness, finish, resiliency, and durability in direct relation to the kinds and proportions of aggregates and other materials used in their mixture.

Asphalt can be combined with a variety of other materials to provide a reasonably resilient or extremely hard surface. The use of such materials as cork, sponge, or rubber in combination with asphalt will yield a fairly-resilient surface. Aggregates such as slag or granite will produce an extremely hard surface when combined with asphalt.

b. Concrete. Concrete has fewer advantages and more disadvantages than blacktop. As a consequence its use has declined.

c. Synthetics. Many different types of synthetic surfaces have been developed for physical education and athletic use. Initially these surfaces were designed for a specific activity such as tennis or track. Improvements in construction now make it possible for these surfaces to have multiple use. One surface can be used for tennis, basketball, volleyball, playground activities, and street games. These surfaces have at least a 4″ base with a leveling course of graded aggregates and a surface course of fine aggregate to provide a smooth, uniform plane on which to place the synthetic playing surfaces. Product specifications will vary with geographic regions. When considering the installation of a synthetic surface, the quality of each commercial product must be carefully evaluated and a list of required specifications met by any contractor bidding on the job. Synthetic surfaces can also be placed over existing surfaces. This should be considered by schools desirous of upgrading current facilities.

Synthetic surfaces have many advantages. They are resilient, durable, non-abrasive, are excellent for multiple use, require little maintenance, come in a variety of colors, and are appropriate for year-round use.

d. Protective playground cushions. Some schools and recreation departments are utilizing 1″ rubber cushions on their hard surface playgrounds, particularly under apparatus. This is a valuable safety feature and is required by ordinance in some municipalities.

2. Turf surfaces:

a. Natural turf. This is the most extensively used turf surface. A properly constructed turf area with appropriate maintenance will provide an excellent surface for the use of many physical education and athletic programs. The four common faults in the construction of turfed fields are:

1. Poor subsurface drainage.

2. Inadequate surface drainage.

3. Improper texture of the soil. The topsoil should consist of a mixture of sand and loam. The amount of clay should not exceed 15 percent.

4. The wrong type of grass. Expert advice should be sought before the type of grass is selected. Weather and soil conditions in different parts of the country favor certain types of grass. The assistance of the local agricultural agent or a nearby agricultural college or experimental station should be sought in order to select the best variety of grass for the fields.

Maintenance must include proper fertilization, liming, mowing and watering. Weed and insect control, aeration, limitation on time, type, and amount of usage and regular repair of damaged areas will, of necessity, be part of an appropriate maintenance program.

b. Synthetic turf. Various synthetic turfs have been marketed since the initial research in the early 1960's. This type of turf has many advantages and should be carefully considered by secondary schools as well as by higher education institutions. It is particularly valuable when outdoor space is at a premium since it can be used on a round the clock basis for many different activities even during severe weather conditions. There are disadvantages associated with this type of turf. There is a high initial installation cost and although maintenance costs are less than for natural turf, it is not as maintenance free as was first thought. Surface heat during hot weather is a problem and it has been found that the turf does lose its properties over an extended period of use and must be replaced. Conflicting research findings have been presented relative to the rate and severity of injuries to athletes using this surface.

For some schools, synthetic turf will be a valuable answer to turf problems. Each school must evaluate the advantages and disadvantages of synthetic turf to determine if this surface would be economically feasible and would make possible a better physical education, intramural and athletic program.

c. Specialized turf systems. Due to discontent with some aspects of artificial turf, attempts have been made to combine the best qualities of natural turf with the wearability of artificial turfs. The Prescription Athletic Turf System, developed at Purdue University and the Hy-Play System of Portland, Oregon are two examples of these systems which are designed with a specialized growing medium for the turf and a carefully designed drainage and heating system. The success of these fields is keyed to proper management and materials that are appropriate for each geographical area. Systems of this type have some excellent features.

The present and future needs of the school, the budget, the amount of space available and the characteristics desired in a turf will determine whether a synthetic, natural, or specialized turf system will be best for an educational institution.

Orientation of fields and courts. For safety of the participants, as well as for equitable playing conditions, fields and courts should be laid out to reduce the effects of the sun's rays. In rectangular fields and courts the flight of the ball is usually parallel to the long axes of the playing area. At the time of the day and year when the sport is being played the direction of the sun's rays should be determined. The playing field or court should then be laid out so that its long axis is perpendicular to the sun's rays. If these directions are followed the play on football, soccer, and rugby fields will be in a north-south direction. In baseball the rays of the late afternoon sun should be perpendicular to a line drawn from home plate through second base.

Fencing. Most play areas should be fenced. A suitable fence for many locations consists of 11 gauge woven wire 10 feet high. This will protect property, provide privacy, reduce supervising problems, and keep balls and other play materials from rolling, flying, or being carried into the streets. Fencing is particularly necessary for tennis courts. If a number of courts are constructed side by side fencing between courts is not necessary.

Lighting. Outdoor athletic areas have been lighted for night use primarily for interschool athletics. In colleges and universities, night lighting has been frequently used for intramural athletics and for student and faculty recreation. Much greater use of all outdoor areas could be obtained, however, if more extensive use of night lighting were made. Not only would the use be appreciably extended but such use would be much more enjoyable when the heat is excessive during the day.

The assistance of lighting engineers should be sought whenever a project involving outdoor athletic areas is contemplated.

Baseball fields. A considerable problem arises in orienting baseball diamonds so that both the players and the spectators will be handicapped as little as possible. For professional games the spectators often receive more consideration than they do for school contests. The school diamonds should be laid out to favor the players, for they are of prime importance and often they play without spectators. For schools it is satisfactory to have the base line from home to first base run directly west. This will considerably reduce interference with vision by the afternoon sun. Adequate backstops should be provided to reduce lost balls and ball chasing in general and to protect spectators. The distance from home plate to the backstop should be 60 feet. This same distance should separate the base lines and the stands or fence.

The construction and care of the diamond is important. The area should be approximately level, with adequate provision for drainage. The pitcher's plate may be elevated on a gradually sloping mound not higher than 18 inches above the surface of the infield. The ground should be rolled in the spring, and the grass should be kept mowed in both the infield and outfield. If the sod is removed from the base paths and other sections of the infield, those areas need care before each game. If water is available, they are customarily wet down, raked, and rolled, after which, first and third base lines are extended, and the boxes at home plate are marked with lime. Permanent markers on the foul lines in deep right and left field are valuable aids in judging fair and foul balls.

Football fields. The football field should be laid out and constructed in such a manner that it will be the most adequate playing area possible. In order that the team defending the least favored goal may be handicapped as little as possible by the sun and the wind the layout must be considered carefully. Since the prevailing winds in most sections of the country blow from the west, and since the sun shines from the west in the late fall afternoon it is often best to lay out the field north and south if possible. Other factors may make this undesirable but, in general, it is well to keep this in mind.

If natural turf is used, the field should be about 8 inches higher in the center than at the sideline and should slope gradually and evenly to the sides of the playing area to allow water to drain off quickly rather than be left to stand in pools any place on the field.

Tennis courts. For school use a battery of from six to eight tennis courts should be a minimum. One or two courts cannot be used for class instruction because they will not accommodate the number of students in a class.

The dimensions of the doubles court are 78 by 36 feet. The recommended size of the area for a court is 120 by 60 feet. This provides a space of 21 feet from the base line to the backstop and 12 feet from the sideline to the edge of the court surface. Fencing 12 feet high should enclose the courts.

Perhaps the most satisfactory layout position for tennis courts would be from northwest to southwest. However, courts as a rule are not placed at an angle, so the north and south position is most common.

Tennis court surfaces are classified as porous and nonporous. The porous surfaces permit some seepage of moisture while the nonporous surfaces are impervious. Porous surfaces include grass, clay, and various types of crushed materials. Concrete and various bituminous combinations are the types of nonporous surfaces in most frequent use.

For secondary schools and colleges and universities the porous type surfaces are not practical. They require too much maintenance and they cannot be used after rainy weather for too long a period of time. There are many regions in the United States, especially in the northern part, where hard surface courts are almost essential if tennis is to be played in the spring of the year.

There are a number of specific tennis court surface preparations that are good. Thousands of tennis courts have commercially prepared surfaces such as Grasstex, Lay-Kold, and Pave-coat. They are resilient, do not radiate heat, glare is eliminated and they are not hard on the legs and feet.

Track. The running track requires a 440 yard oval with a straightaway sufficient for the 120 yard high hurdles. The track should contain at least six lanes, each with a minimum width of 42 inches. When constructing new tracks, procedures should be followed to permit later conversion to metric measurements. The appropriate track and field rule books (National Federation of State High School Associations, NCAA, etc.) should be consulted for technical and competition rules prior to beginning construction of a track.

A convenient arrangement for most schools is that of placing the track around the football field. This is economical of space and places the performers in both sports in positions where they can be observed from the same bleachers.

The development of all weather tracks composed of such materials as (1) fibrous asphalt composition, (2) rubber, sand asphalt-hot mix, (3) rubberized asphalt cold mix, (4) synthetic resin material, and (5) rubber-cork asphalt composition was an important factor in the improvement of track surfaces. This type of track did have some disadvantages. Its resiliency changed with the weather and over a period of time it tended to become excessively hard. Heavy use had an adverse effect on it and it was necessary to control use that was made of the surface. Further research led to the development of other synthetic surfaces which are highly successful and have resulted in the obsolescence of the traditional cinder track. The various commerical synthetic surfaces should be carefully evaluated for cost, construction specifications, durability, and maintenance requirements before deciding on the surface that is best for a specific school. There are numerous advantages of a synthetic track surface:

1. Resiliency contributes to the prevention of shin splints.
2. The footing is always good.
3. Maintenance costs are signficantly reduced.
4. Lane markings are permanent.
5. Condition of surface is always uniform.
6. Appearance of surface is enhanced.
7. Inclement weather does not cause cancellations or postponements of meets because of track conditions.
8. Rubber-soled shoes can be used as readily as spiked shoes.
9. The performance of athletes is not adversely affected by wet weather.
10. Use of the track need not be restricted to the track teams.
11. The surface can be used for different purposes.

INNOVATIVE FACILITIES

Schools must constantly be alert to new construction ideas to maximize the facilities that can be provided for physical education and athletic programs. Such simple designs as an outdoor covered area can significantly increase the use of outdoor space in most geographical areas. Air bubbles are also used extensively for increasing the amount of physical education space that can be provided with limited financial resources. Investigation of different building materials, utilization of the natural terrain, building on roof tops, and varied building designs are examples of approaches that should be investigated to provide the best possible physical education facilities.

Renovation of Facilities

Excellent facilities can frequently be provided at a considerable financial saving by renovating an existing structure. Factors such as cost for renovation as opposed to constructing a new building, portion of present facility that can be salvaged, amount of space that will be available, time element and the availability of construction sites all must be considered when evaluating the advisability of renovation. Renovation can be planned to provide additional space or to make better use of the present space. An addition to the current building is a commonly used procedure to increase the available space. New lighting, multiple use floors, providing large activity modules by removing walls and other barriers, and restructuring areas for specialized use are examples of techniques that have been used effectively in the rehabilitation of physical education facilities.

Athletic Field and Court Layouts

For detailed specifications of athletic field and court layouts for various physical education activities see Appendix B.

SELECTED REFERENCES

Ashton, Dudley and Charlotte Ivey (Editors). *Dance Facilities.* Washington, D.C.: American Alliance for Health, Physical Education and Recreation, 1972.
Bronzan, Robert T. *New Concepts in Planning and Funding Athletic, Physical Education, and Recreational Facilities.* St. Paul, Minn.: Phoenix Intermedia, Inc., 1974.

320 ADMINISTRATIVE RESPONSIBILITIES

Dressing Rooms and Related Service Facilities for Physical Education, Athletics and Recreation. Washington, D.C.: American Alliance for Health, Physical Education and Recreation, 1972.

Ezersky, Eugene M., and Richard Theibert. *Facilities in Sports and Physical Education.* St. Louis: The C. V. Mosby Company, 1976.

Penman, Kenneth A. *Planning Physical Education and Athletic Facilities in Schools.* N.Y.: John Wiley and Sons, 1976.

Planning Facilities for Athletics, Physical Education and Recreation. North Palm Beach, Florida: The Athletic Institute, 1974.

Scholastic Coach. January Issue each year emphasizes Athletic and Physical Education Facilities.

NOTES

1. *Planning Areas and Facilities for Health, Physical Education and Recreation* (North Palm Beach, Florida: the Athletic Institute, 1965), p. 153.

2. *Planning Facilities for Athletics, Physical Education and Recreation* (North Palm Beach, Florida: The Athletic Institute, 1974), pp. 151–155.

3. *Planning Areas and Facilities for Health, Physical Education and Recreation* (North Palm Beach, Florida: The Athletic Institute, 1965), p. 73.

4. *Planning Areas and Facilities for Health, Physical Education and Recreation* (North Palm Beach, Florida: The Athletic Institute, 1965), p. 80.

14

The Purchase
and Care of Equipment

IMPORTANCE

The purchase and care of equipment was not an important responsibility of those in charge of the first physical education programs as very little equipment was used with mass calisthenic programs. As programs became more extensive and diversified and many companies started promoting the sale of all kinds and grades of physical education equipment, the equipment responsibilities of the physical education director became more and more important. Equipment was not a major problem for interscholastic and intercollegiate athletics during their developmental years either, since the athletes furnished most of the equipment that was used. Relatively little equipment was needed since the athletic program was limited to a few sports, the squads were small, and the players were not equipped as elaborately and completely as they are now. Furthermore, the cost of physical education and athletic equipment was considerably less than it is today.

Today, the purchase and care of equipment constitutes one of the director's most important responsibilities. It is the responsibility of physical education and athletic departments to provide quality equipment for every aspect of their programs. Desired educational outcomes will not be attained when insufficient or inadequate equipment is provided. Safety of the participants is of prime consideration for classes and intramurals as well as for interschool athletics. Appropriate safety standards must be used as a basis for determining the kind and quality of equipment that will be purchased. In addition to protecting the student, good equipment contributes to a better learning climate and increased pride in performance. Well-equipped, well-dressed athletic teams have the added advantage of appealing more to the public than unattractive teams do. Equipment expense has become one of the largest items in the physical education and athletic budgets and a great deal of money may be wasted unless equipment is purchased carefully and cared for properly. Many of the expense items in the budget do not lend themselves readily to reductions, but directors have found numerous ways by which they can reduce the expense of equipment without appreciably impairing its effectiveness and appearance. It is essential that every director know equipment thoroughly and be acquainted with the policies, methods, and techniques by which equipment might be bought and cared for most economically.

PROVISION OF EQUIPMENT BY SCHOOL

Practically all schools provide equipment for the instructional and intramural programs with the uniforms furnished by the students. Many schools provide towels and towel service at no cost to students, but some make a charge for this service. In still other schools the provision of clean towels is the responsibility of the student. This means that the student must bring a towel to school, take it home for laundering, and then return it to school every day that it will be needed. This practice is not recommended because of the problems in administering it. Schools should strive to provide all equipment, including uniforms and towels, for students.

For interschool athletics it is highly desirable to have the school furnish all items of equipment including uniforms. Students should not be required to provide all or part of their uniforms because, inevitably, some will be unable to afford to become candidates for teams. Also, some parents will purchase expensive pieces of equipment, such as field hockey and football shoes, that are too large in hopes that they will last for two or three years. Equally undesirable is the practice of using cheap, ill-fitting equipment that has been borrowed or handed down year after year. The provision of all items of athletic equipment by the school is a standard toward which all athletic departments should work. Specialized and personal equipment such as golf clubs, tennis rackets, softball gloves and baseball gloves are normally provided by the athletes. However, each school should have some of these items available for use by students who are unable to purchase their own.

Since the physical education instructional program, the intramural program, and the interschool athletic program are all part of the educational program of the school, equipment that is needed to participate should be furnished by the school. No student should be prevented from participating because of the inability to personally provide appropriate wearing apparel or equipment.

Purchasing Equipment

Physical education. The physical education teachers should be consulted about the equipment that will be purchased for their teaching specialties. They will be conversant with the different kinds of equipment and know what material and type of construction has been found to hold up the best and be most effective and safest for teaching purposes. The physical education director will use the information obtained from the teachers as a guide when purchasing equipment. Individual requests must be weighed in light of the budget and needs of all areas of the physical education program.

The director should be permitted to make purchases without approval of other administrators as long as the budget is adhered to and the school's purchasing procedures are followed. The director is expected to be qualified to know what equipment is best for the program and to be able to purchase the kind and amount of equipment that will contribute to a quality physical education program.

Interschool athletics. The coach and athletic director must work cooperatively when making athletic purchases. The coaches should be best able to make equipment purchases for their squads as they have the practical experience and know what materials and product specifications are needed. The athletic director is responsible for seeing that the equipment requests are in line with the budget and that the amount and type of equipment ordered can be justified.

In some high schools the principal, business manager, and/or the superintendent have the responsibility for approving athletic purchases. This should not be necessary if the athletic progam operates within a budget that has been approved by the board of education.

The inventory. Before equipment is purchased the need for it should be carefully considered. This will necessitate an itemized inventory of the equipment room covering both the amount and the condition of the materials on hand. (See chapter 15.) Some directors can be rightly criticized for being unable to justify amounts of equipment purchased. The inventory is the best insurance against overbuying on some items and underbuying on others. Firsthand information concerning the amount and condition of the stock on hand should always be available and accurate information about equipment requirements for physical education activities and athletic teams should be provided by the directors, teachers, and coaches.

Purchasing Policies

After the needs have been determined the director is prepared to buy. The purchase of equipment involves much more than merely buying goods to the limit of the budget. Every director is anxious to obtain the best service and the longest life in equipment per dollar spent. In order to attain this objective there are some recognized policies of buying which should be followed. Purchasing physical education and athletic equipment is a business proposition and it should be conducted on a business-like basis. There are certain procedures that are recognized as sound in any business. Although each school presents separate problems, there are certain fundamental principles of buying which will operate successfully in most situations.

Standardization of equipment. "Standardization of equipment" is a common expression among directors. By this term is meant the adoption, by a school, of a certain color, type, and style of equipment which is maintained over a period of years. There are advantages in buying certain consistent types of equipment, usually from the same firm. It allows for replacement of the equipment in whole or in part. It maintains quality of material and color. The end result is uniformity over a period of years. Economy is practiced in that items can be matched in varied quantities without having to purchase a complete new outfit each season. Parts and replacements are easily obtained and repairs can be made more successfully. The uniformity of equipment for team members adds color to the organization and strengthens the team morale. There is no question that lack of uniformity may be interpreted as bad buying. The director must be alert to the rapid changes in equipment, however, in order not to be found with a large store of obsolete or extinct types on hand.

Quality merchandise. Informed opinion agrees that the best policy is to purchase the better grades of equipment. The most expensive equipment is not always the best, but it must be recognized that good material will be more expensive than cheap material. It has been proved on numerous occasions that quality merchandise fits better, looks better, wears longer, and can be repaired more advantageously than cheap items. The director must not go to the extreme in paying prices to the point that teams go unequipped on a limited budget, but experience has shown that in the majority of cases, low-cost materials are low-grade materials. The practice of purchasing cheap merchandise for reserve and freshmen teams has not proven to be economical. It is far better to pass down from the varsity squad quality material in good repair than to provide a cheap grade of equipment that may last for the season but gives little promise of being suitable for reconditioning.

Buy within range of ability to pay. This is a sound policy in any business. Credit is easily obtained, and many directors have gone heavily into debt as a result of unrestrained purchasing. Even though many schools operate on a budget, it is possible to spend more for equipment than can be afforded. Buying too much and too expensive equipment has plunged many departments into debt. Buying too much equipment is not as serious a mistake as buying too expensive equipment because the surplus can be used later. Many coaches and directors have been overanxious to equip their teams with the best and have gone to extremes in their buying. Although quality merchandise is advocated, small high schools cannot afford to buy the same grade of equipment that large universities use. When a director overpurchases equipment, the operations of the entire department may be curtailed, and the director's ability as an administrator is questioned. Frequently, schools buy recklessly after financially successful years. As a long-term policy, consistent, regular buying is to be preferred.

Early ordering. The director should not overlook the advantages of ordering equipment early. These advantages include:

1. Early delivery. This is an advantage because opportunity is still available to correct mistakes, make size adjustments, and order additional items, the need for which could not be foreseen when the original order was submitted.

2. Better equipment management, When equipment is delivered early, ample time for marking and storing is available.

3. Better equipment. An early order is more likely to result in exact equipment carefully made to specifications by unhurried craftsmen.

Early buying also aids the manufacturer by providing a better estimation of the expected volume of business. Better materials can be produced at a better price if the labor is spread out over the entire year instead of being accumulated during certain intervals. In addition, the reputable manufacturer has the opportunity to replace materials that are defective or not up to standard.

Equipment dealers will be able to provide information about ordering deadlines. These deadlines differ according to the type of equipment that is being purchased, the manufacturer, the geographic area of the country, and whether the item is a stock item or is to be custom made. As a general rule, equipment on hand should be inventoried and new equipment ordered as soon as the season is completed. The following schedule can be used as a guide for ordering equipment:
Fall sports—order by April 1.
Winter sports—order by July 1.
Spring sports—order by November 1.

The best interests of the school should guide purchasing decisions. Not infrequently some sporting goods dealers, in order to obtain a school's equipment business, have offered gifts to the coach or administrator. A set of golf clubs, a rifle, jacket, fishing tackle or a tennis racket have been given to obtain a favorable decision. Such inducements should never be accepted; it is a violation of professional ethics to do so. Decisions about equipment purchases should be based upon the best interests of the school rather than the personal gain of the individual making the decision.

Purchase from reputable concerns. It is essential to deal with companies that have a proven reputation for sound business policies. A reputable dealer will properly service all accounts. Service to a buyer is an integral part of the manufacturer's product. Reliable companies also guarantee the excellence of their products and this guarantee is worth paying for.

Few directors are accurate judges of textiles, leathers, and other materials used in the manufacture of athletic equipment. Cheaper grades of fabrics, fiber, padding, and leather can be made to look like better-grade materials. The integrity of equipment companies must be relied upon unless the director knows equipment thoroughly. Every administrator will discover that buying from reputable firms will prove more satisfactory and more economical as a long-term policy.

This does not mean that all goods should be bought from the same firm year after year. There are tendencies to form too strong an attachment for a particular manufacturer. This should be avoided. The quality and price of one company's goods may change to advantage or disadvantage. New materials and new processes may enable one firm to excel temporarily in certain items. It is better to keep an open mind regarding the products of different manufacturers.

Take advantage of legitimate discounts. Many discounts that are offered to prospective buyers are, in reality, no discount at all. The amount of the discount is added to the original selling price in order that it might be taken off to attract purchasers. "Two percent within ten days" is, however, a legitimate discount. The seller can afford to offer this discount for the advantage of being paid within ten days after the goods are billed. Some firms offer this discount and the director can save considerable money by taking advantage of it. Many institutions buy in the spring, but on a September 30th dating. The discount period then carries up until October 10th.

Legitimate discounts may also be secured if large quantities of equipment are purchased at one time. The director should take advantage of this discount if purchases are large enough to obtain it.

Bids and specifications. Directors must be aware of state statutes and local policies which will determine the bid procedure that must be followed. Small purchases can be made without bids. This sum will vary and might be $50 in one school district and $250 in another. Informal bids are required on more expensive purchases such as those from $250 to $2,500. Anything over $2,500 would then require public advertising and receipt of sealed bids that would be opened at a public meeting. Bids are a valuable aid in getting the lowest possible price and they provide a fair method of determining which companies should supply the equipment. The usual practice is to require a minimum of three bids.

There are problems with bids. It takes more time and one cannot always be certain that the low bidder will provide the best service. Some unethical companies will submit bids on one item and deliver a cheaper item or attempt to have a poorer piece of equipment accepted. Because of this problem, it is critical that stringent, detailed specifications be written. This is particularly important when the "or equal" clause must be included on bid requests. It is the responsiblity of the director to make certain an "or equal" item is in fact equivalent in all aspects to the requested item. There should be no hesitation in refusing an item even though the reason must be justified in detail. A company which provides inferior equipment or inadequate service should not be permitted to bid on future orders.

Some states now utilize a state contract system whereby vendors, including physical education suppliers, provide a standing bid on specified items for a six or twelve month period. State institutions then buy directly from the vendors who have been awarded a state contract by virtue of being low bidders. School districts also have the option of buying from state contract sources at the bid prices.

Official Equipment

Practically all games or sports have certain items of equipment that must be manufactured to specifications and are commonly marked "official." The specifications may call for a definite weight, length, relative dimensions, certain types of material, or the exclusion of certain materials. The purchaser should be acquainted with such specifications or any changes that may occur from year to year or season to season. Cases have occurred where competitors have been ruled out of an athletic event or records have been refused on the grounds that the implements used were not "official." This may have come about through the ignorance of the purchaser or the misrepresentation of a salesman.

How to Buy

The best buyers study market conditions for proper values. Equipment prices fluctuate and the director who knows when to buy and when to refrain from buying can save money. Although prices are fairly uniform among sporting goods houses, excellent values are frequently offered on certain items by the various companies. If the director records and files the prices of equipment of the different firms, he can compare them when he is ready to buy.

The most effective way to discover how equipment stands up is to use it and check the results. If equipment rooms are properly managed, they should serve as laboratories to check the results of purchasing decisions. It is a simple matter to mark equipment and check it periodically to see how it wears. The perpetual inventory (see chapter 15) will provide information which will help the administrator evaluate equipment durability.

Local Dealers

Preference should be shown to local dealers if they provide the needed items of equipment at prices that are comparable to those of out-of-town firms. Ordinarily, the local dealer is in a position to provide better service within the community. Also, local school support is provided through taxes paid by the business and usually local dealers will support the school physical education and athletic programs in many other ways such as by purchasing ads in the school paper and yearbook. These considerations justify dealing with local firms as long as the difference in price is minimal.

Approval of Equipment by the National Federation[1]

The National Federation of State High School Associations has always been concerned about the quality of equipment that is used in athletics. A positive step was taken in 1970 when the National Federation joined the Athletic Goods Manufacturers Association, the American College Health Association, the National Athletic Trainers Association, the National Collegiate Athletic Association, and the National Junior College Athletic Association to form the National Operating Committee on Standards for Athletic Equipment (NOCSAE). This committee authorizes in-depth experimentation with protective equipment by Wayne State University in Detroit, Michigan. Their goal is to establish standards in the manufacture and use of equipment and to increase knowledge and understanding of the safety, comfort, utility, and legal aspects of athletic equipment. A standard for football helmets has been adopted and only helmets that have a seal attesting to this quality may be worn.

Ordering Equipment

In any type of school, large or small, order blanks should be used in purchasing equipment. It is a poor policy to order verbally. If goods are ordered verbally, there will frequently be an inadequate record of the transaction. When the merchandise arrives it cannot be checked accurately, and in case of a dispute the buyer will not be able to show just what goods were ordered. If verbal orders are necessary because of a time expediency, a follow-up purchase order should be submitted immediately.

If goods are ordered by letter, a carbon copy of the letters should be kept on file. Order blanks are preferable, however. They are uniform in size and can be filed systematically. Furthermore it is desirable to use an order number that will check with the invoice number. The director who uses order blanks and keeps them filed will have a complete record of purchases from which reports for the season or year can easily be made.

The samples in Figures 14-1 and 14-2 are suggested as guides in printing order blanks and vouchers. Letter size, 8½ by 11 inches, is commonly used.

The original copy of the purchase order is sent to the firm with two voucher forms, and the duplicate order, which should be printed on colored stock, is filed until the goods are received. With the duplicate order blanks on file, the purchasing agent or director may readily check up at any time to ascertain when the goods were ordered. When the bill is paid, the duplicate purchase order may be filed with the receipted voucher. When possible, goods should be ordered by catalogue numbers.

The original or white voucher form is filed with the copy of the purchasing order to show payment, and the duplicate is returned to the shipper with the check to show that the bill has been paid. Some firms will return their own voucher forms along with the voucher that was attached to the purchasing order. The vouchers provide for a statement of terms.

EQUIPMENT ORDER BLANK

Department

Name of School

City＿＿＿＿＿＿State

Purchase Order

To. ＿＿＿＿＿＿   Date ＿＿＿＿＿＿

Please deliver the following articles to:

Quality	Article

Please follow directions exactly

I.

Address every package of goods
to:

Director ＿＿＿＿＿＿＿＿＿＿

Department＿＿＿＿＿＿＿＿＿

School ＿＿＿＿＿＿＿＿＿＿

City ＿＿＿＿＿ State ＿＿＿＿＿

Order No. ＿＿＿＿＿

Ship Via. ＿＿＿＿＿＿＿＿＿

II.

Please bill us goods on the
attached voucher forms, returning both the white copy
and the duplicate pink copy.
Be sure to indicate our purchase order number on all
voucher forms.

Purchasing Agent.

Approved by.

Figure 14-1. Equipment Order Blank.

EQUIPMENT VOUCHER

Department

Name of School

City_____**State**

Voucher

To be returned to the Purchashing Agent
All Bills Must Be Rendered In Duplicate On This Form

Our order No. _____ Date _____

Must be shown on all voucher forms.

Deliver to._____ Name of Firm _____

_____ Address of Firm _____

    Street   City   State

Terms _____ Your Order No. _____ Your Invoice No. _____

Quantity	Material	Unit Price	Total Price	Trade Disc.	Net Amount

Appropriation_____ Approved _____

Rec'd O.K._____ Date_____

ure 14-2. Equipment Voucher.

When orders are placed a number of months or weeks in advance, it is well to state that goods are to be billed at a certain date.

At the lower left-hand corner of the sample voucher the word "Appropriation" is marked. This space should be used for indicating the sport or department to which the goods should be charged. The line marked "Rec'd O.K." is to be used when the goods are received by one person and the voucher is approved by another. At times, there will be mistakes in shipping, and when this is the case the fact will be noted in this space after the goods are unpacked.

Some schools use one form for the purchase order and voucher. The form is composed of from four to eight different colored pages with carbons attached. The pages are easily distributed and accuracy is insured since there is not a separate purchase order and voucher. Sets of carbonless paper such as NCR paper can also be used effectively for this purpose.

When schools have a central purchasing department, requisition forms will be submitted by the physical education and athletic director to the purchasing officer. The purchasing officer then submits the purchase order to the appropriate vendor. The requisition must include all the information that will be needed to complete the purchase order.

Considerations in Selecting Athletic Equipment

The Athletic Goods Manufacturers Association[2] has recommended some basic *considerations in selecting athletic equipment.*

1. Design and material. The design must be practical while the material must be thoroughly serviceable. One should be skeptical of a dress-up item where basic design and playability may be sacrificed for eye appeal. Many times the extras and frills serve no functional purpose.

Each year many new fabrics and materials, made from new synthetics and plastics, are introduced. These may or may not be an improvement over an older fabric or material. The physical education administrator cannot afford to have a closed mind and should not hesitate to experiment with new materials.

2. Utility and cost of maintenance. Equipment should be purchased on the basis of utility—that is, it should meet specific game and safety needs. Also, the equipment should be of such quality and construction that it is easy and inexpensive to maintain.

In considering the utility and cost of maintaining equipment be sure to check:

   a. Are there frills on the equipment, making it difficult to maintain?

   b. Will the equipment clean up easily and well?

c. Does the equipment have to be repaired and reconditioned after normal use?

d. Is the equipment too costly to maintain for effective use?

3. Safety factor in protective equipment. In purchasing protective equipment the first consideration must be the safety of the wearer. It is inexcusable to sacrifice the safety of students in order to save a few dollars.

4. Quality and workmanship. There is no substitute for quality in athletic equipment. The materials from which the equipment is made must be of excellent quality. The workmanship is equally important.

5. Source of supply. See "Purchase from Reputable Concerns," p. 326.

6. Price. It is never wise to sacrifice quality for price. Chances should not be taken with untested low-cost equipment. Athletic equipment should never be purchased on the basis of price alone.

Purchasing Specific Items of Equipment

In this section the discussion will center on some specific items of equipment and those features of each which the purchasing agent should bear in mind when making his selection.

Fabrics. A wide variety of fabrics is available for physical education and athletic garments. In addition to cotton and wool and such synthetics as nylon and rayon many other synthetic and plastic fibers are available. These can be combined into an endless variety of fabric materials. Athletic clothing is usually constructed by a weaving or knitting process. The purchaser must be aware of the advantages and disadvantages of the different types of fabrics and buy garments that are best for wear, comfort, and appearance.

One of the problems encountered with fabrics is shrinkage. "Sanforized" garments have been tested for shrinkage in accordance with United States Government-approved tests. They are guaranteed not to shrink more than one percent in width or length.

Colorfastness is one of the desired and necessary qualities of many fabrics. Since garments are subjected to sunlight, perspiration, and frequent washings, the best dyes to use to maintain the color are those known as "vat-dyes".

Shoes. The shoes are very important items of equipment. It is a sound principle to purchase the best shoes that the budget will permit because, in the long run, it will prove economical. Since there are so many different types of leather, tannages, and construction features involved in the manufacture of shoes, it is particularly important to rely upon shoes from reputable manufacturers.

The Goodyear welt construction has been proven by long experience to be excellent for all-around serviceability. Because it is built around a leather insole, this type of construction assures a good foundation for the shoe. This will enable it to take wear and tear, mud, water, and perspiration without losing its shape. Moreover, it is always repairable.

Kangaroo leather used to be the preferred leather for shoes. Slaughter of kangaroos is now limited in Australia and therefore the quality and availability of kangaroo leather is limited. Leathers used include calf, cowhide, pigskin, goat, deer and gazelle with specially tanned calf or cowhide used for top grade baseball, football, soccer, and track shoes. Cotton duck, light duck and nylon are satisfactorily used for shoes in sports such as wrestling and basketball.

A critical consideration in regard to shoes is that they fit properly. Correct size is probably more important in shoes than in any other item of apparel. The consequences of improperly fitted shoes can be extremely serious.

Jerseys. Stretch nylon is used extensively for jerseys as this material will stretch readily and return to its original size. It is stronger, wears longer, and has better abrasion resistance than other fabrics. Blends of stretch nylon, durene cotton, and nylon are also extensively used. Lettering and numbering must be in accord with regulations established by the high school or college organization under whose jurisdiction the team competes.

Inflated balls. Rubber balls of all types have been greatly improved in recent years and, since they are appreciably cheaper than leather balls, they have supplanted the latter in many instances. Rubber balls are used extensively in instructional classes and intramural activities. Some interscholastic and intercollegiate teams employ them at times for practices. Rubber balls are durable, will not lose their shape, and will not pick up moisture. Because of this resistance to moisture, rubber balls are especially valuable for football or soccer practices which are held in the rain or on a wet field. Rubber basketballs, volleyballs, and softballs are also available.

Almost all leather inflated balls are made of cowhide, which does not stretch as much as horsehide. The difference in prices of footballs, basketballs, volleyballs, and soccerballs is due largely to the grade of leather that is used. The choice section of any hide is called the *bend*, which comes from the middle of the upper back of the animal. The section immediately surrounding the bend is termed *back* and is considered the second best part of the hide. The fibers in these two sections of the hide are more closely knit, stronger, and firmer than other types of leather. The third best leather is *rump,* and grouped together as the poorest types are *shank, flank,* and *neck.* These sections have fibers of varying lengths and are usually spongy and coarse. The best balls, with close, small, tight, and firm fibers, will keep their shape, but cheaper balls, of inferior leather, will not. One good ball will give greater service than two inferior balls.

Specialized equipment. Every sport requires some specialized equipment. The list would be too extensive to be included in a book of this type. Physical education directors, athletic directors, teachers, and coaches must research the various types of materials and construction that are used to manufacture clothing and equipment specific to the different sports. Based on this information, intelligent equipment purchases can be made. New products are continually being made available. The director should evaluate the positive and negative features of new as well as extensively used products and use this information as a guide for spending the school's equipment money as judiciously as possible.

The Care of Equipment

A good equipment room is the first essential in the proper care of equipment. A carelessly kept supply room can take a greater toll on the life of equipment than many hours of hard service on the playing fields because equipment spends most of its life in the equipment room. The equipment room must be conveniently located adjacent to the locker and training rooms. It should be large enough to store all of the equipment of the department adequately and provide sufficient space for the handling and repairing of it. Proper lighting and heating are important. The equipment room ought to be well ventilated, dry, free from sweaty walls and pipes, and protected against moths, roaches, rats, and other rodents. The equipment room should be so constructed that shelves and bins can be built against the walls in order to have articles readily accessible for issue. Fairly deep shelves that will accommodate cartons and bulky articles are necessary. Narrower shelves for shoes and smaller articles are desirable. Enough shelves should be available so that nothing need be dumped in the corners or on damp floors. Steel bins and shelves are recommended. A cage-door, sliding type of window with a counter is necessary.

Storage cabinets that can be locked should be provided for expensive and high theft items. This is particularly important if the equipment room is not restricted to full-time equipment personnel. Out of season equipment should be placed in a locked compartment away from the issue area. Separate storage areas for each sport have been found to be the best procedure when individual coaches are responsible for their team's equipment.

Every athletic department needs a drying room in conjunction with the equipment room. Placing wet uniforms in a locker after practice or a game will tend to rot the material and to rust the lockers. With the use of a drying room this problem will be solved, and the department will save a considerable amount of equipment. An inexpensive drying room can be built in most gymnasiums if one is not available.

Equipment Room Management

An equipment room manager is indispensable to the director, teacher, and coach whose presence is required on the field or in the training room when equipment is most wanted by students. Universities and large colleges employ a full-time equipment room manager. A few large high schools can afford a full-time manager, but smaller institutions cannot. A paraprofessional may be employed on a full or part-time basis to take charge of the equipment. This responsibility is sometimes combined with another position. In most high schools the coach must assume responsibility for the equipment room. A common practice, however, is to appoint students to manage the equipment room. In some schools the students are paid, but in many schools the students have this as part of their management responsibility. Student managers are rarely as capable and proficient as full-time managers, but if they are carefully selected and trained, they will discharge their responsibilities satisfactorily.

Student assistants may be used if the equipment room manager requires assistance. No other students should be permitted in the equipment room. When everyone has access to the equipment, the manager faces a hopeless task in preventing loss and preserving order.

Issuing equipment. Every piece of equipment issued should be accounted for. A very desirable method of keeping a record of equipment is through the card system. Each student signs a card on which is recorded the equipment issued. Every sport has a special card of a different color. On each card are listed the equipment items that are issued for that sport. The football cards may be yellow and the basketball cards white. After each card is signed it is filed alphabetically according to its color. Figure 14-3 is an example of a card that might be used.

At the beginning of the school year the equipment manager should assign all lockers, issue equipment to the students upon request of the director or coaches, and handle the daily routine task of managing the towel service. In the course of a season the equipment manager should inspect the playing equipment from time to time. This is done for the

EQUIPMENT RECORD.

FOOTBALL

Name_____			
Address _____			
		Date_____	
		Class_____	

Practice	Out	In	
Pants			
Shoulder Pads			
Jersey			
Under-shirt			
Sox—Inner			
Sox—Wool			
Supporter			Locker
Stockings			No. _____
Shoes			Combination
Special Pads			
Towel			
Sweat-shirt			
Game			
Pants—Rain			
Pants			
Jersey			
Shoes			
Shoes—Rain			
Sox			

Checked out by_____
Checked in by_____

Figure 14-3. Equipment Record.

purpose of culling all equipment that is beginning to wear and of saving the athlete from possible injuries. The material that has been culled should be sent to the repair shop immediately. This means of checking and repairing often saves the department considerable money.

At the end of the playing season the equipment manager and assistants check in all equipment. This can be done far better by clearing the lockers than by having the players check in their own equipment to the stockroom. There are always some players with more equipment than is charged against them, and this is the best method of securing it. Each piece of equipment, when checked in, should be tagged with its size and with the former player's name. This saves the manager time the following season in giving it out to the returning players. Each article should be closely inspected, and those needing cleaning and repairing should be cared for at once. An inventory can be taken at this time in order to determine the equipment consumed during the season. A check can be made at the close of the season to see how the equipment has stood up in comparison with other makes during the previous years.

Some schools check each player's equipment into the equipment room daily. Every player is given a number that is the key to the control of this sytem. This number appears upon the locker to which the player is assigned. It is marked upon each piece of equipment except the white equipment such as towels and socks. The number is also marked on the equipment rack above each player's hook in the equipment room where the equipment is kept at all times. Only the white equipment is retained in the lockers. On reporting for practice, the player comes to the window of the stockroom and gives his or her number to the equipment manager, who goes to the rack and brings the player all the equipment placed under that number. At the close of practice every evening the player returns the practice equipment to the window and the manager replaces it upon the rack. The manager checks the equipment displayed under each number daily and, if any pieces are missing, endeavors to locate them. If any of the equipment is in need of repair, it is attended to immediately. The night before a game the practice equipment is removed from the racks and temporarily stored. Game equipment is substituted in its place upon the racks, and the player follows the same routine on the day of the game as for the practice sessions. This is an excellent system of handling athletic equipment, and it is recommended if a large equipment room is available.

All equipment that is taken from the equipment room must be accounted for in some way. Instructors and coaches or their managers should sign for the equipment they use. Students who check out balls and other equipment for free play should sign for them. Ordinarily, they are requested to return the equipment within a certain time and never to keep it overnight. The practice of students signing for equipment and then permitting other students to return it later should be discouraged. This frequently results in lost equipment. In some schools each student checking out an article for free play exchanges it for an ID card which is not returned until the borrowed items are returned. All equipment should be numbered and each student should then sign for a numbered item.

Use of equipment. The development of the proper attitude among all students regarding their equipment is the most important consideration in the care of equipment. Much equipment is lost or damaged by carelessness or destructiveness. Frequently, varsity athletes do not feel an obligation to treat equipment carefully. Unless all students have a respect for property and are indoctrinated with a desire to care for their equipment properly, considerable damage and loss will be incurred. Students must appreciate the fact that equipment is loaned and not given to them and that they are responsible if it is lost. Petty thievery can best be combated by making each player accountable for everything that is checked out.

Marking equipment. All pieces of athletic equipment of an institution should be marked in some way in order to identify them. The usual way of doing this is to stencil or stamp the name or initials of the school on the equipment. In addition, athletic clothing should have sizes clearly indicated. The identification of the school on athletic clothing does not suffice; the items issued to each player should be numbered and the numbers recorded in the equipment room. This is additional bookkeeping, but it helps to trace missing articles. When this system is known to all the students within a school, it reduces the amount of stealing. Including the year of purchase in the marking system is a good procedure to use in determining the durability of equipment.

Cloth articles may be successfully marked with a stencil and stencil paint or an India ink stamp. Leather goods can be stamped. In some institutions initials are burned into leather goods, but unless this is done carefully, the leather will be damaged. Wooden items of equipment can be marked by burning initials at some convenient spot. Identification labels can be sewed into some articles. Many items of equipment may be purchased already marked. An additional charge is usually made for this service.

Care of Specific Types of Equipment

It stands to reason that not all athletic equipment can be treated, cleaned, or stored in the same way. The materials from which the equipment is made—leather, rubber, fabric, wood, and so forth—require different methods of care. If the persons using it are to get the maximum service from the equipment, they must be familiar with the manner of caring for the various types of apparatus on hand.

Leather balls. The vulnerable part of any leather ball is the stitching. The stitiching can be protected by relieving the pressure inside the ball between seasons. Wiping off moisture and then slowly drying the ball when it is wet rather than forced drying will also protect the stitching. When inflating a ball with a rubber core valve, always moisten the needle, preferably with glycerin. If the needle is moistened with the mouth, remove the moisture from the needle after using it. A rusty needle will injure the core of the valve. The needle should be inserted with a gentle; rotary motion. A pressure gauge should always be used to insure correct inflation. A chart should be available next to the pump or on the wall to indicate the desirable air pressure for the different types of balls. Overinflation should be avoided, inasmuch as it strains the fabric lining and thus affects the shape and life of the ball.

A ball that has been used in the mud should be wiped clean with a damp cloth and dried at the normal room temperature. Leather balls should never be placed near a radiator or hot-air register. To clean a ball that has been discolored, commerical cleaners or saddle soap are recommended. When the leather of a ball has become harsh and rough because of repeated exposure to moisture, an application of a commerical leather dressing or a light mineral oil will prove helpful.

Leather balls should be partially deflated when stored away between seasons. They should be stored in a cool, dry place without objects of appreciable weight upon them.

Rubber balls. The chief enemies of rubber are direct sunlight, heat, grease, and oil. With regard to sunlight and heat, all that can be done is to avoid exposure when possible. Grease and oil should be removed with soap and warm water. Dry-cleaning fluids should never be used on rubber goods. Rubber balls should be stored in a cool, dry bin or box away from heat and sunlight.

Textile fabrics. The manufacturer's instructions should be carefully followed to ensure maximum fabric life, prevent shrinkage, and maintain true colors. Cleaning of equipment should be done by trained and skilled operators. A good policy is to initially clean one item from a new group of garments to make certain the recommended cleaning instructions do not damage the garment. Water temperature, wet versus dry cleaning, the type of detergent, and the cleaning process should be determined by the manufacturer's recommendations.

All woolen items must be protected against moths. Moths will not attack nylon or cotton fabrics. After jerseys are cleaned, they should be stored away by sizes. They should not be stored in open bins where dust will collect but in closed containers.

Leather goods. The most common sources of trouble with leather goods are high temperatures and excessive moisture. There are three types of formations which accumulate on leather, only one of which is harmful. This is green mold, which rots leather. In order to prevent green mold rot, leather articles should be kept in a cool, dry place. When wet, leather equipment should be dried immediately, but the action should not be forced. The article should be dried at normal room temperature without the use of artificial heat. Sun drying and air streams or pressure should never be used.

The proper care of leather shoes is especially important. They are subject to dampness due to perspiration, rain, or snow. This condition tends to remove the tanning oil from the leather, causing it to dry out and crack. In addition, shoes if worn when very wet become misshapen. In caring for wet shoes, lime and mud should first be removed. Warm water should be used if necessary. Oil or grease should then be applied and worked into the leather. Castor oil is especially recommended. If the oil is warmed before application, it is more effective. Oil should be applied to the uppers, and wool grease to the soles. It is important to keep oil and grease away from rubber cleats. Wearing football, baseball, softball, and track shoes on stone or concrete floors should be discouraged.

Before leather shoes are stored away after the season they should be cleaned and oiled. They should be oiled again about the middle of the year. The toes should be stuffed with paper to help the shoe retain its shape. The shoes should be stored in special compartments to promote air circulation and to avoid crushing.

Wooden equipment. Wooden equipment, such as bats, hockey sticks, bows, and lacrosse sticks, are built to last for long periods of time and will do so when properly handled. Moisture is the main source of difficulty. It will damage the wood where the finish has worn away. Consequently, applications of warm linseed oil are recommended whenever the finish of the wood requires it. Equipment should be stored in such a way that warping is prevented. Storage of wooden equipment in a cool, dry place is recommended.

Nets and rackets. Nets that are exposed to dampness will rot. Nets that are used outdoors should be tarred. If they are dipped in creosote every year, their life will be prolonged. They should be taken in during bad weather, kept dry, and repaired at the first indication of damage. If space is available, it is better to hang tarred nets on pegs in a cool, dry area rather than to fold or roll them. Badminton and tennis rackets should always be kept in presses when not in use. Restringing is much less expensive when it is done immediately after a string has been broken. Probably the greatest source of racket problems is too great string tension. This condition greatly increases string breakage and the loss of shape of the frames. At the same time it does not improve the performance of the poor and average players. Expert players use tightly strung rackets, but such equipment is neither necessary nor desirable in physical education and intramural activities. A tension of from 50 to 60 pounds is adequate for such use.

Badminton shuttlecocks. The greatest damage to shuttlecocks comes through careless use. Students should not be permitted to abuse this fragile equipment. Shuttlecocks are also saved when students are prevented from smashing and swinging vigorously until they have developed proper skill and timing. Feather shuttlecocks should be kept in a moist environment since the feathers lose their oils in a dry atmosphere.

Archery tackle. All bows should be unstrung when not in use. On the archery range the bow should be hung on the ground quiver between rounds. When not in use, the arrows should be racked in a dry place. The rack should be so constructed that there are three pressure points on the arrow—two inches from either end, and one in the middle—to prevent warping.

Helmets. Helmets should be cleaned before they are stored away. Leather linings should be cleaned with saddle soap and then have a light coat of castor oil applied. The outside should be cleaned with a recommended solution. In storing helmets the important consideration is to maintain their shape. They can be stored on helmet racks, on helmet hangers, or in the boxes in which they were delivered. They should not be hung by the chin strap. Helmets should not be crushed by having heavy objects placed upon them or by having an individual sit upon them. Throwing helmets should also be prevented. The common practice of carrying helmets in a duffle bag is not recommended.

Hip and shoulder pads. These items of equipment should be cleaned and repaired before being stored. Hip and shoulder pads can be washed with warm water and soap if care is used to avoid getting too much water into materials, such as kapok, which absorb it. Leather parts should be lightly oiled after cleaning. Special forms upon which shoulder pads may be stacked are easily made. Stacking pads more than five or six high will spread the arches of the bottom pads to the point where they lose their body-conforming shape. If space is available, open wooden racks to accommodate not more than two pads to each space is the ideal arrangement. Hip pads should be hung by the belt loop.

Mats. Mats should be washed daily with a mat disinfectant. Mats will last longer if left flat rather than rolled. When mats must be rolled for storage they should be rolled around a cylinder to minimize the pressure that is put on the mat surface. Cuts, tears, and splits in the mats should be repaired immediately with the repair kit that is provided by the manufacturer. A clean surface on which to place mats will protect the mat from damage. Even after many years of use, mats can be recoated and restored to their original condition. Care must be taken when moving mats so they will not be gouged or otherwise damaged. It is recommended that transporters be used when moving large wrestling mats.

Track equipment. Metal shots should be cleaned with steel wool and oiled before being stored away. Steel tapes should be treated similarly. Discuses should be cleaned and shellacked, then placed in a rack, and stored in a room that is not overheated. Javelins should always be hung from a height with the point downward to prevent warping.

Cleaning Uniforms

The great majority of institutions must rely upon commercial cleaners to launder their athletic uniforms. This is a specialized type of work which requires trained personnel and proper facilities. The athletic director would be well advised to seek a cleaner who specializes in this type of cleaning.

Athletic uniforms are among the most difficult-to-clean garments known to the cleaning industry. They are subjected to dirt, perspiration, rough usage, and a variety of stains—grass, blood, resin, iodine, and adhesive tape. In addition, practically all items of the uniform consist of two or more fabrics, each of which may require separate handling.

Excessive heat, whether in the wash water, rinse water, or in drying, will shrink the garment. Generally lukewarm water (100° F.) is recommended. In any case, the rinse water should be the same temperature as the wash water. Automatic tumble dryers and certain forced air methods are dangerous because of the heat.

White garments should always be washed alone. Different colored garments should not be mixed. Colored garments are not adversely affected by water at a lukewarm temperature. High temperatures can be very harmful to colored items. Any bleaching agent will have a serious effect on the fastness of color and therefore should be restricted to white or natural cotton garments.

For certain fabrics, especially brushed and woven wool, dry cleaning is the only safe method. It may also be used successfully to remove dirt and ordinary stains from other garments. However, dry cleaning normally is not sufficient to combat perspiration and perspiration stains. Wet cleaning must be used in such instances.

Any garment, such as two-way stretch football pants, that contains rubber yarn or elastic in the knit fabric should never be dry cleaned. The cleaning fluid will dissolve the rubber threads. The same holds true for water-repellent garments.

Sporting goods manufacturers recommend that the athletic director take a complete uniform to the cleaner in advance of the season to prepare the personnel for the type of cleaning it will require. If the cleaner knows the fabrics involved in the various parts of the uniform, whether or not rubber is used, and the color fastness of the garments, the fabric is much more likely to be cleaned properly.

Repairing Equipment

Physical education and athletic directors would profit by investigating thoroughly the possibilities of repairing their own equipment. The extent to which it should be repaired depends upon the size of the school and amount of equipment handled. In some of the larger institutions the stockrooms are so completely equipped that all equipment can be repaired. The practice in the majority of schools is to make simple repairs and to send the remainder to local repair companies or national reconditioning concerns. Many schools could cut their equipment bill appreciably by enlarging their repairing facilities.

A sewing machine that can sew leather as well as textile materials is indispensable in the equipment room. Such a sewing machine will more than pay for itself in a short time by mending the rips and tears that occur so frequently in all types of athletic materials. Special facilities for sewing footballs, basketballs, and baseballs by hand should be available also.

The repair of shoes is important. The shoes should be inspected frequently in order that damage may be detected at its beginning. Detachable cleats should be shifted around so that they will wear evenly and be of uniform height on all shoes. When the cleats are shifted, the fixtures should be checked to ascertain that they are tight. The old cleats should be used on the practice shoes and the new ones placed on the game shoes. It frequently occurs that when one shoe is useless for further wear, its mate is still in fair condition. These odd shoes should be saved for replacements.

Common sense must be used in repairing equipment. Up to a certain point it is good economy to recondition athletic materials, but beyond that it is a waste of money. Some directors make the mistake of repairing old equipment that will not give them enough service to pay for the repairs made. It is more advisable at times to sell old equipment to cleaning and reconditioning firms and use the money to buy new equipment.

In most schools only minor repairs can be made on athletic equipment. The usual practice is to send all equipment in need of repair to special equipment reconditioning companies. A number of these have developed in all sections of the country. Originally, many of these firms were not adequately prepared to do effective work, but most of those that have survived have developed the personnel, the specialized equipment, and the technical skill to do a superior job of reconditioning athletic equipment. It is the experience of most directors that in the long run it is more economical to turn over the bulk of the repair work to reputable concerns of this type.

School Laundry

The great amount of laundry service which physical education departments need every year, particularly for towels, runs into large sums of money. More and more schools are finding they can reduce this expense considerably by installing laundry units and doing their own laundry. All that is necessary is the purchase of a good washing machine and dryer. The work of laundering the equipment can be done by the equipment manager, the custodian, or student help.

SELECTED REFERENCES

Athletic Handbook. St. Louis: Rawlings Sporting Goods Company, 1974.
Care of Athletic Equipment. Chicago: Wilson Sporting Goods Company.
Cleaning Athletic Garments. Chicago: Wilson Sporting Goods Company.
SPOMER, JOHN, *Athletic Clothing Facts.* Chicago: National Sporting Goods Association, 1975.
SPOMER, JOHN, *Athletic Footwear Facts.* Chicago: National Sporting Goods Association, 1975.

NOTES

1. National Federation of State High School Associations, *Handbook: 1976 and 1977* (Elgin, Illinois), pp. 24–25.
2. Athletic Goods Manufacturers Association, *How to Budget, Select, and Order Athletic Equipment* (Chicago, Athletic Goods Manufacturers Association, 1962), pp. 14–17.

15

Budget Making
and Finance

IMPORTANCE OF EFFICIENT FINANCIAL
MANAGEMENT

Departmental financial management is one of the most important duties of the physical education administrator. This involves the instructional and intramural programs and sometimes the interscholastic program in elementary and secondary schools. Driver education and health education programs are also the responsibility of many physical education administrators. In addition, college and university administrators will have professional preparation programs when majors in physical education, health education, and recreation education are offered within the department. The physical education administrator's duties will include the handling of money, making all kinds of financial transactions, bookkeeping, and preparing budgets. In handling these financial matters, simple and effective procedures are available and should be used.

Any school official who receives and expends funds is expected to employ sound business methods. To do otherwise causes an adverse reflection upon the administrator. Regardless of the size of the institution or the amount of money involved, no teacher or administrator can afford to be careless or ignorant in handling public funds.

Another reason why efficient financial management is important is that maximum benefit must be secured from the revenue available. Most departments never have sufficient funds to provide all the desired services to students. Consequently, available resources must be wisely employed. Almost invariably those departments with the most serious financial problems use the most unbusinesslike procedures. This is particularly true of small high schools and colleges.

Despite the great importance of this phase of their duties, few directors are prepared for the efficient financial administration of the physical education department when they first undertake it. The majority of administrators learn by the trial-and-error method. Experience may be the best teacher; but it is an expensive teacher, particularly where finance is concerned. Large universities and colleges emphasize the importance of special training when they employ an expert to handle the business affairs of the intercollegiate athletic program. The director is frequently selected for his/her business ability. Professional physical education programs should make provision to prepare physical educators for the financial responsibilities that they will encounter in their positions.

THE BUDGET

The budget is a prepared statement of estimated income and expenditures. Although a physical education budget is submitted by the director, it must be the result of the combined efforts of the departmental faculty members and paraprofessionals who have equipment responsibilities. In the same manner, coaches and trainers must assist the athletic director in preparing the athletic budget. Maximum input is thus obtained relative to needs for the various segments of the physical education and athletic programs. In larger departments, it is advisable to elect representatives to serve as a budget committee to facilitate planning for long range as well as immediate needs. Budgets will be planned well in advance of the fiscal period in which they will be used. The fiscal year for most educational institutions is the period from July 1 to June 30. Governmental regulations and local policy will determine the time schedule that must be followed when preparing and presenting a budget.

Line Item Budget

This has been the traditional, incremental budget which has been used for physical education and athletic programs. It is classified as a historical budget in that the specific expenditure items that form this budget are based on information from previous years' budgets together with anticipated changes keyed to such things as escalating costs, increasing or decreasing student population and new programs. Too often these budgets are characterized by the inclusion of programs without seriously analyzing them to see if they are still useful or if resources could be used more effectively if they were reallocated.

Planning-Programming-Budgeting System (PPBS)

This is a comprehensive budgeting process that has been used extensively in private business and by governmental agencies. Great impetus was given to this sytem by its successful use in the Defense Department under the direction of Robert McNamara in the early 1960's. Many educational institutions are using PPBS or are investigating the advantages such a system would have.

PPBS requires the careful establishment of goals and objectives (Planning). Programs are then developed to reach these goals (Programming). The final step is the allocating of resources (Budgeting). One of the prime values of this system is that planning, programming, and budgeting are coordinated. It is necessary to extend the planning over a period of years and each program must be compared to the others to determine how the funds can best be used to attain the goals and objectives that were established. This system provides the administrator with a means of objectively evaluating programs and determining where the resources should be allocated.

According to Hartley, PPBS offers at least four important advantages over traditional practices;[1]

1. information on total system costs is output, or program, oriented.
2. analysis of possible alternative programs and of alternative means of meeting program objectives is more extensive.
3. the planning process is continuous and includes multi-year plans so that future year implications of present decisions are explicitly identified.
4. policy is an ordered process in a well-defined organization which directs major lines of action toward perceptible program goals.

Variations and combinations of the line item budget and PPBS are also used. Even though the budget might be shown as a line item budget, the planning and programming which is involved in PPBS can be utilized to arrive at the budgetary figures. There is difficulty in accurately evaluating many goals of physical education and athletics, and there are intangible goals that administrators might want to consider when making budget decisions. However, the PPBS process is important and its key features should be incorporated into the physical education administrator's budgetary procedure.

THE PHYSICAL EDUCATION BUDGET

Although in some schools the physical education budget includes interschool athletics, most schools prepare a separate budget for athletics. The physical education budget is much easier to prepare when athletics are separated since income does not have to be estimated and it does not involve the amount or variety of expenditures that are present in an interschool athletic budget. For efficient financial planning, it is usually better to prepare a separate athletic budget.

Source of Financial Support

The physical education instructional program should be financed from the school budget the same as any other academic subject. At the college and university level the major program will also be financed with institutional resources. The intramural/recreational program is considered to be an integral part of the educational program and should be supported from regular school funds. As was explained in Chapter 10, college and university intramural/recreational programs are frequently supported, at least partially, by sources such as student fees. Even when this is the case, the cost of facilities and personnel are almost always carried in the institutional budget.

Steps in Preparing the Physical Education Budget

The major items in a physical education budget are capital outlay, new equipment, expendable equipment, and maintenance and repair. These items should be included under these separate headings in the budget. Capital outlay includes all expenditures that increase the value of the school plant, such as additions of any kind to the grounds, new buildings or fixed equipment. Permanent bleachers, tennis courts, or a new shower room are examples of capital outlay. Maintenance and repair items include painting, refinishing, and repair of equipment. This category also includes replacement items in some budgets.

New equipment includes semi-permanent items such as wrestling mats, gymnastic equipment, volleyball standards, and stop watches. This equipment will last for an indefinite period of time. Expendable items are supplies such as balls, nets, shuttlecocks, bats, which are worn out in a relatively short period of time through normal use.

After determining the equipment that will be needed to attain departmental goals in the next fiscal year, the next step is to determine equipment that will need to be purchased. The administrator must know what equipment is on hand and the condition of the equipment. This can best be accomplished by use of a perpetual inventory (Figure 15-1) and a periodic inventory (Figure 15-2). The perpetual inventory should be kept up to date throughout the year by recording when new items are received and/or put into use and when a worn out item is discarded. This inventory has a record of when items were purchased so an approximation as to the remaining life of different items can be made. The inventory information also allows the administrator to evaluate the longevity of similar items purchased from different companies and thereby serves as a guide for future purchases. The periodic inventory should be made as close to the time of the submission of the budget as possible and is used to provide a complete record of the equipment and supplies for which the department is responsible. The items on a periodic inventory can either be alphabetized or grouped by activity or type of equipment and then alphabetized. The periodic inventory total for each item should also be recorded on the perpetual inventory for that item.

The next step is to determine the total amount and type of equipment which will be needed during the next school year. If a line item budget is being used, analysis of budgets for previous years will indicate the amount of equipment normally required. This amount can be used as the starting point for determining over-all requirements. Changes in the number of students, departmental policies, or the nature of the service and intramural programs will increase or decrease this amount. When the estimate of total equipment needed has been obtained, the amount of new equipment to be ordered will be the difference between what is required and what is left over.

In making the estimate of what is needed the administrator should be certain to order an adequate amount. It is better to err on the side of too much rather than too little equipment. This is not to suggest padding the budget, but to recommend liberal rather than ultraconservative estimates. It is preferable to have a small amount of equipment left over at the end of the year rather than to run short.

In some elementary and secondary schools the physical education department is given a budget for supplies (balls, nets, rackets, bows, arrows, shuttlecocks, etc.) based on a certain amount per student in school. All expendable items for the department for the year must be purchased from this budget. In regard to equipment items (trampoline, parallel bars, mats, baskets, etc.) the principal is sometimes allocated a lump sum for such items annually. Priorities are established in light of all the school's educational needs, and funds are allocated accordingly.

After the budget has received the necessary approvals, the equipment should be ordered. Practice varies in this regard. In some schools the physical education administrator is free to order whatever equipment

PERPETUAL INVENTORY FORM

Item _____

Catalog # and Specifications	Number Ordered	Cost		Supplier & Address	Purchase Order #	Invoice Order #	Date Rec'd	Faculty Requesting	Inventory				
		Unit	Total						Date	New	Used	Dis-card	Total

Figure 15-1. Perpetual Inventory Form.

PERIODIC INVENTORY FORM

Page _____

Category of equipment _____

Date of Inventory _____

Item Description	1 New	2 Good	3 Fair	4 Discarded	5 Total	6 Purchased Since Last Inventory	7 Previous Inventory	8 Total	9 Lost (Diff. between Col. 8 & 5)	10 Needed For Program	11 Additional Number Needed (Diff. between Col. 10 & 5)

Figure 15-2. Periodic Inventory Form.

is preferred if total spending does not exceed the money allocated. In other schools bids from several merchandizers must be invited. In this case the administrator must prepare detailed specifications.

The expertise of staff members should be solicited before ordering new equipment. Some staff members may have had more experience with certain items of equipment than the adminstrator, and their recommendations will be very helpful.

THE ATHLETIC BUDGET

Support of Interschool Athletics

Interscholastic and intercollegiate athletics are usually supported in part from the institutional budget and in part from gate receipts and other sources of income. Although most schools include the salaries of coaches from the regular institutional budget and provide for the maintenance and operation of the athletic facilities, many institutions do not go so far as to appropriate funds to meet all of the current expenses of the athletic program.

Ideally, interschool athletics should be financed in the same way as any other school subject. The only justification for interscholastic and intercollegiate athletics is the significant educational experiences they provide. These experiences are so vital and important that they merit financial support from institutional funds. These values of athletics cannot be obtained if the program must be supported by gate receipts. Gate receipts and educational outcomes are incompatible objectives of interschool athletics. Experience has repeatedly demonstrated that athletics are conducted on a much higher plane if they derive their support from regular school funds.

The reason for the failure of many schools to finance athletics properly stems from the philosphy that only curricular activities are deserving of such support. Athletics originated as extracurricular activities and in many schools are still considered in that category. However, there is an increasing trend to regard athletics as an integral part of the school curriculum, and in many states boards of education are empowered to provide financial assistance from regular school funds.

The practice of expecting interschool athletics to be largely self-supporting has led to most of the problems that have developed. The amount of gate receipts is largely dependent upon the success of the teams. The effort to produce winning teams often results in undesirable educational practices. When the public exerts undue influence on the interschool programs, the educational authorities lose control and objectionable policies are frequently followed. Interschool programs must have financial independence if they are to emphasize educational goals with value to the participants being the paramount consideration.

The Educational Policies Commission strongly recommends that the complete costs of the interscholastic athletic program be paid out of general school funds. In some states this cannot be done until permissive legislation is passed. Such legislation should be initiated in those states where it is needed.

The results of financing interscholastic athletics entirely out of tax funds in one city are reported as follows by the Educational Policies Commission:[2]

1. The high school program has ceased to be a commercial enterprise, dependent on gate receipts. Outside pressure for postseason, charity, all-star, and curtain raiser games have been eliminated.
2. More adequate health and safety protection is accomplished by having fewer games and contests, avoiding play during inclement weather, providing safe equipment and safe transportation, and valuing the health of the participant above the winning of the game.
3. Most football games are now played on week-end afternoons, with resulting decrease in such problems as vandalism and rowdyism.
4. All schools within a system are assured of equal quality of equipment and supplies. Through central purchasing savings can be had.
5. Some of the hidden costs of public high school athletic fees are reduced for the student.

Sources of Athletic Income in High Schools

The school board should allocate funds to adequately support the entire athletic budget. The athletic budget must be carefully prepared and justifications provided to show how the money will be used to provide a quality program. Other sources of income are also used in many high schools. When money is obtained from these it should revert to the institutional budget and not affect the amount of money that is available for athletics. The athletic program should not be determined by such factors as bad weather and losing seasons which will reduce gate receipts.

Gate receipts. Gate receipts are an important source of income for some interscholastic programs. Football and basketball are the chief income-producing sports, although even these are not operated at a profit in many small schools. The other interscholastic sports rarely produce a significant profit.

Gate receipts should come predominantly from the adult public. It is an accepted policy to keep admission prices for students at a minimum; some high schools admit all students free. Students should also be given priority when it is necessary to limit attendance at athletic contests because of inadequate seating accommodations.

The philosophy that the interschool athletic program should be subsidized by the institution does not imply that gate receipts should be abolished. Gate receipts are an important source of income for some school districts and charging a fee to the public is helpful to many school administrators in maintaining crowd control. Gate receipts are not objectionable so long as they are incidental. Sufficient funds should be appropriated to insure the adequate operation of the program. The gate receipts would then revert to the institutional budget.

In many high schools all athletic income goes directly into the student activity budget. This includes gate receipts and guarantees that come from games played away from home. In this situation the costs for equipment, travel, medical care, scouting, advertising, towels, laundry, films, officials, and other operational expenses will be defrayed by the student activity budget.

Ordinarily high schools do not have guarantees. The usual procedure is for the home team to keep all gate receipts.

Student activity fees. Another important source of income is derived from the student activity fee. Some high schools have adopted a student activity plan to provide support for all student activities. Under this plan each student pays a prescribed amount and is entitled to admission to all home athletic contests and all other school functions for which there is a charge, such as school plays and concerts. In addition, the cost of the student newspaper and the school annual is defrayed in whole or in part. Most schools also admit students from the visiting institutions to athletic contests at a reduced rate upon presentation of the student body card. Students who do not belong to the student activity association are usually admitted to home contests at a reduced fee.

The income from student body fees is usually apportioned over the various student activities. The allocation may be made by the student council, a student activity board, or a committee that consists of representatives of the various activities.

Booster clubs. Parent and community booster clubs are sometimes organized to support the athletic program. Major equipment items are purchased by these groups and they also assist in the operation of concessions that can provide signficant sums of money for the program. Booster groups sponsor end-of-the-season athletic banquets in some communities. They can be a positive force in a community, but care must be taken that the total athletic program receives support and not only certain segments. An even greater danger of booster clubs is that they will unduly influence the organization and administration of the athletic program. Administration and organization must remain the sole responsibility of the educational authorities. This is another reason why it is much preferred that the athletic program be supported 100 percent by the board of education.

Procedure in Preparing the Athletic Budget

At the end of the season for each sport a careful inventory of the equipment and supplies is made. Based upon this inventory the head coach of the sport makes out a tentative list of the equipment that will be needed for the following year. This list and other estimated costs are reviewed with the athletic director who may or may not modify it in consideration of the anticipated funds. The athletic director submits a total athletic budget to the department chairperson or principal, depending on the school's table of organization. (In some large systems the athletic director from each school submits a budget to the director of athletics for the entire school system who prepares a district athletic budget.) The principal will submit the budget to the superintendent of schools who in turn presents the budget to the board of education for final approval.

Sources of Athletic Income in Colleges and Universities

In the institutions of higher learning the chief sources of athletic income are gate receipts, student athletic fees, activity tickets, and institutional appropriations. Additional sources of revenue may be contributions, subscriptions, concessions, programs, parking fees, rentals, and radio and television broadcasting fees.

Contrary to the popular impression, intercollegiate athletics in the majority of institutions are not self-supporting. Were it not for substantial support from institutional budgets, most intercollegiate athletic programs could not continue. The salaries of coaches and other personnel connected with athletics, as well as the expense of maintaining and operating athletic facilities, come from this source at all but a relatively few universities where high powered football programs provide significant sums of money. Many colleges and universities expect that athletic income will be sufficient to cover such operating expenses as equipment, travel, medical care, laundry, and officiating.

A number of the wealthier private colleges provide for the complete support of intercollegiate athletics in the general budget. All expenses are covered by appropriations. The athletic income is purely incidental and reverts to the institutional budget.

Heavy reliance is placed upon gate receipts in colleges and universities. The bulk of these come from football and basketball. When these two sports must support themselves as well as most of the other sports and pay salaries and provide college buildings and equipment, a situation is created which invites overemphasis by those concerned with athletic direction and management. Educators have been very critical of various uneducational aspects of intercollegiate athletics; yet they themselves are partially responsible for their existence. If the heavy burden on gate receipts could be lightened by adequate financial support, athletics would become more valuable as an educational agency.

Student fees help substantially in supporting the intercollegiate athletic program. Most institutions require a student activity fee and from this fee a percentage is allocated for athletics. In some of the major athletic schools, the students also must purchase individual game tickets or a season ticket, usually at a reduced cost.

Concessions

The income-producing possibilities of concessions have rarely been appreciated in small schools and colleges. In these smaller institutions, where the financial need is the greatest, the concessions are frequently overlooked or, if they are used, they are inefficiently operated. Professional teams and large university athletic departments have discovered that there is substantial revenue in concessions if they are properly handled.

Concessions may be handled by the school itself or by an outside concessionaire. Within the school it may be operated by the physical education or athletic department, the athletic association, or by some student organization. When concessions are handled outside the school, the concessionaire should be selected after competitive bids have been received. In advertising bids the detailed specifications that will govern the concession should be stated and should become part of the concession contract. The concession specifications should indicate the commodities that may be sold. Standards of sanitation and methods of vending should also be explicitly stated.

The contract should provide for payment of a percentage of gross receipts. The flat-sum arrangement may work a hardship on the institution or the concessionaire. Net income should not be used as the basis for determining percentages, as there is invariably the question of what costs the concessionaire will include in determining net proceeds.

For interschool athletic events that draw considerable attendance, the management of the concessions becomes a business operation of such size that high schools and colleges have difficulty handling it effectively. In these instances most of the institutions have found it advantageous to have a concessionaire handle them. Experience has shown that more income has been received from a concessionaire than from a school-operated concession.

Increasing Gate Receipts

The best way to increase gate receipts from high school and college athletics is to have winning teams. However, there are other methods of making athletic contests more attractive to the public. A season ticket sold at a reduced rate is one of the most effective methods of increasing gate receipts. Such a plan guarantees a definite income despite poor teams and bad weather. It also provides funds early in the season when they are needed to get under way. Adults are appreciative of the opportunity because it results in a saving to them. The price of a season ticket varies from 50 to 75 percent of the total cost of tickets to each home game. If season tickets are made transferable, they will prove more attractive to adults.

In many communities reserved seats will appeal to certain adults. Some individuals are willing to pay more if they are assured of a good seat. There are always individuals who are unable to arrive at the game in time to get a good seat and would not attend if reserved seats were not available.

Well-coached teams appeal to the public. Public interest cools quickly when the players demonstrate poor fundamentals and appear disorganized. Many individuals will continue to support a team even in defeat if it gives the appearance of being well coached. In this connection, it is important to schedule opponents of approximately the same strength as the home team. Unevenly matched teams are not good attractions. In addition to being well-coached, teams will appeal more to spectators if they are smartly attired.

One of the strongest attractions and most colorful features of athletic contests is the music, cheering, and pregame and half-time entertainment. Good officiating adds to everyone's enjoyment of a game. Attractive, accurate programs, a good scoreboard and a loud-speaker system with a capable announcer are all factors that provide satisfaction to the spectators.

Other factors that contribute to the comfort and enjoyment of spectators are good seats, convenient entrances and exits, and a sufficient number of clean, readily accessible restrooms. Having good parking facilities available near the athletic field or gymnasium is an important consideration. Contests should always be started at the time advertised.

There is no question whatsoever that night football produces substantially more revenue than afternoon contests. Most of the adult public who find it impossible to leave their work or business in the afternoon are able to attend at night.

The importance of good publicity in increasing gate receipts is well established. The entire matter of publicity is discussed in Chapter 17.

The Control of Finances

In the early days of interscholastic and intercollegiate athletics, the control of finances resided in the hands of the coach or graduate manager. These individuals were rarely called upon to account for the funds of the athletic department, and audits to check the athletic accounts were seldom used. Under these conditions, it is not surprising that a great deal of money was misused and misappropriated. Such financial practices naturally served to increase the evils of commercialization and subsidization.

High schools. Financially and educationally sound methods of handling interscholastic athletic funds have evolved. In general, the trend is for these moneys to be handled in the same manner as other school funds. The practice of having the treasurer or business manager of the board of education handle all athletic funds has much to recommend it. Such a plan centralizes all financial matters and insures a more businesslike procedure. In particular, a more accurate audit is likely to result. The recommended practice is to use a centralized accounting system whereby the responsibility for all financial accounts is centralized in one individual, such as the principal or a designated business manager. A system whereby the various accounts are decentralized and handled separately leads to confusion and inefficiency.

In the centralized accounting system all athletic funds, along with all other activity funds, are deposited with the school treasurer. Records are maintained for all deposits. When purchases are to be made, a purchase order in triplicate must be signed first by the athletic director and then certified by the school treasurer, and the remaining copy is kept by the athletic director. Bills are not paid by the school treasurer until an invoice has been received from the vendor and checked by the athletic director or designee that the materials received correspond with what has been ordered. At periodic intervals, probably once a month, the school treasurer submits a report to the athletic director and principal on the condition of the athletic budget.

The school treasurer should be bonded for the largest sum of money that will be in the fund during the year. The account should be audited by a qualified auditor.

Colleges and universities. As the faculty assumed control of athletics, it undertook to remove the control of finances from the hands of those directly in charge of athletics. Although athletic directors still handle the funds in a number of institutions, the common practice today is to place the handling of athletic finances in the office of the general business manager of the college or university. A number of the larger universities have a business manager within the department. The most satisfactory plan, however, is to have the university treasurer or the university business officer in actual charge of the care and distribution of athletic funds. This individual is usually a highly trained business person, well qualified to handle the funds of the athletic department. Under such a plan, the misuse of funds is reduced to a minimum.

Under this plan, the director may make out a requisition for any needed purchases. This requisition is sent to the purchasing department, where two vouchers are made out and sent to the vendor. The vendor sends the equipment to the athletic department and returns the vouchers with the equipment as bills. The athletic department receives and checks the equipment and vouchers. One of the vouchers is kept on file and the other is sent to the business office, which then pays for the purchase. When the director desires cash, a requisition is made out directly to the business office for the desired amount. Practically all institutions require receipts from the director or coach for cash expenditures.

The above plan has much to recommend it. The director may make purchases as desired, as long as the budget is not exceeded. The director is not deprived of authority to make expenditures.

Special Procedures in Large Cities

Interscholastic athletics in larger cities are usually coordinated by an individual who functions from a central office, usually the superintendent's office. Methods of operation vary from city to city. When funds for athletics are provided by the board of education, gate receipts are returned to the general fund. In other situations the receipts should be pooled and distributed as equitably as possible to all the schools. This insures that each school will have comparable financial resources and no school will have an advantage over any other. Athletic equipment is purchased on a centralized basis, although no school is required to purchase any item it does not want.

Budget Making

The first essential in the efficient management of any enterprise is to plan carefully in advance the income and the expenditures for a fiscal period. This process is essentially what is known as budget making. A budget is merely the complete financial plan, which is based upon the estimated expenditures to be made and the expected income. Budget making naturally originated in connection with business and governmental enterprises. The practice was found desirable and has since extended to most business enterprises and public service organizations, including the schools.

The safest way to avoid deficits in athletics is to adopt budgets that limit the appropriations to the income and then confine the expenditures to the appropriations. The budget results in planned spending. It is the best insurance of an equitable distribution of available funds to all the activities of the athletic department. Examples of the spending of too much money on one sport, resulting in the curtailment of other sports, are not hard to find. The antagonisms and embarrassment that may develop when this occurs could be eliminated if a budget were set up and followed. By means of the budget, the director can show where the money was spent and thus prevent any suspicion of misuse of funds. The need for increased appropriations can be shown and justified more easily and effectively with a budget than without one. Extravagant and foolish buying will be checked, and comparisons with previous years and with other institutions can be made. The budget permits an analysis of the cost of the various sports and reveals where revision can be made, if necessary, with the least loss in the effectiveness of the department.

Procedure in Making a Budget

There are far more poorly constructed budgets than well-constructed ones, since few athletic departments construct them in accordance with the accepted principles of budgetary procedure. Every school presents an individual problem, but there are some fundamental principles that should be observed by any director who is constructing a budget. There is nothing mysterious about making one; nor is it necessary to be a business expert to do it. Any administrator can construct a satisfactory budget by carefully following a few fundamental principles.

Physical education and athletic budgets are ordinarily prepared in March or April. They are made out annually. The director of physical education has the responsiblity for formulating the physical education budget. In colleges and universities the athletic director develops the athletic budget. This same situation prevails in the majority of high schools. However, the principal has this responsiblity in some schools. The superintendent, particularly in smaller schools, frequently carries this assignment. Other groups or individuals with this responsibility are the athletic council and the business manager of athletics.

The steps in constructing a budget are (1) collecting the necessary information, (2) classifying the information, and (3) presenting and adopting the budget.

Collecting the necessary information. The information the budget maker collects is concerned with the expected income and necessary expenditures. In estimating the income for the coming fiscal period, the director must consider carefully all the sources from which revenue may be expected. In regard to student fees, the director will need to consider any factors that may affect enrollment and the students' desire and ability to purchase tickets. The appropriation from the board of education or the board of trustees can be estimated from previous appropriations. The director is usually familiar with the board's policies and will probably know whether any changes in the appropriation are likely. If revenue is anticipated from any additional sources, the amount may be calculated on the basis of previous income from these sources.

The estimate of expenditures proceeds along similar lines. Information about departmental needs should be gathered and compiled continuously. The entire department should be encouraged to inform the director of present and future needs in order to determine accurately where new expenditures are needed most. The director should consult staff members who are in a position to assist in supplying needed information and should keep in constant touch with the supply houses and read current catalogues on the cost of athletic equipment.

Classifying the information. After the information has been gathered it should be classified. This insures uniformity of presentation and provides for accuracy in planning. It facilitates the gathering and compiling of the data, and makes easier the reviewing and revising of the estimates. The form the classification takes should resemble the form of the final budget. All the information is classified under two general heads: one dealing with the information concerning revenue and the other bearing on expenditures. Every item for which an expenditure is contemplated, even though it may amount to only a few dollars, should be reflected in the budget. These smaller items can be segregated under larger headings, but the detailed information should be available if requested.

Presenting and adopting the budget. In colleges, the athletic budget is first approved by the athletic committee or board which usually administers the policies of the department. If no such group exists, the president probably approves it. Final approval of the budget is usually made by the board of trustees or board of regents. High school budgets are first approved by the principal, then by the superintendent, and, finally, by the board of education. At times, the business manager of the college or high school approves the budget before it goes to the board of education or board of trustees. The budget should be adopted before any purchases are made or expenditures entered into for the next year.

Administering the Budget

After the athletic and physical education budgets are adopted, they become the financial program of the department. Should they be followed rigidly? There are some who believe that after the budget has been adopted the expenditures should be made as directed. Others hold to the view that the budget should be reviewed again when the expenditures are actually to be made. The general practice, however, is to follow the budget figures fairly closely. The variation is usually from three to five percent in which the expenditures exceed or fail to match the appropriations.

Practically all budgets make provisions for readjustments. Emergencies are certain to occur, and the budget should be elastic enough to provide for them. There are several different plans that may be followed. An emergency or contingency fund may be set aside in the original budget. But if this fund is too small, the administrator may feel cramped in his efforts to adjust appropriations to unforeseen circumstances. If on the other hand, the fund is too large, it may encourage waste and carelessness and thus defeat one of the main purposes of budget making. The most common plan is to transfer funds from one budgetary item that appears likely not to need all the available money to the item on which the demand has unexpectedly increased. Such transfers, if appreciable, however, must have the approval of the athletic board, the business manager, or (in colleges) the president or his designee.

Proper records should be kept in order that the actual revenue and expenditures may be compared with the budget estimates. These records are invaluable to the administrator when preparing a new budget. In addition, they are of value in making necessary adjustments where indicated in the current budget. The administrator should receive monthly reports to be informed of the relationship of income and expenses with the budget estimates. It is important to know whether actual income is in line with estimates. Information should always be available on the amount appropriated, the amount expended, commitments that must be paid but have not yet been received, and the unallocated balance. If income is much lower than anticipated during the first half of the fiscal period, it might be indicated that expenditures should be reduced in the second half of the period to prevent a serious deficit.

A Practical Budget

Physical education budget. In most situations, the board of education will allocate funds for the physical education program and intramural/recreational program from the general school fund. The primary responsibility is to develop the expenditure portion of the budget. Expendable supplies, new equipment, and funds for maintenance and repair should be provided for each aspect of the programs. Transportation to locations away from the school for classes must be budgeted where this is applicable. The usual procedure is to estimate the cost for each activity in the program and then consolidate this information into the major categories (new equipment, expendable supplies, transportation, officiating for intramurals, etc.). In some situations, additional categories will be needed for office supplies, student salaries, custodial assistance, and clerical work. In most high schools and in smaller colleges these items, together with faculty salaries, are included in the institutional budget.

Athletic budget. Athletic budgets will reflect receipts and expenditures. Anticipated receipts from each sport and other sources (institutional appropriations, donations, etc.) will be shown in one portion of the budget and the estimated expenditures will be presented in the second part of the budget. Expenditures will include anticipated costs of each activity for the fiscal year, office costs and possibly other general costs.

The various expenditure schedules may be itemized in detail. The following classification and codification system is suggested as an aid in keeping a detailed, reliable record of expenditures in the athletic department:

Classification of Activities

A. Football.
B. Baseball.
C. Basketball.
D. Track and cross country.
E. Wrestling.
F. Swimming.
G. Golf.
H. Tennis.
I. Gymnastics.
J. Lacrosse.
K. Field Hockey.
L. General.

Classification of Accounts

Office expense:
011 Dues and subscriptions.
012 Stamps and postage.
013 Telephone and telegraph.

014 Freight, express, and cartage.

015 General.

Printing:

021 Tickets, yearbooks.

022 Advertising—newspapers and magazines.

023 Advertising—posters, schedules, etc.

024 Advertising—photographs and engraving.

025 General printing.

Travel:

031 Team transportation.

032 Scouting.

033 Local transportation.

034 Hotel and lodging.

035 Meals.

036 General travel.

Supplies:

041 Athletic supplies (not equipment).

042 Medical supplies.

043 Grounds and pool supplies.

044 General.

Repairs:

051 Equipment repairs.

052 General repairs.

Wages:

061 Handling bleachers.

062 Ticket takers and ticket sellers.

063 Police.

064 Assistants to medical supervisor.

065 Auditing.

066 Student help in equipment and towel rooms.

067 General.

Equipment:

071 Equipment.

072 General.

Laundry and cleaning:

081 Towels.

082 Dry cleaning.

083 Laundry.

Insurance:
091 Travel.
092 Earnings.
093 Public liability.

Other expenditures:
101 Hospital and dental service.
102 Medical attention.
103 Awards.
104 Guarantees.
105 Officials—fees and expenses.

In those institutions where salaries are paid from athletic revenue, a salaries account should be carried. This would include all salaries that are not paid directly by the institution. The preceding classification is used as follows: every expenditure made is allocated to some activity. Thus, if a telephone bill for football is paid, football is charged with the amount of the bill. Therefore, the item will be recorded as 013A. The 013 refers to telephone and telegraph expense and the A to football. A trip by the tennis squad would be recorded as 031H for the transportation expense, 034H for the hotel expense, and 035H for the meal expense. When all expenditures are classified in this manner as they occur, it is a simple matter to find out what the total expenditures for each activity have been. The coach may employ the above system of recording expenditures in order to know the cost of the various items and activities without recourse to the business office or the school treasurer.

The Accounting Procedure

The proper functioning of the budget and the success of budgetary procedures depend largely upon an adequate accounting system. The director should understand the accounting procedure even though this might not be a primary responsibility. It would be impossible for the director to conduct a department on a businesslike basis without the help of an accounting system. Computerized systems are used in most institutions and provide immediate access to information as well as detailed periodic reports. These reports serve to restrict the expenditures to income. Unanticipated tendencies in cost and income will be revealed in time to revise the budget. The director secures much of the information for drafting the budget from the accounting records. The accounting method protects the director or the coach from charges of carelessness and misuse of funds. The director can base his requests for further financial assistance from the board upon the information supplied by the accounting records.

The individual in charge of the athletic finances is interested in current income and expenses. The accounting method classifies revenue on the receipts side of the budget. However, the recording of current expenditures is more complex. Copies of transactions for which funds have been expended should be kept for use during audits and in checking records. A balance sheet on which expenditures are regularly posted should be maintained in the department office for each account so that the current balance is known by the coach and athletic director. Completed expenditures must be regularly processed in the business office in order that computer printouts accurately reflect the current financial status.

The annual audit. Provisions for regular audits must be made if the budget is to function properly as an instrument of fiscal control. An audit serves as a check on the manner in which the director administers the budget and gives assurance that the budgetary provisions are being carried out. The audit should be made by competent auditors who are not directly connected with the administration of the school funds. A majority of schools follow this practice. Good budgetary procedure requires an external, independent, annual audit.

Expense reports

Following a trip by a school athletic team a report should be made of the expenses that were incurred. Receipts should be obtained for all expenditures and attached to the report form. The use of an expense report form facilitates the accounting of the expenses and is a businesslike procedure to follow. The form that is used should include pertinent information about the contest such as location, date and opponent; the mode of transportation; the number of athletes, coaches and managers making the trip; and the cost of meals, lodging and expenses.

Interschool Financial Agreement

Practically all colleges and large high schools sign contracts with each other for all interschool contests. The practice of making verbal financial agreements still persists in some of the smaller high schools. Such a procedure is hardly businesslike, and it naturally lends itself to misunderstanding and mistakes. In order to make financial agreements between schools more understandable, more explicit, and more binding, regular contracts should be signed by both schools for all contests.

Handling School Funds

Schools are frequently careless in their management of gate receipts. The large sums of money which often are involved should call forth all precautions to insure against loss. Another argument for the sale of tickets in advance of the game is that it prevents the accumulation of large sums of money. Theft insurance is carried by all large schools, and the game manager is usually bonded. Police protection should be provided, particularly when the funds are collected and taken from the ticket offices. Unless the amount is very small, arrangements should be made to deposit the gate receipts in a bank after the game.

It is a cardinal principle in schools as well as in business organizations that all financial transactions should be recorded in some tangible way. For this reason receipts for all purchases are necessary. By the same token, when money is received receipts should be given and carbons retained. Such receipts are essential when the accounts are audited. An accurate record of ticket sales at athletic contests must also be available. Ordinarily this is done by recording the number on the roll prior to and following the game. These data are also necessary for the auditors.

Game Reports

In many schools the athletic director is expected to provide game reports after each contest. This report includes items such as attendance (according to such categories as children, students, general admissions, and so forth), gate receipts, complimentary tickets, expenses, other income, weather conditions, and the score. These reports serve as a valuable record for future use, especially in the preparation of future budgets.

Petty Cash Fund

It is an established business procedure for the administrator to have a small petty cash fund from which to make small purchases. It is much simpler to make small purchases directly rather than to make out a purchase requisition. Receipts for all purchases should be obtained. When the petty cash fund is exhausted, the receipts should be submitted along with the request for an additional appropriation.

SELECTED REFERENCES

AVEDISIAN, CHARLES T., "Planning Programming Budget Systems," *Journal of Health, Physical Education and Recreation,* 43 (October 1972), pp. 37–39.

FORSYTHE, CHARLES E., and IRVIN KELLER, *Administration of High School Athletics* (6th ed.), Englewood Cliffs, N.J.: Prentice-Hall, Inc., 1977.

HARTLEY, HARRY J., *Educational Planning-Programming-Budgeting—A Systems Approach.* Englewood Cliffs, N.J.: Prentice-Hall, Inc., 1968.

NOTES

1. Harry Hartley, *Educational Planning-Programming-Budgeting-A Systems Approach* (Englewood Cliffs, N.J.: Prentice-Hall, Inc., 1968) p. 86.

2. Educational Policies Commission, *School Athletics* (Washington, D.C., National Education Association and American Association of School Administrators, 1955), p. 66.

16

Legal Liability for Injury

Physical educators have become increasingly concerned about the legal implications resulting from injuries which occur while students are participating in the physical education program. It has been estimated that between 350,000 and 400,000 pupil injury accidents occur in physical education and athletics per year, many of which lead to litigation. The possiblity of a public school teacher being involved in legal action resulting from a school-related injury is greater now than at any time in educational history.

The frequency of pupil injury accidents has several implications for physical educators. It is imperative that physical educators, coaches, and administrators know the legal parameters within which they function as determined by statutory enactments and judicial decisions in their respective states. Each is individually responsible for personal acts of negligence and state laws may vary considerably with regard to immunity and subsequent legal attachment to the school district employer. Therefore, the physical educator must be familiar with all facets of the law as it applies to his or her specific position: legal liability, insurance, travel regulations, legal aspects of administration and supervision, curriculum development, segregation of pupils, and design, installation and repair of equipment and facilities.

A further consideration is the moral obligation physical educators have to develop and administer programs which have as their primary concern the total welfare of all students involved. When physical educators understand the legal implications of their work, they should become more sensitive to their responsibilities and, eventually, should develop policies and procedures which would minimize the frequency of student injury.

Administrative Responsibility

It is the physical education department administrator's responsibility to conduct the program in such a way that there will never be a cause for legal action against staff members, administration, or the school district. This can be accomplished by eliminating the common basis for legal action, namely, negligent behavior. It is a difficult assignment for the administrator, nevertheless this is the objective.

Once the administrator knows the legal framework within which the program functions, the entire faculty and staff must be informed of their duties and responsibilities and the department must develop policies, procedures and guidelines designed to prevent negligently-inflicted student injury and subsequent possible litigation. Such policies and procedures would include legal considerations in (1) supervision, (2) curriculum development, (3) methodology, (4) environmental safeguards, (5) segregation of pupils, (6) transportation, and (7) first aid and accident reporting.

Negligence Theory

Negligence is the word ordinarily used in common law terminology to express the foundation of civil liability for injury to person or property, when such injury is not the result of premeditation and formed intention.[1]

The theory of negligence has been established upon the principle that harm which is inflicted as the result of carelessness must be compensated for by the wrongdoers. The harm must result from a wrong or fault which violates the standard of conduct expected of a member of a civilized society.

Negligence, of which the law takes cognizance in imposing liability, depends upon the existence of various essential elements, such as a duty owed by the person charged, and an injury which follows the violation of that duty in such direct and natural consequence that the breach of duty can be said to be the proximate cause of the injury.[2]

To recover in a negligence action the plaintiff must fulfill four basic essentials. First, plaintiff must be able to invoke some principle, theory or rule of law under which he or she claims to be entitled to protection against the conduct of the defendant. This is the duty issue. Second, plaintiff must show that defendant violated his or her duty to the victim with respect to the risk of injury. This is the negligence issue or the violation of duty issue. Third, the plaintiff must show that an injury was suffered as the result of the defendant's conduct, at least in part. This is known as the causal relation issue. Fourth, the plaintiff must show the damages he suffered, the damage issue.[3]

Duty and Breach of Duty Issues

An action to recover damages for an injury sustained by the plaintiff on the theory that it was caused by the negligence of the defendant will not lie unless it appears that there existed, at the time and place where the injury was inflicted, a duty on the part of the defendant and a corresponding right in the plaintiff for the protection of the latter.[4]

In all actions the statement of the duty will vary but in each case it is either stated or assumed and necessarily establishes a standard by which the conduct of the defendant is measured. Since the duty of the defendant in any case is the primary basis of liability, its recognition cannot be overstressed.[5]

Fundamentally, the duty of a person to use care, and his/her liability for negligence, depend upon the tendency of his/her acts under the circumstances as they are known or should be known to him/her.[6] Foreseeability, the reasonable anticipation that harm or injury is a likely result of acts or omissions, therefore becomes an important factor in the duty issue of a negligence action.

The duty issue is unique to each specific case. It is proportioned to any given situation, its surroundings, peculiarities and hazards. The determination of the issue of duty and whether it includes the particular risk imposed on the victim ultimately rests upon broad policies which underlie the law. These policies may be characterized generally as morality, the economic good of the group, practical administration of the law, justice between the parties, and other considerations relative to the environment out of which the case arose.[7] What may be deemed ordinary care in one case may under different surroundings and circumstances be considered negligence. More care and vigilance must be exerted to avoid liability for negligence in dealing with a dangerous agency than with an instrumentality in which danger is not so apparently inherent.[8]

In the final analysis, however, the standard by which the conduct of a person in a particular situation is judged in determining whether she/he was negligent is the care which an ordinarily prudent person would exercise under the circumstances.[9]

Steinhilber has suggested that the "reasonable and prudent physical educator:"

1. Knows the health status of his students and/or players if he has them engage in highly competitive and/or rough activities.
2. Requires medical approval for participation following serious illness or injury.
3. Inspects all classes and personal equipment at regular intervals.
4. Does not expose students to possible injury by using defective equipment.
5. Conducts an activity in a safe area.
6. Foresees possible injury if activity is improperly conducted.
7. Analyzes his teaching and coaching methods for the safety of his students and players.
8. Assigns only qualified personnel to conduct and supervise an activity.
9. Keeps the activity within the ability of the students.
10. Performs the proper act in the event of injury.
11. Does not diagnose or treat injuries.
12. Instructs adequately prior to permitting performance.
13. Keeps an accurate record of all accidents and action(s) taken.
14. Uses school buses or public utility motor vehicles to transport members of athletic teams to and from contests.
15. In cooperation with administration, makes arrangements for adequate care of injured pupils in emergency situations.
16. If he serves as athletic trainer, performs only in areas in which he is directed by medical personnel.
17. Fulfills his duty to supervise within the scope of his employment—especially in situations in which the risk of harm is exceptionally high and in those situations in which it is reasonable to foresee that injury might occur if supervision is not provided.[10]

Causal Relation Issue

It is well to understand that it is not important to the causal relation issue that the defendant's conduct in whole or in part was lawful, unlawful, intentional, unintentional, negligent, or non-negligent. The moment some moral consideration is introduced into the inquiry, the issue is no longer one of causal relation. Causal relation is a neutral issue, blind to right and wrong. It is so easy to think and speak of a defendant's negligence as the cause of a victim's hurt that it is frequently overlooked that causal relation is the beginning point of liability and must be established or tentatively assumed before issues involving duty, negligence, damages, and the defensive issues can be determined. There may be causal relation but no basis for the later inquiries, but in absence of causal relation the plaintiff has no case, and all the other inquiries become moot.[11]

Legal or proximate cause is that cause which, in a natural and continuous sequence unbroken by any efficient intervening cause, produces the injury, and without which the result would not have occurred.[12] It is not necessary to a defendant's liability that the consequences of his negligence should have been foreseen, and it is sufficient if the injuries are the natural, though not necessary or inevitable, result of the wrong.[13]

Liability for negligence, of course, depends upon a showing that the injury suffered by the plaintiff was caused by the alleged wrongful act or omission of the defendant. Merely to show a connection between the negligence and the injury is not sufficient to establish liability for negligence. The connection must be such that the law will regard the negligent act as the proximate cause of the injury.[14]

Damage Issue

The words "damage," "loss," and "injury" are used interchangeably, and within legislative meaning and judicial interpretation import the same thing.

Damage is commonly defined as loss, injury, or deterioration, caused by the negligence, design, or accident of one person to another, in respect to the latter's person or property.[15]

In an action for personal injury the showing of the physical hurt may be sufficient within itself to be a basis for evaluating the damages.[16]

Injury may arise from non-feasance or not fulfilling a legal obligation or duty or contract. It may arise also from misfeasance or the performance in an improper manner of an act which was either the party's duty or contract to perform, and by malfeasance or the unjust performance of some act which he or she had no right to do or which he or she had contracted not to do.[17]

Defenses Against Negligence

Common defenses utilized to counteract actions of negligence include the doctrine of governmental immunity, elements of negligence not proven, assumption of risk, contributory negligence, comparative negligence, and certain technical legal aspects.

While the doctrine of governmental immunity is not a defense in the true sense, it does often provide protection from liability on the basis that the act was done as part of a governmental function. Presently the doctrine of governmental immunity is being seriously questioned and, within the last decade, has been drastically altered or totally abrogated in several states.

Obviously, the best defense occurs when one or more of the four essential elements required in a negligence is not proven—that a duty was not owed the plaintiff, that reasonable care was exercised in the performance of the act, that the act was not the proximate cause of the injury, or that there was not in fact injury to the plaintiff.[18]

Assumption of Risk

The assumption of risk defense is based upon the legal theory of *volenti non fit injuria*—no harm is done to one who consents. It is founded upon the knowledge of the injured, either actual or constructive, of the risks to be encountered, and the individual's consent to take the chance of injury therefrom. It differs from contributory negligence in that contributory negligence implies misconduct while assumption of risk is based upon contract.

Various types of risks are inherent in certain activities and persons engaging in these activities are expected to have a thorough knowledge and understanding of these risks. The participant is then said to have assumed the risks involved upon engaging in the activity. The voluntary assumption of risk—either express or implied—must be adjusted to consideration of age and capacity of the individual to cope with the risks involved. When an *in loco parentis* relationship exists, an adult must not allow a child to become involved in unreasonable or considerable risk.

Assumption of risk applies only to the normal hazards of the activity and may not include defective equipment, dangerous areas, or acts of negligent conduct.

Contributory Negligence

Contributory negligence is:

> . . . any want of ordinary care on the part of the person injured (or on the part of another whose negligence is imputable to him,) which combined and concurred with the defendant's negligence, and contributed to the injury as a proximate cause thereof, and as an element without which the injury would not have occurred.[19]

As the term implies, contributory negligence refers to instances where the plaintiff in some way contributed to his/her own harm. Usually any contributory fault on the part of the plaintiff denies recovery even though the defendant's conduct may have been a substantial cause of the injury. In most jurisdictions contributory negligence is an affirmative defense with the burden of proof on the defendant, but several jurisdictions still require the plaintiff to be free of contributory negligence.[20]

The elements necessary to sustain an action for negligence, except for the duty issue, apply to contributory negligence. In some instances, such as wanton, willful, or reckless misconduct on the part of the defendant, the defense of contributory negligence will not bar recovery. As in negligence, considerations regarding the nature of the activity as well as the age, capacity, and experience of the individual involved must be made in determining the appropriateness of contributory negligence defense. Some legal writers also feel that maintenance of a nuisance should also be an exception to the use of the defense of contributory negligence.[21]

Comparative Negligence

Some jurisdictions allow an assessment of the varying degrees of contributory negligence and a settlement thereon. This is commonly known as comparative or apportioned negligence. This concept had its origin in cases where the defense of contributory negligence barred recovery even though the plaintiff's negligence was very slight and the defendant's quite great. A generally accepted working definition of comparative negligence is:

> . . . that doctrine in the law of negligence by which the negligence of the parties is compared, in the degrees of "slight," "ordinary," and "gross" negligence, and a recovery permitted, not withstanding the contributory negligence of the plaintiff, when the negligence of the plaintiff is slight and the negligence of the defendant gross, but refused when the plaintiff has been guilty of a want of ordinary care, thereby contributing to his injury, or when the negligence of the defendant is not gross, but only ordinary or slight, when compared, under the circumstances of the case, with the contributory negligence of the plaintiff.[22]

Attractive Nuisance

The attractive nuisance doctrine has often been utilized, with varying degrees of success, to attempt to circumvent non-liability created by the governmental immunity doctrine. Regardless of governmental immunity, a governmental agency has no right to create or maintain a nuisance without incurring liability.

Often referred to as the attractive-place doctrine, the attractive nuisance doctrine is quite well explained in the dictum from the following case:

It is our opinion that a possessor of real estate should be subjected to liability to a young child who is injured upon his premises if it be found that the former maintained on, or allowed to exist upon his land, an artificial condition which was inherently dangerous to children being upon his premises; that he knew or should have known that children trespassed or were likely to trespass upon his premises; that he realized or should have realized that the structure erected or the artificial condition maintained by him was inherently dangerous to children and involved an unreasonable risk of serious bodily injury or death to them; that the injured child, because of his youth or tender age, did not discover the condition or realize the risk involved in going within the area, or in playing in close proximity to the inherently dangerous condition; and that safeguards could reasonably have been provided which would have obviated the inherent danger without materially interfering with the purpose for which the artificial condition was maintained.[23]

Governmental Immunity

The doctrine of governmental immunity, often called the doctrine of sovereign immunity or the doctrine of non-liability is believed to have had its genesis in a 1788 English case, *Russell* versus *Men of Devon County.*[24] The entire male population of Devon County was sued to recover damages sustained by plaintiff's wagon due to a bridge, which the county had a duty to maintain, being in a state of ill-repair. Recovery was denied by Lord Kenyon because (a) there was no precedent for the action, (b) there was no legislative intent for actions of this type, (c) there was no fund out of which compensation could be made, and (d) there was "no law or reason for supporting the action." Although the creation of sovereign immunity, the concept that "the King can do no wrong," may not have been the intent of this court, it was the result.

The doctrine of *Russell v. Men of Devon* was generally accepted by the American courts as exemplified by *Mower v. Inhabitants of Leicester,*[25] *Hedges v. The County of Madison,*[26] and *City of Navasota v. Pearce.*[27]

In the late eighteenth and early nineteenth centuries the rule became quite well established that a school district was not liable for the negligent acts of its agents, servants, or officers while they were engaged in a governmental function in the absence of a legislative statute expressly imposing liability. In *Chicago v. Chicago,* in 1927, the court discussed the reasoning behind governmental immunity for schools, a rationale which is still held to in varying degrees in most states:

There are two reasons for this rule: (1) that a school board acts *nolens volens* as an agent of the state, performing a purely public or governmental duty imposed upon by the law, for the benefit of the public and for the performance of which it receives no profit or advantage; (2) since the property which it possesses is held in trust, the payment of judgments in tort would amount to a diversion, or, in some cases, a destruction, of the trust.[28]

The basic issue in governmental immunity is whether the activity which caused the injury was governmental or proprietary in nature.

Municipal corporations exist and function in a dual capacity—one governmental, the other proprietary. Generally, municipalities, as arms of the state, are not liable for negligence in the discharge of their governmental functions, but immunity from liability is not extended to municipalities in the exercise of their proprietary functions.[29]

The task is not as easy as it would first appear to make the distinction between proprietary and governmental functions with regard to the operation of a public school system. The courts in some instances have held that regardless of the nature of the activity, school districts, because of their governmental nature, are powerless to enter into a proprietary function. Other courts have held that school districts may be held liable for injuries which originated in the conduct of a proprietary function. Generally, however, most courts have held that the activities and functions of school districts do not automatically become proprietary, with the resulting loss of immunity, simply because the activity yields some revenue or profit.

Charging admission for athletic contests, leasing school facilities, selling student projects, and certain fund-raising activities are functions which could possibly be considered either governmental or proprietary. The inability of the courts to draw a consistent line between a governmental and proprietary function of a school district, sometimes even in a single jurisdiction, is generally conceded.

Recently an increasing number of courageous courts, by overruling their earlier decisions, have influenced other courts and some legislatures to reject governmental immunity from tort liability over ever-widening areas. The movement is well under way but years of litigation and legislative efforts will be required to establish the limits of govermental tort liability.[30] It is imperative that the physical education department administrator fully understand governmental immunity and its status in that state.

Save Harmless Legislation

When states, by either the legislative or judicial process, partially or totally abrogate governmental immunity, there is usually an accompanying statute or provision which deals with the vulnerability of the individual employee. Collectively, these enactments and statutory provisions are called "save-harmless" legislation.

New York Education Law states in part:

> . . . it shall be the duty of each board of education, trustee or trustees . . . to save harmless and protect all teachers and members of supervisory and administrative staff or employees from financial loss arising out of any claim, demand, suit or judgment by reason of alleged negligence or other act resulting in accidental bodily injury to any person within or without the school building, provided such teacher or member of the supervisory or administrative staff or employee at the time of the accident or injury was acting in the discharge of his duties within the scope of his employment . . .[31]

The California statutory provisions are outlined as follows:

> If suit is brought against any member of the governing board of any school district as an individual, for any act, or omission, in the line of his official duty as a member of the board, or suit is brought against any employee of any school district for any act performed in the course of his employment, the district attorney of the county shall defend the member of the school board or the individual employee upon request of the governing board of the school district, without fee or other charge.[32]

Further statutory provisions provide for the paying of judgments which may be assessed or the reimbursement, without obligation, of the employee if he has paid the judgment.

Oregon's save-harmless statute is slightly different in that it provides for insurance protection but does not, as does California's, provide for complete protection regardless of the amount of the judgment.

> Any county, school district, municipal corporation and any state agency . . . may purchase liability insurance, in such amounts and containing such terms and conditions as it may deem necessary, for the protection of its board or commission members, officers, and employees against claims against them incurred by such board or commission members, officers, and employees in the performance of their official duties. The premiums for such insurance shall be paid out of appropriations or funds available for expenditure by the state agency, district or county purchasing the insurance.[33]

Although worded in different fashions, the intent of the "save-harmless" legislation is to provide a measure of protection for employees of governmental agencies who are charged with negligence in the discharge of duties within the scope of their employment.

Liability Insurance

There presently exists some degree of liability in each of the United States and educators should be aware of the status of governmental immunity, save-harmless legislation, and liability insurance provisions in the states where they practice.

The relationship between tort law and liability insurance is a very interesing but totally uncertain one. With regard to the operation of public school systems, it has been held that, because of the sovereignty of the state, no liability insurance by the state was necessary because no liability existed. Some states have not authorized school districts to purchase liability insurance using the same reasoning upon which they uphold governmental immunity. School district funds are, in fact, trust funds which may not be legally diverted to operations other than the educational enterprise.

In states where school districts are permitted to purchase liability insurance, the trust fund theory is generally set aside because justification for paying insurance premiums is found in the notion that in so doing the educational programs of the school district are protected. It is generally held that a statute authorizing the purchase of liability insurance does not waive governmental immunity, at least not beyond the limits of the policy coverage. Some states have indicated that the authorization to purchase liability insurance waives governmental immunity only for proprietary functions, others for only governmental functions, and some for both.

Since, due to the fact that personal liability for negligence always exists even in the presence of school district coverage, regardless of the statutory provisions regulating a school district's ability to purchase liability insurance from generated funds, an individual teacher, coach or administrator should carefully investigate personal liability insurance options available. In addition to a wide variety of insurance packages available through private carriers, the American Alliance for Health, Physical Education, and Recreation as well as the National Educational Association and various other professional organizations have liability insurance programs available to their members, usually at very low cost.

The availability of various forms of liability insurance has had the effect of extending liability and narrowing immunities to liability.

Common Legal Actions in Physical Education and Athletics

The nature of the most-often litigated cases in physical education and interscholastic athletics involve alleged negligence in (1) care of buildings; grounds and facilities, including purchase and maintenance of equipment; (2) supervision, (3) curriculum development and teaching methodology; (4) first aid and medical assistance, and (5) transportation of pupils.

Buildings, Grounds, Facilities, Equipment

As physical education and interscholastic programs continue to expand, the range of possible liability obviously increases. Students have an inherent right to expect these programs to be conducted in safe environments with properly designed and maintained equipment. To depart from the standard of care which is expected of a "reasonable and prudent" physical educator or coach in assuring safe environments and proper equipment is to invite injury and litigation. Students do not "assume the risk" of unsafe equipment, insecure locker rooms, or fields and courts which have not been periodically inspected.

Courts or fields upon which vigorous, fast-moving activities are conducted, which do not provide "buffer zones," but rather develop contiguous or overlapping areas have generally been held to be negligently designed.[34] Equipment and facilities which, after proper notification, are not repaired have become the bases for other negligent actions.[35] Facilities which could fulfill the legal requirements constituting "attractive nuisances" serve, likewise, as the bases for certain litigations within physical education and athletics.[36] Interscholastic athletics is replete with legal action relating to alleged negligence in issuing and maintaining equipment.[37]

A recent award of $5,300,000.00 was made to a young athlete in federal district court upon the contention that the football helmet which he was wearing at the time of the injury was improperly designed and directly related to the cause of injury. In the area of products liability, there is no longer any doubt that it attaches to any seller of a product, including the maker of a component part of the final product, or when a product is properly made according to an unreasonably dangerous design.[38] Interscholastic coaches should take special precautions in issuing equipment to student athletes and should be very familiar with current research and legislation regarding certain types of equipment.

Supervision

Supervisory deficiencies undoubtedly produce the largest number of legal actions for negligence in physical education and interscholastic athletics. A cardinal principle of supervision requires that instructors exercise active supervision over any assigned class or duty station and never absent themselves or otherwise divide a class so as to render supervision from a single vantage point an impossibility.

To leave a class in the hands of uncertificated personnel has been held to violate some state laws requiring that classes are to be supervised only by personnel holding valid teaching certificates and has been extended in some instances to include teacher aides, paraprofessionals and even student teachers.[39] Attempting, or being assigned, to supervise too many students has been a focal point in several cases.[40] Teacher absence is often cited as the basis for negligent supervision.[41]

Proper supervision also implies a duty on the part of the teacher to protect students from negligently injuring themselves by engaging in activities for which they are not properly suited or which might be inherently dangerous.

Instruction

The development of a curriculum which is both educationally justifiable and legally sound, together with the utilization of reasonable and proper teaching techniques, should be the goal of every administrator. Local school, school district and state teaching guides and syllabi should be kept current and should be strictly observed. Failure to do so has, in some instances, formed the basis for legal action.[42]

The selection of drills, progressions, and activities to be included in the curriculum is of critical importance. A critical evaluation of existing activity offerings should be made periodically to insure that activities included in the curriculum represent the best possible selections to meet stated educational objectives. Courts have often criticized activity selection and, because of their rulings, have even had the effect of virtually removing activities from the curriculum.[43]

Another area often closely evaluated by courts concerns the proper segregation of pupils within an activity, particularly factors relating to age, size, experience, strength and physical capacity which may be deemed as necessary considerations prior to pupil assignment to certain drills and activities. Again, failure to do so often becomes the focal point of a negligence action.[44]

Physical educators and coaches are generally held to have a precise knowledge of the health status of each pupil participant. Further, teachers and coaches are held to know the results of physical examinations and any recommendations resulting therefrom.[45]

First Aid and Medical Assistance

Since it is quite obvious that numerous injuries occur in physical education and interscholastic athletics it follows that substantial legal activity is generated when improper procedures are followed in treating and caring for the injured party. Physical educators and coaches should pay special attention to existing statutory provisions which, in several states, prohibit persons unlicensed to do so from practicing acts which could be construed as physical therapy, hydrotherapy or nursing.

Initial misdiagnosis could lead to mistreatment. Unwarranted or improper movement of an injured student could further complicate an existing condition. The program administrator, together with staff and guidance from the medical profession, should carefully prepare procedures to be followed in emergency situations. Since most physical educators and coaches have received professional preparation in first aid and/or care and prevention of athletic injuries, they will be held to a greater standard of care in rendering first aid than would a classroom teacher with no training in first aid procedures. Teachers and coaches should use extreme caution lest they, in the confusion of the moment, treat a non-emergency situation as though it were an emergency or, in the case of a real emergency fail to act or act improperly.[46]

Transportation of Students

Transportation of pupils by private automobile is a very common practice in public schools today. Coaches transport athletes, teachers take students on field trips, and often older students run errands. Every teacher and administrator should be aware that loaning a car, or using a private automobile to transport students, is a very hazardous undertaking and should be avoided whenever possible.

The courts have held, in some instances, that "the owner of a car is liable for negligence whether he drives the car himself or not. This rule is based upon the presumption that the person driving the car is acting as the agent of the owner."[47]

That the owner or operator of a motor vehicle owes to invited, gratuitous guests more than the duty of exercising ordinary and reasonable care to avoid injuring them, has been abrogated in most states through the enactment of "guest statutes."

Guest statutes state, generally, that "any person who, as a guest, accepts a ride in any vehicle, moving upon any of the public highways of the state, and while so riding as such guest receives or sustains injury, shall have no right of recovery against the owner or driver or person responsible for the operation of the vehicle."[48]

The guest statutes deny recovery on the theory that an operator or owner should not be liable to a guest to whom one is doing a favor or extending a courtesy. There are, however, two extenuating circumstances (1) if the guest has paid for the ride or the owner or operator has in some other way been compensated for the ride, the guest is no longer considered a "guest" under the law but, rather, a "passenger" and as such the driver or owner of the automobile can be held liable for injuries received; (2) if the accident occurred due to gross negligence or willful or wanton misconduct on the part of the driver, then the guest can entertain an action for recovery of damages for injuries sustained. For the most part, the constitutionality of such statutes has been upheld.

However, the Supreme Court of the Sate of California recently declared unconstitutional that state's automobile guest statute as a violation of equal protection of the law.[49] Many leading attorneys predict the California case will be a prime factor in removing similar statutes which presently exist in over forty states.

A good rule to follow is to avoid the use of private transportation whenever possible. If it must be used, observe these guidelines:

1. always try to get a responsible adult in every car.
2. use only safe cars (you may have a duty to inspect).
3. travel together.
4. check state statutes.
5. check insurance coverage (and exceptions).
6. in the event of an accident report *only* to appropriate persons, i.e., police and or *your* insurance agent.
7. carefully investigate the driving history and competency of any potential driver.
8. instruct drivers as to route, speed and road conditions.
9. try to establish riders as "guests" if possible.
10. if you cannot meet *each* of the above criterion, DON'T GO!![50]

Release, Waiver, Emergency Treatment and Accident Reporting Forms

A multitude of forms are utilized in the conduct of programs of physical education and interscholastic athletics. Many actually serve as legal, binding contracts, others provide needed information vital to the administration of the programs, and others, contrary to some popular opinion, serve little, if any, function at all.

Release forms commonly utilized by many school districts to absolve them of responsibility for injuries which might occur, have no legal validity. It is contrary to basic legal principle for a parent to sign away the right of recovery of a minor. The forms do, however, serve a quasi-public relations function of informing the parent of participation.

To require proof of insurance as a condition of participation would likely invite legal action based on some form of discrimination. To fully insure each participant in school physical education and interscholastic programs would place an insurmountable financial burden upon a local school district. Some districts, in an effort to inform parents of their financial responsibilities in this regard, have developed another type of release form. Release forms which seek to absolve the school or school district of financial responsibility for costs of injury treatment and rehabilitation, particularly in the absence of insurance coverage by either the school or the parent, are generally held to be quite binding. Obviously, the school may not absolve itself of liability for damages for injuries negligently inflicted.

Consent for emergency care forms are recommended prior to interscholastic athletic participation. These forms authorize selected school personnel to seek emergency medical treatment for a student in the absence of his/her parents. Given the contemporary status of medical malpractice insurance and the incidence of legal action in this area, it is distinctly possible for a physician, in the absence of a consent for emergency care form, to refuse or substantially delay treatment. A sample form follows:

CONSENT FOR EMERGENCY CARE

STUDENT: _____

Be it known that I, the undersigned parent or guardian of the student above-named, do hereby give and grant unto any medical doctor or hospital my consent and authorization to render such aid, treatment or care to said student as, in the judgement of said doctor or hospital, may be required, on an emergency basis, in the event said student should be injured or stricken ill while participating in an interscholastic activity sponsored or sanctioned by the (state high school athletic association), of which (name of high school) is a member.

It is hereby understood that the consent and authorization hereby given and granted are continuing, and are intended by me to extend throughout the current school year.

Dated this _____ day of _____, 19___,
at _____(city)_____, _____(state)_____.

WITNESS: _____
                                  (Parent or Guardian)

Figure 16-1. Consent for Emergency Care.

Part A. Information on ALL Accidents

1. Name: _____ Home Address: _____
2. School: _____ Sex: M☐: F☐: Age: ____ Grade or Classification: ____
3. Time accident occurred: Hour ____ A.M.: ____ P.M. Date: _____
4. Place of Accident: School Building ☐ School Grounds ☐ To or from School ☐ Home ☐ Elsewhere ☐

5. **NATURE OF INJURY**	Abrasion ____ Amputation ____ Asphyxiation ____ Bite ____ Bruise ____ Burn ____ Concussion ____ Cut ____ Dislocation ____ Other (specify) _____	Fracture ____ Laceration ____ Poisoning ____ Puncture ____ Scalds ____ Scratches ____ Shock (el.) ____ Sprain ____	DESCRIPTION OF THE ACCIDENT How did accident happen? What was student doing? Where was student? List specifically unsafe acts and unsafe conditions existing. Specify any tool, machine or equipment involved. _____ _____ _____ _____ _____
PART OF BODY INJURED	Abdomen ____ Ankle ____ Arm ____ Back ____ Chest ____ Ear ____ Elbow ____ Eye ____ Face ____ Finger ____ Other (specify) _____	Foot ____ Hand ____ Head ____ Knee ____ Leg ____ Mouth ____ Nose ____ Scalp ____ Tooth ____ Wrist ____	_____ _____ _____ _____ _____ _____ _____ _____

6. Degree of Injury: Death ☐ Permanent Impairment ☐ Temporary Disability ☐ Nondisabling ☐
7. Total number of days lost from school: _____ (To be filled in when student returns to school)

Part B. Additional Information on School Jurisdiction Accidents

8. Teacher in charge when accident occurred (Enter name): _____
Present at scene of accident: No: _____ Yes: _____

9. **IMMEDIATE ACTION TAKEN**	First-aid Treatment ____ By (Name): _____ Sent to School Nurse ____ By (Name): _____ Sent Home ____ By (Name): _____ Sent to Physician ____ By (Name): _____ Physician's Name: _____ Sent to Hospital ____ By (Name): _____ Name of Hospital: _____

10. Was a parent or other individual notified? No: __ Yes: __ When: _____ How: _____
Name of individual notified: _____
By whom? (Enter name): _____
11. Witnesses: 1. Name: _____ Address: _____
    2. Name: _____ Address: _____

12. **LOCATION**	Specify Activity Athletic field _____ Auditorium _____ Cafeteria _____ Classroom _____ Corridor _____ Dressing room _____ Gymnasium _____ Home Econ. _____ Laboratories _____	Specify Activity Locker _____ Pool _____ Sch. Grounds _____ Shop _____ Showers _____ Stairs _____ Toilets and Washrooms _____ Other (specify) _____	Remarks What recommendations do you have for preventing other accidents of this type? _____ _____ _____ _____ _____ _____

Signed: Principal: _____ Teacher: _____

Figure 16-2. Standard Student Accident Report Form. (Source: National Safety Council.)

Accident reporting forms should be completely filled out and appropriately filed immediately following the accident for several obvious reasons. They not only focus attention upon the causes of accidents, but also may assist school and school district personnel in defending negligence actions which may arise as a result of injuries. Such reports are basic to the implementation and administration of a safety program in the school. In light of substantial delays which often occur between the time of an accident and subsequent legal action, accident report forms should be filed while the event is fresh in the minds of all involved, including witnesses. (See Figure 16-2)

SELECTED REFERENCES

APPENZELLER, HERB, *Athletics and the Law*. Charlottesville: The Michie Company, 1975.

APPENZELLER, HERB, *From the Gym to the Jury*. Charlottesville: The Michie Company, 1970.

BAKER, BOYD B., "Physical Education and the Law: A Proposed Course for the Professional Preparation of Physical Educators," (Microcarded Doctoral Dissertation, University of Oregon, Eugene, 1970).

LEEBEE, HOWARD C., *Tort Liability for Injuries to Pupils*. Ann Arbor: Campus Publishers, 1965.

VAN DER SMISSEN, BETTY, *Legal Liability of Cities and Schools for Injuries in Recreation and Parks*. Cincinnati: W. H. Anderson Company, 1968.

NOTES

1. 38 *American Jurisprudence* (Rochester, N.Y.: Lawyer's Publishing Company, 1943–), 646.

2. 38 Am. Jur. 642.

3. Leon Green, et. al., *Cases on the Law of Torts* (St. Paul: West Publishing Company, 1968), p. 3.

4. 38 Am. Jur. 652.

5. Green, *Cases*, p. 4.

6. 38 Am. Jur. 665.

7. Leon Green, *The Litigation Process in Tort Law* (New York: The Bobbs-Merrill Company, Inc., 1965), p. 218.

8. 38 Am. Jur. 675.

9. 38 Am. Jur. 676.

10. August Steinhilber, "A 'Reasonably Prudent and Careful' Physical Educator," *Annual Safety Education Review*, 1966, pp. 34–38.

11. 38 Am. Jur. 676.

12. Swayne v. Connecticut Co., 86 Conn. 439; Lemos v. Madden, 28 Wyo. 1.

13. Cowman v. Hansen, 250 Iowa 358, 92, N. W. 2d 682.

14. 38 Am. Jur. 673.

15. *Black's Law Dictionary,* p. 466.

16. Green, et. al., *Cases on the Law of Torts,* p. 3.

17. Samuel G. Kling, *The Legal Encyclopedia.* (New York: Pocket Books, Inc., 1965), p. 544.

18. Betty Van der Smissen, *Legal Liability of Cities and Schools for Injuries in Recreation and Parks* (Cincinnati: W. H. Anderson Company, 1968), p. 94.

19. Railroad Co. v. Young, 153 Ind. 163, 54 N.E. 791; Townsend v. Missouri Pac. Railroad Co., 163 La. 872, 113 So. 130, 54 A.L.R. 538.

20. Green, *Cases,* p. 406.

21. Van der Smissen, *Legal Liability,* p. 97.

22. 3 Amer. & Eng. Enc. Law 367; St. Louis & S.F.R. Co., v. Elsing, 37 Okl. 333, 132 p. 483.

23. Angelier v. Red Star Yeast & Products Co., 215 Wis. 47, 254 N. W. 351.

24. Russell v. Men of Devon County, 100 Eng. Rep. 359, 2 Term. Rep. 667, 16 East 305.

25. Mower v. Inhabitants of Leicester, 9 Mass. 247.

26. Hedges v. The County of Madison, 6 Ill. (1 Gilman) 567.

27. City of Navasota v. Pearce, 46 Tex. 525.

28. Leon Green, et al., *Cases on the Law of Torts* (St. Paul: West Publishing Co., 1968), p. 196.

29. Grover v. City of Manhattan, 424, p. 2d 256.

30. Leon Green, et al., *Cases on the Law of Torts* (St. Paul: West Publishing Co., 1968), p. 196.

31. *New York Educational Law,* sec. 3023.

32. *Deering's California Education Code,* sec. 1043.

33. *Oregon Revised Statutes,* 1963, Tit. 22, C 243, sec. 243.110.

34. Bauer v. Board of Education of the City of New York, 285 App. Div. 1148, 140 N.Y.S. 2d 167.

35. Freund v. Oakland Board of Education, 28 Cal. App. 2d 146, 82 p. 2d 197; Eastman v. McLane, 124 Vt. 445.

36. Saul v. Roman Catholic Archdiocese of Santa Fe, 75 N.M. 160, 402 p. 2d 48.

37. Mitchell v. Hartman, 297 p. 77; Vendrell v. School District No. 26c, Malheur County, 233 Or. 1, 376 p. 2d 406.

38. Pike v. Frank G. Hough Co., 467 p. 2d 229; Stephan v. Sears, Roebuck & Co., 266 A. 2d 855.

39. Brittan v. State, 103 N.Y.S. 2d 485; Spedden v. Board of Education, 74 W. Va. 181; Pierce v. Village of Ravens, 264 App. Div. 456; 36 N.Y.S. 2d 42.

40. Silverman v. City of New York, 211 N.Y.S. 2d 560; Pickett v. City of Jacksonville, 155 Fla. 439, 20 So. 2d 484; Cirillo v. City of Milwaukee, 34 Wisc. 2d 705, 150 N.W. 2d 460.

41. Miller v. Board of Education, N.Y. Sup. Ct., L., Div. L-7241-62; Dailey v. Los Angeles United School District, 84 Cal. Rptr. 325; Kerby v. Elk Grove Union High School District, 1 Cal. App. 2d 246, 36 p. 2d 431.

42. Smith v. Consolidated School District No. 2, 408 S.W. 2d 50; Keesee v. Board of Education of the City of New York, 37 Misc. 2d 414, 235 N.Y.S. 2d 300; Gardner v. State, 10 N.Y.S. 2d 274.

43. Bellman v. San Francisco High School District, 73 p. 2d 596; Yerdon v. Baldwinsville Academy, 374 N.Y.S. 2d 877.

44. Luce v. Board of Education of Johnson City, 157 N.Y.S. 2d 123; Brooks v. Board of Education of the City of New York, 189 N.E. 2d 497; Rodriguez v. Seattle School District No. 1, 401 p. 2d 326.

45. Vendrell, op. cit.; Smith, op. cit.; Pirkle v. Oakdale Union Grammar School District, 253 p. 2d 1; Hale v. Davies, 70 S.E. 2d 923.

46. Mogabgab v. New Orleans Parish, 239 A 2d 456; Duda v. Gaines, 12 N.J. Super. 326, 79 A. 2d 695; Welch v. Dunsmuir Joint Uncon High School District, 326 p. 2d 633; Price v. Mt. Diablo Unified School District, 327 p. 2d 203; Cramer v. Hoffman, 390 F. 2d 19; Sayers v. Ranger, 83 A. 2d 775.

47. Gorton v. Doty, 69 p. 2d 136.

48. Leon Green, et al., *Torts* (St. Paul: West Publishing Company, 1968), pp. 656–661.

49. Brown v. Merlo, 506 p. 2d 212.

50. Herbert Appenzeller, *From the Gym to the Jury* (Charlottesville: The Michie Company, 1970) pp. 147–148.

17

Public Relations in Physical Education

The modern concept of public relations has emerged from the term *publicity*. Schools have been concerned with publicity for many years, but experience has shown that much more publicity is needed to secure public understanding and support. Public relations is much broader than publicity. Although publicity is its major tool, public relations is concerned with *all* the impressions that people receive rather than those obtained only through the various publicity media. Fine[1] points this out in his definition: "Public relations is more than a set of rules—it is a broad concept. It is the entire body of relationships that go to make up our impressions of an individual, an organization, or an idea."

In addition to the information that is transmitted via newspapers, radio, films, television, annual reports, and demonstrations, public relations for physical education involves all the relationships that the various staff members have with students, parents, other teachers, administrators, school board members, and the general public. It also involves the impressions obtained from the secretary, custodian, equipment room manager, and any other personnel associated with the physical education department. It even includes the visual, auditory, and olfactory impressions received from the athletic fields, gymnasium, swimming pool, and locker and shower rooms. As Fine has indicated, it involves "the entire body of relationships" associated with physical education.

Purposes of Public Relations in Education

Inasmuch as the public schools are supported by taxation, an obligation exists on their part to give an accounting of their activities to the public. The schools belong to the people. The public invests heavily in education, and the citizens are entitled to know what is being accomplished with their money. In addition to discharging this responsibility to the public, the schools find it necessary to keep the people informed about their activities in order to obtain the kind of support needed to maintain a high level of efficiency. The cost of public schools is the largest item in municipal budgets, but as long as public confidence and support are maintained this expense is cheerfully borne. Harral[2] points out:

> Administrators and others must strengthen their public relations programs. Education will meet current needs only as the masses of people—the throngs who keep the wheels of society moving—understand the schools and take an active interest in supporting them. Upon the attitudes of the public and its willingness and ability to provide the revenues, the development of education in this country depends. As long as education justifies itself in the minds of those who are instrumental in financing it, the financing will continue. These are bedrock considerations.

Still another purpose of public relations is to rectify mistakes, to clear up misunderstandings, and eradicate negative and antagonistic attitudes. These conditions always exist in the general public, and they are powerful deterrents to good will. It is particularly important to influence these individuals favorably, because they might otherwise become leaders of attacks upon the schools.

Purposes of Public Relations in Physical Education

The purposes of public relations in physical education do not differ from those of the entire field of education. The following statement of detailed purposes of public relations in physical education by Davis and Wallis[3] further clarifies the meaning of this term:

1. To create good will with all pertinent publics (pupils, parents, school personnel).
2. To help pertinent publics understand the reasons for and values of physical education.
3. To inform pertinent publics of present programs and planned changes in programs, policies, etc.
4. To inform pertinent publics of services rendered by the department, and its willingness to serve.

5. To inform pertinent publics of events that have occurred and will occur.
6. To encourage participation in suitable activities related to the program and in the use of available facilities.
7. To inform the publics of the expenditure of funds (probably through the superintendent's annual report).
8. To enlist assistance in suitable projects and other help.
9. To encourage and publicize activities that are as self-supporting as possible.
10. To show reasons for greater financial support if needed (and if approved by the school administration).
11. To rectify mistaken ideas, remove misunderstandings, erase negative attitudes.
12. To guide and promote public opinion in favor of worthy programs of physical education.

Public relations in physical education seeks to create good will for the program, the department, and the personnel involved. The following statement by Miller[4] emphasizes the nature and importance of good will:

> The good will of others is the most precious thing anyone or anything—man or business—can have. It is as fragile as an orchid, and as beautiful; as worthy as a gold nugget, and as hard to find; as powerful as a great turbine, and as hard to build; as wonderful as youth, and as difficult to keep.

Need and Importance of Public Relations in Physical Education

It has been pointed out previously that an obligation exists on the part of all public agencies to report periodically to the community. It was also pointed out that continued public support depended heavily upon an effective public relations program. As Harral[5] says: "public relations seeks to bring about a harmony of understanding between any group and the public it serves and upon whose good will it depends."

Of all areas of public school, physical education, particularly, needs to bring about "a harmony of understanding" among parents, teachers, school administrators, and other citizens in the community. This need stems from the fact that the philosophy, activities, and methods in physical education have changed so greatly in this century that few adults understand and appreciate present-day programs. Most people react in terms of their own experiences. When they recall the physical education they themselves endured, they are not disposed to tax themselves heavily for it.

Far too few physical educators have concerned themselves with reporting and interpreting physical education to the public and school administrators. They have only themselves to blame when the public is unwilling to provide adequate financial support for this phase of the school curriculum. During the depression years of the thirties physical education was eliminated or greatly curtailed in hundreds of communities. School boards and school administrators, when confronted with the problem of operating on reduced budgets, too often considered physical education as a "fad or frill" and acted accordingly.

As education faces expansion in the years ahead because of varied ages in student enrollment, physical education faces a challenging situation. When school costs are increasing so enormously, all items in the educational budget are being scrutinized with great care. Any program or service that cannot be justified in terms of its contribution to the welfare of students will have difficulty in surviving.

Physical educators must justify their existence. It is unfortunately a fact that physical education facilities are the most expensive "class rooms" in our schools. School administrators, school boards, parents, and the general public must be convinced that the funds expended upon physical education pay rich dividends. When these groups understand what physical education can contribute to students in terms of health, vitality, physical fitness, citizenship, sportsmanship, and happiness, adequate support will be forthcoming. Parents will pay for what they want for their children. They always want the best and will unstintingly support what they are convinced is desirable. But they must be convinced.

Human Relations vs. Publicity

It is helpful for the administrator to recognize that there are two broad aspects of public relations, namely, human relations and publicity. By all odds, the most important aspect is human relations which involves personal relationships with people. It has been established that the most effective public relations is carried on through the person-to-person medium.

Publicity, on the other hand, is the use of various methods to disseminate information and to influence public opinion in the direction of intelligent group action and support. The ultimate purpose of publicity should be to create a favorable image and understanding of the physical education program.

Responsibility for Public Relations

The physical education administrator is responsible for the public relations of the department. In fact, this is one of the most important responsibilities. Good public relations aid and abet physical education;

poor public relations damage or even bring about the elimination of the program.

As indicated above, the responsibility for public relations involves two aspects; namely, human relations and publicity. In the human relations phase all those affiliated with the department—teachers, custodians, office and equipment room personnel—are agents of public relations. Students are also public relations agents. They represent a vitally important public and are the recipients of the program. After their exposure to the program they can become powerful agents. Whether they become supporters or enemies of physical education depends upon their experiences in it. Inevitably, all these agents, including the administrator, are involved in public relations in their every contact—every word and action—with other people. Since these contacts have significant implications for the department, the administrator must be concerned with them and do everything possible to assure that the overall result will be favorable and enhance the program.

The administrator cannot discharge responsibility for the public relations of the department unless aware of all the factors which create favorable and unfavorable impressions. It is therefore important to cultivate, promote, and encourage the favorable conditions and to eliminate the unfavorable ones. The administrator must develop a sensitivity about the image of the organization and work unceasingly to improve that image.

Because everyone connected with physical education is a human relations agent it follows that the total public relations program must be a team effort. Ordinarily, staff members have more contacts with students than the administrator does. Since a single agent from a department is capable of doing more damage to public relations than can be overcome by all the remaining members, it is necessary that the administrator give constant and careful attention to the impressions which colleagues are creating.

In addition to the key role in the human relations of a department, the administrator also has the ultimate responsibility for all the publicity which is produced. Through the various publicity media it is possible to communicate with any of the public who cannot be reached personally.

Principles of Public Relations in Physical Education

In this section we shall list and discuss six principles that constitute a sound basis for any public relations program in physical education that is going to be effective.

1. The public relations program must be based upon truth. All facts, data, and interpretations that are reported to the public must be pre-

sented impersonally, unselfishly, and honestly. By the very nature of public relations any misrepresentation will inevitably create adverse public opinion.

2. The best foundation for good public relations is a sound program. The most elaborate public relations program cannot cover the basic defects of a poor program. It should never attempt to do so. The first step in successful public relations is a physical education program that is making a genuine contribution to the lives of students. A limited, poorly taught program can have no other result than bad public relations. The following statement emphasizes this point:[6]

> When the public relations program of a school system rests on a foundation of sound classroom accomplishment, it is like a house built upon a rock. Storms of ill-founded criticism and innuendo will not overwhelm it. Its foundations are sure. On the other hand, the most systematic and skillfully devised publicity cannot maintain the public's confidence or win its approval for a school program that is fundamentally unsound. No shoring up "interpretation" can permanently conceal the shortcomings and failures of misdirected or ineffective teaching. Public relations, under such circumstances, is built on shifting sands. The public cannot hear what is said because it is so acutely aware of what the school program is—or is not.

In this connection it should be pointed out that the program can be far from ideal and still develop good public relations. In schools that have limited facilities, equipment, and time, and large classes, no one expects the physical educator to accomplish what could be done under ideal circumstances. The criterion, however, is how effective is the program *under the circumstances?* In any given situation a superior teacher will produce better results than a poor or mediocre teacher. Many physical educators have obtained improved facilities, equipment, and time allotment because of the excellent public relations that developed from a program that was as good as it could be under unfavorable circumstances.

3. The public relations program should be continuous. Unfortunately, very few physical educators have any definitely planned public relations program for their departments. What few programs do exist are usually of the campaign type, which are not considered as effective in molding public opinion as is a continuous program. The common practice has been to neglect the public relations program until an emergency arises and then to conduct an intensive campaign to secure public support. Although this procedure has some value, it so resembles propaganda that the public develops a more suspicious, defensive attitude than it would if it were supplied regularly with information. Campaigns are more successful if the public has been educated by a continuous program of public relations.

4. Public relations is a two-way process between the community and the schools. The concept of public relations wherein everything originates within the schools and flows to the public is a limited one. The public is capable of providing more than mere financial support, as important as that is. The trend is toward genuine cooperation in planning and working for good schools, with the public giving as well as receiving the ideas. Mutual understanding and teamwork between the community and the school give laymen greater confidence in their schools. In addition, parents are led to a better understanding of the role of the home, the community, and the school in the whole program of education.

A committee of fourteen school administrators made the following observation about public participation in school affairs.[7]

> The significance of public participation in educational planning is that it represents one of the most effective means of helping people talk through the problems of education. Citizens come together to explore, plan, and think through and solve educational problems in co-operation with the board of education and the professional staff. In this manner, by digging deeply into the rich strata that are basic to good education, the individual will grow in experience and knowledge. His view of education will be more complete. From these co-operative experiences will come understandings which lead to better support for the schools and an improved school program.

One of the most promising trends in physical education is the development of physical education advisory committees. In some communities such committees are in operation for a variety of school areas. The committees are considered school board committees, and each member is invited to serve each year, by a letter from the chairperson of the school board. The decision concerning membership of the various committees is made after consultation by the superintendent of schools, the supervisor of the area concerned, and the chairman of the board. The membership consists of from twenty to thirty members, one third of whom are school personnel. The lay members are men and women who represent a cross section by occupation and geographical area throughout the system. The school people also represent a cross section of school personnel, that is, men and women, elementary and secondary teachers, and administrators. One school board member is assigned to each committee. The supervisor of the area is secretary for the committee and provides leadership and direction. The chairperson is elected by the group.

The physical education advisory committee is informed of the work of the past committees and the needs and problems of the physical education class, intramural, and interscholastic athletic programs in all the schools. Problems are discussed, study groups formed, resolutions passed, and the minutes provided for the superintendent, who transmits the committee's resolutions and recommendations to the school board.

5. A knowledge of what the public thinks about the schools is essential. The more school personnel know about the level of understanding and attitudes of the public in regard to the schools, the more intelligent and effective will be the public relations program. Thus, schools have been making increasing use of opinion polls. The advantages of knowing the areas of ignorance and misinformation in the community, the prevailing opinions and attitudes on educational matters, the views of particular groups, and the obstacles that need to be overcome before certain proposals can be implemented are obvious.

This principle has particular implications for physical education. Because of the changes in philosophy, objectives, programs, procedures, and evaluative techniques in the past twenty-five years, it is probably true that the adult population has a more erroneous impression of physical education than most subject areas within the schools.

6. The effective public relations program involves all school personnel. Schools could learn some valuable lessons from business organizations regarding the orientation of all personnel in their public relations responsibilities. The most successful stores devote much effort in training clerks, secretaries, floor walkers, elevator operators, and other personnel to work successfully with people, yet in most schools there is an assumption that everyone will automatically practice good public relations. Good public relations do not happen in the normal course of events; they are the result of a well-planned program, intelligently and continuously executed. The quality of the public relations program is commensurate with the effort put into it.

Relatively few physical education departments have a planned public relations program. Only rarely is this subject discussed in staff meetings or included in departmental policies. Seldom is an organized effort made to familiarize the teaching staff with desirable public relations procedures. Even though there is abundant evidence to the contrary, the presumption apparently exists that the teaching personnel always practices good human relationships. The nonteaching personnel, such as the stenographer, clerk, secretary, custodian, and equipment room attendant, are also important from this standpoint; yet few efforts are made to assure that they treat students, faculty, and the general public in a courteous, dignified, and friendly manner. A brusque secretary or telephone operator, a dirty or unshaven custodian, an uncouth and inconsiderate equipment room clerk can damage the reputation of the physical education department.

Nevertheless, the overall impression of the public toward physical education depends much more upon dedicated, superior teachers than upon any other consideration. The impressions received by students from their teachers are gained over a much longer period of time, and they are more intimate, dynamic, and vital. They relate to matters of much more crucial concern to students. The favorable public image created by the teacher may be adversely affected by discourteous secretaries or custodians; on the other hand, the finest possible impressions created by nonprofessional personnel cannot begin to compensate for an incompetent, selfish, disinterested teacher.

Planning and Organizing the Public Relations Program

A number of factors need to be considered in establishing a public relations program within a physical education department. These factors will depend upon the size of the department and upon the existence of an on-going program for the entire school system as well as the specific school. The most important considerations involved in planning and organizing a public relations program are:

1. The specific purposes of the program should be indicated. These purposes should be discussed and approved by all members of the staff. Unless there is unity and support for the program by all staff members, there is not much point in initiating such a program.

2. The past and present policies and procedures need to be evaluated in terms of the effects that they have had upon the public relations of the department. Data should be collected from students, alumni, parents, faculty, and other groups regarding their reactions to these policies and procedures. Factors that produced misunderstanding and resentment must be eliminated.

3. In the larger departments the best-qualified person should be designated to assume the responsibity for the program. In the smaller departments the physical education administrator must undertake this assignment. There are specific duties that must be regularly performed and others that occur at irregular intervals. When one individual has these duties as part of his or her responsibility, they are more likely to be done promptly and efficiently. Often everyone's responsibility becomes no one's responsibility.

4. If the school or school system has a definite public relations program, the efforts within the physical education department must be integrated with it.

5. The facts to be emphasized in public relations should be determined. In making this selection a public opinion poll might prove very helpful. The decisions concerning features to be emphasized should be made by all staff members.

6. All media for disseminating information should be employed. The various groups within the general public of greatest concern to physical education should be reached by the most appropriate means of communication.

7. The results of the public relations program should be checked from time to time. Such an evaluation is necessary to guide future efforts and to assess what has been accomplished.

8. The public relations program plans and policies should be available in writing. All members of the organization should have a copy and be familiar with it. It should be developed by staff members and should serve as a guide for all members of the department. The entire staff, non-teaching as well as teaching personnel, must be "public relations conscious." Each should know his or her responsibilities and limitations in the program. The written program will be an important instrument in accomplishing these objectives.

Multiple Publics

There is no one public. Formerly, the idea was held that a school or department had relations with a "public." We know now that there are many publics differing in size, organization, interests, methods of communication, and systems of control or guidance. Every religious, political, service, social, and professional organization constitutes a public. Every individual is, ordinarily, a member of several publics.

This concept of publics is important in public relations because the approach to a specific group depends upon its nature and interests. A successful approach to one group may prove ineffective with other groups. One of the lessons which specialists in public relations have learned is that the various media of communication must be planned for specific groups—a shotgun approach is of dubious value.

Concerning physical education, the important public consists of students, parents, other teachers, school administrators, school board members, press, radio, and television personnel, and representatives of related governmental and social agencies. Each of these groups will be considered in greater detail.

Students. By all odds, the most important group from the standpoint of public relations is the student body. Two reasons exist for this situation. In the first place, student reactions to physical education powerfully affect the opinions and attitudes of parents, other members of the family, and friends. Each pupil is a daily reporter on what happens in physical education relationships. What the student thinks and says about school work and teachers is extremely important. If happy and successful in their relationships, they are boosters for the program. No more effective approach could be made to parents. Even though parents might have had a negative attitude toward physical education, they become ardent supporters when their children's reports are enthusiastic and favorable. The instances are legion where parents, convinced of the importance of physical education for their children, have used their influence to bring about improved facilities, equipment, class size, and time allotment. The correlation between *pupil approval* and *public approval* of physical education is very high.

The second reason why students represent such an important group is that they are tomorrow's public. They eventually become the parents, doctors, lawyers, businessmen, school administrators, congressmen, politicians, public officials, college presidents, school board members, and the like. Their attitudes toward physical education are conditioned largely by their own school experiences. Individuals who strongly support physical education and others who are bitterly prejudiced against it are found in every community. To some physical educators belongs the credit for the friends and supporters who have been created; others are responsible for the enemies.

Unfortunately, much harm has been done to physical education in various states and communities by individuals who were antagonistic to it. Some of these individuals obtain positions of power and influence which they employ to the detriment of physical education. Behind the defeats and setbacks that physical education has suffered is the failure of one or more physical educators. Every student who is slighted, neglected, humiliated, or otherwise mistreated, who is frustrated and unhappy in experiences in physical education, has been adversely affected. Upon graduation from school, if the sum total of impressions is negative, the student can hardly be expected to be an enthusiastic supporter.

Parents. The importance of this public has already been emphasized. It has also been pointed out that the support of parents can be obtained by providing them with an excellent program while they are in school and by contributing positively to the health, fitness, skill development, social adjustment, and recreational competencies of their children. Additional ways of increasing the understanding and appreciation of parents are also available to the physical educator and should be utilized.

Administrators have learned that much more needs to be done to educate citizens about their schools. Many of the problems with which education is confronted are due to the ignorance or misinformation of people. Increasingly schools are teaching students about their schools in simple, nontechnical terms—their place, values, organization, operation, and sources of support. Units of study about the school itself merit consideration, along with units on other community agencies and institutions. Children should be educated to understand and appreciate the services of teachers no less than those of policemen, firemen, and postmen.

Such a program would be valuable insofar as physical education is concerned. If high school and college students were taught something of the nature and purpose of physical education, it would do much to spread understanding about this aspect of the curriculum. They would not only communicate what they learn to their parents but they would also acquire a greater appreciation of its benefits, which would carry over into adulthood.

Parents can also be educated via reports, visits to school, demonstrations, parent-teacher meetings, and various types of publicity. The features that are reported are dependent upon what the people want to know about physical education and what they should know. They should know that modern physical educational philosophy no longer conceives of the school as being concerned only with the "three R's" or preparation for a vocation. They should realize the increasing need for physical education—a need that cannot be adequately served by any other agency in the school. Once they have been convinced of its indispensability, they should know how it fulfills its purpose in an educational institution. In other words, parents should be educated to know the objectives of physical education and the means by which they may be attained. They should know about physical education operating at its best.

The major interest of parents in physical education revolves about their children. They are eager to know the progress and achievement of their boys and girls. If a student is not making satisfactory progress, parents want to know why and what might be done to remedy the situation. They are interested in the course of study and the values of the different activities to their child. They might have questions about the teaching procedures and methods of evaluation which are employed. The health and physical fitness of their boys and girls is a matter of vital concern to all parents.

It appears that what parents want to know about physical education corresponds very closely to what they should know. The following items, which are based on the parents' interest and need for information about physical education, are suggested as being of most value for publicity purposes:

1. The progress and achievement of their children.
2. Methods of instruction.
3. Health and physical fitness of their children.
4. The program of activities.

5. Need for physical education.

6. The objectives of physical education.

7. Intramural athletics.

8. Teachers of physical education.

9. Physical education facilities.

10. Attendance and behavior of pupils in physical education.

Other teaching personnel. Another important public for physical education consists of the other teachers within the school system. Good public relations with this group pays valuable dividends. When they comprehend the nature and purposes of the program and are sympathetic, they can be very helpful in interpreting it to students, parents, and the general public. In their advising and counseling functions they can be helpful to both the students and the physical education department. Also, if they are favorably disposed toward physical education, they are unlikely to vote for school policies and regulations that are inimical to it.

Physical educators can win the support of the other teachers in a number of ways. The most important step toward this end is the development of an educationally respectable program—one which merits a place within the schools. Teachers usually obtain from their students a fairly accurate impression of the physical education program. An excellent program will gain their respect. Other teachers admire physical educators who are educators—who exert a wholesome influence upon their students. They lose their respect for physical education when questionable practices, which teach youth undesirable lessons, are tolerated.

Physical educators must also play their role as teachers. They should attend faculty meetings, PTA meetings, and other school functions. They should demonstrate interest in all school activities and should avoid conveying the impression that they are a group set apart from the other faculty. The more they associate with other teachers professionally and socially, the better will their public relations be with this important group.

The support of all faculty members for the interscholastic and intercollegiate athletic program is invaluable, and the cooperation of most of them can be easily gained if the athletic director and coaches demonstrate interest in and support of the purposes of the school. If every effort is made to conduct the athletic program on an educational basis the respect of most of the faculty will be forthcoming. However, faculty members resent pressure from coaches to grant unwarranted concessions to athletes. They dislike overemphasis upon winning, with its concomitants of poor sportsmanship, excessive demands upon the time of the students, and the debasement of academic standards. Other faculty members admire and support the coaches who attend faculty meetings and other staff functions, who consider themselves a part of the school team and cooperate with school policies and purposes, and who are always more concerned about the welfare, character, and ideals of their athletes than anything else.

School administrators and school board members. This is a small but very important public. The status of physical education within a school or a city system can be drastically affected by this group. When the individuals involved become convinced that physical education merits an increased time allotment, more teachers, an additional gymnasium or swimming pool, the improvements are usually forthcoming.

Physical educators can win the support of their principals and superintendents if they become part of the team in trying to accomplish the purposes of the school. School administrators want loyalty and cooperation from their teachers. They do not want teachers who are apparently working toward objectives that have no relationship to those of the school system.

School administrators and school board members are sensitive to public opinion. The best way to win their support is to have favorable information come to their attention from students, parents, other teachers, and the various publicity media. The combination of a good program and good public relations will usually produce the desired results. It is also helpful if the physical educators conduct an effective program of evaluation with which they can demonstrate objectively how the children in the program have developed. An annual report that cites the progress and present status of the program and indicates the needs and problems is invaluable in interpreting the program to this particular public.

Members of the press, radio, and television. The importance of these publicity media emphasizes the necessity to work cooperatively with their representatives. The publicity they can disseminate is invaluable, and the only cost is the time required to cooperate. Physical educators should take full advantage of this opportunity and assist the representatives of these communication media in every way possible. Another important consideration is to treat all individuals concerned impartially. The surest way to damage public relations with personnel of the press, radio, and television is to show preference to one or another.

Representatives of government and social agencies. Good public relations should exist between physical educators in the schools and those in other agencies in the community, such as the Y.M.C.A., Y.W.C.A., boys' clubs, and the municipal recreation department. It is mutually advantageous to all to work cooperatively with each other. Facilities, equipment, and personnel may be shared on occasions. Programs may be cooperatively arranged. Most important of all, perhaps, is the banding together of all professional people when certain emergencies arise. When physical education in the school is under attack, the personnel of other community agencies can be of invaluable assistance.

The Teacher's Role in Public Relations

In the daily interaction of pupil and teacher the most lasting and vital public relations are undoubtedly built. Certainly the teacher has the most associations with pupils, and works more directly and intimately with them than do nonteaching personnel. Consequently, the intrinsic value of teacher-pupil relationships is a major factor in the school's public relations.

Physical education teachers have exceptional opportunities to contribute to the wholesome development of their pupils. The activities are exciting and challenging, and students are enthusiastic about them. The goals—health, physical fitness, skills, wholesome recreation, social adjustment—are vitally important and esteemed by parents and pupils alike. With these advantages physical education teachers are strategically situated to develop outstanding public relations.

Unfortunately, these opportunities are often ignored. Not at all uncommon in physical education are certain undesirable teaching practices and procedures. Among those faculty members who may irrevocably damage the department's public relations are the following:

1. The teacher who tosses out a ball and leaves the area.

2. The teacher who offers the same activities year after year without progression or change.

3. The teacher who ignores the weak and inept to concentrate upon the superior performers.

4. The teacher who never teaches systematically.

5. The teacher who exploits physical education classes to locate and develop varsity performers.

6. The teacher who is sarcastic, abusive, disparaging, and impatient.

7. The teacher who concentrates upon only one objective of physical education to the exclusion of the others.

8. The teacher who is dirty or slovenly in appearance.

9. The teacher who shows dislike or bias toward students because of their physical or mental disabilities, or their racial, social, or religious backgrounds.

10. The teacher who is lazy, weak, and a poor disciplinarian.

Such teachers have a devastating effect upon public relations. Students, parents, other teachers, school administrators, board members, and the general public have nothing but scorn and disrespect for them.

Studies have been made which show the characteristics that students most esteem in their teachers:

1. They like a teacher to be fair and firm, with no favoritism to any pupil or group. They resent teacher bias. Often teachers are adjudged unfair because of an inadequate understanding of their motives. Teachers should be alert in discovering and remedying misconceptions that occur.

2. They like a teacher to be sincere. It is impossible to teach successfully what one fails to practice. Courtesy will not result if the teacher is discourteous. Good sportsmanship cannot be expected if the teacher or coach endorses an illegal play or unsportsmanlike tactic. Pupils quickly discover whether a teacher sincerely believes in and practices such virtues as honesty, courtesy, loyalty, good sportsmanship, and charity.

3. They like a teacher who has an interest in them. They resent being ignored or "brushed off." The informal relationships in physical education provide an ideal setting for students to talk with their teachers about their daily work, studies, future problems, or hobbies. Physical educators can be very effective counselors if they are willing to take the time to talk to their students.

4. They like teachers who make learning interesting. They prefer teachers who motivate learning, who have patience and give them additional assistance, who help them evaluate their progress. They like teachers who are considerate of the opinions of students and who make learning a joint endeavor.

5. They like teachers who know their subject. They quickly discover the teacher who is poorly prepared, and they soon lose respect for this type of teacher.

Some physical education teachers confine their human relations to the classroom. They hold themselves aloof from the community and its various organizations and groups. This is unfortunate from a public relations standpoint. A community likes a teacher, particularly a physical education teacher, to participate in community activities. The people want the teacher to fit in, to observe their customs and traditions. That a teacher's private life is his or her own is largely fiction. Teachers, especially those new in a community, should be sensitive to the behavior codes that differentiate one community from another. They should not necessarily be enslaved to local customs, but they should have an appreciation of prevalent traditions and a consideration for them within the limits of good taste and good sense.

There is also an obligation on the part of all citizens to participate in community enterprises, and every teacher should do so. In most communities physical education teachers are expected to engage in youth activities that relate to their field. The Boy Scouts and Girl Scouts, Y.M.C.A. and Y.W.C.A., service clubs, churches, civic and fraternal groups, and many other community organizations offer many opportunities for physical educators to broaden their community contacts.

Physical education teachers have been unflatteringly stereotyped over the years. They are envisioned as overdeveloped muscularly, attired in sweat clothes, uncouth in their use of language, lacking in the social amenities, and uninterested in scholarly and cultural attainments. By their actions physical educators must invalidate these impressions. They must be aware of these concepts and make a particular effort to eradicate them.

In summary, the role of the physical education teacher in the public relations program is accomplished through good human relations. The value of tact, courtesy, and friendliness toward all with whom he/she comes into contact cannot be overestimated. A dedication to the welfare of all students is essential.

Other Factors Affecting Student Attitudes

It would be erroneous to assume that unfavorable student attitudes are produced only by teachers. Administrative regulations and policies sometimes result in negative reactions from students. Details such as attendance regulations, uniform requirements, grading system and the amount of credit are of much concern to them. Students appreciate the option of taking physical education courses for a letter grade or on a Pass-No Pass basis. They are anxious to have their physical education credits apply toward their graduation requirements and their letter grades be included in the computation of their grade point averages. Students have much less objection to a physical education requirement if they have some choice within the requirement. Life-time sports and co-educational activities appeal to high school and college men and women. Intermediate and advanced as well as beginning courses in popular sports are favored by students. An adequate amount of equipment of good quality is an important consideration.

Unfortunately, many institutions do not have the resources—chiefly facilities—for an adequate physical education program. Faculty members face serious obstacles in their efforts to develop favorable attitudes among their students when the teaching stations are unattractive, inadequate in size, poorly lighted, ventilated, and maintained. Overcrowded, dirty, unsanitary, inadequately lighted, heated and ventilated locker and shower areas would not help public relations. Proper facilities for grooming are also important. The importance of good services provided by the equipment room should also be recognized.

To conduct a physical education program which will gain the support and endorsement of the students requires careful attention to a multitude of factors. It is unrealistic to expect favorable reactions from all of the students all of the time but this is a goal for which to strive. It is a fact that by the application of what we know about student reactions to physical education programs the approval of the great majority can be obtained.

Publicity Techniques and Media

Publicity is an integral part of public relations. It provides an opportunity to communicate with an audience which cannot be reached personally. Many more people can be reached via the various publicity media than through the medium of person-to-person contact. The favorable opinions of this much wider audience are of crucial importance to physical education.

The major publicity media include newspapers, radio, television, films, filmstrips, slides, graphic and pictorial materials, public addresses, anniversary demonstrations, open houses and tours, school publications, bulletin boards and annual reports to parents. So many media are available that a problem is presented in making a selection of the ones to use.

The obvious criterion to employ in determining what media to use is that it should be the best one available for the specific purpose. The particular public or publics for whom the information is primarily intended is another important factor. Expense, time, facility of preparation, and availability are other considerations.

The newspaper. The local newspaper is a powerful factor in molding public opinion. As it reaches practically everyone in the community, it becomes an invaluable means of informing people about physical education. Because of the public's interest in its schools, newspapers are very liberal with space for school news. The only cost for this is the time required to cooperate with the press. Physical educators should take full advantage of this opportunity and assist the representatives of the local papers in every way possible. They should furnish the newspapermen with news regarding physical education in the school and undertake to learn themselves what constitutes news, what are news values, and how news stories are prepared. Such a background is highly desirable, for most physical educators find it necessary to write news stories frequently. In only the larger institutions is there a separate publicity writer whose sole duties are to assemble and prepare the news stories. In the majority of schools, the individual in charge of physical education must prepare the material and either place it in the hands of those responsible for school publicity or give it directly to the newspapers. It is a mistake to depend entirely upon the visits of the reporter in order to get physical education news into the local papers. When the physical education director prepares stories they fall into one of three different types. *News stories* are reports of the events as soon as they are over. They must contain the six basic elements of all newspaper leads: who did what, when, where, why, how. *Advance stories* are notices given out in advance of events, stating in future tense the basic elements. The more important the events, the greater the number of advance stories. *Feature stories* are those in which the writer explains, interprets, describes, and develops in popular form some interesting subject for the purpose of informing, entertaining, or giving practical guidance. The feature story generalizes over many events and a long time, whereas news and advance stores usually treat one specific event at a specific time.

Harral[8] gives the following valuable suggestions for preparing news stories.

1. State facts only, not personal opinions.
2. Tell your story briefly in simple language, then stop.
3. Answer the questions who, what, where, when, and why early in the story.
4. Make the report accurate and coherent.
5. Paragraph and punctuate properly.
6. Be especially careful about names, titles, hours, and subjects.
7. Avoid abbreviations, slang, adjectives, wordiness, and involved sentences.
8. Omit headlines.
9. Submit clean typewritten copy, double spaced.
10. Always get your story in on time.

To this advice we might add that the news story should be written in the third person and should not include too many superlatives.

Harral[9] also makes the following suggestions for effective press relations:

1. Play fair with newspapers if you expect them to play fair with you.
2. Establish personal contacts with members of the newspaper staff.
3. Lose no opportunity to be of service to reporters and editors.

4. Do not send the editor thinly veiled school propaganda or advertising.

5. Since newspapers attempt to mirror life, do not expect them to publish only favorable stories.

6. Newspaper space is valuable. Don't expect too much space to be devoted to news of education.

7. Evaluate your news through the eyes of the editor.

8. Never be too busy to see a reporter.

9. Don't play favorites. Treat all reporters alike.

10. Be as eager to help the reporter to get the details of an adverse story as you would a favorable one.

11. If an editor has been generous in giving space to news of school affairs, don't strain your relationship by continually demanding more.

12. Express your appreciation to reporters and editors.

13. Invite representatives of the press to banquets, receptions, or special occasions.

14. Do not evade or side-step a reporter's questions. He or she may think you have something to hide.

15. Remember that a reporter seeks facts, not hearsay or rumor.

16. Don't be condescending. Reporters deal with all types of people.

17. Plan for dull days by having several tips for feature stories.

18. Don't ask the reporter for favors.

19. Don't expect the impossible. Trust the editor to know news values.

20. Keep an idea file of potential news stories, features, and pictures.

Radio and television. Radio and television are powerful communications media because of the large number of people they reach. They have been effectively used to interpret physical education and to provide the public with essential information. Both of these media welcome programs from the schools and are usually cooperative in making their facilities available.

All commerical radio and television stations are required to devote a certain amount of time to public service programs. Many schools have a regular program scheduled on this basis. Physical education has the opportunity, along with other school activities, to participate. In addition to these sustaining programs, information and announcements may be broadcast by means of spot announcements and newscasts. Many of the same materials prepared for newspapers can be used on newscasts if they are rewritten.

When physical educators have opportunities to present programs over the radio or television, they must seek technical assistance. Ordinarily, the individual with this responsibility for the school system will render this assistance. Radio and television personnel are also available for this purpose.

Films, filmstrips, and slides. These visual aids are being increasingly used by schools to present ideas, activities, and needs. The public has few opportunities to observe the work of the schools, and these media are usually more effective than verbal descriptions.

The production of a film is an expensive undertaking and requires careful planning and experienced direction. A number of the larger school systems have produced excellent films that have justified the expense and effort. Some physical educators have made films of their departmental activities with the assistance of volunteers who possess the technical competence required. Even though they are silent films, they are of value.

Slides and filmstrips can be developed from any good photographs. They are inexpensive to make and can be quite effective, particularly if they are in color. Ordinarily, these aids are used in conjunction with a talk on some phase of the school activities.

Other graphic and pictorial materials. Photographs, charts, graphs, and diagrams are included in this category. The Chinese proverb, "A picture is worth a thousand words," emphasizes the importance of these media.

Photographs tell a story and arouse interest. If they are well done, they interpret, dramatize, inform, and explain. They can be used for reproduction in newspapers and reports, for bulletin boards, exhibits, and window displays. For best results photographs should have a good background, show action, and involve small groups only.

Charts, graphs, and diagrams are valuable in presenting various types of statistical data. Data on budget, school growth, and participation in school activities, as well as comparisons of various types, are much more effectively portrayed by these visual aids than by words.

Public speaking. Physical educators have frequent opportunities to speak before groups. They receive invitations to address P.T.A. groups, service and fraternal clubs, and social civic organizations. All of these invitations should be accepted because they present opportunities for developing good public relations. It goes without saying, however, that the effect of an address depends upon how well it is presented.

The fact that an invitation to speak has been extended indicates that the group has an interest in what the physical educator has to say. Nevertheless, much careful preparation is indicated. There are, of course, a few individuals who can give an excellent address with little preparation, but they are the exception that proves the rule. In general, the quality of the speech will correspond to the amount of time devoted to its preparation.

Mastery of subject matter and interest in it are two prerequisites to effective speaking which the physical education teacher should possess.

Sincerity and enthusiasm are other essentials. Speech authorities urge that speakers make an outline of the major points they wish to cover rather than write the speech out in detail and memorize it. Reading a speech is also considered poor practice. Another common mistake is to try to cover too much in one talk. Practice in delivering the speech is recommended.

Student publications. The student newspaper, the school annual, and the student handbook are important communications media that can be utilized to advantage by the physical educator. These projects are vital to the students, who are grateful for whatever assistance and cooperation they receive from the faculty. Student reporters should be treated courteously and extended all the assistance they require. The student publications can be of great help in giving the students, particularly those working on them, an understanding of physical education.

Annual reports. Many school systems publish an annual report that describes the status, progress, activities, and needs of the schools. In the yearly report to the school administrators and the school board, the physical education administrator should present a fair and honest summary of what has been accomplished in the department and indicate what its important needs are. The presentation is made stronger when the administrator can provide objective evidence rather than personal opinion to support recommendations. For example, if one can present *objective* data that show that local children do not compare favorably with other children or with recommended standards, the report is much more likely to secure helpful action.

Demonstrations. Demonstrations are extensively used by physical educators to promote understanding and support. Correctly used, these media provide an unusually effective means of interpreting physical education to parents and the general public. It is easy to get the public to attend, and it is not difficult to create the understandings that lead to favorable public opinion. In addition to the public relations value, demonstrations are of exceptional educational value to students and teachers alike.

Demonstrations are placed before the public on special occasions, such as Parent-Teachers Night, Open-House Night, Field and Play Days, or whenever the occasion indicates the desirability of one. They should be made annual occasions rather than a device to use only when physical education is in trouble. As an integral part of the physical education program they deserve the time, space, and personnel which are required for their proper execution.

Demonstrations should represent the regular program to the public. They should involve all or as many students as can be used rather than only the outstanding performers. Preparation for the demonstration should not interfere appreciably with the regular program of instruction. The primary purpose is to *inform* the public, not to entertain it. Physical education has outgrown the practice of spending weeks preparing for an exhibition. Experience has shown that this approach damaged public relations rather than improved them. The demonstration should endeavor to present a representative cross section of the program and, at the same time, interpret it to the observers.

Public Relations by National, District, and State Organizations

The national, district, and state physical education organizations should initiate and carry out a definite plan of public relations. In fact, this represents one of their major functions. They supplement the work of local personnel and perform certain services on the national and regional levels which could not be done by individual teachers. The total public relations effort requires an effective program not only on the local level but on the wider state, district, and national levels.

The public relations functions of the national alliance are directed by a professionally trained individual and assisted by other paid personnel, as well as by the national officers. On the district level the public relations efforts must be spearheaded by the officers or special committees of the district association. The state director of physical education, assisted by state association officers, conducts the program on this level.

The functions of these individuals are limited by the funds at their disposal and the needs of their organizations. Some of the things that national, district, and state organizations can do to further the public understanding and support of physical education include:

1. Disseminate and suggest public relations ideas and methods to members of the organization in the field.

2. Prepare and disseminate appropriate material for release to newspapers, radio and television programs, and speakers.

3. Establish cooperative relationships and mutal understanding with related national organizations, such as the American Medical Association, Parent-Teachers Association, American Public Health Association, National Recreation Association, American Legion, and Veterans of Foreign Wars.

4. Publicize conventions, meetings, and speeches.

5. Gather and pass on to members in the field information regarding the newest developments and best practices in physical education.

6. Study all bills that come before the Congress of the United States and state legislatures to ascertain their possible effect on physical education.

7. Take the lead in developing the strategy to be used in promoting certain bills and opposing those detrimental to physical education.

8. Promote an international relations program.

9. Provide a plan and means of getting physical education literature published in educational and other periodicals serving professional groups.

10. Prepare films, books, and brochures that will interpret physical education.

11. Conduct a research program to gather data on important needs and problems.

12. Conduct national and regional conferences on specific areas of physical education, such as facilities, teacher education, and athletics, to solve problems and upgrade the profession.

Public Relations in Interscholastic and Intercollegiate Athletics

Basically, all that has been stated before in regard to physical education public relations applies with equal force to interschool athletics, which constitute one of the important aspects of physical education. Every contact, impression, or relationship that people have with the athletic program of an institution will mold public opinion positively or negatively. Because of the powerful interest of the public in athletics and its tendency to overemphasize winning teams, it is particularly important to cultivate as much good will as possible by effective public relations. In addition, public attendance and support of the athletic program need to be solicited.

Public Relations with Newspapers, Radios, and Television Personnel

An extremely important consideration is the relationship of the athletic director and coach with sportswriters, publishers, and representatives of radio and television. Publicity through these various media, if translated into dollars-and-cents value, would be infinitely more than an athletic department could afford to pay. Yet, practically the only cost of this publicity is the time and effort required to cooperate with the personnel.

It pays to be honest with the sportswriters. There are times when it is desirable to suppress information. On these occasions, more will be gained by taking reporters into confidence and requesting their cooperation than by trying to deceive them or hide the facts from them. Frequently, stories will break which the coach may not wish to have published. If the confidence of sportswriters has been cultivated, they will communicate with the director or coach and often, if asked, refrain from publishing the story. Many coaches make the mistake of trying to build up a belief in the weaknesses of their squad in order to establish a ready alibi for a possible defeat or to gain greater glory for a supposedly unexpected victory. Others go to the other extreme and boast of victories before the game is played. Some coaches are constantly seeking personal publicity. Sportswriters soon see through such tactics, and lose respect for the coach and the team, who thereby lose a powerful source of support. No athletic director or coach can afford to alienate sportswriters.

In those communities that support more than one newspaper, the coach must be careful to be impartial to the representatives of each. Much rivalry naturally exists between the various papers, and the coach may lose the support of all the papers by showing partiality to one. The same situation applies to relationships with representatives of the different radio and television stations in the community.

It is poor economy to be stingy with complimentary tickets for newspaper, radio, and television personnel. When they come to cover a contest, special conveniences should be provided for these representatives. Good seats are essential. If a press box is available, it should be equipped so that the writers and broadcasters get the game information first. This may be done by telephone from the field or by messenger. The press box, naturally, should be equipped with telephones to the outside. The larger universities have a representative from each team in the press box to identify the players and supply pertinent information. Many institutions serve hot coffee and sandwiches to the representatives of the various publicity media. In short, every effort should be made to anticipate the needs of these individuals and to assist them in doing their jobs.

Public Relations with Alumni and Parents

In recent years many coaches have endeavored to develop effective public relations by weekly letters to alumni, supporters, faculty, parents, and other interested individuals. Other coaches have weekly meetings with local groups. Some coaches write letters to parents. All these methods are of value in transmitting correct information to interested groups, and if they are well done, supporters are gained. Much of the antagonism toward coaches and teams is the result of misinformation.

Public Relations with Opponents

Contrary to the opinion of some coaches and rabid fans, opposing teams represent a public with whom good relations are essential. Fundamentally, the Golden Rule should apply in all relations with teams from other institutions. They appreciate courteous, hospitable treatment, and every consideration should be shown to them as guests. Some of the recommended courtesies to be shown visiting teams include:

1. Providing refreshments after the game.
2. Providing official hosts. These individuals—usually managers—should endeavor to provide for every need of the visitors.
3. Providing satisfactory dressing and showering facilities.
4. Accepting all decisions of officials in a sportsmanlike manner.
5. Avoidance of rough tactics by home players.
6. Exemplary behavior of fans of home team.
7. Writing letters of commendation for outstanding qualities exhibited by the visiting team.

Athletic Publicity

Publicity for school athletics should stress the educational purposes and true values of these activities. Many undesirable practices and pressures persist in athletics because the public has never been educated to anything else. The following statement is pertinent:[10]

> The challenge ahead lies in interpeting and promoting the sound educational values inherent in sports. The public has to cultivate the desire to exert its influence in making sound athletic policies stick. The people in the community can be the strongest force in determining that athletics should be conducted chiefly for the good of the players. The right kind of sound, interpretive publicity—and plenty of it—is the crying need. If the schools and teachers and an informed public would fight intelligently the evils in sports practices, it would not take long to remove the evils and to establish athletics as a worthwhile educational activity of value to participants, to school morale, and to community welfare.

The public has been educated to a wrong sense of values largely through the medium of the printed word. This same medium must be used to provide the proper perspective about athletics. This can be done by feature stories primarily. These cannot achieve the desired purpose if they are written in a pedantic style. The human interest stories involved in athletics can be written in simple, everyday language and can bring out incidents involving sportsmanship, sacrifice, teamwork, courage, loyalty, integrity, idealism, leadership, self-discipline, and unselfishness. Every athletic squad has many incidents which, if represented in nonacademic terms, illustrate the educational values of sports.

Athletic publicity in large universities is handled by a special individual or department having that specific duty. In smaller colleges and high schools this function is handled in a variety of ways. Sometimes, capable students may be assigned to take charge of athletic publicity. A few schools have part-time publicity personnel. A member of the faculty with journalistic training may assume the responsibility for the publicity program as part of his or her duties. Frequently, the director or coach must perform this service. It is very important that someone who is responsible to the director or school administrator be assigned to this work if the public is to develop the proper attitude toward school athletics.

Much of the publicity in athletics is directed toward increasing the attendance at games. The following are effective media to use in this connection:

1. Daily newspapers.
2. School newspapers.
3. Radio and television.
4. Popular periodicals.
5. Moving pictures.
6. Posters.
7. Athletic periodicals.
8. Souvenir programs for events.
9. Windshield stickers.
10. Bumper stickers.
11. Buttons.
12. Direct mail and circulars of information.
13. School annuals.
14. School and departmental catalogues.
15. School and departmental bulletins.
16. Reports.
17. Talks by athletic leaders.

The practice has grown up in recent years for all college and high school athletic departments to prepare a "dope sheet," which is made available to all local sportswriters and sportscasters in the area. This brochure contains pertinent publicity material about the team. The names of all squad members, with data concerning the age, height, weight, experience, position, and potential of each, are given. The previous season's record and the outlook for the present season are indicated. The names, experience, and achievements of the coaching staff are also included. Other information includes the schedule, type of offense and defense employed, school colors, nicknames, and the like. The value of such data from the publicity standpoint is obvious.

School athletic games and contests may be effectively advertised in a number of ways. The media listed above are well known. Some of the less known, economical, yet effective methods are herewith suggested:

1. Ladies' day or ladies' night. Admit all ladies free of charge to some particular game or games. This has proved very effective in increasing attendance and gate receipts at professional baseball games, and there is no reason why it should not be successful in interscholastic and intercollegiate contests.

2. Knothole clubs. Admit all children under twelve years of age to all home games, excepting perhaps the homecoming game, for from 10 to 25 cents. This creates a favorable attitude toward the school on the part of the public. Many adults come to the game because they wish to be with their children and take care of them after the game. The knothole club is segregated in a special section and kept there until the game is over. This greatly reduces the problem of watching the fences and gates to prevent the children from stealing into the games.

3. Post card, direct mail campaign. Organize a mailing list of prospective customers, usually alumni. Three days before the game, mail a post card with an appropriate picture on it to all on the mailing list. This card should convey anything of important informational value. The following items are suggested:
   a. Pregame information on opponents.
   b. Names and numbers of outstanding players.
   c. Dates and starting time.
   d. Seating facilities.
   e. Record of opposing team if significant.
   f. Any significant advertising features pertaining to the coming game; for example: the coach of the opposing team, comparative scores, scores of this game in previous years, and all-star players and high-score players.

4. Telephone campaign. Organize a group of volunteer students and have each call ten prospective spectators the day before the game. Divide the list of prospects, usually alumni, among the students, and have them call these people and briefly announce a few pertinent facts about the game.

5. Parents', fathers' or mothers' day. Allow the whole family to come for the price of one ticket. This is a valuable means of introducing the sport to the students' parents. They may find they enjoy it and return on later occasions.

6. Game coupons. Sell four-game coupon books at the start of the school year at reduced prices. These coupons should be transferable and good for any athletic contest during the entire school year. A campaign may be conducted to sell season passbooks to the public at the same rate that students pay. This means a considerable saving to interested individuals and will greatly stimulate attendance among the general public.

7. Advance sale of tickets at reduced prices. This is a sound procedure in advertising the game and increasing sales. Every ticket purchaser becomes a medium of advertising. It also insures a fair crowd and gate in the event of bad weather.

8. Ticket-selling contests. Ticket-selling contests between campus or school groups have been used successfully to promote sales. For a small trophy or prize, much advertising can be secured and ticket sales materially increased.

9. Posters. Attractively designed posters should be placed in strategic locations. Store windows, theater lobbies, restaurants, hotels, and other places that are certain to attract public attention should be utilized. An excellent plan is to post the announcements of the game on all hotel bulletin boards for the benefit of out-of-town visitors.

Radio and Television

The radio has proved to be one of the most effective media for athletic publicity. When interschool athletics were first broadcast, many directors felt that the radio would keep large numbers of spectators from attending the contests. There was even agitation in certain collegiate conferences to ban broadcasts of football games. However, experience has proved beyond the question of a doubt that the radio has greatly increased the number of followers of interschool sports. Many individuals now believe that television will reduce attendance, particularly at small college and high school contests. In fact, data are available to show that attendance has been materially reduced when contests are played at the same time that feature college games are telecast. Many smaller colleges and high schools have been forced to schedule their games on Friday afternoon or evening or Saturday evening to avoid the direct competition with major attractions.

The proposal to eliminate televising athletic contests has been seriously discussed. At the present time the National Collegiate Athletic

Association is controlling the amount of telecasting of contests. Whether television will eventually increase attendance at athletic events as radio has done remains to be seen.

SELECTED REFERENCES

BRONZAN, ROBERT T., *Public Relations, Promotions, and Fund Raising for Athletic and Physical Education Programs.* New York: John Wiley & Sons, 1977.

PESTOLESI, ROBERT A. and WILLIAM ANDREW SINCLAIR, *Creative Administration in Physical Education and Athletics.* Ch. 9 Politics and Public Relations. Englewood Cliffs, N.J.: Prentice-Hall, Inc., 1978.

NOTES

1. Benjamin Fine, *Educational Publicity* (New York, Harper & Row, Publishers, Inc., 1943), pp. 255–256.

2. Stewart Harral, *Tested Public Relations for Schools* (Norman, Okla.: University of Oklahoma Press, 1952), p. 4.

3. Elwood C. Davis and Earl L. Wallis, *Toward Better Teaching in Physical Education,* © 1961. Reprinted by permission of Prentice-Hall, Inc., Englewood Cliffs, N.J.

4. Ben Miller, "Public Relations," *Professional Contributions* # 7. American Academy of Physical Education, 1961, p. 93.

5. Stewart Harral, *Public Relations for Churches* (New York, Abingdon-Cokesbury, 1945), p. 7.

6. American Association of School Administrators, *Public Relations for America's Schools: Twenty-eighth Yearbook* (Washington, D.C., 1950), p. 59.

7. *Public Action for Powerful Schools,* Metropolitan School Study Council Research Studies No. 3 (New York, Teachers College Bureau of Publications, 1949), p. 4.

8. Harral, *Tested Public Relations,* p. 127.

9. Harral, *Tested Public Relations,* p. 135.

10. Clifford L. Brownell, Leo Gans, and Tufie Maroon, *Public Relations in Education* (New York, McGraw-Hill Book Company, 1955), p. 154. Copyright,© 1955, by McGraw-Hill Book Company, Inc. Reprinted by permission of the publisher.

18

Evaluation

Neilson and Jensen[1] propose the following definition of evaluation:

> Evaluation is a process of determining the status of something and of relating that status to some standard in order to make a value judgment.

The administrator must assess all aspects of the organization's operations and compare the results to some criteria or standards which have validity. One needs to determine if expectations have been met.

IMPORTANCE OF EVALUATION

Evaluation is a major responsiblity of the physical education administrator. The need for evaluation is present in any viable, dynamic organization. For only when results are measured against original purposes or stated goals will the administrator be able to judge progress. With the resources at his or her command one is expected to accomplish the objectives for which the organization was created. The administrator is not unlike the coach who constantly evaluates the strengths and weaknesses of his or her team and endeavors to augment the strengths and to eliminate the weaknesses.

The administrator's goal is the greatest possible accomplishment of the organization's objectives. This requires the maximum contribution of all staff members. It is imperative that the physical education administrator evaluate the achievements of staff members individually and collectively to determine how succuessful they have been and how their future efforts may be improved.

The importance of evaluation is aptly expressed by Williams:[2] "Occasionally an administrator or teacher contends that the practical affairs of his work leave no time for attention to *evaluation*. In a sense evaluation is like bookkeeping in business; it indicates direction, and shows degrees of accomplishment. The worth of administrative procedures . . . remains obscure or unknown unless their effects are evaluated."

Aspects of Evaluation

Evaluation has many aspects. Most of the people who are related or involved with a high school or college physical education program will probably evaluate it. Many parents evaluate the effects of the program on their children. Students evaluate their teachers and the program. The teachers evaluate student achievement. Other faculty members evaluate the physical education department. The department chairperson is evaluated by a superior as well as by staff members. He or she in turn evaluates the performance of staff members. Finally, the administrator should do a self-evaluation.

All of these aspects of evaluation are important but there is one that transcends any of the others. This is the evaluation of student achievement. The schools exist primarily for this purpose and their success or failure depends upon how well this objective is accomplished. In reality, if student achievement comes up to expectations, the evaluations of the physical education departments by parents, students, other faculty, and the school administrator are likely to be favorable. Also, an appropriate level of student achievement reflects excellent teacher performance. If student and faculty performance are excellent it is quite likely that the administrator is performing successfully.

Knowledge of Standards Essential

Basic to the administrator's evaluation of the performance of the different aspects of the organization is the knowledge of the standards these aspects should attain. If one is to evaluate an intramural program he or she should have in mind what constitutes an excellent program. Appraisal of the teaching effectiveness of a staff member should be based upon the concept of superior teaching. One of the reasons why so many poor programs exist in our secondary schools and colleges and universities is that the administrator does not have valid aims. One must be familiar with the standards that have evolved over the decades in such areas as curriculum, intramural athletics, interschool athletics, facilities, equipment, evaluation, and staff. Knowledge of these standards is indispensable to the physical education administrator.

Purposes of Evaluation

For the administrator the purposes of evaluation are:

1. To determine the extent to which the objectives of the program are being accomplished.

2. To provide evidence demonstrating the worth and contributions of the program.

3. To determine how the total program compares to recommended standards.

4. To ascertain the teaching effectiveness of each staff member.

5. Where indicated, to encourage staff members to adjust and improve the teaching process and method.

6. To obtain a basis for the periodic rating of faculty members and recommendations for tenure, promotions, and merit salary increases.

7. To determine whether all operations are proceeding according to plan. To correct weaknesses and inadequacies.

8. To provide a check on personal administrative performance.

Evaluation Must Be Continuous

For the administrator evaluation is a continuous process. Decisions such as those involving personnel or budget may be made only once a year but they are based upon judgments that extend over many months. As the administrator carries out responsibilities he or she is constantly making appraisals of every aspect of the operations. This is a desirable situation because evaluations that are based upon many impressions made over an extended period of time are apt to be sounder than those that are hastily made.

EVALUATION OF STUDENT ACHIEVEMENT

The Physical Development Objective

The physical development objective cannot be evaluated with a single test because it involves a variety of components. A test battery with different tests for each of the various components is needed. A number of valid test batteries are available. Various states such as California, Oregon, Washington, New York, Indiana, and Minnesota have developed excellent test batteries. Many universities have done likewise.

Probably the most extensively used physical fitness test is that developed under the sponsorship of the American Alliance for Health, Physical Education, and Recreation.[3] The AAHPER Youth Fitness Test was first published in 1958, with later revisions. National norms are available for each test for boys and girls from the fifth through the twelfth grades. Norms are also available for college men and women.

This AAHPER Youth Fitness Test possesses a variety of advantages. It requires little equipment, and test items are those with which teachers and students are familiar. The battery can be easily and quickly administered, with one exception the items are the same for boys and girls, and the tests can be given from the fifth grade through college. The availability of national norms is a great advantage to the administrator. One is able to compare the performances of students with those of other children of the same ages. In this way the effectiveness of the physical education program can be evaluated. If students are unable to meet the national standards the administrator must determine the reason or reasons. Perhaps the time allotment or facilities are inadequate. The cause might be poorly qualified teachers or the lack of emphasis upon the physical development objective.

The availability of these national standards gives the administrator a powerful lever in the effort to correct the deficiencies of a program. Parents and the general public do not want their children to be appreciably below the level of children throughout the country in various aspects of physical fitness. It is much easier for the administrator to secure what is needed to strengthen the program when unfavorable comparison of local children and youth are shown in comparison to national norms.

If the administrator prefers not to use an already established test battery to evaluate the physical fitness of students there is another alternative. One may use separate tests for each of the various components of physical fitness. Cardiovascular, strength, endurance, and agility tests are available. Table 18-1 gives specific tests of each type.[4]

The Motor Skill Development Objective

To evaluate motor skill development requires more than one test. In fact, a battery of tests is required to assess skill in one sport adequately. Skill tests in a wide variety of physical education activities have been developed over the years. Some of these are excellent tests but many have limitations that preclude their use. Their validity coefficients may not be high enough; they may require too much equipment; they may take too

TABLE 18-1

Cardiovascular Tests	Strength Tests	Endurance Tests	Agility Tests
1. Schneider Tests	1. Physical Fitness Index	1. Runs of Various Distances	1. Burpee Tests
2. McCurdy-Larson Organic Efficiency Test	2. Strength Index	2. McCloy Endurance Ratio	2. Jack Spring
3. Harvard Step Test	3. Cable Tension Strength Tests	3. Drop-Off Index	
4. Tuttle Pulse Ratio Test	4. Kraus-Weber Tests	4. Twelve Minute Run (Cooper)	
5. Hodgkins-Skubic Cardiovascular Efficiency Test	5. Larson Muscular Strength Tests		

long to administer; their reliability may be too low; norms may be lacking; they have too limited applicability; they may not be capable of differentiating abilities at all grade levels. Before a test is used it should be examined for appropriateness in the local situation.

Some of the well-known sport skills tests include:

1. Hyde Archery Achievement Tests.
2. French-Stalter Badminton Skill Tests.
3. Lockhart-McPherson Badminton Test.
4. Miller Wall Volley Test (badminton).
5. Kelson Test (baseball).
6. Leilich Basketball Test for Women.
7. Stroup Basketball Test.
8. Johnson Basketball Test.
9. Knox Basketball Test.
10. Phillips-Summers Bowling Norms.
11. Schmithals-French Field Hockey Tests.
12. Borleske Touch Football Test.
13. Brace Football Achievement Tests.
14. New York State Football Test.
15. Cornish Handball Test.
16. New York State Softball Test.
17. O'Donnell Softball Skill Test.
18. New York State Soccer Test.
19. McDonald Soccer Test.
20. Hewitt Swimming Achievement Scales.
21. Table Tennis Backboard Test.

22. Dyer Tennis Test.
23. Broer-Miller Tennis Test.
24. Russell-Lange Volleyball Test.
25. Brady Volleyball Test.

The Knowledge and Understanding Objective

Physical educators have used knowledge tests for many decades. These tests have usually been of the objective type. The tests may have been constructed by the instructor or they may have been published tests that have been statistically validated. The tests may include any or all of the following areas:

1. Knowledge of skill performance.
2. Rules.
3. Strategy or activity patterns.
4. Protective requirements.
5. Conditioning procedures.
6. Effects of activity upon health.
7. Codes of etiquette appropriate to the activity.
8. Understanding of effective utilization of the organism in movement.
9. Factors affecting performance such as age, sex, drugs, nutrition, fatigue, alcohol, and tobacco.

There are physical education knowledge tests for archery, badminton, basketball, bowling, golf, canoeing, handball, field hockey, folk dancing, ice hockey, riding, softball, tennis, soccer, volleyball, stunts and tumbling, swimming, and track and field.[5]

Unfortunately, none of the above tests have national norms. They would not enable the administrator to evaluate student performance against that of a larger population. However, the American Alliance for Health, Physical Education and Recreation has a project to serve this purpose. The Project on the Measurement of Understandings in Physical Education has been completed and it makes available standardized knowledge tests in physical education, including the activities, the effects of activities on the human organism and factors modifying participation in activities. Standards are available for upper elementary, junior and senior high school students. With these tests and standards the administrator will be able to make comparisons with a wider population on this important dimension. The AAHPER Cooperative Physical Education

Tests are available from the Addison-Wesley Testing Service, Reading, Massachusetts.

The Social Development Objectives

Can the administrator evaluate how much progress the students have made in regard to the social development objectives? Apparently, physical educators do much less evaluation of this objective than they do of physical development, motor skills, and knowledge and understanding. Probably, also, they do much less planning for this objective than the others. The idea is unfortunately prevalent that social development is a concomitant of the physical education program and does not require careful planning and specially designed programs.

Several different types of tests have been used to measure social adjustment. One of the most commonly used measures is the behavior rating scale whereby observers rate the frequency with which certain types of behavior have been observed. The Blanchard Behavior Rating Scale is representative of this type of device (see Figure 18-1). Another approach to the assessment of progress toward the socal objective is by means of a social acceptance determination. These instruments involve students rating their fellow students on the basis of social acceptance. One type developed by Cowell is called the Cowell Personal Distance Scale (see Figure 18-2). Each individual's score in a class or group is obtained by adding the total weighted scores given by all the participants and then dividing by the number of participants. The lower the index, the greater the degree of acceptance by the group. Sociometric techniques involving the use of the matrix chart and sociogram are also of value in determining popularity or isolation among students.

Measures of general social adjustment may also be used to advantage. A number of excellent instruments such as the Washburne Social Adjustment Inventory, The Bell Adjustment Inventory, The Minnesota Multi-phasic Personality Inventory, and the California Psychological Inventory[6] have been frequently and successfully used in physical education.

Self Evaluation[7]

Many administrators never think of evaluating their own leadership. They evaluate everyone else in their organization but for some reason they forget themselves. Yet from the standpoint of the success of the department there is no one whose performance is more important. It is

Name:_____ Grade:_____ Age:_____ Date:_____

School:_____ Name of Rater:_____

BEHAVIOR RATING SCALE

Personal Information	No Opportunity to Observe	Never	Seldom	Fairly Often	Frequently	Extremely Often	Score
Leadership							
1. Popular with classmates.................		1	2	3	4	5	
2. Seeks responsibility in the classroom........		1	2	3	4	5	
3. Shows intellectual leadership in the classroom		1	2	3	4	5	
Positive Active Qualities							
4. Quits on tasks requiring perseverance.......		5	4	3	2	1	
5. Exhibits aggressiveness in his relationship with others...........................		1	2	3	4	5	
6. Shows initiative in assuming responsibility in unfamiliar situations................		1	2	3	4	5	
7. Is alert to new opportunities..............		1	2	3	4	5	
Positive Mental Qualities							
8. Shows keenness of mind..................		1	2	3	4	5	
9. Volunteers ideas........................		1	2	3	4	5	
Self-Control							
10. Grumbles over decisions of classmates......		5	4	3	2	1	
11. Takes a justified criticism by teacher or classmate without showing anger or pouting...		1	2	3	4	5	
Cooperation							
12. Is loyal to his group.....................		1	2	3	4	5	
13. Discharges his group responsibilities well....		1	2	3	4	5	
14. Is cooperative in his attitude toward his teacher.............................		1	2	3	4	5	
Social Action Standards							
15. Makes loud-mouthed criticism and comments		5	4	3	2	1	
16. Respects the rights of others..............		1	2	3	4	5	
Ethical Social Qualities							
17. Cheats................................		5	4	3	2	1	
18. Is truthful............................		1	2	3	4	5	
Qualities of Efficiency							
19. Seems satisfied to "get by" with tasks assigned............................		5	4	3	2	1	
20. Is dependable and trustworthy............		1	2	3	4	5	
21. Has good study habits...................		1	2	3	4	5	
Sociability							
22. Is liked by others.......................		1	2	3	4	5	
23. Makes a friendly approach to others in the group.............................		1	2	3	4	5	
24. Is friendly.............................		1	2	3	4	5	

Source: B. E. Blanchard, "A Behavior Frequency Rating Scale for the Measurement of Character and Personality in Physical Education Classroom Situations," *Research Quarterly* (May, 1936), p. 56.

Figure 18-1. Blanchard Behavior Rating Scale.

Grade

What to do		I would be willing to accept him:					
	Into my family as a brother	As a very close pal	As a member of my gang or club	On my street as a next-door neighbor	Into my class at school	Into my school	Into my city
If you had full power to treat each student in this group as you feel, just how would you consider him? Just how near would you like to have him to your family? Every student should be checked in some one column. Circle your own name and be sure you check every student in one column only.	1	2	3	4	5	6	7
1. Stanley Whitaker							
2. James Southerlin							
3. Parvin Schriber							

Source: Charles C. Cowell and Hilda M. Schwehn, *Modern Principles and Methods in High School Physical Education* (Boston, Allyn and Bacon, Inc., 1958), p. 307.

Figure 18-2. Cowell Personal Distance Scale.

vital that administrators objectively appraise the manner in which they are administering the unit.

Criteria for Self Evaluation

If the department is successful in accomplishing its objectives, if the staff is excellent, and if the program and facilities meet recommended standards, there is every reason to believe that the administrator is successful. However, regardless of the success the administrator has enjoyed he or she knows that perfection has not been attained and can see areas in which improvement can be made.

Criteria that emphasize important aspects of administration are listed below:

1. The administrator has been successful in eliciting 100 percent effort from each member of the organization.

2. The administrator has been successful in securing a fair share of the budget and the resources available.

3. High morale prevails among all staff persons.

4. The department enjoys high respect within the school and in the community.

5. Staff members are loyal to each other and to the departmental objectives.

6. The administrator is fair and impartial to all staff members.

7. The administrator personally sets an example of the values for which the department stands.

8. Consistency characterizes the administrator's decisions and actions.

9. Regular staff meetings are held.

10. The administrator never violates the chain of command.

11. The administrator solicits and respects the opinions of staff members and students.

12. Curriculum development is a cooperative process.

13. The physical education program is accepted on an equal basis with other departments in the school.

14. The organizational objectives are being accomplished.

15. Staff members feel free to express differences of opinion.

16. Channels of communication between the chairperson and staff members and students are open.

17. All staff members participate in the development of departmental policies.

18. Staff members are informed of the reasons when their responsibilities are changed.

Instruments for Evaluating Administrative Leadership

The members of an organization are in a strategic position to assess the quality of the leadership of their superior. However, it is difficult for the administrator to approach staff members directly for their evaluation of his or her performance. There would be an understandable reluctance for them to be frank, particularly if they were critical of the leadership. However, there are some methods by which one can indirectly obtain such information. Some instruments are now available which would give the administrator an indication from colleagues how he or she is performing.

Likert[8] has developed a checklist which, if completed anonymously by all staff members, would enable the administrator to determine whether they regard their leader as exploitive authoritative, benevolent authoritative, consultative, or participative type of administrator. This instrument describes managerial behavior under seven areas as follows:

1. Leadership processes used.
2. Character of motivational forces.
3. Character of communication process.
4. Character of interaction-influence process.
5. Character of decision-making process.
6. Character of goal-setting or ordering.
7. Character of control process.

A variable number of sub-items are listed under each of the above headings.

Halpin[9] and Croft developed an Organizational Climate Description Questionnaire (OCDQ) by which the climate of an organization can be assessed. It includes 64 items divided into eight sub-tests. Four of the sub-tests pertain primarily to the relationships found among the faculty and four to the administrator. By means of a factor analysis six different organizational climates are identified. These are open, autonomous, controlled, familiar, parental, and closed climates. When staff members complete the OCDQ anonymously, the climate as perceived by them is revealed. Since the departmental chairperson is the most important factor in determining the climate, an indication of leadership is determined.

As follow-up to the Halpin and Croft OCDQ, Borrevik[10] developed a similar instrument at the higher education level to better assess the organizational climate that surrounds academic departments in colleges and universities.

A Leader Behavior Description Questionnaire (LBDQ) was developed by the Ohio State Leadership Studies. It originally included 150 items designed to measure nine dimensions of leader behavior. Stogdill[11] developed the LBDQ-Form XII, the current form of the instrument. Form XII is the fourth revision and contains twelve subscales, each of which have five or ten items. This instrument has been extensively used to evaluate administrative behavior. When completed by staff members of an organization, it provides an effective method of determining how colleagues view the administrator.

SELECTED REFERENCES

BAUMGARTNER, TED A. and ANDREW S. JACKSON, *Measurement for Evaluation in Physical Education* (2nd ed.), Boston: Houghton Mifflin Co., 1975.

CLARKE, H. HARRISON, *Application of Measurement to Health and Physical Education* (5th ed.), Englewood Cliffs, N.J.: Prentice-Hall, Inc., 1976.

HALL, J. TILLMAN, et al., *Administration: Principles, Theory and Practice with Applications to Physical Education.* Ch. 6 "Evaluating the Administrator." Pacific Palisades, Calif.: Goodyear Publishing Company, Inc., 1973.

NOTES

1. N. P. Neilson and Clayne Jensen, *Measurement and Statistics in Physical Education* (Belmont, California: Wadsworth Publishing Company, 1972), p. 3.

2. Jessie F. Williams, Clifford L. Brownell, and Elmon L. Vernier, *The Administrator of Health Education and Physical Education* (Philadelphia: W. B. Saunders Company, 1964), p. 319.

3. AAHPER, *Youth Fitness Test Manual* (Washington, D.C.: AAHPER, 1976).

4. Descriptions of these tests are available in *Application of Measurement to Health and Physical Education*, 5th ed. by H. Harrison Clarke (Englewood Cliffs, N.J.: Prentice-Hall, Inc., 1976).

5. For further information on these tests see H.H. Clarke, *Application of Measurement to Health and Physical Education*, 5th ed. (Englewood Cliffs, N.J.: Prentice-Hall, Inc., 1976).

6. For further details concerning these inventories see Carl Willgoose, *Evaluation in Health Education and Physical Education* (New York: McGraw-Hill Book Company, 1961).

7. For evaluation of staff see chapter 4.

8. Likert, Rensis, *The Human Organization—Its Management and Value* (New York: McGraw-Hill Book Company, 1967), pp. 197–211.

9. Halpin, Andrew, *Theory and Research in Administration* (New York: The Macmillan Company, 1966), pp. 148–150.

10. Borrevik, Berge A., Jr., "The Construction of An Organizational Climate Description Questionnaire for Academic Departments in Colleges and Universities," (unpublished Doctoral dissertation, University of Oregon, 1972).

11. Stogdill, Ralph M., *Manual for the Leader Behavior Description Questionnaire—Form XII: An Experimental Revision* (Columbus, Ohio: Bureau of Business Research, Ohio State University, 1963).

APPENDIX A

Methods of Organizing Competition

The kind of tournament to be used will be determined by a number of factors. The type of activity, the time and facilities that are available, the purpose of the competition, and the number of entries must all be considered when selecting a tournament that will be appropriate. The criteria for a tournament that will be used in a class situation will differ from the criteria for an intramural tournament which in turn will differ from standards that will be used to choose a tournament for interscholastic or intercollegiate competition. All types of tournaments have strong and weak points with some serving one purpose well and others serving another.

ELIMINATION TOURNAMENTS

This type of tournament involves the elimination of all competitors until only one winner remains. There are basically five types of elimination tournaments.

Single elimination. The single elimination tournament is the least desirable because it emphasizes the *elimination* of teams and players. For example, in this type of tournament one half of the competitors are eliminated after their first contest. Further, since a single defeat eliminates a contender, the eventual winner often is not the best team or player. Nor does the defeated finalist represent with certainty the second best team or player, since one of the teams or players in the other half of the bracket may be superior. However, despite these disadvantages, there is a place for the single elimination type of tournament. It is short and selects a winner quickly. It is interesting to watch and can be conducted with limited facilities and a large number of entries. The use of the single elimination tournament is justified when the time available is limited.

The first step in arranging a single elimination tournament is to draw for positions. The positions in the brackets are numbered, and each team or player takes the position indicated by the number drawn, as in Figure A-1. In the tournament shown the location of each team was determined by the number that was drawn. Thus, the captain or representative of Team B drew # 1; the representative of Team A drew # 4, and so forth.

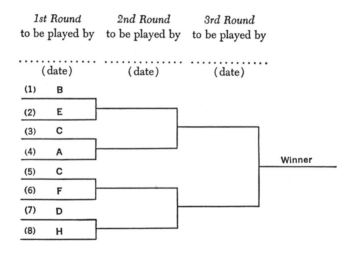

Figure A-1. Single Elimination Tournament.

When the number of entrants is not an even power of two (that is, 2, 4, 8, 16, 32, etc.) "byes" must be arranged so as to avoid having an uneven number of teams or players left to compete in the semifinal or final rounds. All the byes must be placed in the first round. The competition is less intense in the first round, and a rest before play does not provide the advantage of a rest after a game or two. The number of byes should be sufficient to assure a number of contestants for the second round that is an even power of two. This is accomplished by subtracting the total number of entrants from the next higher power of two. For example, with eleven entrants, subtract 11 from the next higher power of two, which is

16. This leaves 5, which is the number of byes. The total number of entrants (eleven) minus the five byes leaves six contestants to play each other in the first round. Three will lose, leaving eight contestants in the second round. As 8 is an even power of two, only two teams can now meet in the final round. The byes should be distributed as evenly as possible between the upper and lower brackets. Figure A-2 shows a sample bracket for thirteen teams.

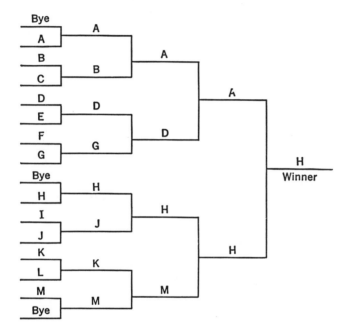

Figure A-2. Single Elimination Bracket for Thirteen Teams.

"Seeding" is a process employed to place the competitors who, by virtue of previous performance and reputation, are considered superior in separate brackets or as far apart as possible in the same bracket in order to minimize their chances of meeting in the early rounds. With two seeded entries one should be placed at the top of the upper bracket and the other at the bottom of the lower bracket. If four entrants are to be seeded the third should be placed at the top of the lower bracket and the fourth at the bottom of the upper bracket. If there are byes, the seeded players get them in the order of their ranking. Thus, number one gets the first bye, number two the second, and so on. No team or player ever receives more than one bye. Seeding should be employed only when the previous record of the teams or players justifies it.

The number of games in a single elimination tournament is always one less than the number of entries. Thus, with thirteen teams entered, 12 games would be required to complete the tournament. The number of rounds required is equal to the power to which two must be raised to equal or exceed the number of entries. With thirteen entrants 4 rounds are necessary to complete the competition.

Consolation elimination tournament. This type of tournament is superior to the single elimination in that it permits each team to play at least twice. A good team that has been eliminated by the champion in the first round may continue to play with a chance to win secondary honors. More games are involved, and greater player interest is engendered.

There are two general types of consolation elimination tournaments. In the first type all the losers in the first round (or those who lose in the second round after drawing a bye in the first round) play another single elimination tournament. The winner of this second tournament is the consolation winner. Figure A-3 is an example of the manner in which a consolation tournament of this type with no byes is arranged. Figure A-4 illustrates the manner in which a consolation tournament including byes may be arranged.

A second type of consolation tournament provides an opportunity for any loser to win the consolation championship, regardless of the round in which the loss was sustained. Figure A-5 is an example of this second type of consolation tournament.

Double elimination tournament. This is a tournament in which a player or a team must be beaten twice to be eliminated; the play continues until all but one have been twice defeated. The double elimination tournament is a step in the direction of a round robin tournament and selects a more

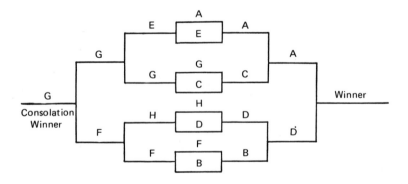

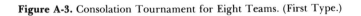

Figure A-3. Consolation Tournament for Eight Teams. (First Type.)

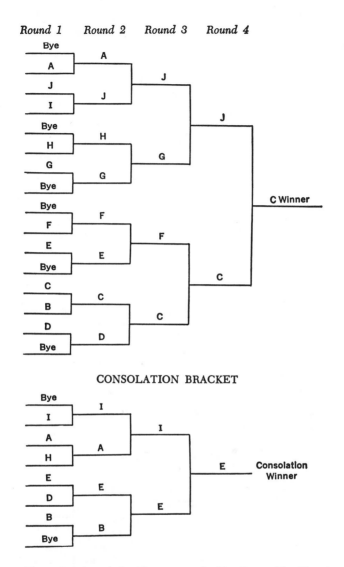

Figure A-4. Consolation Tournament for Ten Teams (First Type.)

adequate winner. It provides for at least twice as much play as in a single elimination tournament and maintains maximum interest. A double elimination tournament of 8 teams will involve either fourteen or fifteen games (Figure A-6).

Bagnall-Wild elimination tournament. This is a modified form of the elimination type of tournament. Its strong point is the selection of true second- and third-place winners; its weakness is the delay following the first round before those who are to try for second or third places can be matched. It should be used when second and third places are of particular

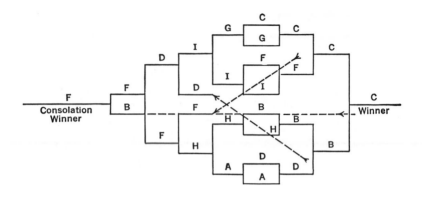

Figure A-5. Consolation Tournament for Eight Teams. (Second Type.)

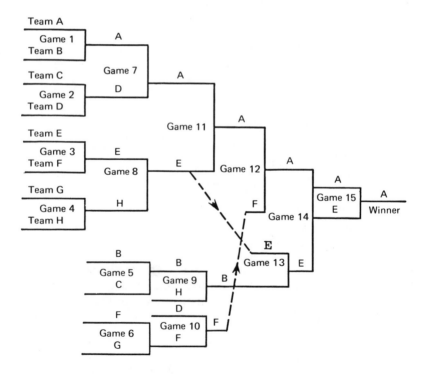

Figure A-6. Double Elimination Tournament for Eight Teams.

significance or when a point system is in operation and points are awarded for these places.

First place is determined by means of straight elimination play. To determine second place all the competitors defeated by the champion previous to the final round compete against each other in an elimination tournament, the winner of which plays the defeated finalist for second place. In Figure A-7, the defeated finalist (A) proves to be best among the teams defeated by the winner and wins second place. However, Team K (defeated by A) does not automatically become third place winner. One of the other teams defeated by A might be better than K. To determine this an elimination tournament is conducted among the teams defeated by A. The winner (second best team in the upper bracket) plays K (second best team in the lower bracket) for third place.

In the event the defeated finalist (Team A) should lose in the match for second place, Team K becomes second-place winner. This automatically leaves Team A the third-place winner.

The playoffs for second and third place should not await the playing

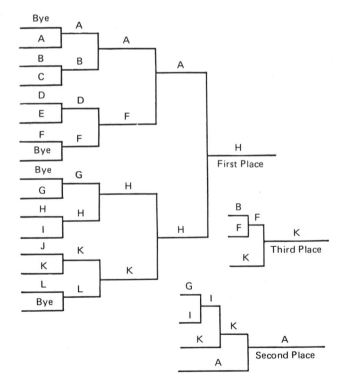

Figure A-7. Bagnall-Wild Tournament for Twelve Teams.

of the finals match. As soon as it is determined that Teams A and H are to be the finalists the elimination competition between the teams defeated by each of the finalists should begin. Thus, before the finals, Teams B and F and G and I should play matches. This will reduce the amount of play after the winning finalist has been determined.

Mueller-Anderson Playback Tournament. An advantage of this tournament is that there is a place ranking for all entries. Another advantage is that each player or team plays the same number of games. This tournament requires a longer period of time to complete than does a single elimination tournament. Although there might be some loss of interest on the part of losing teams, enthusiasm remains high as there is motivation to finish the tournament with as high a ranking as possible. Figure A-8 illustrates an eight team tournament with the place ranking of each team.

Round Robin Tournaments

If sufficient time and facilities are available, the round robin tournament is the best type of tournament to employ. It produces a true winner, ranks the other competitors, permits all participants to continue play until the end, and does not require one contestant to wait until others have played the next round.

Regular round robin. In the round robin tournament, each team or player plays each other competitor in the league. In a single round robin

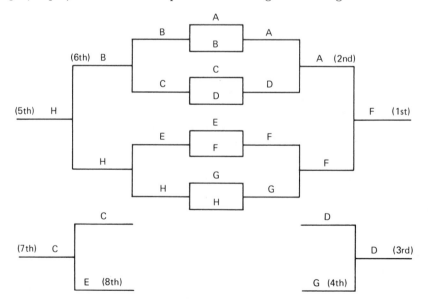

Figure A-8. Mueller-Anderson Playback for Eight Teams.

one game is played with each other team or player; in a double round robin two games are played with each of the opponents.

The positions of the teams at the end of a round robin tournament are determined by percentages. Each team's percentage is obtained by dividing the number of games won by the total games played. For example, if a team played eight games and won seven, its percentage would be .875. In cases of tie games, the customary procedure is not to count such contests as games played when the percentages are computed. A better plan is to count a tie as half a victory and half a defeat. Thus, a team that wins seven games, loses four, and ties one would have a percentage of .625 (7.5 ÷ 12).

The British and Canadian systems of determining team standings in round robin tournaments are somewhat different. In the Canadian system, two points are awarded for each victory and one point for each tie. Thus, if a team wins twelve games, loses three, and ties one, its total points would be 25. The team with the greatest point total is the winner. The British carry this one step further. They determine points as in the Canadian system, but the point total obtained is then divided by the total possible points (total games played multiplied by two). In the example just given, the team's percentage would be .781 (25 ÷ 32).

The formula for determining the total number of games to be played in a round robin tournament is n $(n- 1)/2$ with n representing the number of teams in the tournament. Substituting for n in an eight-team league, the formula is $8(8- 1)/2$ or twenty-eight games. Since there are eight teams involved, eight is used; since each team plays every team but itself, eight minus one is used; and since it takes two teams to play one game, it is necessary to divide by two.

To draw up a round robin schedule, place as many numbers as there are teams in two vertical columns. The numbers should be arranged consecutively down the first column and up the second. With each number representing a team, this arrangement provides the pairing for the first round. Thus, Team # 1 plays Team # 8; Team # 2 plays # 7; Team # 3 plays # 6, and Team # 4 plays # 5 in the first round. To obtain pairings for subsequent rounds, rotate the numbers *counterclockwise* around one of the numbers that remains fixed. In the example given in Table 1, number one is fixed with the other numbers rotated around it.

TABLE 1

Round 1	Round 2	Round 3	Round 4	Round 5	Round 6	Round 7
1 vs. 8	1 vs. 7	1 vs. 6	1 vs. 5	1 vs. 4	1 vs. 3	1 vs. 2
2 vs. 7	8 vs. 6	7 vs. 5	6 vs. 4	5 vs. 3	4 vs. 2	3 vs. 8
3 vs. 6	2 vs. 5	8 vs. 4	7 vs. 3	6 vs. 2	5 vs. 8	4 vs. 7
4 vs. 5	3 vs. 4	2 vs. 3	8 vs. 2	7 vs. 8	6 vs. 7	5 vs. 6

When an uneven number of teams is entered the same plan is used. However, in this case the bye should be placed in one of the positions and the other numbers rotated about it. The number opposite the bye signifies the team that receives the bye in that particular round. In the example given in Table 2, the bye is placed in the upper left-hand corner and the other numbers are rotated *counterclockwise* around it. Another method of drawing up a round robin tournament is illustrated in Figure A-9. Schedules for even numbers of teams follow one general plan; those for odd numbers of teams do likewise except that the schedule is drawn for the next greater even number and the last vertical column to the right represents the byes.

TABLE 2

Round 1	Round 2	Round 3	Round 4	Round 5	Round 6	Round 7
Bye 7	Bye 6	Bye 5	Bye 4	Bye 3	Bye 2	Bye 1
1 vs. 6	7 vs. 5	6 vs. 4	5 vs. 3	4 vs. 2	3 vs. 1	2 vs. 7
2 vs. 5	1 vs. 4	7 vs. 3	6 vs. 2	5 vs. 1	4 vs. 7	3 vs. 6
3 vs. 4	2 vs. 3	1 vs. 2	7 vs. 1	6 vs. 7	5 vs. 6	4 vs. 5

The letters in Figure A-9 represent teams, and the numbers playing days. Numbers at the intersection of the various vertical and horizontal columns indicate that the team represented in the columns concerned play on the playing day indicated by the number. That is, 7 on vertical F

Eight Team Schedule

	A	B	C	D	E	F	G	H
A		1	2	3	4	5	6	7
B			3	4	5	6	7	2
C				5	6	7	1	4
D					7	1	2	6
E						2	3	1
F							4	3
G								5
H								

Nine Team Schedule

	A	B	C	D	E	F	G	H	I	Bye
A		1	2	3	4	5	6	7	8	9
B			3	4	5	6	7	8	9	2
C				5	6	7	8	9	1	4
D					7	8	9	1	2	6
E						9	1	2	3	8
F							2	3	4	1
G								4	5	3
H									6	5
I										7
Bye										

Figure A-9. Round Robin Schedules.

and horizontal C means F plays C on the seventh playing day; likewise E plays B on the fifth playing day. These relationships can be noted in the arrangement of the numbers in the schedule. All numbers are in regular order except those in the last column to the right (1 following 7 is in regular order when 7 is the largest number). The last column to the right starts with the largest odd number, then goes to the smallest even number and on up through the even numbers in order, then starts with the smallest odd number and continues through the remaining odds in order. The numbers in this last vertical column, except the first and last, are always one less than the first number in the horizontal column.

The Lombard round robin. The Lombard tournament is a unique form of round robin competition in which the entire tournament is completed in a day or several hours. This is accomplished by playing abbreviated contests. This type of tournament should not be thought of as a substitute for regular round robin competition. Rather it is a special type of tournament which can be used effectively under certain conditions.

Assuming a tournament of seventeen basketball teams and a playing time of 32 minutes, which is the customary length of high school basketball games, the tournament works as follows. Each team meets every other team or plays 16 short games. Therefore, divide 32 by 16 to give the length of time of these abbreviated games, which is exactly two minutes. Eight courts and sufficient officials to conduct 8 games at a time are required. Each team is assigned a scorer, who keeps a record of its scores for all games in one column and scores of all opponents in another. All teams start play at one time, play two minutes, and shift to another court to play another opponent until a complete round robin tournament of two-minute games is played. The scores for each team are totaled for the 16 games. The opponents' score is then subtracted from each team's own score. The four teams with the largest positive scores are selected to play a regular round robin to decide the winner and other ranking places if desired. In the event of a tie for fourth place after the first round robin of two-minute periods, the tying teams play for the right to enter the final tournament.

Since the players of the various teams have played only the equivalent of one full-time game, the first round of the final tournament of four teams can be played the day of the abbreviated round robin. Then all teams can go home, and the four remaining contenders can return the next Saturday to complete the tournament. This assumes that they live within a radius of forty or fifty miles.

During World War II the Lombard tournament, used somewhat differently from that indicated above, was extensively and effectively employed in the army. Its great value lay in the fact that an entire round robin tournament could be completed within a period of several hours.

For example, a Lombard round robin tournament in basketball in a league of twelve teams (66 games) can be completed in less than four hours if two courts are available and six-minute games are played. If more courts are available the time may be further reduced. The Lombard tournament worked very successfully with from 6 to 12 teams playing on two or three courts. In this way, teams alternate playing and players have a chance to rest. For this reason, it is an excellent tournament for players who are not yet in condition to play full-length games. The best length of basketball games proved to be from five to six minutes.

To assist in scoring the Lombard tournament, a scoreboard such as indicated below has been found helpful. For each game played, two scores must be recorded, one for each team. A team's scores are recorded and added *horizontally*. If Team #4 defeated Team #1 by a score of 10 to 5, Team #4's score would be +5, and Team #1's score would be −5. If Team #2 defeated Team #3 by a score of 6 to 0, its score would be +6, and Team #3's score would be −6 points. These scores are recorded as shown in Table 3. The Lombard type of tournament can also be employed effectively for volleyball, speedball, soccer, touch football, cage ball, handball, badminton, squash, and tennis. When used for volleyball, handball, squash, badminton, and tennis, only one game or set should be played against each opponent.

TABLE 3

	Games							Total	Score
	#1	**#2**	**#3**	**#4**	**#5**	**#6**	**#7**		
Team #1	−5								
Team #2	+6								
Team #3	−6								
Team #4	+5								
Team #5									
Team #6									
Team #7									
Team #8									

Combination Tournaments

An excellent tournament for intramural purposes should (1) provide for even or well-matched competition, (2) be neither too long nor too short, (3) exclude none from competition after a game or two, (4) require few or no competitors to play a great many more games than other participants, and (5) select a true champion. There are several forms of combined elimination and round robin tournaments that meet these requirements reasonably well.

For purposes of illustration, a combination elimination round robin elimination tournament is presented for 20 basketball teams in Figure A-10. Two rounds of a double elimination tournament are played first to classify the competitors into four leagues. To do this, seed teams as well as possible and play the first round; then have winners play winners and losers play losers. Place those who won twice in the first league; those who won one and then lost one in the second league; those who lost one and then won one in the third league; and those who lost two in the last league.

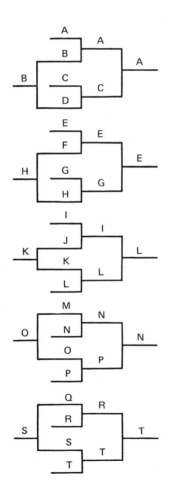

Figure A-10. Elimination Bracket (for a Combination Elimination Round Robin Tournament).

Now that the teams are classified, play a round robin schedule for each league. Each team will then have played six games, two in classifying and four in its league. Place the first- and second-place winners of leagues one and two and the first-place winners in leagues three and four in the final championship tournament. This will discourage the practice of losing in the classifying rounds in order to gain a place in a weaker league. A double elimination tournament is recommended for these six teams; but if time is short, a straight elimination may be necessary. A round robin tournament may be used but it is not to be recommended, since most of the teams are already eliminated, and the remaining six would need to play much more than the other teams.

An interesting method of providing even more participation is to group the place winners in each league together in single elimination tournaments. For example, put all first-place winners together as in the above example; do likewise with the second-place teams in each league. Similar tournaments are drawn up for the teams in third, fourth, fifth, and sixth places (see Figure A-11).

At times, the space and time available are not adequate to permit even an elimination tournament for a large number of entries. When this

Figure A-11. Single Elimination Tournament for Finalist.

occurs in certain sports the number of participants can be quickly reduced by holding a qualifying round in which only the best performers qualify for the finals. Such sports as track and field, swimming, golf, bowling, and foul shooting are well adapted to the use of qualifying rounds. For example, in a golf tournament all the contestants may play a qualifying round and the sixteen players with the best scores thus play a single elimination tournament for the championship. To simplify tournament play the number of entries which qualify is usually a power of two.

Challenge Tournaments

This form of tournament is desirable when the activity is such that it can be carried on by the players independently without formal schedules. It is used for single or dual competition rather than team sports. Tennis, golf, handball, squash, badminton, wrestling, horseshoes, and archery are the activities for which this type of competition is most commonly used.

A challenge tournament affords competition with contestants of near equal ability. It provides an opportunity for all competitors to continue play since none is eliminated. It is entered into with more zest in situations where all the players know each other. This type of tournament is useful in selecting team members in individual sports. When used this way, the players at the top of the ladder represent the institution in interschool competition. The ladder tournament is widely used by wrestling coaches to select the competitors in each weight each week.

There are two common types of challenge tournaments, the ladder and the pyramid (see Figure A-12). Contestants' names are inscribed on

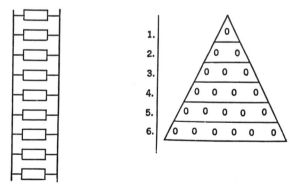

Figure A-12. Challenge Tournament.

cards that can either be placed in slots or hung on hooks. Placing the players on the ladder or in the pyramid in the order in which they sign up will furnish an incentive for all who are interested to sign up quickly. Positions may also be determined by the various players drawing numbers from a hat. Only if the time is short is seeding to be recommended.

Rules governing play for the various forms will differ somewhat, and local factors will also modify them, but in general the following rules, with minor modifications, will suffice.

1. It must be definitely stated what constitutes a win.

2. Players may advance by challenging and defeating, or by gaining default from defending player (player challenged).

3. A player may challenge two players above him. That is, C may challenge A or B.

4. If the challenger wins, only players involved change places; if the defender wins, positions remain as before, and the defeated challenger may not challenge the same player again for a week.

5. Challenges must be met in the order that they are made.

6. After two contestants have played, they cannot play each other again until each has played once with another contestant.

7. In some challenge tournaments the rule exists that a player must defeat someone in his own horizontal row before he can challenge someone above him.

8. A defender must play within three days after receiving a challenge.

9. There is no acceptable excuse, except inclement weather, for failure to play within the time limit stated in rule six; if defender cannot play within set limit, he must forfeit.

10. In case of difficulty concerning challenging and acceptance of challenges, set up a challenge board or require all challenges to be dated and handed to tournament manager, who will then post them.

11. In the pyramid form a player may challenge any player in the rank above; that is, any player in rank five may challenge any player in rank four, who may in turn challenge any player in rank three, and so on.

12. The player at the top of the ladder or pyramid at the end of a specified period of time is the winner.

The Funnel Tournament

The funnel tournament is a combination of the ladder and challenge type tournaments. It works best with activities like handball, badminton, table tennis, and horseshoes. It is played off in a manner similar to a challenge tournament. A player must defeat someone in his/her own horizontal row before he/she can challenge into the next row. The top six positions are played as a ladder tournament. When more than 20 contestants are entered in the tournament the additional participants are placed on the bottom row (see Figure A-13).

The Tombstone Tournament

This is not a widely known tournament yet it has been used very effectively for group and individual competition. It involves a cumulative score, and the person or team that accumulates the best record over a specified period of time or achieves a predetermined goal in the shortest time is the winner. For example, in swimming, each entrant indicates on a chart the distance he has swum each day. At the end of the stipulated

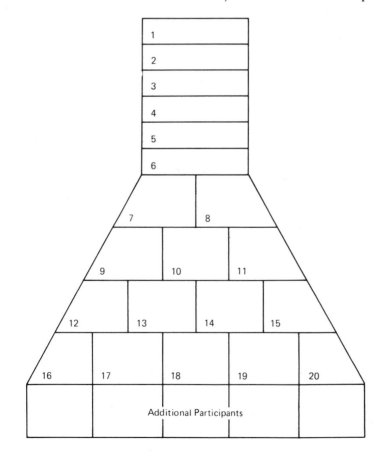

Figure A-13. Funnel Tournament.

| | June 1 | | June 2 | | June 3 | | June 4 | | June 5 | |
Entries	Daily Record	Total Score	Daily Record	Total Score	Daily Record	Total Score	Daily Record	Total Score	Daily Record	Total Score
Jones, H.	44	5068	66	5134	22	5156				—
Henry, B.	60	4896	60	4956	88	5044				
Brown. W.										
Marsh, M.										

Note—Scores are recorded in pool lengths.

Figure A-14. 100-Mile Swim (8800 Pool Lengths).

period of time the contestant who has swum the greatest distance is the winner. If the distance is established, such as 100 miles, the winner would be the individual who first negotiated this distance. A chart such as that shown in Figure A-14 should be used to record the performance in this type of tournament.

The above procedure may be used for competitions in hiking, chinning (one trial per day), pushups, situps, distance running, broad jumping, shot-putting, football punt for distance, and many similar events. For example, in basketball free throwing, it could be specified that each person was to take twenty-five throws each day. At the end of a month (or some other specified period) the player who has made the greatest number of baskets is the winner. In horseshoes, each player might play three games every day and record the total ringers made. After a definite number of rounds, the player with the most ringers is the winner. In archery each player might keep his daily score, and the winner would be that contestant who had accumulated the greatest number of points by a certain date.

In such events as the shot put, broad jump, and football punt each player may be given three or five trials, counting only the best performance. Additional practice each day is encouraged.

In all these events it is obvious that all competitors should compete under the same rules and conditions. When this type of tournament is conducted among widely separated units, it is necessary to select events that are little affected by varying weather conditions and facilities. The progress of the tournament in such a situation is made known to the various competitors either by telephone or mail.

The tombstone tournament may be used for group as well as individual competition. When the number of competitors in each group is the same, the group total may be computed each day until the end of the tournament. For example, to determine the winner in the standing broad jump each competitor would jump five times each day and count the best jump. If all the competitive groups were of the same size, the total distance jumped each day could be computed. At the end of the tournament, the group that had jumped the greatest distance would be the winner.

If the groups are not exactly the same size, it is necessary to obtain group averages. The group average would be scored every day, and the group with the greatest total at a set date would be the winner.

APPENDIX B

Athletic Field and Court Layouts[1]

1. Badminton
2. Baseball
   a. Regulation
   b. Little League
3. Basketball
4. Deck Tennis
5. Field Hockey
6. Football
   a. 11-man
   b. 8-man
7. Handball (Four wall)
8. Horseshoes
9. Lacrosse
10. Paddle Tennis
11. Soccer

[1]Courtesy of Wilson Sporting Goods Company.

12. Softball
13. Squash
14. Table Tennis
15. Tennis
16. Track
    a. Quarter mile
    b. "Staggered" distances
    c. Field Events
17. Volleyball
18. Wrestling

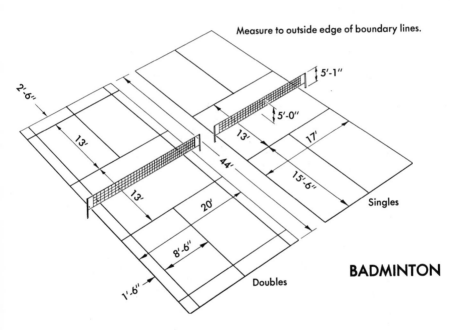

BADMINTON

BASEBALL DIAMOND

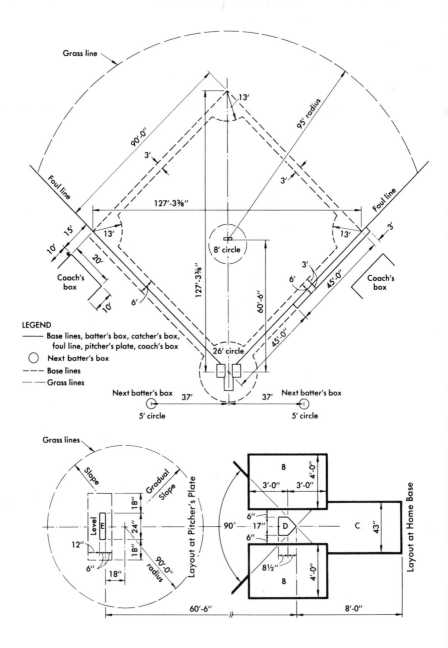

LEGEND
——— Base lines, batter's box, catcher's box, foul line, pitcher's plate, coach's box
○ Next batter's box
- - - Base lines
— — Grass lines

BASEBALL
(Little League)

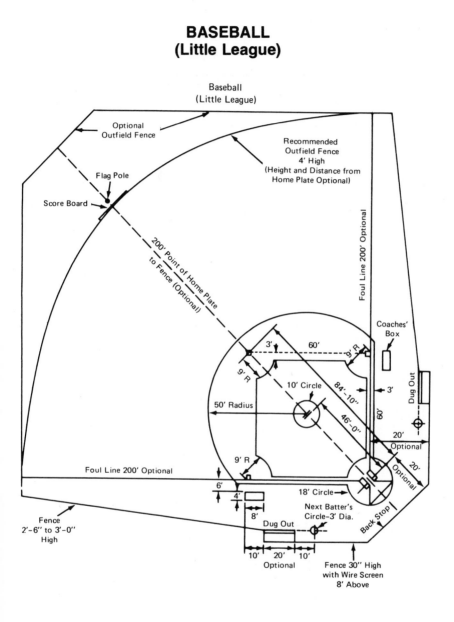

Baseball
(Little League)

Optional
Outfield Fence

Recommended
Outfield Fence
4' High
(Height and Distance from
Home Plate Optional)

Flag Pole

Score Board

Foul Line 200' Optional

200' Point of Home Plate
to Fence (Optional)

Coaches'
Box

3' 60' 9' R

9' R

84'-10"

10' Circle

50' Radius

46'-0"

3'

60'

Dug Out

20'
Optional

20'
Optional

9' R

Foul Line 200' Optional

6'

4'

18' Circle

Back Stop

Fence
2'-6" to 3'-0"
High

8'

Next Batter's
Circle-3' Dia.

Dug Out

10' 20' 10'
Optional

Fence 30" High
with Wire Screen
8' Above

BASKETBALL COURT

Left end shows large backboard for college games.

Right end shows small backboard for high school, Y.M.C.A., A.A.U., optional.

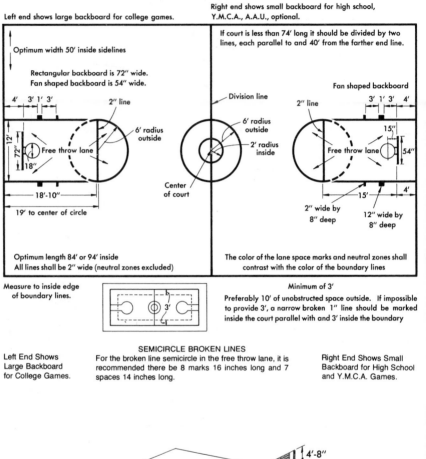

Optimum width 50' inside sidelines

Rectangular backboard is 72" wide.
Fan shaped backboard is 54" wide.

4' 3' 1' 3'

2" line

12'

72'

18"

Free throw lane

6' radius outside

If court is less than 74' long it should be divided by two lines, each parallel to and 40' from the farther end line.

Fan shaped backboard

3' 1' 3' 4'

Division line

2" line

6' radius outside

2' radius inside

15"

Free throw lane

54"

18'-10"

19' to center of circle

Center of court

15'

4'

2" wide by 8" deep

12" wide by 8" deep

Optimum length 84' or 94' inside
All lines shall be 2" wide (neutral zones excluded)

The color of the lane space marks and neutral zones shall contrast with the color of the boundary lines

Measure to inside edge of boundary lines.

3'

Minimum of 3'

Preferably 10' of unobstructed space outside. If impossible to provide 3', a narrow broken 1" line should be marked inside the court parallel with and 3' inside the boundary

SEMICIRCLE BROKEN LINES

Left End Shows Large Backboard for College Games.

For the broken line semicircle in the free throw lane, it is recommended there be 8 marks 16 inches long and 7 spaces 14 inches long.

Right End Shows Small Backboard for High School and Y.M.C.A. Games.

4'-8"

9'

40'

12'

Singles

3'

17'

18'

Doubles

DECK TENNIS

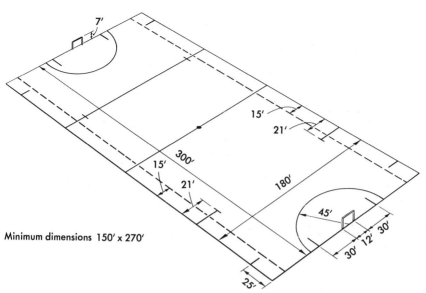

Minimum dimensions 150' x 270'

FIELD HOCKEY

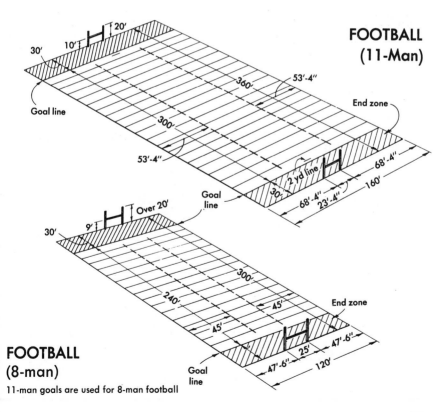

FOOTBALL (11-Man)

Goal line

End zone

Goal line

FOOTBALL (8-man)

11-man goals are used for 8-man football

Goal line

End zone

Goal line

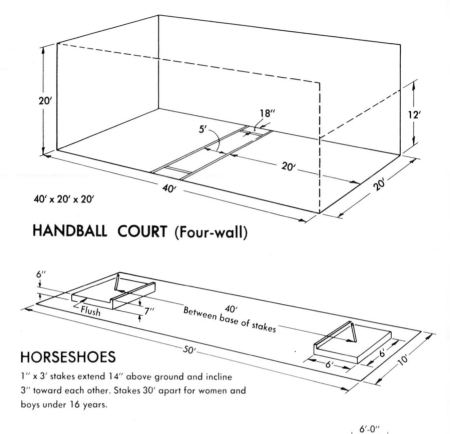

HANDBALL COURT (Four-wall)

40' x 20' x 20'

HORSESHOES

1" x 3' stakes extend 14" above ground and incline
3" toward each other. Stakes 30' apart for women and
boys under 16 years.

LACROSSE FIELD

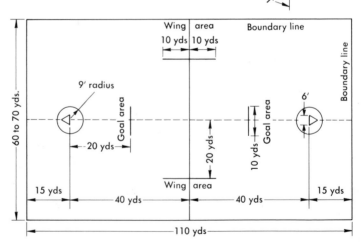

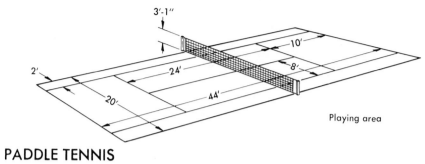

PADDLE TENNIS
(Bat Tennis)

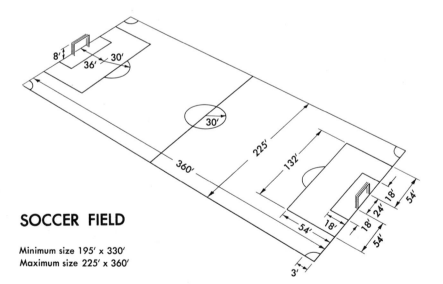

SOCCER FIELD

Minimum size 195' x 330'
Maximum size 225' x 360'

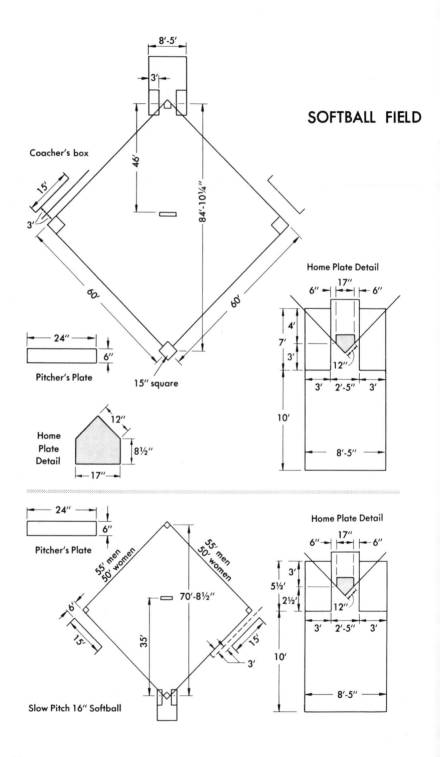

SOFTBALL FIELD

8'-5'

3'

Coacher's box

46'

84'-10¼"

15'

3'

60'

60'

24"

6"

Pitcher's Plate

15" square

Home Plate Detail

6" ← 17" → 6"

4'

7'

3'

12"

3'   2'-5"   3'

10'

8'-5"

12"

Home Plate Detail

8½"

17"

24"

6"

Pitcher's Plate

55' men
50' women

55' men
50' women

70'-8½"

6'

15'

35'

15'

3'

Home Plate Detail

6" ← 17" → 6"

3'

5½'

2½'

12"

3'   2'-5"   3'

10'

8'-5"

Slow Pitch 16" Softball

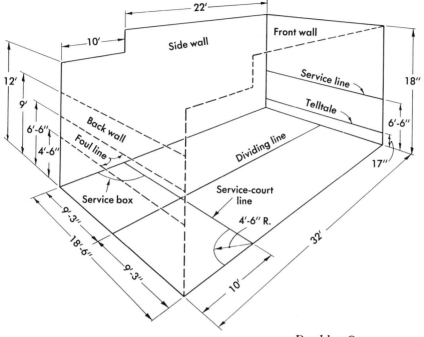

SQUASH COURT

Doubles Court
45' x 25' x 20'

Front Wall—20' High
Side Walls—20' x 31'
Back Wall Telltale Line—7'
Service Line—15'

TABLE TENNIS TABLE

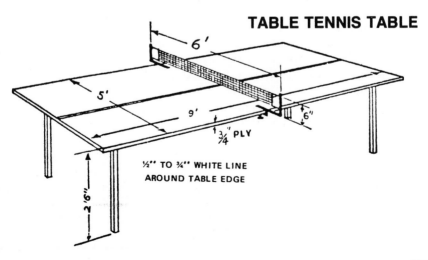

½'' TO ¾'' WHITE LINE
AROUND TABLE EDGE

¾'' PLY

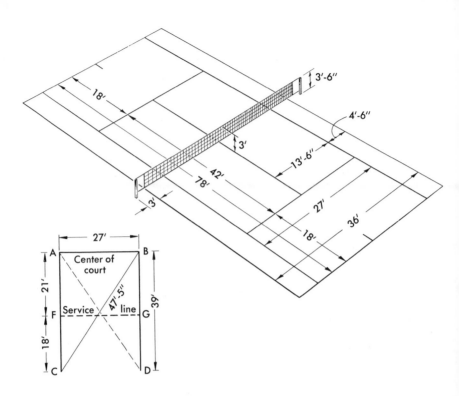

TENNIS Singles and Doubles

HOW TO LAY OUT A TENNIS COURT

First spot place for net posts, 42 feet apart. Measure in on each side 7½ feet and plant stakes 27 feet apart at points A and B in diagram.

Then take two tape measures and attach to each peg—one tape 47 feet 5¼ inches, the other 39 feet. Pull both taut in such directions that at these distances they meet at point C. This gives one corner of the court. Interchange the tapes and again measure to get point D. Points C and D should then be 27 feet apart. Put in pegs at C and D and measure 18 feet toward net and put in pegs to denote service lines.

Proceed in same way for the other half of court and add center line from service line to service line—distance 42 feet. Then add 4½ feet on each side for alleys. Alleys should then be 2 feet inside posts on each side. Put in permanent pegs to mark all corners.

Measure to outside edge of boundary lines.

QUARTER-MILE TRACK
Approved by the National Federation of
State High School Associations

Handicaps—When races, run in lanes, start on the straightaway and relay exchanges are made on the straightaway, the "staggered" distance may be determined from the following tables. These figures apply to all tracks that are laid out with semicircular turns, regardless of the number of laps to the mile.

For 30-Inch Lanes

No. of turns to run	4	3	2	1
Hdcp., Lane 2 over 1	27' 2½"	20' 4⅞"	13' 7¼"	6' 9⅝"
Lanes 3, 4, 5, 6, 7, and 8 over next inside lanes	31' 5"	23' 6¾"	15' 8½"	7' 10¼"

For 36-Inch Lanes

No. of turns to run	4	3	2	1
Hdcp., Lane 2 over 1	33' 6"	25' 1½"	16' 9"	8' 4½"
Lanes 3, 4, 5, 6, 7, and 8 over next inside lanes	37' 8⅜"	28' 3¼"	18' 10¼"	9' 5⅛"

For 42-Inch Lanes

No. of turns to run	4	3	2	1
Hdcp., Lane 2 over 1	39' 9½"	29' 10⅛"	19' 10¾"	9' 11⅜"
Lanes 3, 4, 5, 6, 7, and 8 over next inside lanes	43' 11¾"	32' 11⅞"	21' 11⅞"	11'

For 48-Inch Lanes

N. of turns to run	4	3	2	1
Hdcp., Lane 2 over 1	46'	34' 6"	23'	11' 6"
Lanes 3, 4, 5, 6, 7, and 8 over next inside lanes	50'	37' 6"	25'	12' 6"

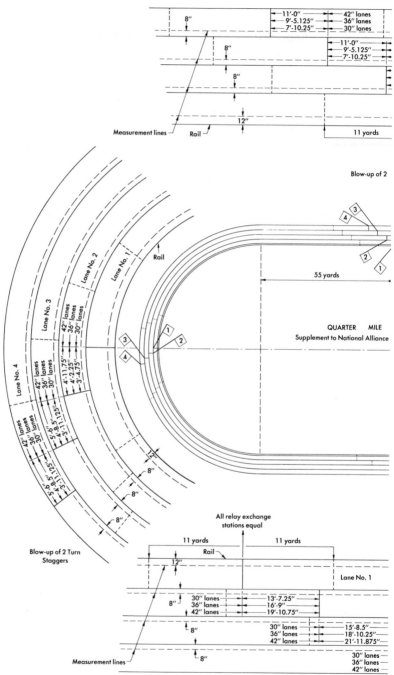

Blow-up of 2

Rail

55 yards

QUARTER MILE
Supplement to National Alliance

Blow-up of 2 Turn
Staggers

All relay exchange
stations equal

Measurement lines

Blow-up of 2 Turn Staggers

MILE

Legend:

.125" = ⅛"
.25" = ¼"
.375" = ⅜"
.5" = ½"
.625" = ⅝"
75" = ¾"
.875" = ⅞"

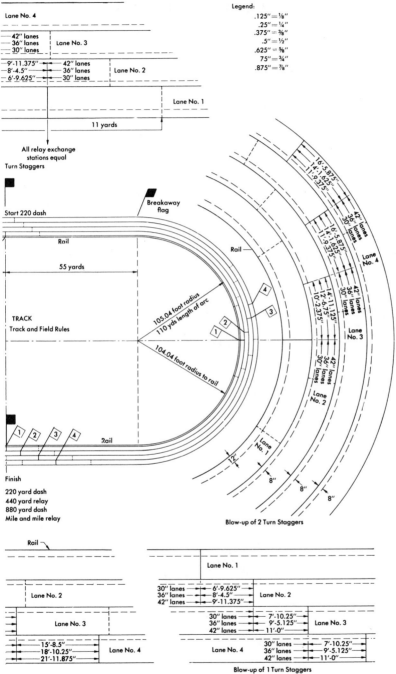

Lane No. 4

42" lanes
36" lanes   Lane No. 3
30" lanes

9'-11.375"   42" lanes
8'-4.5"   36" lanes   Lane No. 2
6'-9.625"   30" lanes

Lane No. 1

11 yards

All relay exchange
stations equal
Turn Staggers

Start 220 dash

Breakaway
flag

Rail

55 yards

Rail

TRACK
Track and Field Rules

105.04 foot radius length of arc
110 yds length of arc

104.04 foot radius to rail

Lane
No. 4

Lane
No. 3

Lane
No. 2

Lane
No. 1

16'-5.875"
14'-1.625"
11'-9.375"

16'-5.875"
14'-1.625"
11'-9.375"

42" lanes
36" lanes
30" lanes

42" lanes
36" lanes
30" lanes

14'-11.125"
12'-6.75"
10'-2.375"

42" lanes
36" lanes
30" lanes

12"

8"

8"

8"

Finish

220 yard dash
440 yard relay
880 yard dash
Mile and mile relay

Blow-up of 2 Turn Staggers

Rail

Lane No. 2

Lane No. 3

15'-8.5"
18'-10.25"
21'-11.875"   Lane No. 4

Lane No. 1

30" lanes   6'-9.625"
36" lanes   8'-4.5"   Lane No. 2
42" lanes   9'-11.375"

30" lanes   7'-10.25"
36" lanes   9'-5.125"   Lane No. 3
42" lanes   11'-0"

30" lanes   7'-10.25"
Lane No. 4   36" lanes   9'-5.125"
42" lanes   11'-0"

Blow-up of 1 Turn Staggers
and break at flag after first turn with start from
chute or without chute

465

TRACK (FIELD EVENTS)

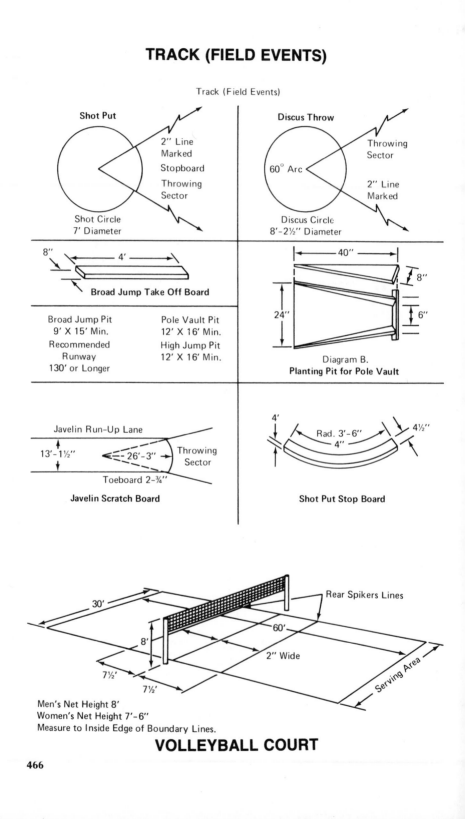

Track (Field Events)

Shot Put

2" Line Marked
Stopboard
Throwing Sector

Shot Circle
7' Diameter

Discus Throw

60° Arc

Throwing Sector

2" Line Marked

Discus Circle
8'-2½" Diameter

8"

4'

Broad Jump Take Off Board

Broad Jump Pit
9' X 15' Min.
Recommended
Runway
130' or Longer

Pole Vault Pit
12' X 16' Min.
High Jump Pit
12' X 16' Min.

40"

8"

24"

6"

Diagram B.
Planting Pit for Pole Vault

Javelin Run-Up Lane

13'-1½"

26'-3"

Throwing Sector

Toeboard 2-¾"

Javelin Scratch Board

4'

Rad. 3'-6"

4"

4½"

Shot Put Stop Board

30'

Rear Spikers Lines

60'

8'

2" Wide

7½'

7½'

Serving Area

Men's Net Height 8'
Women's Net Height 7'-6"
Measure to Inside Edge of Boundary Lines.

VOLLEYBALL COURT

WRESTLING MAT
(Interscholastic Wrestling)

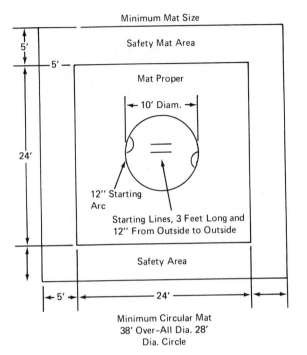

Minimum Mat Size

Safety Mat Area

Mat Proper

5'

5'

← 10' Diam. →

24'

12" Starting Arc

Starting Lines, 3 Feet Long and 12" From Outside to Outside

Safety Area

← 5' →|← 24' →|

Minimum Circular Mat
38' Over-All Dia. 28'
Dia. Circle

Intercollegiate Wrestling:

Minimum size: 32 feet by 32 feet or a circular area 32 feet in diameter

Maximum size: 42 feet by 42 feet or a circular area 42 feet in diameter

Protection mat around wrestling area—minimum of 5' required

APPENDIX C

Duties of a Physical Education Administrator[1]

Office Management

1. Interpret current problems and trends to principal.
2. Keep regular office hours for appointments.
3. Handle routine correspondence.
4. Prepare notices and announcements.
5. Implement departmental reports.
6. Interview salesmen or other commercial people for department.
7. Serve on miscellaneous committees.
8. Prepare yearly departmental records.
9. Prepare and keep miscellaneous departmental records.
10. Other duties.

Finance

1. Prepare the budget for:
   a. physical education program.
   b. athletic program.

[1]John Hansan, "A Job Analysis of Secondary School Men Physical Education Administrators," (unpublished Doctoral dissertation, University of Oregon, 1969).

    c. intramural program.

    d. other.

2. Approve requisitions for departmental purchases.
3. Authorize departmental purchases.
4. Supervise departmental accounting.
5. Keep departmental accounts.
6. Develop cost analysis for all phases of the program.
7. Evaluate per capita costs of program.
8. Other duties.

Facilities

1. Interpret departmental facility needs for school and community in terms of educational needs.
2. Participate in planning and gaining approval of new facilities (local and district).
3. Participate in planning for remodeling of present departmental facilities.
4. Supervise departmental facilities for safety hazards, sanitary conditions, repair and maintenance.
5. Plan scheduling and use of departmental facilities.
6. Other duties.

Public Relations

1. Implement district policy for public news releases to papers, TV, etc.
2. Interpret departmental program to community, students, and faculty.
3. Visit schools for speaking engagements.
4. Inform public of events that have occurred or will occur.
5. Inform the public of departmental expenditures in the yearly reports.
6. Evaluate the total effect of the public relations program for school and department.
7. Promote or conduct public physical education demonstrations (PTA, etc.).
8. Attend miscellaneous community civic meetings.
9. Clear news releases involving school policy with school administrator.
10. Provide in-service public relations training for departmental faculty.
11. Develop procedures for pupil-teacher conferences.
12. Other duties.

Personnel

1. Provide in-service training for department faculty.
2. Orient new department faculty into school and community.
3. Develop philosophy and objectives of department with faculty.
4. Interpret school policy to department faculty.
5. Promote professional growth within department.
6. Develop practices and procedures to avoid legal liabilities within department.
7. Delegate departmental duties to faculty and staff.
8. Conduct departmental staff and faculty meetings.
9. Insure up-to-date first-aid requirements for faculty.
10. Discuss departmental problems with staff and faculty.
11. Recommend and interview new faculty for department.
12. Develop policies governing employment of staff.
13. Evaluate faculty and staff.
14. Plan and implement departmental faculty assignments, including teaching load.
15. Supervise student teachers.
16. Supervise departmental faculty and staff.
17. Other duties.

Professional Growth and Contributions

1. Serve on local, district, state and national committees of professional organizations.
2. Attend clinics, workships and professional meetings.
3. Attend graduate school.
4. Write, edit, or collaborate in writings for books and other publications.
5. Work with others in research projects such as filling out questionnaires, etc.
6. Other duties.

Purchase and Care of Equipment and Supplies

1. Inspect department equipment and supplies for safety and cleanliness.
2. Develop and implement plans for purchase of departmental equipment and supplies.
3. Provide departmental plan for inventory of equipment including storage and identification.

4. Provide plan for issue and return of department equipment and supplies by pupils.
5. Develop plan for distribution of department equipment and supplies and all types of instructional materials.
6. Prepare directions for care and use of department equipment.
7. Assume legal responsibility for departmental equipment with regard to safety, etc.
8. Other duties.

Intramural Athletics

1. Assign intramural Director.
2. Develop and implement plans for:
   a. awards
   b. developing and assigning of officials.
   c. competitive units.
   d. scheduling time for participation.
   e. program of activities.
   f. insurance coverage.
   g. general organization.
3. Develop and implement evaluation program for intramurals.
4. Other duties.

Interscholastic Athletics

1. Check eligibility of athletes.
2. Develop plan for excuses for athletes for game participation.
3. Schedule contests for athletic teams.
4. Prepare lists of approved officials.
5. Develop program of competitive activities.
6. Supervise athletic contests.
7. Evaluate athletic programs in terms of educational objectives.
8. Attend league meetings as school representative.
9. Develop practices and procedures for:
   a. ticket sales and gate receipts.
   b. athletic team travel.
   c. physical examinations and injuries.
   d. athletic awards.
   e. athletic insurance.
   f. contracts for athletic contests.
   g. practice periods for athletic teams.
10. Other duties.

Instructional Program

1. Advise with professional preparation institutions regarding teaching program.
2. Prepare teaching schedules for department faculty.
3. Coordinate adapted program.
4. Visit faculty in the teaching situation.
5. Develop and implement plan for evaluation of department instructional program.
6. Supervise student teachers.
7. Work with curriculum consultants in analysis or development of department curriculum.
8. Develop courses of study or syllabi for department.
9. Participate in planning workshops.
10. Read and comment on lesson plans prepared by department faculty.
11. Coordinate health instruction program.
12. Develop practices and procedures for:
    a. class size.
    b. pupil classification.
    c. student leaders.
    d. excuses.
    e. requirements (physical education).
    f. substitutions for physical education requirements.
    g. class management.
    h. transfer of students.
    i. grading.
    j. safety.
    k. showering.

Name Index

Subject Index